Lecture Notes in Computer Science 2802

Edited by G. Goos, J. Hartmanis, and J. van Leeuwen

T0226283

Springer
Berlin
Heidelberg
New York
Hong Kong
London
Milan
Paris
Tokyo

Dieter Hutter   Günter Müller
Werner Stephan   Markus Ullmann (Eds.)

Security in Pervasive Computing

First International Conference
Boppard, Germany, March 12-14, 2003
Revised Papers

 Springer

Series Editors

Gerhard Goos, Karlsruhe University, Germany
Juris Hartmanis, Cornell University, NY, USA
Jan van Leeuwen, Utrecht University, The Netherlands

Volume Editors

Dieter Hutter
Werner Stephan
German Research Centre for Artificial Intelligence, DFKI
Stuhlsatzenhausweg 3, 66123 Saarbrücken, Germany
E-mail: {hutter,stephan}@dfki.de

Günter Müller
University of Freiburg, Institute for Computer Science
Friedrichstrasse 50, 79098 Freiburg, Germany
E-mail: mueller@iig.uni-freiburg.de

Markus Ullmann
BSI
Godesberger Allee 183, 53175 Bonn, Germany
E-mail: Markus.Ullmann@bsi.bund.de

Cataloging-in-Publication Data applied for

A catalog record for this book is available from the Library of Congress.

Bibliographic information published by Die Deutsche Bibliothek
Die Deutsche Bibliothek lists this publication in the Deutsche Nationalbibliografie;
detailed bibliographic data is available in the Internet at <http://dnb.ddb.de>.

CR Subject Classification (1998): C.2, D.2, D.4.6, H.5, K.4.1, K.4.4, K.6.5

ISSN 0302-9743
ISBN 3-540-20887-9 Springer-Verlag Berlin Heidelberg New York

Springer-Verlag is a part of Springer Science+Business Media

springeronline.com

© Springer-Verlag Berlin Heidelberg 2004
Printed in Germany

Typesetting: Camera-ready by author, data conversion by Olgun Computergrafik
Printed on acid-free paper   SPIN: 10980521   06/3142   5 4 3 2 1 0

Preface

The ongoing compression of computing facilities into small and mobile devices like handhelds, portables or even wearable computers will enhance ubiquitous information processing. The basic paradigm of such pervasive computing is the combination of strongly decentralized and distributed computing with the help of diversified devices allowing for spontaneous connectivity via the Internet. Computers will become invisible to the user, and exchange of information between devices will effectively be beyond the user's control.

Assuming a broad usage of more powerful tools and more effective ways to use them the quality of everyday life will be strongly influenced by the dependability of the new technology. Information stored, processed, and transmitted by the various devices is one of the most critical resources. Threats exploiting vulnerabilities of new kinds of user interfaces, displays, operating systems, networks, and wireless communications will cause new risks of losing confidentiality, integrity, and availability. Can these risks be reduced by countermeasures to an acceptable level or do we have to redefine political and social demands.

The objective of this 1st International Conference on Security in Pervasive Computing was to develop new security concepts for complex application scenarios based on systems like handhelds, phones, smartcards, and smart labels hand in hand with the emerging technology of ubiquitous and pervasive computing. Particular subjects were methods and technology concerning the identification of risks, the definition of security policies, and the development of security measures that are related to the specific aspects of ubiquitous and pervasive computing like mobility, communication, and secure hardware/software platforms.

We received 51 submissions. Each submission was reviewed by three independent reviewers and an electronic program committee meeting was held via the Internet. We are very grateful to the program committee members for their efficency in processing the work within four weeks and also for the quality of their reviews and discussions. Finally the program committee decided to accept 19 papers. We are also very grateful to the four invited speakers for their vivid and stimulating talks.

Apart from the program committee, we would like to thank also the other persons who contributed to the success of this conference: the additional referees for reviewing the papers, the authors for submitting the papers, and the local organizers, and in particular Hans-Peter Wagner, for a smooth and pleasant stay in Boppard.

June 2003

Dieter Hutter, Günter Müller,
Werner Stephan, Markus Ullmann
Program Co-chairs SPC 2003

Organization

SPC 2003 was organized by the German Research Center for Artificial Intelligence in Saarbrücken and the German Bundesamt für Sicherheit in der Informationstechnik in Bonn.

Executive Committee

Program Co-chairs   Dieter Hutter (DFKI GmbH, Germany)
     Günter Müller (University of Freiburg, Germany)
     Werner Stephan (DFKI GmbH, Germany)
     Markus Ullmann (BSI, Germany)
Local Arrangements   Hans-Peter Wagner (BSI, Germany)

Program Committee

Michael Beigl	University of Karlsruhe, Germany
Joshua Guttman	MITRE, USA
Dieter Hutter	DFKI Saarbrücken, Germany
Paul Karger	IBM Watson Research, USA
Friedemann Mattern	ETH Zürich, Switzerland
Catherine Meadows	Naval Research Lab, USA
Guenter Mueller	University of Freiburg, Germany
Joachim Posegga	SAP, Germany
Kai Rannenberg	University of Frankfurt, Germany
Kurt Rothermel	University of Stuttgart, Germany
Ryoichi Sasaki	Tokyo Denki University, Japan
Frank Stajano	Cambridge University, UK
Werner Stephan	DFKI Saarbrücken, Germany
Moriyasu Takashi	Hitachi Ltd., Japan
Seiji Tomita	NTT Information Platform Laboratories, Japan
Markus Ullmann	BSI, Bonn, Germany

Invited Speakers

Friedemann Mattern	ETH Zürich, Switzerland
Hideyuki Nakashima	Cyber Assist Research Center, AIST, Japan
Frank Stajano	Cambridge University, UK
Markus Luidolt	Philips Semiconductors, Austria
Paul Karger	IBM Watson Research, USA

Additional Referees

L. Fritsch	M. Kinateder	H. Rossnagel
P. Girard	D. Kügler	H. Vogt
J. Hähner	M. Langheinrich	S. Wittmann
T. Heiber	P. Robinson	
R. Kilian-Kehr	M. Rohs	

Sponsoring Institutions

Deutsches Forschungszentrum für Künstliche Intelligenz GmbH, Saarbrücken, Germany

Bundesamt für Sicherheit in der Informationstechnik, Bonn, Germany

Table of Contents

Authentication and Trust

Secure Infrastructures

Smart Labels

Verification

Hardware Architectures

Workshop

The Age of Pervasive Computing –
Everything Smart, Everything Connected?
(Abstract of Invited Talk)

Friedemann Mattern

Institute for Pervasive Computing
ETH Zurich, Switzerland
mattern@inf.ethz.ch

Abstract. Given the continuing technical progress in computing and communication, it seems that we are heading towards an all-encompassing use of networks and computing power, a new era commonly termed "Pervasive Computing". Its vision is grounded in the firm belief amongst the scientific community that Moore's Law (i.e. the observation that the computer power available on a chip approximately doubles every eighteen months) will hold true for at least another 10 years. This means that in the next few years, microprocessors will become so small and inexpensive that they can be embedded in almost everything – not only electrical devices, cars, household appliances, toys, and tools, but also such mundane things as pencils (e.g. to digitize everything we draw) and clothes. All these devices will be interwoven and connected together by wireless networks. In fact, technology is expected to make further dramatic improvements, which means that eventually billions of tiny and mobile processors will occupy the environment and be incorporated into many objects of the physical world.
Together with powerful and cheap sensors (and thus the ability to sense the environment), this progress in processor and communication technology will render everyday objects "smart" – they know where they are, and they may adapt to the environment and provide useful services in addition to their original purpose. These smart objects may form spontaneous networks, giving rise to a world-wide distributed system several orders of magnitude larger than today's Internet.
It is clear that we are moving only gradually towards the ultimate vision of Pervasive Computing. Much progress in computer science, communication engineering, and material science is necessary to render the vision economically feasible and to overcome current technological hurdles. However, the prospects of a world of things that virtually talk to each other are fascinating: many new services would then be possible that transform the huge amount of information gathered by the smart devices into value for the human user, and an entire industry may be set up to establish and run the underlying infrastructure for the smart and networked objects.
Clearly, there are also many issues on the political, legal, and social level to consider. Privacy is certainly a primary concern when devices or smart everyday objects can be localized and traced, and when various objects we use daily report their state and sensor information to other objects. The repercussions of such an extensive integration of computer technology into our everyday lives as Pervasive Computing advocates it, are difficult to predict and only time will tell whether this technology does contribute to a better and more enjoyable world or, on the contrary, promote a more totalitarian regime.

D. Hutter et al. (Eds.): Security in Pervasive Computing 2003, LNCS 2802, p. 1, 2004.
© Springer-Verlag Berlin Heidelberg 2004

Cyber Assist Project
and Its Security Requirement
(Abstract of Invited Talk)

Hideyuki Nakashima

Cyber Assist Research Center
AIST Tokyo Waterfront, 2-41-6 Aomi,
Koto-ku, Tokyo 135-0064, Japan
h.nakashima@aist.go.jp

1 Introduction

The Goal of the Cyber Assist Project is realization of a ubiquitous, or pervasive, information society in which all can benefit from assistance of information
processing technology (IT hereafter) in all situations of daily life.

Traditional IT is accessible only through computers sitting on a desktop. Its
accessibility is broadening recently with the spread of mobile devices including
mobile phones with i-mode. Nevertheless, such technology is used only by a small
portion of people in rather limited scenarios of their everyday lives. IT should
be able to support human in every aspect of everyday life with information
processing units embedded in the environment which communicate with portable
or wearable personal devices. Keywords are "here, now and me". IT will be able
to help human daily life by automatically booking a seat in a train according
to an individual schedule, by guiding a user through a shopping mall while
providing necessary information about goods, or automatically calling a taxi or
requesting bus service when needed. Through this technology, we believe that
IT can boost the quality of life in economy, politics, culture, and education.

To widen the range of opportunity for receiving assistance from IT, computers
should be able to share the semantics of tasks with humans. We must pull
computers from their digital world into our physical world by providing various
sensors and visual and acoustic recognition technologies. For instance, if a mobile
phone can understand that its holder has a visitor and is discussing an important
issue, it may be able to automatically forward incoming calls to a secretary.

We need new network architecture to support the technology. It must be capable of dynamic reconfiguration and connection with very low latency, creating
"responsive" network technology.

Another technology necessary for semantic sharing is worldwide document
processing with tagging, ontology, and semantic search as proposed in the Seman-
ticWeb project. We cooperate with that movement and will develop "intelligent
content" technologies.

D. Hutter et al. (Eds.): Security in Pervasive Computing 2003, LNCS 2802, pp. 2–5, 2004.
© Springer-Verlag Berlin Heidelberg 2004

2 Cyber Assist Project

Our project is classified as follows. We have two main targets:

1. Situated information support
2. Privacy protection

We also have two main approaches:

1. Location-based communications
2. Intelligent contents

The four cross-sections yield the following research issues:

2.1 Semantic Structuring

A major cause of information overload and the 'digital divide' is the semantic gap between humans and computers; humans are adapted to dealing with deep meaning, while machines excel at processing explicit syntax. The only feasible way to fill this gap systematically is to make the semantic structure of information content explicit so that machines can manage them too. [Hasida 2000]

2.2 Non-ID Communication

There exist two global communication networks: the telephone network and the Internet. Telephone systems use a phone number as a global ID to reach each telephone in the world. Communication over the Internet is based on IP-addresses, which are also a global ID for each processing unit connected to the network. When communication is overheard, it is easy to connect content to recipients using those global IDs. In a ubiquitous computing environment, the majority of communication is computer to computer: frequency is much larger in magnitude. If ubiquitous computing follows this tradition, it may endanger privacy protection. For instance, if someone discovers the IP address of a TV set, all programs a user watches may be monitored. It is therefore recommended to use locally- resolved IDs wherever possible. It is even better to use no IDs at all.

One candidate for non-ID communication is to use physical location as a target address of communication. We call this location-based communication. We are testing various methods for location-based communication using optical and radio connections.

2.3 Location-Based Services

The main (positive) target of our project is situated information support. If a server knows the user's situation, it can provide more fine-tuned information support without querying the user's selections. There may be many keys to this; we regard location as a most prominent physical property.

One form of location-based service is to provide information only to a certain area of 3D space. For example, in a museum, detailed information of an entry is broadcast to the area in front of an exhibition, but only to those facing it.

As a communication device to receive such information, we developed a very simple compact battery-less information terminal called CoBIT [Nishimura 2002]. In our design, devices embedded in the environment play many important roles. CoBIT is equipped with a reflective sheet whose location can be identified easily from cameras mounted in the environment. Then an infrared beam is projected toward the direction from a LED scanner that is capable of tracking CoBIT movement . Note that there is no need for any ID to establish communication. Physical location of the terminal is an essential and unique key of the device. The infrared signal is modulated using a sound wave; CoBIT replays it as auditory information. The infrared beam itself is the power source of CoBIT; thus, there is no need to have any internal power supply. Cameras in the environment will see the reflection from the reflective sheet of CoBIT to know its location, direction and movement (gesture). Therefore, CoBIT functions as a two way communication terminal even without its own internal power source.

In ubiquitous computing, many devices in the vicinity of the user are used. How does one know which devices are near to the user, and free to use? The location of user may be given by the name of the building, or longitude and latitude of GPS positioning. Those must be converted from one to another. Multiagent architecture plays important roles for access control of those devices. We are developing location identification (including conversion between coordinates and names) and access control architecture called Consorts [Kurumatani 2003].

2.4   Tally Method

In old movies, there were plots employing a map of hidden treasure split into two and possessed by two participants. Two of them must get together to unveil the location. We are seeking a digital version of similar technology. Double encryption is an obvious candidate. But once data is decoded, it is plain data and both participants can copy it freely. What we seek is protected data that can be used only when both of tally holders are present.

These days, a customer's personal data may be gathered by each individual service provider. For instance: a mail order company has a customer's record of purchase; a mobile phone company has a record of outgoing and incoming phone calls as well as history of the trajectory of the mobile phone device with accuracy of cellular area of its connection station; a hospital has a record of a patient's past treatment and medical examinations. If those data are gathered into a single database, it may contain a large amount of personal information. Such accumulation itself is dangerous from the perspective of privacy protection. On the other hand, if those data are used for the benefit of the individual only, they may constitute a valuable personal database. We are seeking a solution to this problem. We seek to protect privacy information while using all data for the sake of the individual. One compromise is that those data be used only when the target person, or their software agent, is present.

We have no solution to this problem at the moment. We believe that clever use of a physical property like location could solve the problem.

References

[Hasida 2000] Koiti Hasida: GDA: Annotated Document as Intelligent Content. Invited talk at COLING 2000 Workshop on Semantic Annotation and Intelligent Content, Luxembourg. 2000.

[Nakashima 2002] Hideyuki Nakashima: Cyber Assist Project for Situated Human Support, Keynote Speech, Proc. The Eights International Conference on Distributed Multimedia Systems, Knowledge Systems Institute, ISBN 1-891706-11-X, pp. 3-7, 2002

[Nishimura 2002] Takuichi Nishimura, Hideo Itoh, Yoshinov Yamamoto and Hideyuki Nakashima: A Compact Battery-less Information Terminal (CoBIT) for Location-based Support Systems, In Proceedings of International Symposium on Optical Science and Technology (SPIE), 4863B-12. 2002.

[Kurumatani 2003] Koichi Kurumatani: Social Coordination with Architecture for Ubiquitous Agents: CONSORTS, Proc. of International Conference on Intelligent Agents, Web Technologies and Internet Commerce IAWTIC'2003 (Vienna), in Proceedings CDROM (2003).

Security in Pervasive Computing

(Abstract of Invited Talk)

Frank Stajano

University of Cambridge
http://www-lce.eng.cam.ac.uk/~fms27/

The audience of SPC 2003 needs no introduction to the Mark Weiser vision of ubiquitous computing: the etymological meaning of "computing present or found everywhere" is not to be taken in the narrow sense of "a computer on every desk" but rather in that of embedding computing and communication capabilities into all the everyday objects that surround us.

Various embodiments of this vision have been proposed over the past fifteen years by researchers from all over the world, covering the whole spectrum of implementation maturity from thought experiments to well-engineered commercial solutions. From self-contained information appliances such as Norman's hypothetical "home medical advisor" to the microscopic embedded RF-ID tags proposed by the Auto-ID Center that allow the washing machine to refuse to wash your precious white shirts until you remove the red sock that got in there by mistake, the idea of computing devices pervading our environment is now much closer to reality than to science fiction.

Moving from one computer per company in the 1960s to one computer per desktop in the 1990s to *hundreds* of computers per person in the current decade is an enormous quantitative change. So large, in fact, that it becomes also a quantitative one. Many old solutions will not scale by so many orders of magnitude. Recycling obsolete paradigms may lead to expensive mistakes—particularly in the field of security.

Authentication is an area in which the advent of pervasive computing will require new ideas and new strategies. We have relied for a long time on passwords as the primary mechanism for authenticating a user to a computer; this solution was never particularly user-friendly ("invent a password, including funny characters and numbers, that you won't forget or write down, but that nobody could possibly guess"), but it is obvious that it will never scale to the scenario of hundreds of computers per person.

Interestingly, the very first computers—of ENIAC and EDSAC vintage—did not require passwords to be accessed: one would just walk up to them and load a punched paper tape in the reader. Neither did the first personal computers, before they were linked up into LANs or the Internet. These are examples of the "Big Stick" security policy model: *whoever has physical access to the device is allowed to take it over*. In its simplicity, this policy is a very good match for many real-world situations. It is effective, sensible and reasonably easy to enforce. In many pervasive computing usage cases it will be a better strategy than passwords. Big Stick, however, is not suitable for every situation. Think of a vending machine or, for a more extreme example, a safe.

A central new problem in the pervasive computing scenario is therefore that of "Secure Transient Association": pairing up a master and a slave device so that the slave will

D. Hutter et al. (Eds.): Security in Pervasive Computing 2003, LNCS 2802, pp. 6–8, 2004.
© Springer-Verlag Berlin Heidelberg 2004

obey the master, will stay faithful to that master even when under physical control of hostile principals, but also will switch allegiance to a new master if the original master tells it to do so.

The solution is the "Resurrecting Duckling" security policy model. The slave device behaves like a newborn duckling that is permanently imprinted to whatever it first sees at birth. The "mother duck" master device is the only entity that can fully determine the behaviour of the duckling; this total control even allows the mother duck to order the duckling to "commit suicide" and be born again, at which point the duckling may get imprinted to a new mother duck. One crucial aspect of this policy model is its explicit reliance on a tamper resistance element in the duckling, to prevent the "assassination" case in which someone other than the mother duck attempts to cause the duckling's death so as to re-imprint it to itself. The Duckling policy fruitfully applies to a very wide range of practical applications—from universal remote control of home appliances to wireless car keys and from biomedical devices to thermonuclear warheads.

Pervasive computing brings convenience but also risk. Many things happen automatically, which is a relief, but their side effects are not always fully anticipated. Location-based services allow applications to customize their service to you based on where you are; but are you happy for the application provider to know your whereabouts on an ongoing basis, every few minutes, at city-block resolution? What about every few seconds and at sub-metre resolution? Protecting location privacy will be a challenge. We have designed a scheme based on frequently-changed pseudonyms, so that applications could provide their location-based service to customers protected by anonymity; and then we have tried to break it, simulating a malicious application that aimed to find out the identities that the users were attempting to protect. There is still much useful work to be done in this area.

Since the deployment of pervasive computing will have such a wide-ranging impact on society, we security professionals have to examine the proposed scenarios with critical eyes, imagining all the ways in which things could go wrong, and bearing in mind all the parties for whom things could go wrong.

Having previously mentioned authorization, for example, the security question that should be asked more often is: *authorized by whom?*. The obvious answer used to be *by the owner of the machine*; but this is no longer necessarily true in the new world of "Digital Restrictions Management". I bought a Sony Minidisc to record my lectures in digital format, only to discover that I can't take a backup of these discs. I am the owner of both the recorder and the copyright of the recording, and yet I can't get at my own bits... Who is the bad guy being kept out?

As architects of this new digitally endowed world of pervasive computing, we technical people have an ethical duty to pay attention to the fair requirements of all the parties involved—especially those without the money, lobbying power or technical astuteness to speak up for themselves.

This invited contribution was just a high level overview as opposed to a research paper. Readers interested in the details of my actual work on this topic may choose to follow the selected references provided below.

References

1. Frank Stajano. *Security for Ubiquitous Computing*. John Wiley and Sons, 2002. ISBN 0-470-84493-0. http://www-lce.eng.cam.ac.uk/ fms27/secubicomp/.
2. Alastair Beresford and Frank Stajano. "Location Privacy in Pervasive Computing". *IEEE Pervasive Computing* 2(1):46–55, 2003. http://www-lce.eng.cam.ac.uk/ fms27/papers/2003-BeresfordSta-location.pdf.
3. Frank Stajano. "Security For Whom? The Shifting Security Assumptions Of Pervasive Computing", in *Software Security—Theories and Systems*, LNCS 2609, pp. 100–111, Springer, 2003. http://www-lce.eng.cam.ac.uk/ fms27/papers/2003-Stajano-shifting.pdf.

The Importance of High Assurance Security in Pervasive Computing

(Abstract of Invited Talk)

Paul A. Karger

IBM Thomas J. Watson Research Center
PO Box 704,
Yorktown Heights, NY 10598, USA

This talk will focus on the benefits that high assurance security (EAL6 or higher) can provide to pervasive computing devices. High assurance security is essential to defeating the attacks of sophisticated penetrators, and must be combined with countermeasures to defeat a variety of physical attacks, including threats such as power analysis, RF leakage, and fault insertion. The argument will be supported with examples from IBM's work on development of a high-assurance smart card operating system, but will also discuss issues for such devices as cell phones and PDAs. Difficulties encountered in the Common Criteria evaluation process are also presented.

D. Hutter et al. (Eds.): Security in Pervasive Computing 2003, LNCS 2802, p. 9, 2004.
© Springer-Verlag Berlin Heidelberg 2004

A Methodological Assessment of Location Privacy Risks in Wireless Hotspot Networks

Marco Gruteser and Dirk Grunwald

Department of Computer Science
University of Colorado at Boulder
Boulder, CO 80309
{gruteser,grunwald}@cs.colorado.edu

Abstract. Mobile computing enables users to compute and communicate almost regardless of their current location. However, as a side effect this technology considerably increased surveillance potential for user movements. Current research addresses location privacy rather patchwork-like than comprehensively. Thus, this paper presents a methodology for identifying, assessing, and comparing location privacy risks in mobile computing technologies. In a case study, we apply the approach to IEEE 802.11b wireless LAN networks and location-based services, where it reveals significant location privacy concerns through link- and application-layer information. From a technological perspective, we argue that these are best addressed through novel anonymity-based mechanisms.

1 Introduction

Pervasive computing promises near-ubiquitous access to information and computing services. Indeed, advances in mobile computing and networking, both wireless and the higher penetration of wired networks, have increased the spatial and temporal coverage of computing services. Users can access computing services from virtually anywhere, anytime.

Wireless networks also provide the ability to approximately track the location of users. Moreover, specialized location sensing technology has seen a dramatic reduction in price. These developments spurred an immense interest in exploiting this positional data through location-based services (LBS) [1–4]. For instance, LBS could tailor their functionality to the user's current location, or vehicle movement data could improve traffic forecasting and road planning.

The ability to track users' location, however, also creates considerable privacy concerns. For example, these privacy risks received attention through discussions about the use of IMSI Catchers [5], which can identify and locate GSM mobile phones, and several cases of monitoring the movements of rental cars through GPS receivers[1].

---

[1] At least in one case [6], a rental car company used GPS technology to monitor the driving speed of their customers. When the company-set threshold speed limit of 79mph was exceeded, the company automatically charged a USD 150 speeding fee per occurrence on the customer's credit card. The fines were later found illegal, however the company is still allowed to track its cars [7].

D. Hutter et al. (Eds.): Security in Pervasive Computing 2003, LNCS 2802, pp. 10–24, 2004.
© Springer-Verlag Berlin Heidelberg 2004

Many different technologies are affected by these location privacy risks. Moreover, an adversary can potentially derive location information at different layers of the network stack. For example, at the physical layer through triangulation of the wireless signal, or at the network layer through DNS names of intermediate routers.

Effective privacy-enhancing technologies need to address these privacy risks according to their significance. At the data collection stage, this requires a framework and methodology for comparing and evaluating the privacy risks associated with different technologies. Specifically, this paper provides the following key contributions:

- A preliminary framework and methodology for identifying, comparing, and evaluating the significance of location privacy risks in network-related technologies.
- A case study that applies this methodology to IEEE 802.11b wireless LAN hotspot networks.
- A discussion of research directions to address the identified privacy challenges.

The remainder of this paper is structured as follows. Section 2 provides background in wireless networks, location-based services, and the resulting location privacy challenges. Section 3 then details the methodology for identifying and assessing location privacy risks. This methodology is applied to WLAN networks in Sect. 4. After covering related work that enhances location privacy in Sect. 5, we describe research directions for improving location privacy in WLAN networks in Sect. 6.

2 Background

In recent times, digital wireless networks revolutionized the telecommunications and networking industry. Wireless networks offer at least two key advantages over their wired counterparts. First, they allow for user mobility by untethering users from fixed communications stations such as desktop PCs or landline telephones. Second, they can achieve broad spatial coverage with less deployment effort due to the reduced need for installing cables.

Successful digital wireless networking standards include the Global System for Mobile Communications [8] for mobile phones and IEEE 802.11b [9] for wireless local area networks (WLAN). While the telecommunications industry is struggling to absorb the high initial investment costs for deploying higher bandwidth, packet-switched mobile phone networks (3G networks), WLAN technology has emerged as a cost-effective alternative for providing wireless network access in restricted areas.

WLAN hotspots are deployed in many residential homes, universities, and industry campuses. More recently, commercial wireless access services have also been offered to the public at coffee shops, airport lounges, and hotels. The term hotspot illustrates that WLAN provides higher bandwidth than 3G networks—11 Mbps compared to a target of 2 Mbps for 3G networks in Europe—but focuses the signal on a much smaller area of interest, typically with a radius of approximately 150 feet. Thus, WLAN networks achieve less spatial coverage than mobile phone networks, but concentrate the coverage on key areas. However, researchers (e.g. Negroponte [10]) envision WLAN access points to route messages between different hotspots. Thus, access points would form a mesh network that greatly increases coverage beyond a single WLAN network. Larger distances between wireless networks could be bridged through wired connections or specialized antenna equipment.

2.1 Location-Based Services

Mobile computing has enabled users to access computing services at many different locations. In addition, location sensing or positioning technology allows automated tracking of users' positions. Particularly well-known is the Global Positioning System [11], which determines location through reference signals emitted by satellites. In 2002, Motorola unveiled a GPS chip that is small and cost-effective enough to be included in a wide range of consumer devices. The chip only measures about 50 square millimeters and costs $10 in volume quantities [12]. According to Tim McCarthy, business director for GPS at Motorola's Automotive Group's Telematics Division, position awareness has a bright future: "All of a sudden, starting 10 or 15 years ago, every electronics device had a clock. I see position awareness going down that same path. It's just a question of how long it takes" [12]. Ambuj Goyal, IBM, goes further in predicting prices for GPS chips to drop to a few cents [13]. Many other location sensing technologies are described in a survey by Hightower [14]. In the United States, widespread deployment of such technologies is encouraged by the Federal Communications Commission since it mandated that locating mobile phones must be possible for emergency purposes [15].

Thus, location-based services (LBS) have emerged, which combine positioning technology with the mobile Internet. Location information becomes an additional input parameter to customize the service. For example, the Webraska Corporation [16] offers applications ranging from navigational services that provide driving directions over point-of-interest or accommodation finders to automotive fleet management. These applications transmit the user's current position over a wireless network to the server hosting the location-based service. Location information also proved useful for customizing functionality to the user's current situation. For example, context-aware tour guides [17] automatically adjust the presented information and menu options to the user's current location.

2.2 Location Privacy

These advances in location sensing and communication technology have significantly decreased the effort to track an individual's movements. Historically, the current location and the history of movements of an individual were little known to other parties. Only through cooperation of the individual or intensive investigative effort could this information be obtained. Today, positioning technologies can easily determine a subject's position, improved database and storage technology permits permanent recording and wide distribution of this data, and data mining enables the detection of movement patterns.

Not surprisingly, information privacy concerns have mounted globally [18–20]. Issues range from detailed, publicly available satellite imagery over data collection on the Internet to DNA databases. In surveys, consumers reiterate their concern for privacy. For example, according to one survey 94% of web user have denied a request for personal information and 40% have provided fake data [21].

In the United States, Privacy risks related to *location* information have been identified in the Location Privacy Protection Act of 2001 [22]. While public disclosure of location information enables a variety of useful services, such as improved emergency assistance, it also exhibits significant potential for misuse. For example, location information can be used to *spam* users with advertisements or to learn about users medical conditions, alternative lifestyles, or unpopular political views. Inferences can be drawn from visits to clinics, doctors' offices, entertainment districts, or political events. Such conclusions can be particularly annoying for subjects if they are inaccurate. In extreme cases, public location information can lead to physical harm such as in stalking or domestic abuse scenarios. Karger and Frankel provide a more detailed discussion of security and privacy risks in Intelligent Transport Systems [23].

Location information is valuable for location-based services because it implicitly conveys characteristics that describe the situation of a person. However, the foregoing examples illustrate how adversaries can exploit the same information to cause harm to a person. Phil Agre also warns us of such location privacy issues [24]. Specifically, he is concerned about a widespread deployment of automatic face recognition technology. He fears "spottings markets" that trade information about the times and locations where people have been identified[2]. Wireless networking could provide an even easier means for spotting people.

3 Methodology

A location privacy threat describes the risk that an untrusted party can locate a transmitting device *and* identify the subject using the device. We make the assumption that a

---

[2] Excerpted from Phil Agre [24]: "My candidate for Privacy Chernobyl is the widespread deployment in public places of automatic face recognition. [...] And that's just the start. Wait a little while, and a market will arise in "spottings": if I want to know where you've been, I'll have my laptop put out a call on the Internet to find out who has spotted you. Spottings will be bought and sold in automated auctions, so that I can build the kind of spotting history I need for the lowest cost. Entrepreneurs will purchase spottings in bulk to synthesize spotting histories for paying customers. Your daily routine will be known to anyone who wants to pay five bucks for it, and your movement history will determine your fate just as much as your credit history does now. Prominent firms that traffic in personal movement patterns will post privacy policies that sound nice but mean little in practice, not least because most of the movement trafficking will be conducted by companies that nobody has ever heard of, and whose brand names will not be affected by the periodic front-page newspaper stories on the subject. They will all swear on a stack of Bibles that they respect everyone's privacy, but within six months every private investigator in the country will find a friend-of-a-brother-in-law who happens to know someone who works for one of the obscure companies that sells movement patterns, and the data will start to ooze out onto the street.

Then things will really get bad. Personal movement records will be subpoenaed, irregularly at first, just when someone has been kidnapped, but then routinely, as every divorce lawyer in the country reasons that subpoenas are cheap and not filing them is basically malpractice. Then, just as we're starting to get used to this, a couple of people will get killed by a nut who been [sic] predicting their movements using commercially available movement patterns. Citizens will be outraged, but it will indeed be too late ..."

subject sporadically sends and receives messages, likely from different locations in the area covered by the wireless network. The adversary seeks to obtain information from these messages. An assessment of location privacy risks should proceed accordingly. Based on the data subject's messages, it should analyze how location information can be obtained, how originators can be identified, and who has the means to do so.

3.1 Locating

The originator can be located through a variety of mechanisms, for example eavesdropping when the originator explicitly reveals location information to a LBS or triangulating the wireless signal. A careful analysis of the information contained in each layer of the network stack reveals possible approaches for location determination. These approaches are then characterized according to the following privacy-enhancing criteria.

User Choice. Location systems differ widely on how much control a user has over the system. An ideal system would allow users to hide while still providing full functionality; however, in practice a user usually experiences inconveniences. For example, the signal of a mobile phone may be located through triangulation. The user can prevent this by switching the phone off; however, the user is then unable to receive or originate phone calls.

Restricted Coverage. Location sensing technologies are often restricted to function only in certain areas (spatial coverage) or during certain times (temporal coverage). Spatial coverage can range from near universal for the GPS system to occasional for a credit card-based location tracking. In the credit card case, location information is only available at point of sale terminals, which are sparsely distributed over populated areas. Furthermore, it is restricted to the occasions when a subject uses a credit card at the terminal.

Lower Resolution and Accuracy. In their areas of coverage, location sensing technologies achieve different resolutions. Higher resolution conveys significantly more information. Consider a system that achieves 1 km resolution versus a system with 1 meter resolution. The first system reveals information such as the city name and district. The latter system can additionally disclose the exact building and even room, where a subject is located.

3.2 Identifying

Identification of the subject means that an adversary learns the real-world name of a subject, such as legal name and address of residence. Network addresses, for instance, are not necessarily considered identifying information, since not every party can correlate a network address to a real-world name and address. Rather, we consider network addresses *pseudonyms*, information that can help identifying a subject.

Note that locating and identifying are not completely independent tasks, since distinct location information helps in identifying subjects. Assume that a user does not disclose her identity but includes precise location information in a transaction. The recipient could correlate the location with location information obtained through other means to identify the user. For example, when the transaction originates from a private residential driveway, it can be easily linked to a public address database. This likely reveals the originator and violates location privacy. Even if the location information itself is less sensitive, it can be used to link other private information (e.g., the content of the transaction) to the user.

Location information can identify the sender of an otherwise anonymous message, if the information is correlated with public knowledge or observations about a subject's location. Consider the case where a subject sends a message M to a location-based service and an adversary A gains access to the subject's location information L. Then, sender anonymity is threatened by location information in the following ways.

Restricted Space Identification. If A knows that space L exclusively belongs to subject S then A learns that S is in L and S has sent M. For example, consider the owner of a suburbian house sending a message from his garage or driveway. The coordinates can be correlated with a database of geocoded postal addresses, such as provided by Geocode [25], to identify the residence. An address lookup in phone or property listings then reveals the owner and likely originator of the message.

Observation Identification. If A has observed the current location L of subject S and finds a message M from L then A learns that S has sent M. For example, the subject has revealed its identity and location in a previous message and then wants to send an anonymous message. The later message can be linked to the previous one through location information.

These identification approaches require high-resolution location information. Specifically, the resolution needs to be high enough to distinguish a subject from other persons and to pinpoint her at a restricted space or to uniquely match the observation.

A more sophisticated identification approach depends on the ability to link messages, but allows lower resolution location information. Linking messages means determining that two or more message stem from the same originator, whose identity is not necessarily known. The approach accumulates location data over periods of time to prepare a movement profile. For example, an adversary could learn from the profile that the morning commute takes a subject from a certain suburb to a certain work location. By filtering residential addresses and work address the subject might be identified.

The ability to link messages provides another advantage for the adversary. If the originator of a set of messages is already identified it can be easier to link new messages to the existing set than to use other identification mechanisms on the new messages. One technique for linking messages is based on pseudonyms. If two messages contain the same pseudonym, they most likely stem from the same originator.

If the subject transmits her location with high resolution and frequency, the adversary can, at least in less populated areas, also link messages based on physical constraints and knowledge of the area. For example, maximum speeds of data subjects are known. Furthermore, an adversary might use road maps, which describe likely travel paths and give clues about the expected speed. The adversary could then link messages received from different locations based on this spatio-temporal analysis.

3.3 Data Collectors

Finally, an important consideration is *who* has access to the location data. We characterize the data collectors as follows:

Dispersion. Measurements stations can be geographically distributed and potentially belong to different organizations. This increases the effort of collecting data, because for effective cross-organizational surveillance, data must be compiled into a central database. We characterize relationships according to the degree of cooperation and data sharing between different network operators or LBS providers.

Trust and Recourse. Trust relationships between data subjects and service providers can differ substantially. Here, we consider only trust related to location privacy, not other concerns such as reliability or security. The relationship can range from complete mistrust to a contractual relationship. In the complete mistrust scenario, the network operator is likely unknown to the data subject or even a known privacy offender. A legally binding privacy contract with a reputable company typically establishes a higher level of trustworthiness compared to an unknown provider.

4   Wireless LAN Risk Assessment

In a case study, we apply the described methodology to a wireless LAN and location-based services environment. The following subsections provide an analysis of possible approaches to determine location information, link messages, or identify subjects.

4.1   Determining Location

Resolution. Most easily, location information can be obtained, when the subject explicitly includes it in the messages. For example, the current location of the subject, as determined by a GPS receiver, could be sent to a LBS that provides driving directions to a specific destination. In this case, both LBS providers and network operators have access to the location information. However, even if location information is not explicitly included in the message, the following mechanism can gather it.

Coarse location information can be obtained at the network layer. While IP-addresses are not assigned according to geographic locations, the hierarchical structure leads to a geographic concentration of address ranges. For example, all addresses within the subnets assigned to a university campus are typically collocated. However, proxies and firewalls are a common obstacle, since they can hide the true address.

The techniques to determine the location of regular internet hosts can be categorized dependent on their information source: DNS name clues and registration information, network delay measurements [26], and web service registrations. DNS names of routers usually include geographic clues such as city names. Therefore *traceroute*-based mechanisms [27] reveal an approximate location. Another widely used approach queries WHOIS servers for the registered contact address information. The geoclustering algorithm [26] combines a clustering technique based on routing information with location information gathered from user registrations at popular web services. Its median error distance varies from below 50 kilometers to several hundred kilometers.

At the physical and link layer, access points can estimate the position of a transmitter based on proximity. If packets are received from the transmitter, it must be within range of a typical 802.11b system - around 50-100 meters. Higher resolution is provided by triangulation mechanisms of which several systems for indoor WLAN installation have been developed [28–30]. They measure the signal strength of received packets to determine position. Together with Bayesian signal processing approaches, resolutions up to 1m can be achieved. However, it is not clear, whether these high resolutions can also be obtained in outdoor mesh networks because the distance between WLAN base stations is likely greater than in an indoor setting.

Coverage. Information included in the application layer and network layer are visible to servers and all parties whose routers a packet traverses. However, only parties in range of the transmitter can access information in the link and physical layer. Therefore, accessibility to link layer information is typically restricted to a smaller set of wireless network operators. However, these risks cannot be ignored considering the astonishing density of access points found in major metropolitan areas. Figure 1 shows the density of access points in downtown Chicago. The map was obtained from the Wireless Geographic Logging Engine [31], which collects and merges data from the *Netstumbler* WLAN monitoring software [32]. Judging by the density of access points, it is difficult to use a WLAN network without being detected by other parties.

Fig. 1. IEEE 802.11b Access Points in Downtown Chicago

User Choice. Most of the described mechanisms do not offer the user a choice whether he allows others to locate the device. For the physical and link layer approaches, the choice is made implicitly, when the user activates the wireless network card. Even when the card is not actively used for data traffic, it will transmit beacons that are sufficient for the location determination mechanisms. At the network layer, the choice is similarly implicit. When the user communicates with any network entity, his network address will be visible to intermediate routers and the communication partner.

GPS location information differs in that position is calculated in a client-side receiver. No signals are emitted from this receiver, which would enable remote parties to determine the location of the receiver. In the GPS case, the user can make an explicit choice to disclose the locally determined location information to another party, for instance to a LBS.

4.2   Identifying a Subject

Pseudonym-based approaches for linking messages are possible on all layers of the network stack. At the application layer user or login names help in linking messages to the same originator, even if the user hides his real identity. The IP-address also provides an easily accessible pseudonym at the network layer. However, IP-addresses tend to change more frequently than service logins, because many clients are configured with dynamic IP addresses, which are assigned on a temporary basis through the Dynamic Host Configuration Protocol. More static identifiers are also available at the link layer, where MAC addresses provide a simple way to identify packets originating from the same transmitter.

4.3   Data Collectors

As illustrated in figure 2, several entities can be distinguished to clarify whose location privacy should be protected from which adversaries:

Data Subject. The data subject is the person to whom the private information relates. The subjects access services over the network through client devices such as laptops, PDAs, or in-car PCs. They typically move among different cells of the wireless network as they go about their daily life.

Wireless Network Operator. Wireless network operators maintain base stations, which form the wireless network. An operator can maintain any number of base stations. Some operators will only have a single base station, while others set up multiple clusters of base stations. Wireless network operators have access to network and application layer information if they act as routers. In addition, they can also access link and physical layer information if packets are directly received from the client device. Even if packets are intended for another access point, wireless network operators may be able to eavesdrop on the information.

Location-Based Service Providers. Location-based services can be provided by arbitrary servers connected to the wireless or wired network. Over the network, LBS providers can typically access only network and application layer information. However, they may receive partial location information from other sources.

The same party might exhibit multiple roles. For example, a person could install a set of base stations, provide a location-based service, and use the wireless network himself. However, more typically, different companies act as the LBS provider and the wireless network operators.

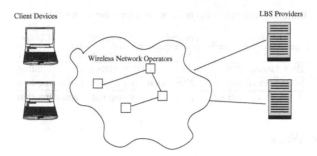

Fig. 2. Architectural context

Since wireless access points are relatively inexpensive, many different parties will act as wireless network operators. Thus, trust relationships will also differ. In some cases, a formal contract may be established between data subjects and the network operators. This contract is likely part of the service agreement under a subscription-based plan. Such a plan typically provides wireless coverage at lucrative hotspot locations, for example in coffee shops[3]. In these cases, service providers may be trustworthier. However, network operators can also enter into roaming agreements, which allow data subjects to use the same access plans on different networks, but also to share collected data. Additionally, data subjects are then likely to use services from network operators without a direct contractual agreement. Moreover, we expect also many little-known entities to act as wireless network operators. Service and privacy will most likely not be governed by a contract. The relationship between data subjects and LBS providers exhibits a similar range of trust characteristics.

Unfortunately, WLAN location privacy issues are further complicated because other parties can easily overhear communications. Everybody can install an access point and thus act as a network operator. Even when data subjects' wireless cards are not associated with the access point, link layer information is visible. In fact, not even an access point is required for monitoring wireless users. Some wireless cards, those based on Prism chipsets, can emulate an access point through software and thus provide the ability to monitor other subjects. When such access points are operated in the vicinity of medical clinics or other privacy sensitive areas, major privacy issues arise.

4.4 Summary

Table 1 summarizes the location determination mechanisms. The most accurate location information is either included at the application layer or can be determined through triangulation at the link layer. Based on this information, identification of a subject is possible for both wireless network operators and LBS providers (if the subject chooses to reveal the location). This leads to significant privacy concerns, especially because of the ease with which untrusted network operators can overhear and locate a subject's communications.

---

[3] Such as the service delivered by T-Mobile to many US Starbucks coffee shops.

Table 1. Characterization of location determination mechanisms

Method	Accuracy	Coverage	Choice
GPS	10m	Near-universal	explicit
IP-Address, DNS	50km +	address dependent	implicit
WLAN Proximity	50-200m	Densely populated areas	implicit
WLAN Triangulation	1-10m	Densely populated areas	implicit

5 Related Work

Prior work on privacy aspects of telematics and location-based applications has mostly focused on a policy-based approach [33, 34]. Data subjects need to evaluate and choose privacy policies offered by the service provider. These policies serve as a contractual agreement about which data can be collected, for what purpose the data can be used, and how it can be distributed. Typically, the data subject has to trust the service provider that private data is adequately protected. In contrast, the anonymity-based approach de-personalizes data before collection, thus detailed privacy-policies and safeguards for data are not critical. Specifically, the IETF *Geopriv* working group is addressing privacy and security issues regarding the transfer of high resolution location information to external services and the storage at location servers. It focuses on the design of protocols and APIs that enable devices to communicate their location in a confidential and integrity preserving manner to a location server.

Snekkenes [35] presents concepts for specifying location privacy policies. These concepts enable access control decisions based on the identity of the requestor and purpose of the request. In addition, time, location, speed, and identity of the located object influence the decision. In the policy specifications, accuracy of temporal, location, and identity information is modeled using a lattice. However, the author concludes by expressing doubt that the average user will specify such policies.

The Mist routing project for mobile users [36] combines location privacy with communication aspects. It focuses on the problem of routing messages to a subject's location while keeping the location private from the routers and the sender. To this end, the system is comprised of a set of mist routers organized in a hierarchical structure. The leaf nodes have knowledge of the location of users but not their identity. They refer to them through handles (or pseudonyms). Each user selects a higher-level node in the tree, which acts as a semi-trusted proxy. It knows the identity of the user but not his exact location. The paper then presents a cryptographic protocol to establish connections between users and their semi-trusted proxies and mechanisms to connect to communication partners through their proxies. The paper does not address the problem of sending anonymous messages to external location-based services.

Mobile IP enables hosts to transparently migrate between different networks by registering the current location with a home agent that tunnels all traffic to the current network. Thus, adversary can track the location of a host by observing the registration messages and the payload messages through the tunnel. The Non-Disclosure-Method [37] method places several rerouting security agents between home and foreign network. Security agents forward messages in encrypted form; therefore, it is hard to trace the path of a message if the security agents are spread over several administrative domains. This method hides the care-of network address of a host from intermediary routers, but it does not address explicit application layer information, provide anonymity with respect to a server, or anonymity with respect to the foreign agent.

Narten and Draves propose privacy extensions for stateless address autoconfiguration in IPv6 [38]. Server-less address autocofiguration in IPv6 can use the MAC address of network interfaces as part of the network layer IP-address. Thus the MAC address becomes visible to servers and intermediaries outside the local area network. This enables such outside entities to track movements of mobile nodes between different networks. The proposed solution switches the network address periodically. New addresses are generated through iterative applications of the MD5 message digest algorithm on the previous network address and the actual MAC address.

Location privacy has also influenced the design of location sensor systems. The Cricket system [39] places location sensors on the mobile device as opposed to the building infrastructure. Thus, location information is not disclosed during the position determination process and the data subject can choose the parties to which the information should be transmitted. However, this solution does not provide for anonymity. Similarily, Smailagic and Kogan [40] addressed privacy in a WLAN location sensing system.

6 Research Directions

We believe that the multi-faceted issue of location privacy must be addressed through a variety of means encompassing legislative, self-regulation, and technological approaches. This discussion focuses on the technological approaches at the data collection stage. As alluded to before, an invasion of location privacy requires that an untrusted party can locate a person *and* identify the person. This suggests at least three alternative approaches to enhance location privacy. First, the data subject establishes trust in the unknown party before it reveals location information, for example through an exchange of privacy policies and privacy preferences. Second, the untrusted party can learn the identity of the subject, but is unable to locate the subject. And third, the untrusted party can locate a subject, however, the subject remains anonymous.

The first approach requires the data subjects to read, understand, and evaluate the privacy policy of every service provider, before they interact with this service. Especially for spontaneous usage of services, this poses a significant burden on the data subject. Moreover, a privacy policy does not provide protection of the data. For example, company insiders could steal private data or data might be inadvertently disclosed over the Internet during software maintenance operations. If a company wishes to employ data protection technology, this significantly complicates the computing architecture and poses a high processing overhead. This approach is most appropriate for services offered by a well-known, reputed company, with which a customer whishes to engage on a longer-term basis. It cannot address privacy issues related to access points operated by unknown parties.

The second approach does not satisfy the requirements of most LBS, since a LBS needs to receive location information to perform its function. However, it could be useful for certain classes of services that work with aggregate data from a large number of individuals. The individuals could hide their true location information through data perturbation, while the service provider can still draw inferences about the distribution of values over a large population. Agrawal and Srikant [41] demonstrated such an approach for data mining applications. However, it is unclear whether the population size would be large enough in the context of LBS. In addition, it is difficult to hide location information from network operators, since they can have access to physical or link layer information. Directional antenna designs could provide a degree of protection, but would require hardware changes to wireless network cards.

The anonymity-based approach seems most promising in the WLAN and LBS context. If data remains anonymous, privacy policies and technological safeguards are not necessary. In addition, service users can reveal their true location provided that the data is not sufficiently distinctive to disclose the identity of the user. Location information could be slightly perturbed, so that it preserves anonymity but is still useful for LBS. Protection from network operators could be achieved through address switching approaches. When network and MAC address change, linking of messages becomes more difficult. Thus, network operators would be unable to track users' movements. However, address switches must be well timed so that network operators cannot link new and old addresses based on location information. If a subject is relatively alone and stationary, address switching might not be effective.

7 Conclusions

This paper presents an approach for identifying and evaluating location privacy risks in network technologies. The methodology distinguishes between location determination mechanisms, identification mechanisms, and the trust relationships between the data subjects and potential data collectors. It characterizes location determination mechanisms according to data resolution, coverage, and user choice.

In the WLAN case study, we found obtaining high-resolution location information relatively easy, provided that the user activates his network card. In addition, access points are densely distributed in highly populated areas, and in many cases, the operators of access points are not known to the data subjects and thus not trustworthy. This causes significant location privacy concerns.

Specifically, we draw the following conclusions. First, accurate location information obtained through GPS or WLAN triangulation can be sufficiently distinctive to identify subjects. Second, the presented methodological approach proved useful in identifying and comparing the location privacy risks in the WLAN case study. WLAN exhibits significant privacy risks because of the availability of inexpensive hardware and the determination of position with high resolution. Finally, anonymity mechanisms that reduce the identification risks of location information itself and hide identifiers from untrusted access points are a promising research direction.

Acknowledgments

Paul Chou and my colleagues at the IBM T.J. Watson Research Center encouraged me to research location privacy challenges. The anonymous referees provided useful comments on a draft of this paper.

References

1. Mike Spreitzer and Marvin Theimer. Providing location information in a ubiquitous computing environment. In *Proceedings of the 14th ACM SOSP*, pages 270–283, 1993.
2. Andy Harter, Andy Hopper, Pete Steggles, Andy Ward, and Paul Webster. The anatomy of a context-aware application. In *Mobile Computing and Networking*, pages 59–68, 1999.
3. Rui Jose and Nigel Davies. Scalable and flexible location-based services for ubiquitous information access. In *In Proceedings of First International Symposium on Handheld and Ubiquitous Computing, HUC'99*, pages 52–66. Springer Verlag, 1999.
4. C. Bisdikian, J. Christensen, J. Davis II, M. Ebling, G. Hunt, W. Jerome, H. Lei, and S. Maes. Enabling location-based applications. In *1st Workshop on Mobile commerce*, 2001.
5. Dirk Fox. Der imsi-catcher (in german). *Datenschutz and Datensicherheit*, 21(9), Sep 1997.
6. Robert Lemos (ZDNet News). Car spy pushes privacy limit. http://zdnet.com.com/2100-11-530115.html?legacy=zdnn, Jun 2001.
7. Robert Lemos (ZDNet News). Car rental gps speeding fines illegal. http://www.mvcf.com/news/cache/00400/, Jul 2001.
8. M. Rahnema. Overview of the gsm system and protocol architecture. *IEEE Communications Magazine*, 31(4):92–100, 1993.
9. IEEE. IEEE standard 802.11b - wireless LAN medium access control (MAC) and physical layer (PHY) specications: High speed physical layer(PHY) in the 2.4 GHz band, 1999.
10. Nicholas Negroponte. Being wireless. *Wired Magazine*, Oct 2002.
11. I. Getting. The global positioning system. *IEEE Spectrum*, 30(12):36–47, December 1993.
12. John Spooner (CNET News). Motorola: New chip will bring gps to all. http://news.com.com/2100-1040-959085.html, Sep 2002.
13. Ambuj Goyal. In talk given at NIST pervasive computing conference. 2001.
14. J. Hightower and G. Borriello. A survey and taxonomy of location sensing systems for ubiquitous computing. UW CSE 01-08-03, University of Washington, August 2001.
15. J. Reed, K. Krizman, B. Woerner, and T. Rappaport. An overview of the challenges and progress in meeting the e-911 requirement for location service. *IEEE Personal Communications Magazine*, 5(3):30–37, April 1998.
16. Webraska Mobile Technologies. Webraska website. http://www.webraska.com/.
17. Keith Cheverst, Nigel Davies, Keith Mitchell, and Adrian Friday. Experiences of developing and deploying a context-aware tourist guide: the guide project. In *Proceedings of MOBICOM*, pages 20–31. ACM Press, 2000.
18. The Economist. The end of privacy, 29th Apr 1999.
19. The Economist. The coming backlash in privacy, 9th Dec 2000.
20. Michael Froomkin. The death of privacy? *Stanford Law Review*, 52:1461–1543, May 2000.
21. Donna L. Hoffman, Thomas P. Novak, and Marcos Peralta. Building consumer trust online. *Communications of the ACM*, 42(4):80–85, 1999.
22. Location privacy protection act of 2001. US Congress, Sponsor: Sen. John Edwards (D-NC), Contact: Maureen Mahon, Legislative Assistant, Sen. Edwards / 202.224.3154 / fax 202.228.1374, http://www.techlawjournal.com/cong107/privacy/location/s1164is.asp, 2001.
23. P. A. Karger and Y. Frankel. Security and privacy threats to ITS. In *Proceedings of the Second World Congress on Intelligent Transport Systems*, volume 5, Yokohama, Japan, Nov 1995.
24. Phil E. Agre. Red rocks eater news service — notes and recommendations. http://commons.somewhere.com/rre/1999/RRE.notes.and.recommenda14.html, Dec 1999.
25. Tele Atlas North America, Inc. Geocode website. http://www.geocode.com/.
26. Venkata N. Padmanabhan and Lakshminarayanan Subramanian. An investigation of geographic mapping techniques for internet hosts. *Proceedings of SIGCOMM'2001*, page 13, 2001.

27. Ram Periakaruppan and Evi Nemeth. Gtrace — a graphical traceroute tool. In *13th Usenix Systems Administration Conference — LISA*, Seattle, WA, Nov 1999. Nov 7-12.
28. Paramvir Bahl and Venkata N. Padmanabhan. RADAR: An in-building RF-based user location and tracking system. In *INFOCOM (2)*, pages 775–784, 2000.
29. Paul Castro, Patrick Chiu, Ted Kremenek, and Richard Muntz. A probabilistic room location service for wireless networked environments. In *Proceedings of Ubicomp*, Atlanta, GA, Sep 2001.
30. Andrew M. Ladd, Kostas E. Bekris, Algis Rudys, Lydia E. Kavraki, Dan S. Wallach, and Guillaume Marceau. Robotics-based location sensing using wireless ethernet. In *Proceedings of MOBICOM*, pages 227–238. ACM Press, 2002.
31. Wireless geographic logging engine. http://wigle.net/gpsopen/gps/GPSDB/, Oct 2002.
32. Netstumbler software. http://www.netstumbler.com, Oct 2002.
33. J. Cuellar, J. Morris, and D. Mulligan. IETF Geopriv requirements. http://www.ietf.org/html.charters/geopriv-charter.html, 2002.
34. Sastry Duri, Marco Gruteser, Xuan Liu, Paul Moskowitz, Ronald Perez, Moninder Singh, and Jung-Mu Tang. Framework for security and privacy in automotive telematics. In *Proceedings of the second international workshop on Mobile commerce*, pages 25–32. ACM Press, 2002.
35. Einar Snekkenes. Concepts for personal location privacy policies. In *Proceedings of the 3rd ACM conference on Electronic Commerce*, pages 48–57. ACM Press, 2001.
36. Jalal Al-Muhtadi, Roy Campbell, Apu Kapadia, M. Dennis Mickunas, and Seung Yi. Routing through the mist: Privacy preserving communication in ubiquitous computing environments. In *International Conference of Distributed Computing Systems*, 2002.
37. A. Fasbender, D. Kesdogan, and O. Kubitz. Analysis of security and privacy in mobile IP. In *4th International Conference on Telecommunication Systems Modeling and Analysis*, Nashville, TN, Mar 1996.
38. T. Narten and R. Draves. RFC3041—privacy extensions for stateless address autoconfiguration in ipv6. http://www.faqs.org/ftp/rfc/rfc3041.txt.
39. Nissanka B. Priyantha, Anit Chakraborty, and Hari Balakrishnan. The cricket location-support system. In *Proceedings of the sixth annual international conference on Mobile computing and networking*, pages 32–43. ACM Press, 2000.
40. Asim Smailagic and David Kogan. Location sensing and privacy in a context-aware computing environment. *IEEE Wireless Communications*, 9:10–17, oct 2002.
41. Rakesh Agrawal and Ramakrishnan Srikant. Privacy-preserving data mining. In *Proc. of the ACM SIGMOD Conference on Management of Data*, pages 439–450. ACM Press, May 2000.

Protecting Access to People Location Information

Urs Hengartner[1] and Peter Steenkiste[1,2]

[1] Computer Science Department
[2] Department of Electrical and Computer Engineering
Carnegie Mellon University
{uhengart,prs}@cs.cmu.edu

Abstract. Ubiquitous computing provides new types of information for which access needs to be controlled. For instance, a person's current location is a sensitive piece of information, and only authorized entities should be able to learn it. We present several challenges that arise for the specification and implementation of policies controlling access to location information. For example, there can be multiple sources of location information, policies need to be flexible, conflicts between policies might occur, and privacy issues need to be taken into account. Different environments handle these challenges in a different way. We discuss the challenges in the context of a hospital and a university environment. We show how our design of an access control mechanism for a system providing people location information addresses the challenges. Our mechanism can be deployed in different environments. We demonstrate feasibility of our design with an example implementation based on digital certificates.

1 Introduction

Ubiquitous computing environments, such as the ones examined in CMU's Aura project [1], rely on the availability of people location information to provide location-specific services. However, location is a sensitive piece of information and releasing it to random entities might pose security and privacy risks. For example, to limit the risk of being robbed, individuals wish to keep their location secret when walking home during the night. Therefore, only authorized entities should have access to people location information.

Whereas location information has received increased attention, its access control requirements have not been studied thoroughly. Location information is inherently different from information such as files stored in a file system, whose access control requirements have been studied widely. Location information is different since there is no single point at which access needs to be controlled. Instead, a variety of sources (e.g., a personal calendar or a GPS device) can provide location information. In addition, different types of queries can provide the same information (see Section 3.4). Therefore, a system providing location information has to perform access control in a distributed way, considering different services and interactions between queries.

The contribution of our work is threefold. First, we discuss challenges that arise when specifying access control policies for location information in different environments. Second, we provide the design of an access control mechanism that is flexible enough to be deployed in different environments, having multiple sources of location

D. Hutter et al. (Eds.): Security in Pervasive Computing 2003, LNCS 2802, pp. 25–38, 2004.
© Springer-Verlag Berlin Heidelberg 2004

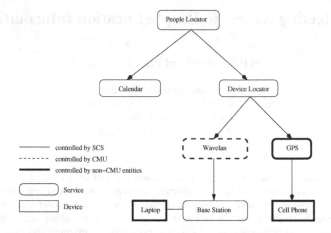

Fig. 1. Example location system. Clients query the People Locator service for the location of a person. This service forwards a query to the Calendar service and to the Device Locator service. The Device Locator service locates a person by locating her devices; namely, it queries the Wavelan service for her laptop and the GPS service for her cell phone.

information. Third, we present an implementation of the proposed mechanism, which is based on digital certificates.

The outline of the rest of this paper is as follows: We introduce the architecture of a people location system in Section 2. In Section 3, we discuss several challenges that arise when specifying location policies. We explain how we deal with multiple sources of location information in Section 4. In Section 5, we present the design of our access control mechanism. We discuss our prototype implementation in Section 6. We comment on related work in Section 7 and on our conclusions and future work in Section 8.

2   People Location System

In this section, we introduce the architecture of a people location system that exploits different sources of location information.

We assume that the location system has a hierarchical structure. Figure 1 shows an example of such a system, as it could be deployed in CMU's School of Computer Science (SCS). The nodes in the graph are either services or devices, the arrows denote which service contacts which other service or device. The *location system* is a composition of multiple *location services*. Each location service either exploits a particular technology for gathering location information or processes location information received from other location services. Location information flows in the reverse direction of a request (not shown in the figure). A location service can be implemented either on a single host or on multiple hosts to improve scalability and robustness.

There are two groups of location services. The first group consists of services that are aware of the location of people. The second group includes services that are aware of the location of devices. These services locate a user indirectly by locating the device(s) the user is carrying with her. The People Locator service, the Calendar service, and the Device Locator service belong to the first group. The People Locator service aggregates information received from other services. The Calendar service looks at people's appointments to determine their current location. The Device Locator service maps a query for a person to potentially several queries for her devices and contacts corresponding services in the second group. In our example, this group of services consists of the Wavelan service and the GPS service. The Wavelan service keeps track of the location of wireless devices by identifying their base station. The GPS service retrieves the location from GPS-enhanced mobile phones. We believe that our location system can easily incorporate other location services (e.g., Microsoft's Radar [2] or MIT's Cricket [3]).

A basic assumption in our work is that different organizations may administer the various services. In our example, SCS's computing facilities control the Calendar service, CMU's computing facilities administer the Wavelan service, and a phone company runs the GPS service.

3   Location Policies

Location queries can originate both from people and from services. In the rest of this paper, we are going to call an entity that issues a query a *location seeker*. A query can ask either for the location of a user (*user query*) or for the people in or at a geographical location, such as a room in a building (*room query*). Based on these two basic queries, it becomes possible to build more sophisticated queries or services that provide location-specific information.

To prevent location information from leaking to unauthorized entities, we employ location policies. An entity can access location information about a person or about the people in a room only if permitted by that person's and that room's location policy, respectively. In this section, we examine location policies and present requirements that need to be provided by the access control mechanism of a people location system.

3.1   User and Room Policies

Corresponding to the two types of queries, there are two types of location policies: user policies and room polices. A user policy states who is allowed to get location information about a user. For example, "Bob is allowed to find out about Alice's location". Similarly, a room policy specifies who is permitted to find out about the people currently in a room. For example, "Bob is allowed to find out about the people in Alice's office".

In addition, both user and room policies should be able to limit information flow in other ways. Namely, we believe that at least the following properties should be controllable:

Granularity. A policy can restrict the granularity of the returned location information. For example, a user policy can state that the building in which a queried user is staying is returned instead of the actual room (e.g., "CMU Wean Hall" vs. "CMU Wean Hall 8220"). A room policy can require that the number of people in a room is returned instead of the identity of the people in the room (e.g., "two people" vs. "Alice and Bob").

Locations/Users. User policies can contain a set of locations (e.g., buildings or rooms). The location system will return location information only if the queried user is at one of the listed locations. For example, "Bob is allowed to find out about Alice's location only if she is in her office". Similarly, room policies can include a set of users. The answer to a room query will include only users listed in the policy (provided they are in the room).

Time Intervals. Location policies can limit time intervals during which access should be granted. For example, access can be restricted to working hours.

Earlier work (e.g., by Spreitzer and Theimer [4]) lets users place boundaries on room policies. Namely, users can specify whether they want to be included in results to room queries. While this approach is appropriate for some scenarios, it is not for others. We argue that in most cases, the owner of a room should always be able to find out who is in her room, regardless of the user policies of the users in her room.

3.2   User vs. Institutional Policies

Depending on the environment, different entities specify location policies. For some environments, a central authority defines policies, whereas for others, users set them. In addition, some environments might give both users and a central authority the option to specify policies.

In general, governments and companies probably do not want the location of their employees or the people in their buildings to be known to outsiders, whereas this information can be delivered to (some) entities within the organization. In such cases, a central authority would establish the location policies such that no information is leaked. For other environments, such as a university or a shopping mall, the institution behind the environment cares less about where an individual is or who is in a room. For these cases, it should be up to an individual to specify her user policy. We examine some example environments in more detail in Section 3.6.

In the rest of the paper, we are going to call the entity that specifies location policies *policy maker*. A location system should be flexible enough to support different policy makers, depending on the environment.

3.3   Transitivity of Access Rights

If Bob is granted access to Alice's location information, should he be allowed to forward this access right to Carol? If Ed is given the right to find out about the people in his office, should he be allowed to grant this privilege also to Fred? In short, should access rights to location information be transitive?

There is no simple answer to this question. Again the answer depends on the environment. The location system should let policy makers explicitly state whether they want access rights to be transitive. Note that even though a user might not be allowed to forward his access rights to other users, he could still issue queries on their behalf. The only way to deal with this problem is to take away the access right from this user.

3.4 Conflicting Policies

User and room policies can conflict. For example, assume that Alice does not allow Bob to locate her, but Carol allows Bob to locate people in her office. If Alice is in Carol's office, should the location system tell Bob about it? There are multiple ways for dealing with this issue:

- The system ignores the room policy when answering a user query. Similarly, it ignores the user policies for a room query. In our example, Bob would thus see Alice if he asks for the people in Carol's office, but he would not be allowed to ask a user query for Alice.
- The system looks at both policies for any request and returns information only if it is approved by both of them. Bob would thus never see Alice being in Carol's office.
- The user and room policies are established in a synchronized fashion so that no conflicts arise. For example, Leonhardt and Magee [5] suggest authorizing user/room pairs. Alice and Carol's location policies would thus have to be rewritten.

The approach that fits best depends again on the environment in which the location system is deployed.

3.5 Privacy Issues

Location policies can contain personal data that users might want to keep private. For example, a user might grant access rights to his friends and thus define a set of friends. The decision about who is (not) in this set can be delicate, and the user wants to keep the identities of people in the set secret. A location system should allow users to keep their policies secret.

3.6 Example Environments

In this section, we discuss how location policies are specified and applied in two different environments; a hospital and a university environment.

Hospital. Medical data, such as patient information, is typically protected based on a multilateral security model, which protects information flow between compartments. For example, only doctors taking care of a patient have access to her medical data, but not every doctor in the hospital. A similar model is required for location information. Only the doctors of a patient should be able to locate her. In addition, a patient should be able to allow other people (e.g., her husband) to locate her. To fulfill these requirements, the hospital has a central authority establish policies. It can give the patient the right to include additional people in her user policy.

Room policies should be established by the central authority to protect the patients' privacy. User and room policies do not need to be synchronized for the hospital scenario.

Patients might be allowed to specify transitive user policies, whereas doctors should not be able to forward an access right given to them in a user policy. Room policies should not be transitive.

University. In a university setting, students and faculty members specify their user policies. However, room policies are established by a central authority.

For an office, the authority is likely to give the right to establish its room policy to the occupant of the office. For lecture rooms and hallways, the authority typically would set the room policy such that room and user policies become synchronized. That is, upon receiving a room query, the location system consults the user policies of users in the room/hallway before returning their identity. For offices, user and room policies are typically not synchronized.

User policies might be transitive, whereas for room policies, the institution may decide not to let the occupant of an office transfer the right to other people.

4   Service Trust

As explained in Section 2, a location system can consist of multiple location services. Some of these services, such as the People Locator service shown in Fig. 1, do not generate their own location information. Instead, they process location information received from other services. To avoid information leaks, the location system must ensure that only services that implement access control checks are given location information.

One way to implement this condition is to require that the user or room policy grants a service access to location information before it is given this information. This option is appropriate for services that must be able to issue requests for location information. For example, the Device Locator service shown in Fig. 1 has to create queries for devices upon receiving a user query. However, for services such as the People Locator service, this option gives the services more privileges than they really need. The People Locator service only forwards requests received from clients. By granting it the right to issue requests, we increase its exposure in case of a break-in. If an intruder breaks into the service and begins issuing requests, the location system will grant access to these requests.

Due to these reasons, we introduce the concept of *service trust.* If a service, such as the People Locator service, is trusted, it is given location information, even if it is not allowed to issue requests. For a particular query, a service needs to be trusted by the policy maker that defines the corresponding user or room policy. Therefore, for a hospital, the set of trusted services should be defined by the central authority. For a university, each user and each owner of a room define their own set of trusted services. The trust assumption is that the service implements access control as follows:

In the first step, the service checks whether the policy maker has granted access to the entity issuing the request. Only if this check is successful, the service proceeds to the second step, else access is denied. In the second step, the service checks whether the entity from which it received the request corresponds to the entity that issued the request. If it does, access is granted. If it does not, the service has to verify whether the policy maker trusts the entity before access is granted. Else access is denied.

How can we verify whether a service fulfills its trust assumption? We require services to sign whatever location information they return to achieve non-repudiation. Therefore, an entity trusting a service can reactively identify misbehaving services and revoke the trust in them.

5   System Design

Based on our discussion in Sections 3 and 4, we now present the design of our access control mechanism for a people location system. We build on three main concepts. First, services respond to a location request only after performing a location policy check that verifies that the location seeker has access. Second, services verify that the service from which they receive a forwarded request is trusted before returning an answer to it. Third, services can delegate both location policy and service trust checks to other services; delegation can be used to eliminate redundant checks. In this section, we motivate and discuss these concepts.

5.1   Digital Certificates

For implementation purposes, we assume that location policy and trust decisions are stated in digital certificates. A digital certificate is a signed data structure in which the signer states a decision concerning some other entity. There are various kinds of digital certificates. Our implementation is based on SPKI/SDSI certificates [6], which we discuss in Section 6.1.

We introduce the following notation for expressing a policy or trust decision:

$$A \xrightarrow[scope]{type} B . \tag{1}$$

A is the entity making a decision concerning B. The type of decision is described above the arrow (*policy* or *trust*). In decisions of type *policy*, A gives B access to some location information, that is, these decisions express location policies. In decisions of type *trust*, A specifies that she trusts service B. A can limit the scope of a decision by stating the scope below the arrow (e.g., whose location policy is specified).

As shown before, there are two types of certificates: location policy certificates and trust certificates. When there is a request, a service must first check whether the location policy grants access to the issuer of the request. The service tries to build a chain of location policy certificates from itself to the issuer of the request. Each certificate in the chain needs to give the next entity further down the chain access to the requested location information. In addition, any constraints listed in the certificate (e.g., time or location based) must be fulfilled to have the policy check succeed. We elaborate on location policy certificates in Section 5.2. If a service receives a forwarded request, it must also check whether the service from which it got the request is trusted. Similar to the location policy check, the service tries to build a chain of trust certificates from itself to the forwarding service. We discuss trust certificates in Section 5.3.

5.2   Location Policy Check

If an entity is allowed to retrieve a user's location information, then there must be a certificate specifying whether and what type of information it can retrieve. (We limit the description of our design to user policies. Room policies are dealt with in a similar way.) For example, a certificate could state that Bob can locate Alice at a coarse-grained level. If Bob then tries to locate Alice, a service receiving his location request needs to check the existence and validity of a certificate permitting this access.

A location service does not have to be aware of the identity of the entities that have access rights. If Bob can prove that he is allowed (by presenting a digital certificate), he will be granted access. This solution makes dealing with unknown users easy. Solutions proposed earlier (e.g., by Leonhardt and Magee [5]) rely on policy matrices consisting of querying users and users whose location can be queried and thus rely on the system being aware of the identity of querying users.

In addition, some digital certificates (such as SPKI/SDSI certificates) can give rights both to single entities and to groups of entities. That is, with a single certificate, Alice can, for example, give all her friends access.

Depending on the environment, different entities issue certificates. For the two environments introduced in Section 3.6, certificates are specified as follows:

Hospital. We show some of the certificates issued in the hospital environment: (PL denotes the People Locator service, C the central authority, S the surgery ward, and D_S^C all doctors that are classified by C as belonging to S.)

$$(a) \quad PL \xrightarrow{policy} C \qquad (b) \quad C \xrightarrow[A]{policy} D_S^C \qquad (c) \quad D_S^C \longmapsto B \ . \quad (2)$$

First, the administrator of the People Locator service enables the central authority to decide about all the patients' location policies. Second, the authority gives all doctors in patient A's ward access to her location. Third, the authority certifies that doctor B belongs to the surgery ward. Note that this certificate is a membership certificate (denoted by the special arrow) and does not grant any rights on its own.

If B inquires about A's location, the People Locator service deduces that B has access to A's location since it can combine certificates 2(a), (b) and (c) in a chain of certificates and conclude

$$PL \xrightarrow[A]{policy} B \ . \tag{3}$$

In addition to certificate 2(b), the authority also issues a certificate that gives patient A the right to let additional people locate her. A can do so by issuing corresponding certificates.

University. In the university environment, the administrator of the People Locator service gives student or faculty member A access to her location information:

$$PL \xrightarrow[A]{policy} A \ . \tag{4}$$

A can define her own location policy by issuing additional certificates.

5.3 Service Trust Check

Trust decisions are also stated in digital certificates. As an example, we show how the Device Locator service handles trust decisions for the two environments introduced in

Section 3.6. Typically, the Device Locator service is not directly contacted by users, but by other services (e.g., the People Locator service).

Hospital. The administrator of the Device Locator service (DL) lets the central authority specify the trusted services used for answering patient queries. The authority states that all services run by the hospital (T_C) are trusted. The authority also states that the People Locator service is in this set. The certificates look as follows:

$$(a) \quad DL \xrightarrow{trust} C \qquad (b) \quad C \xrightarrow{trust} T_C \qquad (c) \quad T_C \longmapsto PL \ . \quad (5)$$

Upon receiving a forwarded user query from the People Locator service, the Device Locator service combines these certificates and concludes that the People Locator service is trusted.

University. In the university scenario, users specify their trusted services. The Device Locator service thus gives student A the right to define this set. Assuming A trusts the People Locator service, the certificates look as follows: (T_A denotes the set of services trusted by A.)

$$(a) \quad DL \xrightarrow[A]{trust} A \qquad (b) \quad A \xrightarrow[A]{trust} T_A \qquad (c) \quad T_A \longmapsto PL \ . \quad (6)$$

5.4 Delegation

Entities in our system grant other entities particular kinds of rights. For example, Alice grants Bob access to her location information. It is up to Alice to also grant Bob the right to forward the access right to a third entity. If she does so, Alice effectively delegates the right to decide about her location policy to Bob. In the remainder of this paper, we are going to use the term *delegation* whenever an entity grants access rights to a second entity and it also permits the second entity to grant these rights to a third entity.

In the rest of this section, we elaborate on delegating policy and trust decisions. In addition, we explain how users can delegate trust decisions to an organization.

Location Policy and Trust Checks. Each trusted location service has to implement location policy and trust checks. However, to reduce overhead or in the case of low processing power, not every service has to build the potentially long certificate chains itself. It can delegate this task to some other service. For example, the Device Locator service is likely to delegate location policy checking to the People Locator service since the People Locator service needs to build a certificate chain for each request anyway. After validating the chain, the People Locator service issues a new certificate that directly authorizes the location seeker. It gives this certificate to the Device Locator service, which thus does not have to validate the entire chain again.

Organizations. If there are lots of services available, it is cumbersome for a user to issue a certificate for each service that she trusts. We assume that trust in a service is closely tied to the entity that administers this service. For example, a user might trust all the services run by her company. Therefore, we give users the possibility to state in a certificate that they trust all the services in a particular organization. The organization then generates a certificate for each of the services that it runs. In this situation, a user effectively delegates the decision about which services she trusts to the organization, and she relies on the organization to do the right thing. For the university environment, certificate 6(b) could thus look as follows:

$$A \xrightarrow[A]{trust} T_C \ . \tag{7}$$

5.5 Privacy

Location policy and trust certificates can be stored in a database from which anyone can retrieve them. However, since location policies contain personal information, policy makers might want to restrict access to the certificates. We now discuss two methods to limit their exposure. The first method keeps policies secret from location seekers, the second one from the location system. Both methods do not require any changes to the access control mechanism of the location system, they differ only in the way the mechanism is deployed. Note that a location seeker can obtain some policy information implicitly by issuing queries to the location system. If the location seeker is denied access, it concludes that the policy forbids access. Similarly, by analyzing the returned location information, it might be able to deduce that it has only coarse-grained access.

For both methods, we assume that each policy maker has a trusted host where it keeps its issued certificates. If the policy maker is a central authority, the trusted host can be the authority itself. If the policy maker is an individual, the trusted host is a designated host. This host has to be available all the time so that it can provide certificates upon a request. An individual has to make a trade-off between its privacy concerns and the convenience provided by its chosen solution. If the individual is willing to trust an organization, it can have the organization run a centralized repository for it. If it is not willing to trust an organization, it needs to set up its own repository.

To prevent policy information from leaking to location seekers, we have the trusted host control access to the certificates stored with it. Only location services entitled by the issuer of a certificate are allowed to access a certificate. This method increases the load on a location service since the service can no longer require location seekers to provide any certificates required for answering the request. Instead it has to retrieve them itself. Delegation or storing certificates in an encrypted form could reduce some of the load on a location service.

To prevent policy information from leaking to the location system, a policy maker has all queries go through its trusted host, which runs access control. The certificate chains expressing the location policy are rooted at the trusted host. If the access control check succeeds, the trusted host issues a request to the People Locator service. The trusted host is the only entity that has access to the location information offered by the People Locator service. A variant of this method is to implement the People Locator service in a completely distributed way. That is, each policy maker runs its own People Locator service on its trusted computer. This solution is similar to the one introduced by Spreitzer and Theimer [4]. However, running and administering a complete People Locator service is a potentially heavyweight operation.

5.6 Discussion

Let us summarize the main advantages of our location system:

No Bottleneck. Certificates do not need to be kept at a centralized node, and there is no bottleneck through which each request has to go. The services perform access control independently of each other and approve a request only if it is supported by certificates.

Support of Unknown Users. The system does not need to know the identity of location seekers. All the system requires is a digital certificate that grants access to the entity.

Support of Group Access. With a single certificate, an entire group of entities can be given access to someone's location information.

Transitivity Control. SPKI/SDSI certificates allow handing out non-transitive access rights. In a valid certificate chain, all but the last certificate in the chain need to allow transitivity of access rights.

We have been able to use digital certificates for expressing location policy and trust decisions in both of our example environments. Therefore, the mechanism for controlling access to location information is identical. Similarly, we can use the same tools for building and proving certificate chains in both environments. However, setting up these mechanisms and tools is environment-specific. We now discuss some of the differences.

User Interfaces. Most probably, there are going to be different user interfaces in different environments. In the hospital case, there is a strong emphasis on being able to define groups and assigning them access. In the university case, users are more likely to authorize other people directly. Though the actual interfaces might differ, they would both create location policy (and trust) certificates in the background.

Types of Chains. The types of chains checked upon a query also depend on the environment. Either a service checks only the user or room policy chain or it checks both chains. For example, when processing a room query about the people in a lecture room in a university, the location system first checks the room policy of the room. If this check succeeds, the system will check the user policy for each of the people in the room. The system returns only location information about people for whom this latter check succeeds.

6   Implementation

6.1   Digital Certificates

To implement the policy and trust decisions introduced in Section 5, we rely on SPKI/SDSI certificates [6]. Authentication and authorization based on these certificates does not require a global naming structure. Instead, the authentication and authorization step are merged, and a certificate gives access rights directly to a public key. There are tools that evaluate chains of SPKI/SDSI certificates and that decide whether requests should be granted access.

In the example below, we show a SPKI/SDSI certificate in which Alice (issuer) gives Bob (subject) access to her location information (i.e., $A \xrightarrow[A]{policy} B$ using our notation). The type of access is described after the keyword **tag**. Note that the certificate has to be accompanied by Alice's signature (not shown here).

```
(cert    (issuer  (public_key:alice))
         (subject  (public_key:bob))
         (propagate)
         (tag (policy alice
              (* set (* prefix world.cmu.wean) world.cmu.doherty.room1234)
              (* set  (monday (* range numeric ge #8000# le #1200#))
                      (tuesday (* range numeric ge #1300# le #1400#)))
              coarse-grained)))
```

Alice gives access to Bob's public key (denoted by public_key:bob). The keyword **propagate** states that Bob is allowed to give the granted right to some other entity by issuing another certificate. If Alice decided not to let Bob forward his access right, she would omit this keyword. Bob can locate Alice only if she is either in Wean Hall or in Room 1234 in Doherty Hall and on Monday between 8am and 12pm and on Tuesday between 1pm and 2pm. Also, Bob can locate Alice only at coarse-grained granularity.

6.2   Location System

We have implemented a subset of the location system shown in Fig. 1. The system consists of the People and Device Locator services and location services that proxy to several calendar systems, that locate devices connecting to CMU's wireless network, and that exploit login and activity information.

We use SSH at the transport layer to achieve mutual authentication of entities and confidentiality and integrity of information. Access control is entirely based on SPKI/SDSI.

Location information and SPKI/SDSI certificates are transmitted between services using the Aura Contextual Service Interface [7], which is a protocol running over HTTP and which exchanges messages encoded in XML. Our SPKI/SDSI implementation has been implemented in Java and is based on previous work [8]. There is an HTML-based front end to the service that lets users specify location policies and conduct searches. The front end makes dealing with certificates transparent to users. Currently, the certificates are stored in a centralized database.

In our system, if Alice directly gives Bob access to her location information in a certificate, it takes about 0.6 sec on a Pentium III/500 to add this certificate to the certificate chain for Alice and to verify the entire chain upon a request.

7 Related Work

Several location systems [2, 3, 9, 10] have been proposed. They are based on only one location technology, are implemented only within one administrative entity, and/or do not address the various access control issues mentioned in this paper. We discuss two notable exceptions:

Spreitzer and Theimer's location system [4] is based on multiple technologies. Each user has her personal agent that gathers location information about her and that implements access control. The authors design the system to work in an environment with different administrative entities, although the actual implementation runs only within a single entity and the authors do not mention how users specify trusted services. A key difference from our system is that users in a room, not the owner of a room, determine the room policy of this room.

Leonhardt and Magee [5] argue that user and room policies need to be consistent. They propose an extension to the matrix-based access control scheme. We believe that having consistent user and location policies is difficult to achieve when policies are established independently of each other. The authors do not discuss how policies are established in their system.

There has been some previous work about authorizing intermediate services, for example, Howell and Kotz's quoting gateways [8]. Howell and Kotz focus on intermediate services that create new requests upon receiving a request and thus need to be authorized to issue requests. However, in scenarios like ours where some services only forward requests, this model would give too many capabilities to intermediate services. Our model of trust avoids this risk.

The Instant Messaging / Presence Protocol working group [11] proposes to return wrong information instead of denying access to information. We refrain from such a solution since it erodes trustworthiness into the location system. Also, if a location seeker tried to validate the wrong location information, it could still conclude that it was actually denied access. As an alternative to the proposed method, we suggest that policy makers build wrapper services that access the location system and that translate "access denied" messages. For example, the wrapper service could return a busy signal when a user temporarily does not want to be disturbed and thus decides not to be locatable.

The Location Interoperability Forum [12] and the Geopriv working group [13] discuss privacy aspects of user queries. The former suggests that location seekers should not be able to learn about the content of location policies. The latter proposes to protect the identities of both location seekers and located entities. We have presented a mechanism for hiding location policies and the identity of location seekers in Section 3.5. Protecting the identity of located entities strongly depends on the actual location service. For example, a user can buy a prepaid phone card when using a GPS-enhanced phone and hide his identity from the GPS location service.

8 Conclusions

We have analyzed the challenges in controlling access to people location information and presented the design of an access control mechanism. The design relies on several key concepts: policy certificates for expressing location policies, trust certificates for dealing with services belonging to different organizations, and delegation for avoiding redundant access control checks and to lower the burden on users. We have shown feasibility of our design with an example implementation, which we are currently deploying at Carnegie Mellon.

We have been able to formulate all of our policy and trust decisions using SPKI/SDSI certificates. These certificates provide a high degree of flexibility. A ubiquitous computing environment poses new challenges on access control that cannot be easily satisfied by conventional mechanisms. We believe that due to their flexibility, SPKI/SDSI certificates are a promising approach and deserve further investigation on their usability in such environments. Namely, these certificates could potentially not only protect access to people location information, but also to other kinds of information that is gathered in a similar way as people location information.

Acknowledgments

We thank Glenn Judd and the anonymous reviewers for their comments. This research was funded in part by DARPA under contract number N66001-99-2-8918 and by NSF under award number CCR-0205266. Additional support was also provided by Intel.

References

1. Garlan, D., Siewiorek, D., Smailagic, A., Steenkiste, P.: Project Aura: Towards Distraction-Free Pervasive Computing. IEEE Pervasive Computing **1** (2002) 22–31
2. Bahl, P., Padmanabhan, V.: RADAR: An In-Building RF-Based User Location and Tracking System. In: Proceedings of IEEE Infocom 2000. (2000) 775–784
3. Priyantha, N., Chakraborty, A., Balakrishnan, H.: The Cricket Location-Support System. In: Proceedings of the Sixth Annual International Conference on Mobile Computing and Networking (MobiCom 2000). (2000)
4. Spreitzer, M., Theimer, M.: Providing Location Information in a Ubiquitous Computing Environment. In: Proceedings of SIGOPS '93. (1993) 270–283
5. Leonhardt, U., Magee, J.: Security Considerations for a Distributed Location Service. Journal of Network and Systems Management **6** (1998) 51–70
6. Ellison, C., Frantz, B., Lampson, B., Rivest, R., Thomas, B., Ylonen, T.: SPKI Certificate Theory. RFC 2693 (1999)
7. Judd, G., Steenkiste, P.: Providing Contextual Information to Ubiquitous Computing Applications. To appear in *Proceedings of IEEE International Conference on Pervasive Computing and Communications (PerCom 2003)* (2003)
8. Howell, J., Kotz, D.: End-to-end authorization. In: Proceedings of the 4th Symposium on Operating System Design & Implementation (OSDI 2000). (2000) 151–164
9. Harter, A., Hopper, A.: A Distributed Location System for the Active Office. IEEE Network **8** (1994) 62–70
10. Ward, A., Jones, A., Hopper, A.: A New Location Technique for the Active Office. IEEE Personal Communications **4** (1997) 42–47
11. Day, M., Aggarwal, S., Mohr, G., Vincent, J.: Instant Messaging / Presence Protocol Requirements. RFC 2779 (2000)
12. Greening, D.: Location Privacy. http://www.openmobilealliance.org/lif/ (2002)
13. Cuellar, J., Morris, J.B., Mulligan, D.: Geopriv requirements. Internet Draft (2002)

Smart Devices and Software Agents:
The Basics of Good Behaviour

Howard Chivers, John A. Clark, and Susan Stepney

Department of Computer Science, University of York,
Heslington, York, YO10 5DD, UK
{chive,jac,susan}@cs.york.ac.uk

Abstract. In this paper, security requirements for software agents and smart devices are derived by working from typical requirements for existing systems, exploring the changes that are envisaged as systems become more highly distributed, then identifying what these imply for a device or service in a pervasive environment. A similar treatment is given to threats, which give rise to both security requirements and design issues. This approach provides insights into security requirements that will be significantly different from today's distributed system policies: they demonstrate that pervasive computing requires a qualitative change in security policy and practice. The paper also explores trade-offs between security complexity and device functionality, and argues that the degree of policy management required in a device will be an important factor in this balance.

1 Introduction

The increasing use of software based mobile devices is already evident in familiar objects such as car control systems, navigation aids, and mobile telephones. A good illustration of the development such devices into general-purpose application platforms is the evolution of mobile telephones.

We envisage a trend towards an environment where computer applications will be hosted on a wide range of platforms, including many that are small, mobile, and regarded today as candidates only for restricted functionality. This highly distributed computing world [1] is becoming known as *pervasive*. Large scale distributed processing is also a theme in traditional computing: the Grid community is enabling collaboration by distributed services [2], and this parallels the evolution of the Internet towards service delivery [3].

This world will be sufficiently different from today's distributed systems to demand a re-evaluation of the requirements and mechanisms for security. New issues include the policies required and how they are distributed, the effect of device context and the dynamics introduced by mobility, and the need to consider distributed security mechanisms and their effect on the system as a whole.

Distributed security implies that security requirements and mechanisms need to be considered in the design of smart devices and their applications, whatever their scale. This paper derives security requirements for such devices by evaluating the issues that emerge in a pervasive environment, within a framework based on current system security requirements and practice (for example, [4]).

D. Hutter et al. (Eds.): Security in Pervasive Computing 2003, LNCS 2802, pp. 39–52, 2004.

There are system functions (for example, billing, licensing,) and properties (for example, safety) that are outside this scope. It is likely that solutions to these will also introduce new security requirements.

2   Security Requirements

Existing system security requirements are often grouped under the headings of Identification and Authentication, Policy, Administration, Accountability and Audit, Confidentiality, Integrity and Availability, and Assurance. This section takes each of these in turn, outlines typical current security requirements, discusses new concerns that arise in a pervasive environment, and then summarises the implications for hosting environments.

Terminology. The following terms are used: *subject* – an actual end user. *principal* – an authenticated subject, or software acting on that subject's behalf. *object* – a data item or software service. *device* – a physical device that provides a software environment (hosting environment) for a service. *service* – a software application, usually uniformly packaged for remote invocation. *agent* – a service that carries out a function on behalf of a subject; some authors define agents as mobile and/or autonomous, the more general sense is intended here. *device* or *resource manager* – the person capable of setting the security policy of a service.

2.1   Identification and Authentication

Systems are required to reliably identify a subject and also associate attributes (rights, roles, privileges) with that identification. Distributed systems support remote identification by providing an authentication mechanism between principals and remote objects (for example, between a user client and a server); authentication can be in either direction or both, depending on the application.

Issues. A fundamental change in the nature of identification is introduced by the need for agents to operate autonomously, invoking services on behalf of a user at times when the user is not present at the system. Consider a complex device (for example, a telescope) controller – it would be able to invoke services for a user that would be unsafe to allow a user to invoke directly, and when the user is not necessarily present. Since many services will need to invoke further services, and may do so with authority that is distinct from their user's, there is an inevitable blurring of the once clear distinction between principals and objects in the system; the result is the need for the identification of devices in addition to users.

The limits of individual identity present a further problem. It is clear that if an agent is able to invoke remote services in the system, then it will often need unique identification. But what of smart devices that provide relatively restricted services (for example, a car engine controller)? The history of such a device will build a unique state (for example, service record), and it may perform customised functions specific to individual users (for example, driver preferences). The result is that despite the fact that the equivalent non-smart device may have been *fungible* (readily exchanged), the smart equivalent may acquire a unique identity.

The process of identification and authentication needs to deal with the dynamic and mobile nature of smart devices. This is illustrated by the current security issues with Wireless LANs or the protocols required to authenticate a mobile phone [5].

Attributes of Principals. At its simplest, identification is the binding of an identifier with an actual individual. Identification infrastructures also often support user attributes (for example, actual name, organisation, project roles) that can be referenced via the identifier. In the case of incompatible roles (for example, bank official/customer) it is sometimes necessary to authenticate user-as-role, but it is generally preferable to provide user attributes separately to the authentication mechanism. In a distributed system with diverse applications, the range of user attributes that needs to be managed expands to meet application requirements (for example, include credit card details). Thus we see a trend toward separate identity attribute management services, such as [6].

This design tactic of packaging a security mechanism as a service that can act on behalf of federations of users or resources is an important scalability enabler, and is likely to become a design theme in very large-scale systems; however, the functional convenience of packaging user attributes in this way needs to be weighed against the potential risk to individual privacy.

Finally, although the discussion of attributes has focused on users, there is a similar need to establish and promulgate attributes for devices (for example, type, location, software environment), some of which may need to be dynamic.

Implications. Devices and their services need to meet the following concerns:

- Identity is required for devices as well as people.
- A rich and potentially dynamic set of identity-associated attributes needs to be supported and promulgated; privacy concerns will limit implementation options.
- Mutual authentication is needed between devices, and must be able to deal with dynamic location and communication.
- Designers must consider if smart devices are intended to be fungible, bearing in mind the overhead of maintaining individual, as opposed to collective, identity.

2.2 Policy

A policy is a set of security rules that specify what actions are allowed in a system, together with other ancillary information such as how, where and when to log events. The essence of most policies is to be able to identify the subjects and objects and to define the accesses allowed between them. A typical example is the well-known access mechanism in UNIX, which provides read/write/execute object attributes for owner/group/all subjects.

In current distributed systems the most common approach has been to extend identities across the network, either directly or by a mapping global into local identities [7], and then rely on the local policy.

Issues. Perhaps the most radical change is to question what such policies are designed to achieve. Protection of system resources has tended to be the key goal, with less emphasis on privacy, which has been treated as an aspect of confidentiality. However, users have an expectation that personal data will be used only for the purpose for which it was provided, and the fact that this is transparently not the case in today's networks is a growing cause of concern. The European Union Directive on data [8] also seeks to ensure uniform privacy standards in EU member states, including their external trading practices. Pervasive computing increases the threat to privacy by increasing the scope for location tracking, by holding a richer set of user attributes in the system, and by delegating rights based on user attributes to software agents.

The policies implemented in a pervasive system therefore need to take privacy into account to a far greater extent. This trend is illustrated in the Shibboleth project [9] where it is possible to authenticate with attributes other than identity (for example, team membership) and only those attributes necessary to invoke services are propagated.

Authorisation. In existing systems the local security policy determines if a given subject is authorised to access services or data. A fully distributed world exposes the range of concerns embedded in such a policy. Consider a user accessing third party data, using a project budget to pay for computing services. The authorisation takes into account what services the project is authorised to access, and the policies of the data owner and the resource manager, as well as user attributes. In a distributed system these parties may be separate, and a hosting environment needs to dynamically compile the concerns of these stakeholders before authorising a transaction.

A number of researchers [10,11] have proposed *trust management systems* that include chains of signed attributes as well as user delegations, with an authorisation function that is able to traverse and resolve the resulting threads of authority. Other researchers [12,13] have proposed policies that explicitly deal with privacy. Trust management systems are capable of expressing flexible distributed policies; it remains to be seen if they are sufficiently dynamic for the pervasive environment, and if they are able to accommodate emerging privacy requirements.

Aggregation Constraints. Some policies can be expressed only as an aggregation (for example, project budget, permitted departmental storage). These resource constraints pose difficulties for distributed systems since they apply to collections of users and their applications that would otherwise be independent. To optimise utilisation of such a resource, the policy implementation generally requires a mediating service, together with late or dynamic binding to agents requiring access to the resource.

Mobility. Mobility changes the physical and the software context of a device, with both direct and indirect effects on its security policy. The direct effect is the constraint placed on a device by its location. This may be physical (for example, temperature), availability of local services (for example, logging), available communication methods, and, particularly when crossing national boundaries, legal, social or safety requirements. Indirect effects are that policy stakeholders (users, data owners etc) may not wish to apply the same policies in different locations; for example: it may not be lawful to export an algorithm; a data owner may not wish to place data in a competitor's location; smart cards may work only in the proximity of their owner. This places a requirement on devices to be able to infer their physical [14] and network contexts, and update their security policy accordingly.

Scalability. The type of policy and its distribution mechanism may present scalability problems in devices, and may shape the forms of policy that are possible, and their implementation. For example, the current Grid approach of substituting local for global identities has the problem that policies are of dimension subjects X resources: in principle each device needs to know every subject. Again, federation services are likely to provide the key (for example, CAS [15]).

Implications. This discussion of policy illustrates the scope and complexity of the distributed security problem. However, devices may have limited computer power, intermittent communication capability, and restricted ability to sense their environment (for example, smart cards are generally not powerful enough to execute a full range of cryptographic algorithms). Thus they may not be able to implement complex security policies. However, simply avoiding security concerns is not a solution: we have already noted user concerns about privacy, and security mechanisms are also needed to support integrity and availability.

One resolution is to balance limited security with limited functionality. For example, a smart car controller may have a simple security policy (for example, odometer may not be written except by increment, only service centers can update service history), with the policy fixed for the life of the device. The penalty for such a fixed policy would be that it would not be possible to execute arbitrary software services (for example, vehicle entertainment or navigation) if that later became desirable.

We therefore propose that device designers categorise smart devices from the perspective of how flexible they need to be in terms of policy management:

- *Fixed Policy.* A smart device with fixed security characteristics.
- *Updateable policy.* A device where a limited number of pre-set attributes can be updated (for example, user of a smart lock).
- *Flexible policy.* A device that is capable of updating its policy from services in its environment. (for example, to support dynamic response to changing device context).

Other device security requirements that emerge are:

- The device must be able to trace and resolve authorisations and attributes from several external stakeholders (subject, resource manager, subject's organisation or virtual affiliation, etc.), relating to what actions are permitted.
- Privacy may require Authentication by means other than identity, and may limit the use to which a subject's attributes can be put.
- The authorisation process must support a dynamic policy environment, to accommodate both changing context and resource allocation policies.

2.3   Administration

Security administration involves the configuration management of security functions, policies and mechanisms. Administrators also manage intrusion detection mechanisms, and the technical and administrative responses to an attack.

Issues. Policy management requirements follow from the nature of the policy. The identification of stakeholders who are the source of permissions and constraints is the root of the policy configuration. In conventional systems the administrator maintains a table of users who act as owners for objects; the distributed equivalent is a list of stakeholder services from which policy constraints may be obtained. This trend is already illustrated by the storage of root Certificate Authority public key certificates in many systems. Similarly, instead of internally managing user attributes, the resource manager needs to maintain a list of trusted services that can authenticate a service request. So, management of fundamental security data is still required in pervasive systems, but the data are likely to be in a different form.

These requirements can again be interpreted in ways that are appropriate to the device or application. Consider a smart device that is able to associate itself with a user based on proximity. The underlying security requirement remains: the device is able to call on a known system service that authenticates that user. If the device has a flexible policy, the manager must be able to specify how that service is to be obtained.

Intrusion Detection. Open distributed systems are constantly under attack, and are constantly penetrated by attackers; the challenge is to use their size and diversity to self-heal. To a limited extent this is achieved today: the size of the Internet makes the detection of attack mechanisms likely before they have been widely exploited, and there are commercial (for example, suppliers of anti-virus software), educational, and governmental (for example, the CERT co-ordination center http://www.cert.org/) organisations who are prepared to fund the ongoing research and promulgate results. The lesson for distributed systems is to design them in such a way that large or systematic attacks are likely to cause observable behavior, which can then be investigated. Conventional security wisdom can help in the design of smart devices with such properties: devices should be configured to regard confusion (for example, invalid service requests, failed authentication) as a potential attack and support some form of external signaling mechanism (section 2.4).

Containment. An important containment strategy is *least privilege*: operate every service with only the privilege necessary to carry out the required function. This is not just good security practice, but generally good design practice, since it tends to trap the propagation of errors. Other forms of containment may also be possible in highly distributed systems, for example, the duplication of services with voting on the result, or detection of inconsistencies within a session.

Intrusion Response. In a distributed system, problems are likely to originate from outside of the boundary of any given resource manager, but the actions required (such as establishing interim service, tracking and isolating the cause, damage assessment and repair) all require organisational co-ordination and an accurate and shared understanding of system dynamics. Needing agreements between all pairs of management organisations to determine responsibility and action for problem tracking does not scale, so this is another case where federations are necessary.

Implications. Security administration places many requirements at the organisation and system level, and few on individual devices. However, there are some:

- The need to support policy management by maintaining root locations of services from which policies can be obtained.
- The need for mechanisms to detect unexpected or inconsistent invocation, which require a supporting service of accountability and audit (section 2.4).

2.4 Accountability and Audit

The usual requirements for accountability are to associate a subject with a security event, to be able to select which events are recorded and to ensure that records are preserved and retrievable for analysis. Current practice in distributed systems leaves security logging to the local system, but ensures that the identification can be traced to an original subject. There are emerging distributed notification and logging application frameworks (for example, Apache log4j), but we are not aware of their use for security.

Issues. Privacy requirements (section 2.2) create an immediate problem for accountability: if a user is identified only as a member of a group, who is to be held accountable for any subsequent misuse of the system? This requires a new approach to accountability; there are a number of possible solutions, including the use of session pseudonyms that could be traced to a user by their local administration, but even these may risk aggregation attacks on privacy. It is clear that users' policy requirements and accountability are no longer independent issues.

The preservation and retrieval of a security log presents practical problems in a fully distributed system. The straightforward answer of requiring a distributed network logging service resolves the problem for more complex devices (subject to a design that is robust and scalable) but not all devices will be able to persist data, and communication may be intermittent. This is another instance where it is necessary to find a mechanism appropriate to the scale of the device. For simple devices it may be sufficient to raise an alarm when an attempt at misuse is detected, by entering an externally detectable 'safe state'. If the device can be reset only by its resource manager, who is able to retrieve any stored information about the incident, then the requirement will have been met.

Implications. Accountability and logging cannot be avoided, since the overall system needs to detect and respond to misuse. Where possible an application should use a distributed logging service to record events; where that is not feasible this requirement may be met in simpler ways that still allow the detection of attacks.

2.5 Confidentiality

Confidentiality in present systems is supported by associating owners with objects, and allowing owners to place access constraints on those objects. Where requirements for confidentiality or privacy are particularly important (for example, credit cards) then access constraints inside systems are supported by communication confidentiality services. Communication Confidentiality is also required for some system functions, for example the distribution of cryptographic keys.

Issues. There is no reason to suppose that access control of objects within a device will be less important that it is at present: it is a fundamental mechanism supporting the practice of least privilege in a system, including the separation of system and application software. Least privilege mechanisms are also needed to support user privacy; however, the discussion above (section 2.2) indicates that privacy requirements are more extensive than confidentiality, and justify separate consideration.

Again, there may be a problem with devices without the capability to support the equivalent of an operating system kernel. One possible solution is for such devices to be stateless, maintaining state for the delivery of a service to a single invoker, then disposing the state before a change of use (for example, see [16]).

Confidentiality has been a relatively unimportant aspect of communications, except for special cases: for example, defence applications, or the protection of credit card and similar information. This is already changing as communications become more open; the evolution of mobile telephone protocols illustrates the process and the extent that confidentiality can become a user concern. A similar process is taking place with wireless LANs; users are recognising that broadcasting business communications may not be desirable, and even if they are not concerned about their data the use of encryption denies an attacker an easy option for mapping a system prior to mounting an active attack. Information about location, or which devices are communicating, may also need to be contained for privacy reasons. A greater need for communication confidentiality is therefore consistent with the vulnerability of increasingly open communication methods and also with privacy requirements.

Some researchers [17] suggest that software agents will be mobile to the extent that they will move between host environments while they are executing. Even assuming that the security policy in the new host makes this feasible, static access restrictions on internal objects would have to be preserved in transit, and this may also require an end-to-end confidentiality service.

Multi-way security context. Consider a tree of service invocations, the leaves of which need to communicate in order to carry out their function. This is a common model for computing tasks, with a scheduler at the root of the tree, but is equally applicable to delivery chains such as video streaming. The agents in the delivery chain communicate with their logical neighbors, perhaps via intermediate physical devices that are not part of the process. They need to authenticate each other as valid parts of the same service, and ensure end-to-end process integrity and perhaps confidentiality. System security mechanisms are needed to ensure that the security context of a complete process is shared by the services within the process, and is not otherwise accessible.

Implications. Devices need to support internal access control, if necessary in the simple form of a stateless service.

Confidentiality becomes a more prevalent communications requirement, because more accessible methods of communications are likely to be used. A device also needs the ability to build communication security services to collaborating devices via intermediaries that are not part of the same security context.

2.6   Integrity and Availability

The primary focus of integrity is maintaining service and defending against accidental or deliberate acts that can degrade or deny service to users. Quality of service is usually defined and measured in terms of non-functional attributes that users can perceive, such as latency, volume of storage or throughput.

Issues. The ultimate contract for quality of service is likely to remain with the user or organisation prepared to pay for a service, but distribution complicates the picture: it becomes difficult to establish how each individual device contributes to overall quality, and particularly difficult to instrument marginal failure. The problem is illustrated by the need to provide sophisticated logging services in current distributed applications [18]; these difficulties are compounded in a more dynamic environment.

Conflicting user policies are possible, for example, one user's advertising may be another's junk mail. As at present, when such conflicts become offensive to one user, or consume appreciable resource, action is necessary at the system level to restore a balance. How such control is to be exercised in a pervasive system is yet to be established, and highlights the tension between agent autonomy and system stability.

The perception of availability by a user depends on the application. At present, denial of service attacks seek to disable a server by the exhaustion of one or more of its resources. As distributed systems become used for both critical and commonplace functions, then less dramatic modulations of service may become important to users: consider the opportunity cost to a stockbroker of delayed market data.

At the same time increasing numbers of devices increase the access opportunities for attackers (section 3), and the nature of some devices is such that failure may be permanent, either for physical reasons (the device itself, or inability to access it), or because the only safe response to an attack is to disable itself.

Implications. The need to defend against attacks on service integrity will grow rather than reduce; devices should be designed to resist resource exhaustion attacks, for example, by rationing as resources approach saturation. Other forms of defense need to be applied at the system level, including intrusion detection and response.

2.7 Assurance

Assurance that a device is able to support the security policies it claims is based on the isolation and identification of its security mechanisms and the lifetime protection of those mechanisms through measures such as change control, configuration control, and operating procedure management.

Issues. Almost none of the current assurance practices can be applied to a complete distributed system. If system level assurance is required, new assurance mechanisms have to be developed based on reasoning about system properties, while assuring the properties of devices and services individually.

One aspect of assurance that becomes important in pervasive systems is establishing that a device is what it claims to be: at one extreme that it has not been impersonated, at the other that it will enforce any claimed restrictions on its own behaviour. The former may be a question of identity, the latter a question of assurance, which is technically difficult to achieve over the lifetime of a mobile smart device. Furthermore, the question of demonstrating that a host is actually running a given piece of software has, at present, no solution (see summaries at [19,20]).

Implications. Some assurance in the implementation of security mechanisms in smart devices is necessary; the design principle of separating security and functionality is applicable to all devices with security mechanisms.

Mechanisms need to be developed to provide dynamic assurance of both software environments and mobile code.

3   Threats

The following discussion highlights those threats that are either new, or more prominent, in pervasive systems.

3.1   System Composition

The potential for vulnerabilities due to system composition is, in large part, driven by the specific policy management and authorisation system, and how they resolve inconsistencies that result from different users' perspectives. Some other issues that arise in the composition of the system include:

Critical failure points. Single points of failure can be categorised as physical or logical. Even network topologies with good scaling or distance properties may be disproportionately vulnerable to the physical failure of specific nodes or links, and networks with 'border' devices that concentrate traffic are obvious physical targets.

Logical failure can occur at any point in the design and implementation process, but the resulting vulnerability may become widely dispersed in the system. Design flaws include faults in protocols or encryption algorithms. Implementation flaws include physical failures, such as vulnerabilities in RF receivers, and software defects such as implementation errors in protocol libraries.

Aggregation. Although the need for user privacy can been expressed in a policy, such policies may be vulnerable to being bypassed by data aggregation. This is an extension of the problem of propagating trust via delegation: how does a user meaningfully restrict the use of data in services that are invoked only indirectly?

Pervasive network attacks. Network Worms and Viruses are well-established threats, and will remain so. With very large networks, however, it may be possible to construct self-perpetuating dynamic attacks that operate at the network rather than the component level. A familiar example is a cycle of emails triggered by inadvertent circular re-direction; other mechanisms of devising cycles or waves in a highly functional network are likely to emerge, with the possibility of large-scale persistent denial of service.

Implications. The designer of a device or service must avoid design features that could create a local vulnerability or point of attack. It is also be necessary to show that device policies do not result in undesirable emergent system behavior [21] that could be exploited by an attacker, or invoked by accident.

3.2   The Local Context

The local context of a device is its physical environment, the communications and sensors it may access, and neighboring devices. The general threat is that an attacker may subvert the local context to mislead a device about some aspect of its environment, either causing damage or mis-invoking functionality.

Physical. If the device has sensors then it may be possible to manipulate them directly, or use extreme temperatures or other environmental factors to modify device performance.

Many forms of communication are subject to physical attack, and the ease with which this can be carried out determines the true threat. Active remote attacks against wireless networks are now commonplace, and there is a danger that 'WarDriving' could be extended to using electromagnetic pulse weapons; even simple weapons could damage RF circuitry. Passive attacks on communications could be an unacceptable risk to confidentiality and privacy, and could enable system mapping prior to an active attack.

Software. There is a risk that subverted or spoof devices could be introduced into the network (for example, an IP masquerading attack or Trojan Horse service) and manipulate the system to violate its security policies (for example, migrate data in violation of confidentiality). An important case is where a subverted host seeks to migrate an attack through the system. Historically, most methods by which a remote device can be induced into executing software have been used to propagate Trojan Horse attacks (for example, opening emails with active content, buffer overflow attacks), and so any feature that executes remote code is a potential vulnerability. Protecting a host against an agent, and an agent against a host, are still unsolved problems [18,19].

Denial of Service attacks tend to use expected service requests in unexpected ways or numbers, eventually modifying a device's capability by exhausting or saturating a physical resource (cpu cycles, memory, file pointers, etc.). There is little new in principle about this form of attack, but novel types of device introduce new services and resource constraints that may then be exploited. For example, communications that use calling channels or ports can be saturated before their bandwidth is exhausted.

A common limitation in smart devices is power (either instantaneous power or total energy) and this needs to be treated similarly to avoid denial of service based on power exhaustion (see 'Sleep Deprivation Torture', [15]).

Implications. The current experience with wireless LANs is that pervasive functionality may provide points of access that can also be exploited by an attacker. Such access points include 'anonymous' logins, accounts without passwords and developer and system administration back-door services, as well as broadcast information about services. Capabilities of this sort need to be subjected to careful security risk assessment.

Designers should be aware that the first stage of an attack might be to *map* the system. Mechanisms that make mapping hard provide useful defense in depth, particularly if an attacker risks detection during the mapping phase. In the case of broadcast communications, encryption may be valuable for just that purpose, even if it is too weak to provide long-term confidentiality.

Authorisation is needed between co-operating devices to avoid spoof device attacks. It is less clear how to defend against remote subverted software; such attacks tend to be identified by their actions or by other fingerprints (for example, signature control ports). Since migration of code may become one of the enablers of pervasive computing, it deserves special attention: devices that feature the capability to run such a service must defend against the importing Trojan Horse software, for example, by ensuring that it executes in an encapsulated software environment.

Devices should be design to minimise hard failure on resource exhaustion including device power, for example, by resource rationing strategies.

Redundancy may increase the difficulty of environmental manipulation as an effective attack on the system, even if such manipulation is effective against individual devices.

3.3 Devices

Devices, which may be small and mobile, are vulnerable to a variety of attacks resulting from their physical nature. Modern smart cards are a good example: it is possible to obtain them legitimately and then attack them at leisure, and even to assemble large collections for study. Physical theft or substitution is also not difficult. Their relative size and portability limits the designer's capability to protect the device, so they may have limited tamper proofing and be vulnerable to a wide range of environmental attacks.

In practice it may be difficult to dispose of device state: although the device may faithfully prevent access to old state, and perhaps even 'zero' memory or magnetic media, there are physical remenance mechanisms in most forms of storage that could leave the device vulnerable to a determined attacker with physical access.

Implications. The physical design of a device is a security mechanism, designers must minimise the possibility of physical remenance and device substitution.

3.4 The User's Perceptions of security

From the security point of view, users are naïve, so security mechanisms that are designed to involve the user's judgment are vulnerable. Current examples include manual agreement to PKI certificates and the management of private keys. Users are also conditioned by a set of assumptions about security based on past experience: the use of mobile telephones is a good example of a presumption of privacy that was not originally supported by the technology, and is still not supported by the environment where users choose to make personal or business calls. The principal threats are:

- *Social engineering.* Persuading a user to do something incorrect, such as resetting a password or simply misusing the system [22].
- *Confusion.* A user acting incorrectly because of lack of understanding (accepting a new PKI certificate from the wrong source), or carrying our a normal action in the wrong environment (typing a password into a spoof screen).

Implications. Device designers should be aware of users preconceptions and work within them. For example – given a pen and diary, either could become smart and store the data, but users are accustomed to the fungibility of pens and the need to protect and store diaries.

On a positive note, attackers may also be confused about the overall properties of a very large system and so the successful implementation of distributed intrusion detection may well allow early detection of potential attacks, in a similar way that many virus types are reported before they are found 'in the wild' (for example, see CERT co-ordination center statistics).

4   Conclusions

This discussion of security, drawing from the perspective of existing system requirements, rather than from the device technology, effectively illustrates the range of security requirements that are required for host environments in pervasive systems. The question of security is unavoidable; it is not possible to build a reliable and effective computing infrastructure if the devices supporting the system do not include security mechanisms.

The practical problems of size and low computing power of many devices can be mitigated by a careful consideration of the balance between security complexity and required functionality, and we offer some suggestions along these lines. In particular, we classify the degree of policy management required in a device into three types: *fixed policy*, *updateable policy* (perhaps just one policy attribute, such as user) and *flexible policy* (able to update its policy from services in the environment). We believe that this is a useful indicator of security complexity and will be of value to designers seeking to achieve this balance.

Although the purpose of this paper is to elicit requirements for devices, we note that there are a number of open questions at the system level; they include:

- How should security policies be expressed and implemented to combine the interests of multiple stakeholders, implement privacy, and express aggregated constraints in a dynamic environment?
- How should users, devices, and resources be federated to facilitate scalability, and what services are required to support these arrangements?
- How can a balance be achieved between the needs of privacy and accountability?
- How can security assurance be provided for large distributed systems?

By starting our analysis from a classical security perspective, rather than a device perspective we provide an insight into security requirements for devices and software agents. The result, however, is rather more than a simple extension of today's distributed system policies; the security issues in a pervasive computing world are qualitatively as well as quantitatively different, to the extent that the success of pervasive computing requires the re-invention of system security practice.

References

1. M. Weiser. The Computer for the 21st Century. *Scientific American*, **265**(3), 1991.
2. I. Foster et al. *The Physiology of the Grid: An Open Grid Services Architecture for Distributed Systems Implementation*. Global Grid Forum. 2002. http://www.gridforum.org/ogsi-wg/
3. H. Kreger. *Web Services Conceptual Architecture*. IBM. 2001. http://www-3.ibm.com/software/solutions/webservices/pdf/WSCA
4. US Department of Defence. Trusted Computer System Evaluation Criteria (Orange Book). DoD 5200.28-STD. 1985.
5. *Network Related Security Features*. 3rd Generation Partnership Project, GSM 03:20. 2001.
6. Liberty Alliance. *Liberty Architecture Overview*. 2002. http://www.projectliberty.org/

7. I. Foster et al. A Security Architecture for Computational Grids. In *Proc 5th ACM Conference on Computer and Communications Security*. pp. 83–92. 1998.
8. Directive 95/46/EC on the protection of individuals with regard to the processing of personal data and on the free movement of such data. In *The European Union*. 1995.
9. M. Erdos, S. Cantor. *Shibboleth Architecture*. Internet2. 2001. http://middleware.internet2.edu/shibboleth/
10. M. Thompson et al. Certificate-Based Access Control for Widely Distributed Resources. In *Proc 8th Usenix Security Symposium*. Washington, D.C. 1999.
11. N. Li, J. C. Mitchell, W. H. Winsborough. Design of a Role-Based Trust-Management Framework. In *2002 IEEE Symposium on Security and Privacy*. IEEE Computer Society. pp. 114–130. 2002.
12. S. Fischer-Hübner, A. Ott. From a Formal Privacy Model to its Implementation. In *Proceedings of the 21st National Information Systems Security Conference (NISSC '98)*. Arlington, VA. 1998.
13. X. Jiang, J. A. Landay. Modeling Privacy Control in Context-Aware Systems. *IEEE Pervasive Computing*. **1**(3): pp. 59–63. 2002
14. H.-W. Gellersen, A. Schmidt, M. Beigl. Multi-Sensor Context-Awareness in Mobile Devices and Smart Artifacts. *Journal of Mobile Networks and Applications* (Special Issue on Mobility of Systems, Users, Data and Computing in Mobile Networks and Applications (MONET)). 2002.
15. L. Pearlman et al. A Community Authorisation Service for Group Collaboration. In *Proceedings of the IEEE 3rd International Workshop on Policies for Distributed Systems and Networks*. 2002.
16. F. Stajano, R. Anderson. *The Resurrecting Duckling: Security Issues in Ad-Hoc Wireless Networks*. AT&T Laborotories. 1999.
17. H. S. Nwana. Software Agents: An Overview. *Knowledge Engineering Review*. **11**(3): pp. 205–244. 1996.
18. D. Gunter et al. Dynamic Monitoring of High-Performance Distributed Applications. In *Proceedings of The 11th IEEE International Symposium on High Performance Distributed Computing*. 2002.
19. W. M. Farmer, J. D. Guttman, V. Swarup. Security for Mobile Agents: Issues and Requirements. In *Proc. 19th NIST/NCSC National Information Systems Security Conference*. pp. 591–597. 1996.
20. G. Karjoth, J. Posegga. Mobile Agents and Telcos' Nightmares. *Annales des Telecommunications*. **55**(7/8): pp. 29–41. 2000.
21. S. Stepney. Critical Critical Systems. In *Formal Aspects of Security FASEC '02*. LNCS, Springer. 2003.
22. G. Cybenko, A. Giani, P. Thompson. Cognitive Hacking: A Battle for the Mind. *IEEE Computer*. **35**(8): pp. 50–56. 2002.

Dependability Issues of Pervasive Computing in a Healthcare Environment

Jürgen Bohn[1], Felix Gärtner[2,*], and Harald Vogt[1]

[1] Eidgenössische Technische Hochschule Zürich (ETHZ),
Department for Computer Science, Distributed Systems Group,
CH-8092 Zürich, Switzerland
{bohn,vogt}@inf.ethz.ch
[2] École Polytechnique Fédérale de Lausanne (EPFL),
Departement de Systèmes de Communications, Laboratoire de Programmation Distribuée,
CH-1015 Lausanne, Switzerland
fcg@acm.org

Abstract. This paper proposes that the healthcare domain can serve as an archetypical field of research in pervasive computing. We present this area from a technological perspective, arguing that it provides a wide range of possible applications of pervasive computing technology. We further recognize that pervasive computing technology is likely to create concerns about the security of healthcare systems, due to increased data aggregation, ubiquitous access, and increasing dependency on technical solutions. But we also justify why the same technology can help building more robust, more dependable systems that increase the quality of healthcare. We identify building blocks that are necessary to achieve this goal: a pervasive middleware, appropriate handling of exceptional situations, and dependability assertions for small devices.

1 Introduction

Today, we see Weiser's vision of ubiquitous computing [39] steadily taking shape. Small embedded devices (like those that allow us to communicate always and everywhere) have changed the way in which we perceive the world. But the biggest changes surely still lie ahead. One difficulty of the research in pervasive computing is to estimate and predict what will be the central paradigms, the central applications, the central technologies that will have the greatest impact. Basically, there are two ways to find answers to this question: On the one hand, researchers build systems and apply them to experiment with them in sometimes rather artificial and therefore unrealistic application environments to estimate their usefulness. On the other hand, it has been attempted to define the paradigms of pervasive computing first and then try to derive useful applications from that. Many different prototypes, methodologies and concepts have therefore evolved, often unrelated and incomparable in usefulness. We believe that this is partly due to the fact that in pervasive computing no *prototype application scenario* for the experimentation of pervasive technologies exists which

---

* Work was supported by the Deutsche Forschungsgemeinschaft as part of the "Emmy Noether" programme.

D. Hutter et al. (Eds.): Security in Pervasive Computing 2003, LNCS 2802, pp. 53–70, 2004.

- is realistic and easily motivated to the public,
- in which industrial and governmental interests guarantee research support, and
- which is challenging enough to offer a multitude of interesting research questions to pursue.

This is unsatisfactory since similar prototype problems exist in other research domains, like the well-known robot soccer (Robocup) challenge in artificial intelligence and robotics [36]. The advantage of such a scenario is that research efforts can be concentrated and solutions can be better compared.

This paper has two main goals. The first goal is to present the application of pervasive technology in medical and healthcare environments, like the hospital, as a suitable scenario for research in pervasive computing that satisfies the conditions stated above. The second goal is to take up some of the research questions from the area of dependable systems, outline and discuss the problems involved, and present some general architectural solutions in the context of the hospital scenario.

There has been some related work in the areas of healthcare, pervasive computing and dependability [4, 8, 9, 14, 18, 25, 32, 37], but this work either does not focus on dependability [8, 9, 14], concentrates on the dependability aspects of a single particular problem [4], or does not focus on pervasive computing [18, 25, 32, 37]. In contrast, we give a general dependability analysis of a healthcare system which is built using pervasive technology.

This paper is structured as follows: In section 2 we outline the general vision of a healthcare environment enhanced by pervasive computing technology and argue that this area is ideal to serve as an archetypical field of research in pervasive computing. Section 3 presents remote monitoring of a patient's health state—an application made possible by the combination of new technologies—and discusses its dependability issues. Section 4 deals with the question of how to provide highly available access control to pervasive devices in a hospital environment. In Section 5, we show that auditing is an essential instrument for providing dependability assurances in the healthcare domain. It turns out that the same infrastructure used for auditing purposes also proves useful for other purposes, especially for process improvement. Section 6 concludes the paper.

2   Pervasive Computing Technology in a Healthcare Environment

One of the major consequences of pervasive computing is the *disappearing computer*, i.e. computing (and communication) power is increasingly embedded into devices and everyday artifacts. When people interact with these "smart objects", they might not be aware of the fact that in the background, data reflecting their current situation and behavior is collected, exchanged, and processed. This processing is going on, in many cases, for the benefit of users, but could also be carried out in the interest of other parties. This gives room to privacy and security concerns. However, in a healthcare environment, the benefits might easily outweigh the risks. Patients are willing to give up a big portion of their privacy for the sake of medical treatment, though that must not lead to disadvantages outside this context.

In this section we argue that the application of pervasive computing in the hospital not only contributes to improvements of healthcare, but also leads to a number of challenging research problems.

2.1 New Diagnostic and Monitoring Methods

Advances in biomedical technology directly contribute to improvements in therapy and medical treatment. Nanotechnology, for example, has the potential to make treatments possible, which have been unthinkable before, by injecting autonomous machines into the human body. These nanomachines, equipped with sensors and communication capabilities, can even transmit valuable information to devices that reside outside the body.

Assuming that a large amount of information is being made available through sensors and monitoring devices, great potential lies in information processing and its linking to other information sources. As an example, consider a hospital where a patient is constantly monitored, and the findings are linked to diagnostic information. Then, it would be possible to advise the hospital canteen to prepare special food for this particular patient, and to adapt the patient's specific medication according to his current health condition. In Section 3 we elaborate on the security issues of remote health monitoring.

2.2 Procedural Improvements

According to [25], thousands of patients die each year in hospitals due to (mostly avoidable) medical errors, imposing substantial cost on national economy. This study was performed in the U.S., but similar numbers are likely to apply in other countries. It is assumed that improving the procedures related to treatment can help prevent many medical errors (see recommendations at [1]). This clearly indicates that high potential lies in the application of pervasive computing technology to process improvement.

For example, medication errors are a severe problem in healthcare. In the U.S., such errors are estimated to account for 7000 deaths annually [16], and are often due to bad handwriting and similar problems [30]. Such errors could be largely eliminated through better auditing capabilities, introduced by pervasive computing technology, such as RFID (cf. Section 5).

Auditing and the availability of location information can also help to improve other processes within a hospital. Decisions are often based upon information about the physical location of a person or an object. For example, if a patient gets into a critical condition, the system could locate the patient and the nearest doctor, and call her to the scene. Location is also a basic feature in detecting context knowledge about entities. Consider for example a doctor in an operating room; it is very likely that this particular physician is currently busy and shouldn't be contacted on matters of low urgency. There are a large variety of localization systems available [20], varying in location precision, environmental constraints, infrastructural requirements, and—of high importance in a hospital—compatibility with other device types (one major issue that might restrict deployment in a hospital is electromagnetic interference with medical devices).

2.3   Economical Benefit

Pervasive technology allows to have patient data accessible to authorized users at any time and at any place. Doctors do not need to be accompanied with a large folder of diagnostic files. All written information as well as X-ray images and other data are accessible on touchpads in the patient's rooms, the offices, on handheld devices, through headsets and wherever else they are needed. This allows working personnel to concentrate better on their work.

New technology might improve productivity, but it also introduces costs for deployment, administration, maintenance, etc. Although healthcare is an area on which people are willing to spend a significant part of their income, the amount of money that can be spent on new treatment methods, the benefit of which is mostly marginal, is certainly limited. We recognize this fact, but taking into account the prospective proliferation of pervasive computing technology, its cost might as well drop below the level where its application in the healthcare domain becomes economically attractive.

2.4   Dependability Issues

The areas which have been described above lie at the heart of the operational abilities in healthcare. Introducing technical equipment into these areas imposes a non-negligible probability of failure and hence the (possibly life-threatening) danger of not being able to perform a service when it is needed. Furthermore, patient data which is accessible in a pervasive way and (f)lying around almost everywhere must be protected to preserve integrity and confidentiality. The dependability issues do not only stem from the increased scale and complexity of a system consisting of pervasive technology. Some of the issues, like the difficulty to define and protect the borders of a pervasive system or the confusion caused by a malfunctioning system which is an unnoticeable part of the environment, are a direct implication of the "pervasiveness". Access control is a particular aspect in this context. We will discuss the issue of pervasive access control in section 4.

3   Remote Health Monitoring

In this section, we look at an example of what can be called typical pervasive computing technology applied to the problem of monitoring medical sensor data that is collected from the patient in real-time. Such systems are being developed for monitoring a variety of vital parameters, often based on standard computing and communication technology [14, 32]. The ultimate health monitoring device would be a tiny sensor, implanted in the patient, equipped with a ever-lasting battery, and communicating directly to a responsible physician. Today's systems consist of tiny implanted sensors communicating to intermediary devices that are typically attached to the patient's clothing. An intermediary device collects data from the sensor and transmits it to a medical center, using public (UMTS) and private (WLAN) communication infrastructure. Processing the data at the medical center may result in simply logging it (for future reviews), giving feedback to the patient (about his current status, not only in critical situations, possibly annotated by a physician), or triggering an alarm, directing an emergency team to the patient.

Messages from the medical center to the patient may also result in configurational adjustments of the intermediary device or the sensor itself. This could be used, e.g., to increase the frequency of data transmissions in more critical situations, or switching from batch transmissions to real-time transmissions if the physician considers it necessary. The intermediary device could also act as a relay station for other devices, such as a "smart pillbox" that offers the patient an optimal dose of medication [8]. This results in a feedback loop which is vulnerable to interferences and attacks. For example, slightly inaccurate measurements could result in different doses that may harm the patient. Therefore, this feedback loop must be protected against outside manipulations.

The collected data itself, or data about medication, must be considered sensitive, and its confidentiality must be ensured. Otherwise, conclusions about the patient's health state could be drawn. The protection of medical information in our context is mainly a task of the "background" system, where data is stored, processed, and made available to clinicians. Access control policies for such systems should follow the guidelines given in [4, 18]. A monitoring system has different requirements, though.

Who might be interested in attacking such a system? After all, since no written records are created by default, an attack has to be carried out on a technical level. We imagine the following scenarios. A greedy relative might want to find out about the health state of an elderly patient, and even try to change the medication in a way that shortens the patient's life time. Or, a competitor of the system's manufacturer might try to render the system useless by executing extensive denial-of-service attacks on the equipment, hoping to persuade patients and physicians to switch to their own product. If data can be easily extracted from the system, these attacks might be feasible. The rest of this section shows which parts of a monitoring system are especially vulnerable.

3.1 Basic Requirements

In applications where the timely delivery and processing of sensor data is crucial, the communication link between an intermediary device and the medical center must offer a high degree of *availability* and *quality* of data transmissions. This could be achieved by using redundant, diversified technologies, such as 802.11 and UMTS. However, if neither of them is available, at least the patient and the medical center should be notified about the failure. Note that the use of public infrastructures, such as UMTS and public WLAN access points, makes it harder for denial-of-service attacks to stay undetected, since the common incentive to keep these infrastructures available is higher than for proprietary infrastructures.

Availability of the background system is essential in order to provide timely feedback to the patient. This imposes strict requirements regarding robustness and scalability on that part of the system.

Auditing capabilities (cf. Section 5) are of utmost importance whenever messages result in changes to the sensing equipment. All changes must be *accountable* to some system decision, either made by an autonomous process, or by a clinician. In the end, somebody must take *responsibility* for the messages being sent. Otherwise, failures due to system errors become more likely. This means that some (life critical) messages can only be sent when authorized by a responsible clinician. The full authorization information must be transmitted to the patient device, which should keep an independent log, making it impossible for the clinician to deny his decision.

Usability is a crucial feature for equipment that is handled by the patient.

The following paragraphs describe some basic issues in providing fundamental security features of medical systems: confidentiality, integrity, availability, and accountability. We will not further go into details of other requirements, such as safety. We assume that all medical devices are designed and built according to established safety engineering principles and that (partial) system failure cannot result in severe harm to the patient.

3.2 Capturing Sensitive Data

The *confidentiality* of medical data is compromised if an unauthorized person gets hold of it in clear text. In the simple model of remote health monitoring we present here, there are many possible attack points where sensitive data could be acquired. They differ in costs, and it turns out that, for this attack, the most vulnerable part is the (implanted) sensor itself, because it is the (computationally) weakest device involved in the monitoring process.

Capturing transmitted data over a public wireless network may be technically simple. Legislation in many countries requires that law enforcement agencies are able to intercept messages in the clear. But the weakening of security mechanisms to allow this also enables attackers to acquire the same messages. Therefore, public wireless networks should only be used if end-to-end confidentiality of data is ensured. Today's computing capabilities should allow for sufficient encryption of sensitive data on the intermediate device before it is transmitted to the background system. However, then *key management* becomes a crucial issue. When the device is handed over to the patient, a secret shared by the device and the background system can be stored on the device. This secret could be used to derive encryption keys for data transmissions. The shared secret must be sufficiently protected in order to deter attackers. On the intermediary device, a smart card token could be used for this purpose. In the background system, a (expensive) highly protected system area is required.

If an attacker is able to place a receiver very close to the victim patient, it might be possible for him to acquire sensitive data directly from the implanted sensor. It is unlikely that sensors will be equipped with sufficient computing power to perform cryptographic functions. Whatever the computing power of a sensor might be, it will be most likely spent on sensing tasks instead of (most of the time unnecessary) cryptographic functions. The best countermeasure against this kind of attacks might be the use of proprietary transmission techniques, but as such devices become more widespread, it gets cheaper for attackers to acquire these. Besides, insiders could be bribed to reveal technical details of the technology, allowing attackers to build their own receivers.

A similar attack is stealing the intermediary device after it has collected (and has still stored) sensor data. If the intermediary device is designed in a way that makes (physical) tampering obvious, the damage could be contained, since only a (small) subset of sensor data might be compromised, and the patient wouldn't reuse the device. But since such a device will most likely be equipped with a maintenance interface (wired or wireless), this API forms a potential vulnerability. In this case, an audit record of the maintenance access, that is also transmitted to the monitoring center, might reveal the unauthorized reading of the data. Note that shutting off the sensor or the intermediary device completely against potentially unauthorized access might hinder access in emergency cases. It is not obvious how to distinguish a malicious access from an access in case of an emergency.

3.3   Manipulating Data

The manipulation of data in a health care system could have a fatal impact, therefore the integrity of data is of major importance. That means that at all places where data is kept or in transit, its integrity must be protected.

Sensors measure data and run it through a (simple) processing step. The output of this step is regarded as the original data. For auditing purposes, it is required that this data is stored in the audit log in its original form. Intermediate processing steps must not alter the original data, since only the original data can be ultimately attributed to the sensor.

The authenticity of sensor data cannot be certified directly by the sensor itself, due to computational restrictions. However, the intermediary device can keep record logs of incoming sensor data, and certify the findings on its own behalf. This makes it technically impossible to firmly attribute data to the sensor, but by the use of certain means, the trust in the authenticity of the data can be increased. Such means might include checks on the plausibility of sensor findings (if disproportionate values are received, the medical center is able to detect a fault), the use of redundant intermediate devices, and regular synchronization with other measurements.

A sensor receiving a control message, e.g. to change its configuration, must make sure that the message is originating from an authorized process and is being delivered when it should be. Again, due to likely restricted computing capabilities within a sensor, the sensor might not be able to verify the authenticity of a message by itself. It relies on the intermediate device to do so. In contrast to the collection and transmission of sensor data, which can be done by a bunch of different devices, controlling the sensor should be reserved for a special, trusted device. Such a device can verify the authenticity of messages. Explicitly requiring the patient to use a certain device makes sure that the patient is aware of the change.

3.4   Denial of Service

A system fault or an attack resulting in denial-of-service (DoS) is perceived by the patient as the intermediary device reporting constantly its inability to receive acknowledgements for its data transmissions. The device might be able to send its data, but it has no way making sure that the data is received. The patient might call the medical center on the issue, and if the center reports that the data was received, the patient might manually acknowledge the receipt. However, if the medical center does not receive any data, it will inform the patient about it. The audit logs should then enable the security officer to trace down the system fault.

There are many possibilities of performing a DoS attack on a weakly protected monitoring system. Transmission links can be jammed, batteries within the sensor and the intermediary device be drained, the communication interfaces of the medical center could be overloaded (e.g., by a conventional DoS attack in the Internet), computationally intensive processes be injected in the center's processing plants.

3.5 Impersonation and Insiders

An attacker might trick a patient into handing him his monitoring equipment by pretending to be a technician or a physician. This is similar to "ordinary" criminals who enter a victim's household under false allegations, stealing valuables or robbing the victim on his own grounds. The attacker might exchange devices with fakes, or install additional equipment for surveillance. As we have already seen, the sensors will most likely not be equipped with sophisticated cryptographic mechanisms, so this is a feasible way of getting sensor data. This problem can be (partially) solved on a higher level through patient awareness. In principle however, there is no technical way of preventing an attacker from acquiring the patient's trust. It is noteworthy that, in companies, most security relevant attacks leading to damage are executed by insiders, who misuse trust laid in them by the victim.

3.6 Emergencies

A typical difficulty in securing medical devices is the requirement of override procedures for emergencies. Everybody knows situations where "regular" procedures, considered safe under ordinary circumstances, threaten to do more harm than benefit, and must be replaced by unusual, possibly dangerous actions. As a rule, formulated in [18], a responsible person must always be able to switch off all security mechanisms and act as he considers appropriate in case of an emergency. The change of the system into emergency mode has to be recorded for future review. Penalties act as a deterrent to abuse of this mechanism.

What does that mean for pervasive computing in healthcare? Suppose a number of devices, invisibly performing their tasks for the benefit of the patient. Patient and physicians might not even be aware of them. However, they must be able to shut them down, or switch to emergency mode, immediately and completely. Assuming that devices cannot detect emergency modes by themselves, there must exist external means to perform this operation. One feasible solution could be a special device, carried by medical personnel, which is able to switch all surrounding devices into emergency mode.

4   Dependable Access Control

Pervasive computing technologies allow accessing confidential patient data always and everywhere. This information must be protected from unauthorized access and modification. In this section we present the design of a highly available access control service. It is similar to the well-known Kerberos system [31], but tailored for a pervasive environment with some degree of fixed infrastructure. In this section, a hospital will serve as example deployment area.

4.1 Dependability Architecture

The electronic equivalent to a patient's medical record on paper is a dedicated database which we see at the center of any system in the hospital environment. Usually, hospitals and other healthcare institutions already have large commercial databases installed, but the mechanism to access this data (based on passwords) is usually not flexible enough to be useful in a pervasive environment. Hence, a central design decision is to separate the management of data from the mechanism to control access to it.

An access control mechanism contains data itself, namely the information of whom to grant access to what. We assume that the mapping from users to objects that defines the access control is given by the security policy of the institution which runs the system. Usually, this is based on a role- and location-based access control mechanism [6]. A user is associated with a digital identity that he carries with him and can be communicated to the access control system. Using a common challenge-response protocol [29], the system can validate the identity of the person and on success return a digital certificate which enables the access. The challenge is now to ensure the availability and integrity requirements of the service.

To ensure availability, access control data has to be replicated at points which are assumed to fail independently [11]. The infrastructure must provide for a set of *access control servers*, which are distributed in the area of the institution. These servers must be physically protected and surveilled. Interaction with the service is performed at certain identifiable *access points*. These may be touch-screens, doors, handhelds or other small devices at a specific location. The distribution of servers and communication facilities must ensure that from every access points, a certain number k of access control servers are reachable. Usually, k will be some number larger than 2. Since k is intuitively a measure of the dependability of the system, the value of k should be chosen as large as possible given the institutional (financial) and locational (area layout) restrictions. It is possible to vary this number according to the security requirements in certain areas of the hospital. For example, k should be at least 3 for access points in publicly accessible areas. In highly sensitive areas where physical access is already limited (like an administration building or an intensive care unit), $k = 2$ or even $k = 1$ should be sufficient (see Figure 1).

The underlying concepts of the access control mechanism rely on a combination of two established mechanisms: agreement protocols and secret sharing. The idea is that in order to grant access to a certain resource, the k access servers in the vicinity of the access point query their access control database and form an agreement on whether or not to grant the access. If they decide to allow access and a subsequent main database query (for patient data) is necessary, the involved servers will jointly calculate a certificate which is made available at the access point for further actions. Otherwise the response may simply be the opening of a door or the activation of a signal on a navigation display.

The agreement is reached using an agreement protocol for the *Byzantine failure model* [26]. In the current setting, theoretical investigations show that at least 3 distinct nodes are needed to tolerate at most one Byzantine process. However, in many cases where the faults are not so malicious, 2 servers or even one are sufficient. Note that reaching agreement using optimistic Byzantine agreement protocols [15] is practical

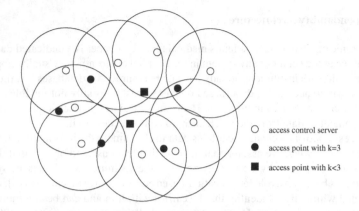

○   access control server

●   access point with k=3

■   access point with k<3

Fig. 1. Sample layout of access points and their connection to access servers.

today. The assumption that access servers may be stolen or completely compromised implies that for $k \geq 2$ no single server may contain enough information to derive and produce valid certificates. This is achieved through standard secret sharing approaches [34]. In these approaches, a secret key is distributed across a set of nodes in such a way that only a certain fraction together is able to compute the secret again. In the case of $k = 3$, at least two servers need to be fully compromised to be able to derive secret key information.

4.2 Summary

The above architecture is highly distributed. Access points for which the necessary access servers are still available can operate autonomously. In case where even this number of servers is unavailable, access points must provide for manual override mechanisms in case of emergencies. These override mechanisms contain devices that allow to log the required data for later audit or raise an alarm. An advantage of the architecture is that it is simple, it exploits the connectivity available to pervasive devices, and it allows to embed the resources necessary to do cryptographic computations into the environment, thus relieving small devices (like the access points) from such heavy duty tasks.

5   Auditing

Auditing in general can be characterized as the accumulation and evaluation of evidence about information to determine and report on the degree of correspondence between the information and established criteria [3, 5].

With a pervasive computing infrastructure in place, it becomes feasible to run a fully computerized electronic 24h accounting process: The ubiquitous infrastructure has means to uniquely sense and identify objects within the hospital. Furthermore, it is providing the technical means for pervasive access to all information and services. Thus the infrastructure is holding a key position: First, it is able to keep a complete record of all objects that are used or accessed in the hospital. Second, it is in a position to log all services and data transactions that are carried out. In addition, such an infrastructure may operate during day and night and analyze the continuously collected data in real-time.

In the following, we will sketch a potential pervasive security auditing service in the hospital environment and describe its basic requirements. Further, we will demonstrate that such an auditing service has favourable side-effects which can contribute to increase the safety and efficiency of health care and business processes within the hospital.

5.1 Security Auditing

As a rule, health care services have to comply with established national standards and legislation of the respective countries. For example, in the United States, the Health Insurance Portability and Accountability Act (HIPAA) [21,33] defines standards for electronic health care transactions and data exchange. It also addresses the security and privacy of health data.

However, in a hospital transformed by pervasive computing technology, it is impossible to verify that its operation satisfies established standards and legal requirements if no data on processes and events is accumulated. Therefore, in order to enforce a security policy in the hospital environment, it is required that all security related data is recorded during operation. The task of analyzing the collected data can then be delegated to an automated security auditing process as described above. This process should then cover all data and information that is relevant to security in the hospital. Figure 2 shows an example of typical auditing information as it may be collected by a pervasive computing infrastructure in the hospital.

In general, whenever a device or a user is authorized to perform a certain task, this event should be liable to supervision and security auditing. Also, whenever standard procedures or regulations are violated, these incidents should be recorded, too. This includes the case of emergencies, e.g. when restrictions are rightfully countermanded in order to avert damage to patient life. In the following paragraphs we give some concrete examples for processes and events that are relevant to security auditing in the hospital environment:

Access control mechanisms in the hospital require means to authenticate and authorize users and devices. For example, this is the case in the following situations:

- Doctors are authorized to have ubiquitous access to medical patient records of their patients only. They may read or edit these records according to the provided medical treatment.
- Patients are equipped with devices for remote monitoring and diagnostics. These devices may be adjusted during operation, either automatically by a medical system or manually by authorized medical staff.
- Pervasive access control is operational throughout the hospital: Doctors, patients, and visitors automatically gain access solely to those areas and rooms which they are authorized to enter.

Fig. 2. Visualization of security auditing information as it may be logged by a pervasive computing infrastructure to cover the prescription of a patient's medicine.

For safety reasons, there are means to countermand the various access restrictions in the case of an emergency. For example, to activate an emergency override may be legitimate in the following situations:

- If a clinical emergency occurs, doctors may be required to read records of patients other than their own. For example, if a patient monitoring device detects a critical anomaly in the patient's health condition, the nearest doctor and not the physician who has been initially assigned to the patient is called to assist.
- In the case of a fire alarm, patients or hospital staff have the right to open doors and enter rooms that normally are off-limits.
- Medical devices that detect technical problems or malfunctions, e.g. due to low battery level or signal interference, call a technician or hospital staff for troubleshooting. If the functioning of a device is vital to the patient's health, a doctor may have to change its configuration or programming even though he does not possess the necessary permissions.

The situations described above should all be covered by a security auditing mechanism in the hospital.

5.2 Dependability Issues

As it is the case with any technical infrastructure, a security auditing mechanism in the hospital, too, is subject to service disruption and unauthorized manipulation attempts.

On the one hand, it is therefore necessary to protect the network and computer equipment against a variety of traditional attacks, including denial of service attacks, hacking, the introduction of Trojan horses, etc. The security auditing service will therefore have to include "classic" security auditing features [27, 38] such as intrusion detection [2, 13] or a firewall [35]. In particular, to protect a heterogeneous and highly distributed pervasive computing infrastructure, the security mechanisms have to give special attention to its physical distributedness. For instance, in the pervasive hospital, a distributed intrusion detection system [10] is required to cope with distributed attacks.

On the other hand, the *quality* of a security audit heavily relies on the composition of the collected data, especially its integrity, confidentiality, authenticity, completeness, and quality: First, it must be ensured that the auditing is performed according to well defined rules and regulations, and that it is tamper proof against manipulation attempts on behalf of malicious third parties. This calls for *security* mechanisms that protect the *integrity* and *confidentiality* of data used for auditing. For example, confidential sensor data should be encrypted and transmitted over secure channels only. It should be impossible to forge data that is collected by the auditing service. Neither should the content of the data be revealed during the process of data collection, e.g. to prevent eavesdropping and to protect the privacy of patients. Second, it must be possible to associate collected data with the originating sources (sensors). For the sake of credibility and *authenticity*, only data from authenticated and trusted sources should be considered for the auditing process. This could be achieved by introducing a local public key infrastructure and digitally signing available data at its source. Third, the infrastructure service that is performing the auditing has to function according to the specification at all times, that is even in the presence of transient disturbances and component failures. For example, if the occurrence of an emergency condition is not duly recorded, a doctor may be reprimanded for taking actions that exceed his authorisations even though he rightfully overrides applicable regulations in order to save the life of a patient. Therefore the auditing infrastructure needs to support *fault tolerance* and meet stringent *availability* requirements to achieve the highest possible level of *completeness* of data. This includes support for disconnected operation [24] to handle states of transient disconnectivity. For example, distributed sensors might have to buffer data during intermittent unavailability of (wireless) network connectivity. Last but not least, the *quality* of the accumulated data is depending on various factors: For instance, the number of sensors that are placed in the infrastructure and the density of their distribution determine the granularity and accuracy of a positioning service. However, inaccurate position information is again counterproductive to location-based services such as automated access control or smart notification. So low data quality must not lead to wrong conclusions when analysed by the auditing process.

Further issues are the robustness and scalability of the security auditing infrastructure. In the first place, the auditing facilities in different sections of the hospital should work independently. For example, if there's a fire on one floor of a building, the auditing mechanisms on other floors should not be affected. This requires a form of decentralized management. The *robustness* of a decentralized auditing infrastructure may benefit from results in the in the research fields of self-organization and self-stabilization. Concerning *scalability*, a security auditing mechanism as described has to cover a great number of mobile or highly distributed devices and objects. However, this aspect is closely related to the scalability of pervasive computing systems in general and not specific to auditing.

5.3 Safety and Efficiency

In this section we demonstrate in which way a generalized, fully automated auditing process can contribute considerably to the safety, efficiency and effectiveness of processes in the hospital environment.

Safety. As mentioned above, medication errors constitute a severe problem in hospitals (cf. section 2.2). In this context, many healthcare IT professionals believe the best way to address the medical errors issue head-on is to install robust information systems that help physicians make the right decisions at the right time for the right patients [37].

Now, pervasive computing may contribute noticeably to increase the *safety* of health care processes. A fully automated real-time auditing mechanism is the basis for on-the-fly surveillance and validation of health care processes. The accumulated, persistently stored data may provide insightful evidence for a later evaluation of emergency incidents, too. Concerning the technical realization, all trays, meals, pill boxes etc. in the hospital may be tagged, e.g. using RFID technology. Antennas mounted in various places in the hospital – inside the patient's bedside table, for instance – are then in a position to identify all objects that appear nearby. This information is then recorded by the auditing mechanism, which in turn makes this data available to other applications. A real-time 24h safety protection service could then evaluate and analyse the safety relevant data, thus performing a *safety audit*. The result of the safety audit may be the sending of a notification message, the triggering of an alarm, or the activation of certain emergency procedures. Such a safety audit may improve the safety of health care processes by (1) *validating allotment processes*, (2) *detecting incompatibilities in patient treatment*, and (3) *surveilling the adherence to safety regulations*:

First, the safety auditing mechanism may help to to validate that drugs, infusions or meals are not confused during their allotment. So if trays actually have been confused and a patient does not receive the proper medication, both the patient and/or medical staff will be alarmed the moment the wrong tray is laid onto the patient's bedside desk.

Second, if a patient requires a certain medication or infusion, e.g. during an emergency, the safety auditing service automatically verifies that a prescribed drug or infusion does not conflict with the patient's medical history or with other drugs he takes. Also, a patient who wears a cardiac pacemaker or has metal screws inside his body, e.g. due to an earlier operation of a fracture, should not undergo a nuclear spin tomography (MRI); the enormous magnetic field might interfere with his implant or the metal in his body in a very unfavorable way, possibly leading to severe injuries or death of the patient. But on entering the antechamber of the tomograph, the safety auditing service can identify the patient and recognize the incompatible treatment. As a consequence, an alarm bell is triggered and both the patient and the doctor are warned about the imminent health risk.

Third, operations on the wrong patient or foreign objects left in patients' bodies after surgery are common problems in hospitals [37]. Now, a safety auditing mechanism helps to prevent cases of incidental medical malpractice. For example, a smart op-box that knows the whereabouts of medical equipment – including pliers and perishable objects such as pads and bandages – may closely monitor the usage of tools and equipment during surgery. It may tell the surgeon which items are still in the box, have been disbanded in the waste basket or are still in use [19]. Thus the surgeon knows at all times whether there are still pieces of medical equipment missing and potentially left in the patient, or if all the equipment has been safely removed. Generally, by making use of identification and localisation capabilities, the auditing mechanism may also be used to verify that the right patient turns up at the right place and gets the right treatment.

Efficiency and Effectiveness. In the hospital domain, computer-based information systems have become common today, covering both administrative as well as medical functions. The Healthcare Informatics magazine, for instance, keeps a record of healthcare management and information systems that have been installed in the recent years [22]. However, in general, these systems share the lack of full automation. They have to be operated manually by hospital personnel, e.g. by using (mobile) computer terminals to enter new data.

A pervasive computing infrastructure, in contrast, allows pervasive information access and automatic data collection, which has been recognized to improve the effectiveness and efficiency of patient care [9]. The accumulation of data provides full coverage regarding space (all buildings, objects, people) and time. Furthermore, it enables both an immediate and time decoupled (asynchronous) analysis and availability of the collected data: certain data may trigger actions the very moment it has been recorded. These capabilities allow to increase the *efficiency* and *effectiveness* of *patient treatment* [17], *facility management* [7, 23], *supply chain management* [28], and *accounting and billing*. For example, in hospitals it is commonplace that doctors and other medical staff spend many hours after their usual shifts to write diagnoses into patient's files and register the performed treatment with the electronic accounting system, so that the corresponding health insurance company may be billed. With a pervasive auditing infrastructure in place, these tasks can be automated to a large extent. The time a patient spends in certain diagnostic and therapeutic environments, e.g. physiotherapy, massage, X-ray examination, computer tomography, etc., can be captured implicitly during the day. This may be achieved by analyzing the location of a patient, the prescriptions he received and the medical records that have been accessed by the physician.

5.4 Summary

A pervasive computing infrastructure is particularly suited to provide a fully automated security auditing service. Still, there are a number of dependability issues that have to be resolved before we can fully exploit the potential benefits of an automated auditing process in the hospital environment. Further, it has been described how a pervasive auditing mechanism can also contribute to increase the safety and efficiency of health care and business processes within the hospital.

Finally we wish to sound a cautious note, too, because the existence of a safety protecting service may lead to a false sense of safety. While it may provide some additional means to improve the safety within the hospital, it cannot guarantee to do so absolutely, at all times and under all circumstances. The ultimate responsibility, control and final judgement still must remain in the hands of health care personnel. Possible social implications of pervasive computing technology in the hospital environment will need closer examination, too. For further information on potential real-world implications of pervasive computing, see [12].

6   Conclusion: A Research Agenda

Apart from promoting healthcare as an application scenario, the technical part of this paper has raised a number of questions which we group and summarize in the following fundamental agenda for research:

– Pervasive middleware: In a general application setting of pervasive technology like a hospital, developers must decide which parts of the solutions should work in isolation and which parts can be delegated to a basic infrastructure. How could such a *pervasive middleware* incorporate services that satisfy the demands of domain-specific applications like remote monitoring and auditing?

– Secure degradation: The problem of dealing with *emergency situations* is obvious in the healthcare domain. This does not only refer to override mechanisms for access control, but also to fail-safe design of pervasive health monitoring and health control devices. How can pervasive technology be designed to maintain security and a basic service both in normal and emergency situations? What rules of thumb exist for the design of "secure or reliable degradation"?

– Hierarchy of devices and properties: There will always be devices which are so small so that they cannot ensure an arbitrary level of dependability (e.g. sensors with small batteries and no cryptographic functionality). Is there a way to group or classify pervasive devices into a hierarchy of *dependability properties*, such that requirements can be stated more easily? For example, auditing requires to maintain a minimal level of trustworthiness and authenticity of sensor data. Can the class of devices that fulfill this requirement be exactly specified?

We wish to further investigate these issues and motivate researchers to perform work in this area.

References

1. Agency for Healthcare Research and Quality. http://www.ahcpr.gov/qual/errorsix.htm, February 2003.
2. J. Allen, A. Christie, W. Fithen, J. McHugh, J. Pickel, and E. Stoner. State of the Practice of Intrusion Detection Technologies. Technical Report CMU/SEI-99TR-028, Software Engineering Institute, Carnegie Mellon University, Pittsburgh, PA 15213-3890, USA, 2000.
3. American Accounting Association (AAA). Home page. http://accounting.rutgers.edu/raw/aaa/.
4. Ross J. Anderson. A Security Policy Model for Clinical Information Systems. In *IEEE Symposium on Security and Privacy*, 1996.
5. Alvin A. Arens and James K. Loebbecke. *Auditing: An Integrated Approach*. Prentice Hall, 8th edition, October 1999.
6. Jean Bacon, Ken Moody, and Walt Yao. Access Control and Trust in the Use of Widely Distributed Services. In *Middleware 2001*, volume 2218 of *Lecture Notes in Computer Science*, pages 295+. Springer-Verlag, 2001.
7. Fred D. Baldwin. Putting your assets to work. *Healthcare Informatics*, April 2001.
8. Jakob E. Bardram and Henrik Baerbak Christensen. Middleware for Pervasive Healthcare. In *Advanced Topic Workshop: Middleware for Mobile Computing*. IFIP/ACM Middleware 2001 Conference, http://www.cs.arizona.edu/mmc/, 2001. http://www.pervasivehealthcare.dk/.

9. Mary Jean Barrett. The evolving computerized medical record. *Healthcare Informatics*, May 2000.
10. Tim Bass. Intrusion Detection Systems and Multisensor Data Fusion. *Communications of the ACM*, 43(4):99–105, 2000.
11. P. Bernstein, V. Hadzilacos, and N. Goodman. *Concurrency Control and Recovery in Database Systems*. Addison-Wesley, 1987.
12. Jürgen Bohn, Vlad Coroama, Marc Langheinrich, Friedemann Mattern, and Michael Rohs. Allgegenwart und Verschwinden des Computers – Leben in einer Welt smarter Alltagsdinge. In Ralf Grötker, editor, *Privat! Kontrollierte Freiheit in einer vernetzten Welt*. Heise-Verlag, Hannover, February 2003.
13. Douglas J. Brown, Bill Suckow, and Tianqiu Wang. A Survey of Intrusion Detection Systems, 2001.
14. C. Kunze and U. Grossmann and W. Storkand and K. D. Müller-Glaser. Application of Ubiquitous Computing in Personal Health Monitoring Systems. In *Biomedizinische Technik*, volume 47 of *Beiträge zur 36. Jahrestagung der Deutschen Gesellschaft für Biomedizinische Technik*, pages 360–362, http://www.vde.com/de/fg/dgbmt/, 2002.
15. Christian Cachin, Klaus Kursawe, and Victor Shoup. Random Oracles in Constantinople: Practical Asynchronous Byzantine Agreement Using Cryptography. In *Proceedings of the Symposium on Principles of Distributed Computing*, pages 123–132, Portland, Oregon, 2000.
16. cnn.com. Medical errors kill tens of thousands annually, panel says. http://www.cnn.com/HEALTH/9911/29/medical.errors/, November 1999.
17. Edmund DeJesus. Disease management in a warehouse. *Healthcare Informatics*, September 1999.
18. Ian Denley and Simon Weston Smith. Privacy in Clinical Information Systems in Secondary Care. *British Medical Journal*, 318:1328–30, May 1999.
19. Christian Flörkemeier, Matthias Lampe, and Thomas Schoch. The Smart Box Concept for Ubiquitous Computing Environments. In *Proc. of Smart Objects Conference SOC*, 2003.
20. Jeffrey Hightower and Gaetano Borriello. Location Systems for Ubiquitous Computing. *Computer*, 34(8):57–66, August 2001.
21. The Health Insurance Portability and Accountability Act (HIPAA). http://www.hipaa.org/.
22. Healthcare Informatics. On record: New contracts and installations. *Healthcare Informatics*, 1997–today.
23. Alan Joch. Right place, right time. *Healthcare Informatics*, May 2000.
24. J. J. Kistler and M. Satyanarayanan. Disconnected Operation in the Coda File System. *ACM Transactions on Computer Systems*, 10(1):3–25, 1992.
25. Linda T. Kohn and Janet Corrigan, editors. *To Err Is Human: Building a Safer Health System*. National Academy Press, 2000. http://books.nap.edu/books/0309068371/html/index.html.
26. L. Lamport, R. Shostak, and M. Pease. The Byzantine Generals Problem. *ACM Transactions on Programming Languages and Systems*, 4(3):382–401, July 1982.
27. Teresa F. Lunt. Automated Audit Trail Analysis and Intrusion Detection: A Survey. In *Proceedings of the 11th National Computer Security Conference*, Baltimore, MD, 1988.
28. Charlene Marietti. Delivering the goods: How healthcare can plug the leak of billions of supply-chain dollars. *Healthcare Informatics*, August 1999.
29. Alfred J. Menezes, Paul C. Van Oorschot, and Scott A. Vanstone. *Handbook of Applied Cryptography*. CRC Press, Boca Raton, FL, 1997.
30. Maryann Napoli. Preventing medical errors: A call to action. *HealthFacts*, January 2000.
31. B. Clifford Neumann and Theodore Ts'o. An authentication service for computer networks. *IEEE Communications*, 32(9):33–38, September 1994.
32. Péter Várady, Zoltán Benyó, and Balázs Benyó. An Open Architecture Patient Monitoring System Using Standard Technologies. *IEEE Transactions on Information Technology in Biomedicine*, 6(1):95–98, March 2002.

33. McGraw-Hill Healthcare Information Programs. Industry Report: Health Insurance Portability and Accountability Act. *Healthcare Informatics*, 2000.
34. Michael O. Rabin. Efficient Dispersal of Information for Security, Load Balancing, and Fault Tolerance. *Journal of the ACM*, 36(2):335–348, April 1989.
35. Marcus J. Ranum. Thinking About Firewalls. Technical report, Trusted Information Systems, Inc. Glenwood, Maryland, 1993.
36. http://www.robocup.org/, February 2003.
37. Lisa Stammer. Seeking SAFETY. *Healthcare Informatics*, October 2000.
38. Gene Tsudik and R. Summers. AudES: An Expert System for Security Auditing. In *Proceedings of the AAAI Conference on Innovative Application in Artificial Intelligence*, 1990.
39. Mark Weiser. The Computer for the 21st Century. *Scientific American*, pages 94–104, September 1991.

Protecting Security Policies in Ubiquitous Environments Using One-Way Functions

Håkan Kvarnström[1,2], Hans Hedbom[3], and Erland Jonsson[1]

[1] Department of Computer Engineering
Chalmers University of Technology
SE-412 96 Göteborg, Sweden
{hkv,erland.jonsson}@ce.chalmers.se
[2] Telia Research AB
Vitsandsgatan 9, SE-123 86 Farsta, Sweden
[3] Department of Computer Science
Karlstad University
SE-651 88 Karlstad, Sweden
hansh@ce.chalmers.se

Abstract. This paper addresses the problem of protecting security policies and other security-related information in security mechanisms, such as the detection policy of an Intrusion Detection System or the filtering policy of a firewall. Unauthorized disclosure of such information can reveal the fundamental principles and methods for the protection of the whole network, especially in ubiquitous environments where a large number of nodes store knowledge about the security policy of their domain. To avoid this risk we suggest a scheme for protecting stateless security policies using one-way functions. A stateless policy is one that only takes into consideration, the current event, and not the preceding chain of events, when decisions are made. The scheme has a simple and basic design but can still be used for practical implementations, as illustrated in two examples in real-life environments. Further research aims to extend the scheme to stateful policies.

1 Introduction

The protection of computers and information systems is vital to the success of virtually every enterprise. Distributed system architectures connecting a large number of computers raise questions on how to better protect the information and resources of these systems. Access-control services such as firewalls [3][4], are most often used to control access to systems and services, but the use of access-control components only may constitute a single-point-of-failure. A flaw in an access-control component could lead to loss or theft of information or computer resources by allowing an intruder to circumvent existing security measures. Intrusion detection systems (IDS) [13] are techniques that attempt to detect unauthorized activities and suspicious events (behavior), that is, events that violate the effective security policy of a certain domain. They provide a second line of defense, allowing intrusions to be detected in the event of a breach in the perimeter defense. Furthermore, intrusion detection systems allow detection of misuse or suspicious user behavior.

D. Hutter et al. (Eds.): Security in Pervasive Computing 2003, LNCS 2802, pp. 71–85, 2004.
© Springer-Verlag Berlin Heidelberg 2004

Our work addresses a problem not often recognized, that is the security of the intrusion detection system itself. This is important for several reasons. First, it is obvious that the functionality of the IDS, i.e. its ability to operate as expected, depends strongly on the security of the IDS itself, i.e. its ability to resist attacks. If an intruder succeeds in mounting an attack against the IDS, either by taking it over, corrupting its input data or its detection policy, or in other ways duping the IDS, it will no longer generate alarms for attacks launched against the target system. A report by Newsham and Ptacek [15], identifies several successful attacks against existing intrusion detection systems. Further, the information contained in the IDS (e.g. audit data) may be misused by an intruder to gain knowledge about the target system (e.g. weaknesses, protocols used etc.) that would indeed facilitate attacks. However, the most serious problem, especially in large distributed systems, is that the IDS or other security mechanisms could contain information such that the unauthorized disclosure of it would endanger the security of the whole computer network. Examples of sensitive information are overall security properties, lists of trusted hosts and information about unprotected vulnerabilities and dubious system configurations. Pervasive computing can be highly distributed, which seriously alters the threat model for an intrusion detection capability. We argue that traditional IDS designs are vulnerable when operating in such environments.

The argumentation above holds for firewalls as well, and indeed for any security mechanism that stores policies or other security-related information. Here we will mainly discuss IDSs. A primary issue for an IDS is how to conceal its policy. This can be achieved by using encryption, as discussed by Neumann [11] for the NIDES system [12]. His method requires storing keys on the local host, which virtually means that anyone that gains access to the host also gains access to the key and thereby the policy. Hiding the key does not help in the long run, as Shamir and van Someren demonstrates in [14]. Besides, as intrusion detection systems extend from mainly having been a centralized component to a distributed computing platform (e.g personal firewalls), key distribution becomes an issue. A high degree of distribution also increases the risk of the policy being disclosed as a result of increased exposure.

Here we suggest a policy protection scheme using one-way functions which to our knowledge, has not been discussed previously. Thus, this is a first attempt towards this type of protection. In particular, we suggest a method for protecting stateless security policies. We are aware that stateless policies can only be used to describe a limited set of policy rules but are nevertheless convinced that they can serve as a starting point for discussion and for constructing schemes to handle more complex types of policies for firewalls and IDSs.

2   The Need for Policy Protection

2.1   Policies

Security mechanisms such as IDSs and firewalls are equipped with a decision function for when an IDS should send an alarm or whether a firewall should block or allow network traffic. To make these decisions the systems use some form of rule set (or rule base) as the basis for the decision. We call this rule set the *detection policy* in the IDS case and the *filtering policy* in the firewall case. When there is no need to separate the two we will collectively refer to them as a policy. Examples of policies are:

- Rules for access-control to objects (e.g. access control lists)
- Misuse signatures
- Statistical user or system normal behavior

The policy is usually expressed in a description language describing the *event* or *combination of events* that is considered inappropriate (or, in the firewall case, usually appropriate). In this paper, we define an event the occurence of a single activity which is registered and stored in an audit log. The mechanisms presented in this paper are not limited to events of a certain type or having certain characteristics, as long as they can be coded or described as a (binary) string. A typical event would be an audit log record describing user activity (e.g. accessing a web page, logging into a service etc.). Table 1 shows five events generated as a result of remote logins to a server host.

Table 1. Five events generated by remote logins to the host "jellybean".

| Jun 24 18:19:42:jellybean sshd[1084049]: log: Connection from 192.168.0.1 port 56722 |
| Jun 24 18:21:12:jellybean sshd[3472342]: log: Connection from 192.168.0.244 port 16239 |
| Jun 24 19:29:14:jellybean sshd[1265421]: log: Connection from 192.168.0.123 port 54346 |
| Jun 24 20:19:01:jellybean sshd[9934742]: log: Connection from 192.168.0.220 port 16222 |
| Jun 24 21:45:41:jellybean sshd[1124234]: log: Connection from 192.168.0.11 port 201 |

A rule in a filtering policy could state for example that connections between the internet and the intranet are allowed only if they originate from the intranet. A rule in an IDS could state that logfile entries containing the string "login successful" and having a time stamp between 11pm and 4am indicate a possible intrusion.

A typical intrusion detection system's rule base can be divided into two parts, the first part consisting of a set of well-known (standard) attack signatures, often provided by the supplier of the IDS. This part is updated regularly, similar to virus scanners. The second part of the rule base consists of site-specific threats and vulnerabilities, which may be unique to the target system that it protects. For example, the target system could be configured to run old versions of software for compatibility with legacy systems or to use applications and protocols known to be vulnerable to attack such as NFS and NIS. In the next section, we show that the latter type of rule base poses a threat to the target systems.

2.2 The Need for Protection

The basic reason for using an IDS is to improve the security of the target system by adding a second layer of defense. However, there are also inherent security concerns for this second layer as it may introduce new security risks [7][8]. These concerns involve the protection of information and information flow within the IDS and how the information can be used for illicit purposes. This section discusses the security properties of an IDS and argues that the confidentiality aspect of the detection policy is one of the most important requirement.

Confidentiality and Integrity of Audit Data. Audit data generated by the target systems within an IDS domain may contain sensitive information not to be disclosed outside the domain. The information may be about users and target systems or may be application related data. In some cases, the mere existence of an event may be confidential as it reveals some form of activity. Audit data should neither be subject to insertion, deletion or alteration as demonstrated in a paper by Ptacek and Newsham [15]. On the other hand, a breach of confidentiality or integrity of audit data presents less of a risk than in the case of policies. The result of a confidentiality or integrity breach can often be limited to a missed detection or a false alarm.

Confidentiality and Integrity of the Policy. Similarly, an attacker may break into an intrusion detection system and disable the detection mechanism so that target system attacks can be launched without being disclosed. However, if and when the attack is eventually detected, the system can be taken offline, at which integrity can be restored and it is finally brought back into operation. The damage is limited to the loss of detection capability over a period of time. In contrast, if the rule base is disclosed during the attack, the attacker can learn about inherent vulnerabilities of the target system, knowledge that would remain even when the integrity of the IDS is restored. The inherent vulnerabilities of the target system may not be possible to fix and, hence, permanent damage has occurred. Thus, the main reason for our concern about the confidentiality of the rule base is that a breach of confidentiality is irreversible.

As an example, consider a target system running NFS to share files between clients. A policy rule could be defined to detect the use of NFS (UDP) packets containing certain strings (e.g. /etc/passwd) between a certain NFS client and a dedicated server. If such a policy rule were stored in cleartext in the rule base, an attacker would learn about the inherent vulnerability that exists and possibly exploit it to gain access to the information in the system. However, this particular attack signature is target-specific and an attacker may not discover the vulnerability when a vulnerability scan of known attacks is made.

Our experience in applying intrusion detection systems is that the rule base containing target-specific attack signatures increases rapidly as the complexity (e.g. the number of hosts and services) of target systems grows. This is different from the standard attack rule base, which is not affected by the complexity of the target system. However, vendors can utilize our protection scheme to protect their rule base as it may provide a competitive advantage not to disclose the workings of attacks not known to competitors. Also, by keeping the rule-base confidential, software vendors (e.g. virus scanners and IDS) could include detection of innovative attacks (i.e attacks not yet known to the hacker community) without the risk of reverse-engineering the policy for the purpose of writing malicious code to exploit the vulnerability.

3   Architectural Implications

An increased use of network encryption and virtual private networks providing end-to-end security between systems, makes it difficult for intrusion detection systems to monitor events in the target system or in the network. One solution to this problem is to execute the detection system on the end-systems, at which the encryption terminates (e.g. a personal IDS). This means that the security policy will be distributed, giving a distributed intrusion detection architecture (IDA) [7]. It is clear that the IDS' ability to protect its detection policy is highly dependent on the intrusion detection architecture.

An IDS is distributed when the different components of the detection system are distributed in some respect. Fig. 1 illustrates a distributed intrusion detection architecture where components are located in different domains.

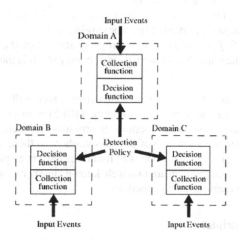

Fig. 1. A distributed intrusion detection architecture (IDA).

In a strictly centralized system, the detection policy is known only to a small part of the system, while in a distributed intrusion detection architecture, the policy is distributed to all of the decision functions that participate in the system (as described by Fig. 1). In addition, the end-systems are not dedicated to detecting intrusions (i.e. many other applications execute on the systems), which alters the threat model for the IDS. An end-system such as an office PC is often under the control of the user, which makes it more difficult to enforce the security policy in practice. Thus, the detection policy may be known to a possibly large number of entities. This implies that the security of the policy is dependent on the security of all the entities that have knowledge of the policy and of the security of the distribution channel. Deploying IDS capabilities to ubiquitous environments may result in a vast number of entities having knowledge about the policy. Hence, we need security mechanisms to allow the distribution of policies without risk of compromising its confidentiality.

4 Protecting a Policy Using One-Way Functions

One way of solving the problem of how to protect the policy may be to use strong one-way functions. In this section we discuss this concept and how they can be used to protect stateless policies.

4.1   The Concept of One-Way Functions

One-way functions are one of the fundamental building blocks of cryptography. Many security mechanisms providing such security services as authentication, integrity protection and confidentiality depend on the unique properties provided by one-way functions. Informally, a one-way function [6] is a function $f : S \rightarrow T$, where S and T are any two sets, such that:

1. for any $x \in S$, $f(x)$ is "easy" to compute,
2. given the information that $f(x) = y$, there is no "feasible" way of computing x for any reasonably large proportion of the y belonging to T,
3. for any $x, z \in S$, $f(x) \neq f(z)$. This property states that the function must be collision free in the sense that no two values of S may result in the same y belonging to T.

Assuming that set is sufficiently large, an exhaustive search will be computationally infeasible. The UNIX password protection scheme [10][5] is an example of a security mechanism making use of one-way functions. It provides confidentiality of the users' passwords, thus preventing disclosure of the passwords even though the password file itself is disclosed. Several candidate one-way functions have been proposed. Factoring and the discrete logarithm problem are two well-known "hard" mathematical problems that are often used to create one-way functions.

4.2   Protection Principle

Informally, the policy classifies an incoming event (or sets of events) into predefined categories such as *legal events, intrusion attempts, intrusions* etc. In its simplest form a security policy states what patterns or signatures of events are authorized/unauthorized. A *default accept* policy would search for events having a certain signature and classify them as unauthorized whereas a *default deny* policy makes the assumption that all events are unauthorized except those that explicitly matches a defined signature. Most rule-based IDSs have taken a default accept standpoint due to the difficulty of defining all authorized events, while most firewalls have a default deny policy, only letting through the events matching the policy.

The following simple example show how signatures can be used to detect policy violations in a default accept policy. Consider a set of input events, $x_1, x_2, \ldots, x_n \in X$, all of which are represented by k-bit binary strings. Further, the set $u_1, u_2, \ldots, u_m \in U$ is the set of "signature strings" that identifies an unauthorized event. Whenever $x_i = u_j$, where $i \leq n, j \leq m$, the event being analyzed matches a detection signature and an alarm is raised. The detection scheme is fairly simple as it only involves comparing events over X with all strings in U searching for identical pairs. Now consider the set $u'_1, u'_2, \ldots, u'_m = f(u_1), f(u_2), \ldots, f(u_m) \in U'$, where f is any cryptographically strong one-way function. A hash is calculated and stored for each signature. Because of the inherent properties of the one-way function, it is hard to deduce any $u \in U$ given $f(u) \in U'$. Thus, U' can be made publicly available without compromising the secrecy of U. The computational effort to successfully deduce $u \in U$ is equal on average to an exhaustive search of $1/2$ of the domain of U. Thus, assuming $u_1, u_2, \ldots, u_m \in U$, where $|u|, u \in U$ has a binary length of k bits. The computational effort to find $u \in U$ given $f(u) \in U'$ would (in average) require 2^{k-1} operations.

Detecting policy violation in the default accept case is a straightforward process of applying the same one-way function to all input events $x \in X$ and compare the resulting values to the stored values of U'. If a match is found, the input event is an unauthorized event and an alarm is raised. Many intrusion detection systems utilizes simple string matching to find unauthorized patterns in the input data. For example, an IDS could search a UNIX syslog looking for strings containing the pattern "su root failed" which would indicate a failed attempt to gain administrative privileges on the system. If one-way functions are used to hide the string patterns, it is very hard for an intruder to identify the detection policy of the system.

Policy violations in the default deny case can be handled in a similar manner as discussed above. The only difference in this case is that U, and thus U', will contain permitted events and actions are taken if $f(x), x \in X$ is not a member of U'.

5 Handling Variabilities

In a normal case one input value will lead to a unique output value from the one-way function, meaning that even a small change in the input value will generate a completely different result. This is a desired property in the traditional use of one-way functions but undesirable in the policy case. This section discusses reasons for handling variabilities in the stateless policy case and offers ideas about how this may be achieved by different methods and elaborates on what we believe to be the shortcomings and merits of the different methods.

5.1 Why Do We Need to Handle Variabilities?

When describing rules in a policy it is useful to be able to handle variables and express intervals. This means that the protection scheme for the policy must also be able to handle this variability in some way. For example, it may be desirable to state in the policy that certain actions are forbidden to all users or that a given user is not allowed to login to certain network addresses. If we divide the information into fields, there will be fields containing variables in both the cases above. In the first case the value in the forbidden action field will be constant while the value in the user field is variable (FIX<Action>, VAR<User>). In the second case the value in the user field is constant but the value in the network field is variable (FIX<User>, VAR<IP Address>). The variability in the latter case could be defined as the the range of network addresses that are permitted or not permitted.

5.2 A First Approach

One naive approach toward handling variability may be to apply the one-way function on every possible combination of field contents, although this would lead to a very large collection of values that need to be compared. This might be tolerable in small systems, but would be unacceptable in large systems. The next approach would be to skip the variable fields and simply apply the one-way function on the fixed fields. This solves the problem in the first case, where we do not care who the user is, i.e all possible values of the user field are considered illegal, but does not solve the problem in the second case above since not all of the possible values in the network field might be considered illegal. It also has a serious side effect. By applying the function about selected fields only, we are giving away information on which fields we are interested in, which in turn could point an intruder towards the kinds of attacks we are looking for.

5.3   Using Fuzzy Commitment to Handle Intervals

Fuzzy commitment is a a way of doing commitment suggested by Ari Juels and Martin Wattenberg [9]. It is essentially a method that accepts a certain amount of fuzziness (i.e variability) in the witness[1] used. Its main use is in the area of authentication by means of biometrics (e.g. fingerprints etc.), where it is almost impossible to get exactly the same result from two consecutive scans of the same object. For example, a thumb is never placed in the same way twice on a thumb scanner. Juels et al. show that using a combination of error correction methods and one-way functions one can create a commitment scheme that will accept different witnesses as long as they differ only up to a controllable threshold. In essence the method works as follows: Assume that we have a witness x and an error correction function f that corrects codewords from the set C. Now, choose a $c \in C$ and calculate $d = x - c$. Commit c by using a strong one-way function and store d. To decommit c a user has to give a witness x' that is sufficiently close to x so that the correction function can correct $x' - d$ to c. The amount of fuzziness accepted is thus dependent on the number of errors accepted by the correction function and on the value d.

Fuzzy commitment can be used to handle intervals in the following way. The basic idea is to let all the values in an interval hash to the same cryptographic hash-sum. In this case we do not really need a proper error correction function but merely a function that groups values together. Such functions can be used in fuzzy commitment, e.g. Juels et al. [9] use a lattice rounding function rather than a proper error correcting function as an example of how the scheme works. The lattice rounding function in their example is a function that rounds points in the plane to the nearest multiple of 100x100. If we interpret the values in the variable fields as integers, we can use a function that truncates values downwards to the nearest multiple of the selectable integer i, e.g. if $i = 10$ then $0 \ldots 9 \to 0, 10 \ldots 19 \to 10$ and so on. We call this function g. Such a function can easily be generalized by making i a parameter of the function (e.g. $g(i,x) = i\lfloor x/i \rfloor$). Let witness x represent the lower end of the interval and let i be the width of the interval. Randomly choose $c \in C$ where $C = \{\forall c \in C : ix\}$, where x is an integer. Calculate all other parameters according to the rules above. To test later whether a witness x' is within the interval the calculations described above for decommitment are used exchanging f with g.

---

[1] The witness is the value that is to be committed or the value that is compared with a committed value after it has been transformed with a strong one-way function.

Example (Commitment). This simple example shows how integer intervals can be committed. The commitment scheme can be applied to any type of variability, however, using a suitable encoding of the input fields.

Assume that we want to commit the integer interval $234 \ldots 243$. In this case $i = 10$ since the width of the interval is 10. Set C will be all integer multiples of 10 and we randomly choose $c = 410$ from this set. Since the lower end of the interval is $234, x = 234$ and $d = x - c = 234 - 410 = -176$. c is then committed using a strong one-way function.

Example (Decommitment). Assume that the commitment in the example above has been made. Further assume that we want to find out whether 240 is within the interval i.e $x' = 240$. We first calculate $c' = x' - d = 240 - (-176) = 416$. By applying function g on 416, the result is 410. We then commit 410 using the same strong one-way function as in the example above and compare the results.

5.4 The Shortcomings of Using Fuzzy Commitment

The great disadvantage of using fuzzy commitment is that the error correction function will give the codeword in the clear as output. With this value and the known value of variable d, it is very easy to calculate the interval. The implications of this is that one lucky guess will reveal the whole interval. This is a small problem if the set of possible values is large as compared to the values within the interval range. In this case, the probability of guessing a correct value is small, and an exhaustive search is highly time consuming. However, in many "real world" cases of specifying intervals for detection purposes, the set of possible values will be small and/or the intervals will be very wide. The probability of a lucky guess is thus high and it is relatively easy to make an exhaustive search. In this light, fuzzy commitment by itself is not a perfect solution to the interval problem. In the next section we discuss a method to make it more difficult to make this deduction.

5.5 Making Value Deduction Harder

The possible input values for the one-way function are usually few enough to permit an exhaustive search. This is basically because we are dividing the input stream into fields and separately applying the one-way function to each field but also because we in essence are dividing the possible values of the fields into equivalence classes, thereby making it easier to find one input value that maps to a valid output value. Of course, one could divide the data in such a way that the input fields would be large enough. We believe, however, that there are natural divisions in most applications based on the format of log entries and other data structures in the system. The individual fields in these structures usually have a small domain of possible input values, but the combined structure in itself has a much larger domain. By applying the function repeatedly in a tree-like manner it is possible to use the input domain of the structure as the input domain of the resulting one-way function and still be able to handle variabilities as previously discussed. The method works as follows:

1. Calculate the individual fields of the structure by applying an appropriate method, i.e a one-way function on the fixed fields and a method for handling variability on the variable fields. Note that the method for handling variablility includes the application of a one-way function.
2. Concatenate the resulting values pair-wise and apply a one-way function to each of the pairs
3. Repeat step 2 until only one value remains. This is the value that is compared with the policy.

The process above is graphically described in Fig. 2. It can be generalized by always applying the method for variability and restricting the variability for the fixed fields, e.g setting the interval length to 1 if the fuzzy commitment approach is used.

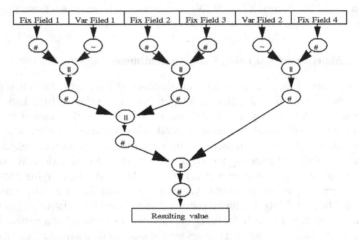

= One-way function
~ = Method for handling variability (including application of a one-way function)
‖ = Concatenation

Fig. 2. Method one for handling variabilities.

If all the fields in the structure are variable or if the structure is small the domain may still be too small. However, it is significantly larger than the input domain of the individual fields.

An alternative to the method described above is the following:

1. Calculate the individual fields of the structure by applying an appropriate method (i.e. a one-way function on the fixed fields and a method for handling variability on the variable fields).
2. Concatenate all the resulting values and apply a one-way function to the concatenated value.

This process is graphically described in Fig. 3. The big difference between the first approach and the second approach, besides a reduction in the use of one way functions,

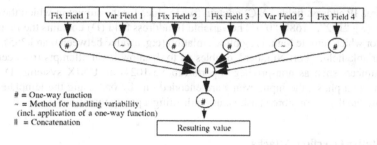

Fig. 3. Method two for handling variabilities.

is that the former can be used to implement a hierarchical matching scheme. Thus, matches can be found for individual fields. This may be useful if it is necessary to adapt the matching path based on intermediate hash values in the tree (e.g applying different field structures for different categories of attacks).

6 Examples of the Proposed Protection Scheme

This section gives two simple examples of how the method presented in here can be used. The first illustrates how the audit logs in Table 1 on page 73 can be used for detection and how variability is achieved. A second example shows how a simple snort [17] rule can be protected using our scheme. Snort is an open source network intrusion detection system capable of performing real-time traffic analysis and packet logging on IP networks.

6.1 Remote Login Policy Violations

In the first example, a template is constructed that will be used for filling in information contained in the logs (Table 1 on page 73).

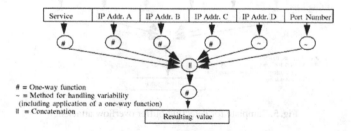

Fig. 4. Template for detecting remote login policy violations.

In Fig. 4 four fixed fields and two variable fields are used to encode an event for remote login attempts. The service field contains the name of the service "sshd". The first three IP address fields (A-C) contain fixed values for the subnet in which the IDS resides (e.g "192", "168", "0"). The variable IP address field (D) contains the range of hosts for which remote login is a policy violation (e.g. a value between 0 and 255). The last variable field, "Port Number", enables us to disallow login attempts from certain port numbers such as non-privileged ports (above 1024) on UNIX systems. During the detection phase, the input events are encoded one by one using the template and compared to the set of stored hash values indicating a policy violation.

6.2 Buffer Overflow Attacks

The second example shows how we can protect a simple snort rule with the purpose of detecting a buffer overflow attack. The rule base of snort (i.e. the detection policy) consists of rules matching bit patterns in the header/payload, ranges of IP numbers and port numbers, header bits etc. The following simple rule (Table 2) aims to detect a buffer overflow attack in an application X. The signature of the attack is characterized by the hexadecimal value "94B5 C1AF FFCB 16EF" followed by the string "/bin/sh". The rule also defines the vulnerable targets to have an IP address in the range 192.168.1.0-255. Any source address originating from any TCP port will trigger an alert as long as the attack is targeted at port 7890.

Table 2. Snort rule detecting a buffer overflow attack.

```
alert tcp any any -> 192.168.1.0/24 7890
(content: "|94B5 C1AF FFCB 16EF|/bin/csh";offset: 3; depth: 22; msg:
"Buffer overflow attack in Application X!";)
```

During detection, a template is used that is similar to that in the first example.

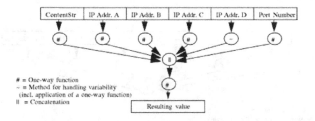

Fig. 5. Template for detecting buffer overflow attacks.

Note that the templete can be reused for all rules having similar parameter values. To gain flexibility, the snort's rule description language may be extended to describe the templates needed for each rule. The offset and depth parameters can guide the process of filling in the correct bit string in the first field of Fig. 5.

To reverse engineer the above rule, an exhaustive search over all possible policies would be necessary. The 72-bit *ContentStr* (64-bit hex value + 8 bit text string) alone would theoretically require 2^{72} operations. By eliminating illegal combinations of machine code and arguments, the search space can probably be reduced. However, we have not further studied the entropy of machine code for various platforms nor have we found any studies discussing the topic. The entropy would yield a rough estimate of the effective search space. In addition, the port number adds another 16-bits of complexity. Note that all fields must contain correct values for the resulting value to match a valid signature. This prevents a divide-and-conquer attack in which the fields are broken one by one.

7 Discussion and Future Work

There are a number of open questions regarding the protection of policies using one-way functions. Below we discuss some of them and give indications for future work.

First, we have only discussed the protection of stateless policies, i.e. policies that take only the current event into consideration. We are fully aware that this poses a certain limitation, but the concept is nevertheless useful and applicable as our examples show. A more elaborated protection scheme for stateful policies could be used to describe more complex threats and attacks and we are currently working to develop such a scheme.

Second, we have discussed the need to handle variability and suggested solutions as to how to handle intervals although with some limitations. One limitation is the disclosure of the variable range once a single value is found. In order to solve this problem we would need a strong cryptographic one-way hash function that generically and controllably would hash different values to one hash value. Basically, this function must divide the possible values of the variable into equivalence classes based on the values in which we are interested and then hash the individual members of each equivalence class into one hash value. In order for this to be generic, the function must be able to take the relation that defines the equivalence classes as a parameter and it must be possible to define arbitrary relations without disclosing the individual values. We do not know of such a function, nor whether it is possible to construct it. Collisionful one-way hash-functions are described in the literature e.g. [6][1][2], but they do not solve the problem discussed above. Moreover, even if the interval disclosure problem were solved, a range could almost as easily be found using linear search once a single value within the range has been found.

Finally, there is the question of performance. Some of the systems, e.g. IDSs in large computer systems or firewalls in high capacity networks, must be able to handle large amounts of information in a limited time. The performance of an IDS described in this paper is likely to be significantly lower than a traditional signature-based intrusion detection system. We do not claim this scheme to be efficient but instead focus on confidentiality properties and the feasibility of protecting the policy from unauthorized disclosure. In a real-life system, traditional signature detection techniques can be used to detect well-known attacks and be complemented with this technique for attacks that are target-specific. This would limit the decrease in performance to a minimum.

8 Conclusion

This paper discusses the problem of protecting the security policy of a security mechanism, such as an intrusion detection system or a firewall operating in distributed or ubiquitous environments. We have noted that the policy contains sensitive information that can be misused by an attacker in order to avoid detection or to render the detection system useless. Still worse, it could provide information that would facilitate intrusions into the target system or even extend to logically connected systems within or outside of the actual network. Thus the policy is crucial for the function of the security mechanism and the system it is supposed to protect.

We have suggested that one-way functions may be used as a means to protect the policy. This approach has certain shortcomings, however. Foremost of these is that normal one-way function schemes can only be used on constant values, so that even small variations in input values give completely different output values. This is a desirable property for the ordinary use of one-way functions. In our case, however, we would like a complete equivalence class of data to be hashed into one specific hash value and have suggested a clustering method based on fuzzy commitment that would accomplish this for some, but not all, types of variability in the input data. The drawback of clustering is that it increases the probability of guessing a correct match or carrying out an exhaustive search. It is also a fact that the very nature of intrusive events puts a bound on the possible cases, thereby making it easier to make a good guess. To counter this we have suggested a method that expands the possible domain by grouping values together and repeatedly applying one-way functions in a tree-like manner, thereby making guessing and exhaustive searches more difficult. Finally, we present two concrete examples of how to apply our protection scheme in real-life situations.

References

1. S.Bakhtiari, R. Safavi-Naini and J. Pieprzyk. On the Weakness of Gong's Collisionful Hash Function. Journal of Universal Computer Science vol 3, no.3, pp 185-196. Springer Pub. Co, 1997.
2. S.Bakhtiari, R. Safavi-Naini and J. Pieprzyk. On Selectable Collisionful Hash Functions. The Australian Conference on Information Security and Privacy, LNCS No. 1172, pp 287-292, Springer Pub. Co., 1996.
3. D.B. Chapman and E.D. Zwicky. Building Internet Firewall. O'Reilly & Associates, Inc. September, 1995.
4. W.R. Cheswick and S.M. Bellovin. Firewalls and Internet Security: Repelling the Wily Hacker. Addison-Wesley. 1994.
5. D.C. Fieldmeier and P.R. Karn. UNIX password security - ten years later. Advances in Cryptology CRYPTO 89, LNCS 0302-9743; 435 pp:44-63, Springer cop., 1990.
6. L. Gong. Collisionful keyed hash functions with selectable collisions. Information Processing Letters 55, pp 167-170, Elsevier, 1995.
7. H. Hedbom, H. Kvarnström, E. Jonsson. Security Implications of Distributed Intrusion Detection Architectures, In Proceedings of the 4th Nordic Workshop on Secure IT systems - Nordsec 99, pages 225-243; Stockholm, Sweden.
8. H. Hedbom, S. Lindskog, E. Jonsson. Risks and Dangers of Security Extensions. In Proceedings of IFIP Working Conference on Security and Control of IT in Society-II, SCITS-II, Bratislava, Slovakia, June 15-16, 2001. To appear

9. A. Juels and M. Wattenberg. A Fuzzy Commitmen Scheme. In Proceedings of the Second ACM Conferens on Computer and Communication Security CCS'99. Singapore, 1999.
10. R. Morris and K. Thompson. Password security: A case history. Communications of the ACM, 22(11):594-597, November 1979.
11. P.G. Neumann. "Architectures and formal representations for secure systems", Final Report; SRI Project 6401; Deliverable A002, 1995.
12. Next-generation Intrusion Detection Expert System (NIDES) - A Summary, SRI, Computer Science Laboratory, 1995.
13. S. Northcutt. Network Intrusion Detection : An Analyst's Handbook. New Riders. 1999.
14. A. Shamir, Nico van Someren, "Playing hide and seek with stored keys", Weizmann Institute of Science, Israel; nCipher Corporation Limited, England, 1998
15. T. H. Ptacek, T. N. Newsham, "Insertion, Evasion, and Denial of Service: Eluding Network Intrusion Detection", Secure Networks, Inc.
16. S Staniford-Chen, B Tung, P Porras, Cliff Kahn, D Schnackenberg, R Feiertag, M Stillman, The Common Intrusion Detection Framework - Data Formats, Internet Draft, September, 1998.
17. M. Roesch. Snort - Lightweight Intrusion Detection for Networks; In Proceedings of the USENIX LISA '99 Conference, November 1999

Enforcing Security Policies via Types*

Daniele Gorla and Rosario Pugliese

Dipartimento di Sistemi e Informatica, Università di Firenze
{gorla,pugliese}@dsi.unifi.it

Abstract. Security is a key issue for distributed systems/applications with code mobility, like, e.g., e-commerce and on-line bank transactions. In a scenario with code mobility, traditional solutions based on cryptography cannot deal with all security issues and additional mechanisms are necessary. In this paper, we present a flexible and expressive type system for security for a calculus of distributed and mobile processes. The type system has been designed to supply real systems security features, like the assignment of different privileges to users over different data/resources. Type soundness is guaranteed by using a combination of static and dynamic checks, thus enforcing specific security policies on the use of resources. The usefulness of our approach is shown by modeling the simplified behaviour of a bank account management system.

1 Introduction

Code mobility is a fundamental aspect of global computing; however it gives rise to a lot of relevant security problems like, e.g., *secrecy* and *integrity* of data and program code. Indeed, in mobile distributed systems/applications, other than attacks to inter-process communication over the communication channels (e.g. traffic analysis, message modifications/forging), several other kinds of attacks could take place. For instance, malicious mobile processes can attempt to access private information, or modify private data of the nodes hosting them. Hence, a server receiving a mobile process for execution needs to impose strong requirements to ensure that the incoming process does not violate the secrecy and jeopardize the integrity of the information. Similarly, mobile processes need tools to ensure that their execution at the server node does not compromise their integrity (e.g. modification of process code) or secrecy (e.g. leak of sensible data). Such problems have increasingly importance due to the spreading of security critical applications, like, e.g., electronic commerce and on-line bank transactions. Moreover, global computing environments, like e.g. the Internet, are highly dynamic and open systems. In these environments static information could be partial, inaccurate or missing, therefore for ensuring security properties a certain amount of dynamic checks is needed (e.g. mobile agents should be dynamically checked at run-time when they migrate).

Code mobility strongly restricts a safe use of cryptography, that is one of the most used techniques for ensuring security in distributed systems. In fact, because of attacks like those mentioned before, we can hardly imagine to use mobile processes carrying

* This work has been partially supported by EU within the FET - Global Computing initiative, project MIKADO IST-2001-32222, and by MIUR project NAPOLI. The funding bodies are not responsible for any use that might be made of the results presented here.

D. Hutter et al. (Eds.): Security in Pervasive Computing 2003, LNCS 2802, pp. 86–100, 2004.

confidential data (e.g. private keys) with them, or host nodes with classified information accessible to all incoming processes (whatever their source node be). Hence, the use of security mechanisms that back up and supplement cryptographic mechanisms becomes a major issue when developing systems of distributed and mobile processes where the compliance with some security policies must be guaranteed.

Several alternative approaches have been exploited to enforce security policies in distributed computing systems. The approaches may differ in the level of trust required, the flexibility of the enforced security policy and their costs to components producers and users. A comprehensive security framework could result from the combination of complementary features. Approaches like *code signing* and *sand-boxing* (for instance, consider the Java implementation of these concepts [23, 20]) have low costs but cannot enforce flexible security policies (signed components may behave in arbitrary ways and the user must trust the component producer, while sand-boxed components are isolated and cannot interact with each other).

Type systems can be sensible and flexible language-based security techniques, like [32] shows. Recently, a number of process/programming languages supporting process distribution and mobility have been designed that come equipped with type systems that guarantee some kind of security properties, see, e.g., [24, 15, 16, 25, 8]. However, to the best of our knowledge, the type system we present in this paper is the first that exploits the source of mobile processes for granting them different privileges over different kinds of data (thus, e.g., preventing dangerous operations over specific sensible data). These desirable features can be found in real systems like, e.g., UNIX, where different users can have different privileges and different files can be manipulated with different allowed operations.

Our type system permits expressing and enforcing security policies for controlling the access of host resources by possibly malicious mobile processes. It is expressly designed for the process calculus μKLAIM [21] that puts forward a programming paradigm where there is a clear separation between the programmer level and the net coordinator/administrator level. Programmers write processes, while coordinators write nets, hence manage the initial distribution of processes and set the security policies for accessing the resources. The policies are specified by assigning each node of a net a type expressing the operations a process is allowed to perform once spawned at it. Hence types are part of the language for configuring the underlying net architecture and must be taken into account in the language operational semantics. Other than to express security policies, types are used to record processes intended operations, but programmers are relieved from typing processes because this task is carried on by a static type inference system. By using a combination of static and dynamic type checking, our system guarantees the absence of run-time errors due to lack of privileges. As an application of our approach we model the simplified behaviour of a bank account management system where the compliance with the bank security policy must be enforced.

The rest of the paper is organized as follows. We present the syntax of μKLAIM in Section 2, its type system in Section 3, and its operational semantics in Section 4, that also contains the type soundness results. In Section 5, we illustrate an application of our approach to model a bank account management system. Finally, in Section 6 we point

Table 1. μKLAIM Syntax

$N ::= \mathbf{0}$	(empty net)	$a ::= \mathbf{read}(T)@\ell$		(process actions)
$\quad\mid l ::^\Delta P$	(single node)	$\quad\mid \mathbf{in}(T)@\ell$		
$\quad\mid N_1 \parallel N_2$	(net composition)	$\quad\mid \mathbf{out}(t)@\ell$		
$P ::= \mathbf{nil}$	(null process)	$\quad\mid \mathbf{eval}(P)@\ell$		
$\quad\mid a.P$	(action prefixing)	$\quad\mid \mathbf{newloc}(u:\Delta)$		
$\quad\mid P_1 \mid P_2$	(parallel composition)	$T ::= F \mid F,T$		(templates)
$\quad\mid A$	(process invocation)	$F ::= f \mid !x \mid !u:\pi$		(template fields)
		$t ::= f \mid f,t$		(tuples)
$e ::= V \mid x \mid \ldots$	(expressions)	$f ::= e \mid \ell$		(tuple fields)

out a few concluding remarks and comment on related work. Due to lack of space, in this extended abstract we omit some technical details and all proofs; they can be found in the full paper [22].

2 The Process Language μKLAIM

In this section we briefly present the syntax and informally describe the semantics of μKLAIM [21], a calculus to program distributed and mobile processes communicating asynchronously via shared data. Due to lack of space, some formal aspects (akin to those presented in [21]) are omitted.

The syntax of μKLAIM is reported in Table 1. We assume the existence of the following countable sets: $\mathcal{A}$, *process identifiers*, ranged over by $A, B, \ldots$; $\mathcal{L}$, *localities*, ranged over by l; $\mathcal{U}$, *locality variables*, ranged over by u; $\mathcal{V}$, *basic values*, ranged over by V. We let ℓ to range over $\mathcal{L} \cup \mathcal{U}$, x over value variables, π over sets of *capabilities* and Δ over *types* (capabilities and types are formally defined in Section 3).

The syntax of *expressions*, ranged over by e, is deliberately not specified; we just assume that expressions contain, at least, basic values and variables. *Localities* l are the addresses of nodes. *Tuples* t are sequences of actual fields f, that contain information items (expressions, localities or locality variables). Tuples are collected into multisets called *tuple spaces* (TSs, for short). *Templates* T are used to select tuples in a TS; they are sequences of actual and formal fields F. The latters are used to bind variables to values and are written $!x$ or $!u:\pi$ (the set of capabilities π constraints the use of the address dynamically bound to u and is crucial for the type checking).

Processes are built up from the inactive process **nil** and from the basic operations by using prefixing, parallel composition and process invocation. For the sake of simplicity, we assume that each process identifier A has a *single* defining equation $A \stackrel{\triangle}{=} P$ and all these equations are available at any locality of a net. Recursive behaviours can be modelled via process definitions.

μKLAIM supplies five different basic operations, also called *actions*. $\mathbf{out}(t)@\ell$ adds the tuple et resulting from the evaluation[1] of t to the TS located at ℓ. The presence of

---

[1] Tuple/template evaluation consists in replacing each expression with the value resulting from its evaluation.

the evaluated tuple et in the TS at ℓ is represented by putting in parallel with the process located at ℓ the auxiliary process $\mathbf{out}(et)$. Operation $\mathbf{eval}(Q)@\ell$ sends process Q for execution to ℓ, where a run-time typechecking of the incoming code will take place: if Q does not comply with ℓ's security policy the operation is blocked. Operation $\mathbf{in}(T)@\ell$ evaluates T and looks for a matching[2] tuple et in the TS located at ℓ; if et is found, it is withdrawn and the values it contains are used to replace the corresponding variables of T within the continuation process, otherwise the operation is suspended until a matching et is available. Operation $\mathbf{read}$ behaves similarly but leaves the accessed tuple et in the tuple space. Operation $\mathbf{newloc}(u : \Delta)$ dynamically creates a new net node with a fresh address whose security policy is specified by type Δ. The last operation is not indexed with an address because it always acts locally; all the other operations explicitly indicate the (possibly remote) address where they will take place.

Nets are finite collections of nodes where processes and tuple spaces can be allocated. A *node* is a triple $l ::^{\Delta} P$, where locality l is the address (i.e. network reference) of the node, P is the (parallel) process located at l and Δ is the type of the node, i.e. the specification of its access control policy. The nodes of a net can be thought of both as physically distributed machines and as logical partitions of the same machine. As we already said, the TS located at l is part of P because evaluated tuples are semantically represented as special processes.

3 A Capability-Based Type System

In this section we introduce a type system for μKLAIM that permits granting different privileges to processes coming from different nodes and constraining the operations allowed over different kinds of data. Thus, for example, if l trusts l', then l security policy could accept processes coming from l' (that will be called l'-processes) and let them accessing any tuple in l's TS. If l' is not totally trusted, then l's security policy could grant l'-processes the capabilities for executing **in/read** only over tuples that do not contain classified data.

3.1 Capabilities

Capabilities are used to specify the allowed process operations and are formally defined as

$$ \mathcal{C} \triangleq \{e, n\} \cup \{ \langle c, p \rangle \ : \ c \in \{i, r, o\} \wedge p \subseteq_{\blacksquare \mathbf{n}} \mathcal{P} \} $$

where $\mathcal{P} \triangleq (\mathcal{L} \cup \mathcal{V} \cup \{\mathbf{from}, -\})^{+}$ is the set of all *patterns*. Capabilities e and n enable process migration and node creation (i.e. operations **eval** and **newloc**, resp.). A capability of the form $\langle c, p \rangle$ enables the operation whose name's first character is c (i.e. **in** if c is i, and so on); operation arguments must comply with the finite set of patterns p if $p \neq \emptyset$, and are not restricted otherwise (in this case, we write c instead of $\langle c, \emptyset \rangle$). Like

---

[2] An evaluated tuple matches against an evaluated template if both have the same number of fields and corresponding fields match; formal fields of a given type match values of the same type and two values match only if identical.

Table 2. Capability Ordering Rules

$$\{\langle i,p \rangle\} \sqsubseteq_{\Pi} \{\langle r,p \rangle\} \qquad \frac{\mathcal{T}(p') \subseteq \mathcal{T}(p)}{\{\langle c,p \rangle\} \sqsubseteq_{\Pi} \{\langle c,p' \rangle\}} \qquad \frac{\pi_1 \subseteq \pi_2}{\pi_2 \sqsubseteq_{\Pi} \pi_1} \qquad \frac{\pi_1 \sqsubseteq_{\Pi} \pi_1' \qquad \pi_2 \sqsubseteq_{\Pi} \pi_2'}{\pi_1 \cup \pi_2 \sqsubseteq_{\Pi} \pi_1' \cup \pi_2'}$$

tuples and templates, *patterns* are finite, not empty sequences of fields; *pattern fields* may be localities, basic values, the reserved word **from** (denoting the last locality visited by a mobile process) and the 'don't care' symbol $-$ (denoting any template field). Thus, for instance, the capability $\langle\, i\, ,\, \{("public", -), (3, -, \mathbf{from})\}\, \rangle$ enables the operations **in**$("public", !x)@...$ and **in**$(3, !u : \pi, l)@...$ for an l-process, while disables operation **in**$("private", !x)@... $.

We use π to denote a non-empty subset of $\mathcal{C}$ such that, if $\langle c,p \rangle \in \pi$ and $\langle c',p' \rangle \in \pi$, then $c \neq c'$. Π will denote the set of all these π.

We say that a template *complies with* a pattern if the template is obtained by replacing in the pattern all occurrences of **from** with a locality, and any occurrence of '$-$' with any template field allowed by the syntax. Given a non-empty set of patterns p, we write $\mathcal{T}(p)$ to denote the set of all templates complying with patterns in p. By definition, $\mathcal{T}(\emptyset)$ denotes the set of all templates. Since tuples are also templates (see Table 1), the previous definitions also apply to tuples.

Notice that the definition of pattern fields affects, via the relation 'complies with', the ability of our types to control the tuples accessed by process operations. However, our framework is largely independent of the choice of a specific set of fields. For instance, we could also permit fields of the form $-_\delta$, for any type δ of legal values, with the idea that, when defining the relation 'complies with', an occurrence of $-_\delta$ could be replaced by any value/variable of type δ. In μKLAIM, this corresponds to adding only fields $-_\mathcal{L}$ and $-_\mathcal{V}$; in this way, a finer control could be exercised on the tuples accessed by processes because we could distinguish between a tuple field containing a locality from one containing a basic value.

We now introduce an ordering between capabilities, $\sqsubseteq_{\Pi}$; formally, it is the least reflexive and transitive relation induced by the rules in Table 2. The chosen ordering relies on the following assumptions: (i) if a process is allowed to perform an **in** then it is also allowed to perform a **read** over the same arguments, (ii) if a process is allowed to perform a **read/in/out** over arguments complying with patterns in p then it is allowed to perform the same operation over arguments complying with any set of patterns p' that has at most the same 'complying templates' as p, and (iii) if a process owns a set of capabilities π_2 then it also owns any subset π_1.

3.2 Types

Types, ranged over by Δ, are functions of the form

$$\Delta : \mathcal{L} \cup \mathcal{U} \cup \{\mathbf{any}\} \rightarrow_{\mathbf{fin}} \left((\mathcal{L} \cup \mathcal{U} \cup \{\mathbf{any}, \mathbf{from}\} \rightarrow_{\mathbf{fin}} \Pi \cup \{\emptyset\}) \cup \bot \right)$$

where $\rightarrow_{\mathbf{fin}}$ means that the function maps only a finite subset of its domain to meaningful values (i.e. values different from $\bot$ and $\emptyset$). With abuse of notation, we use $\bot$ to also denote the empty type, i.e. the function mapping all its domain to $\perp$. Moreover, by letting λ to range over $\mathcal{L} \cup \mathcal{U} \cup \{\textbf{any}, \textbf{from}\}$, we shall write a Δ different from $\perp$ as a non-empty list $[\lambda_i \mapsto [\lambda_{i,j} \mapsto \pi_{i,j}]_{j=1,...,k_i}]_{i=1,...,n}$. Types are used to express the security policies of nodes. Intuitively, if the type Δ of a node with address l contains the element $[l' \mapsto l'' \mapsto \pi]$, then l'-processes located at l are allowed to perform over l'' only the operations enabled by π. The reserved word **any** is used to refer any node of the net. If it occurs in the domain of Δ then it collects the privileges granted to processes coming from any node of the net (i.e. $[\textbf{any} \mapsto l'' \mapsto \pi]$ grants all processes the privileges π over l''). If **any** is contained in the domain of $\Delta(l')$, for some l', then it is used for denoting the operations that l'-processes located at l are allowed to perform over any node of the net (i.e. $[l' \mapsto \textbf{any} \mapsto \pi]$ grants l'-processes the privileges π over all net nodes). The reserved word **from** stands for the last node visited by a process and is used to grant privileges over this node whatever it is; thus, for instance, $[\textbf{any} \mapsto \textbf{from} \mapsto \pi]$ grants l'-process spawned at l the privileges π over l'. The type $\perp$ expresses total absence of privileges.

For the type Δ of a locality l to be l–*well-formed* the following conditions must hold:

1. The keyword **from** can occur only in the function $\Delta(\textbf{any})$.
2. For each $\ell \in dom(\Delta)$, it holds that $\Delta(\ell) \preceq \Delta(l)$, where relation $\preceq$ holds true if and only if for all $\lambda \in dom(\Delta(\ell))$ it holds that $\Delta(l)(\lambda) \cup \Delta(l)(\textbf{any}) \sqsubseteq_\pi \Delta(\ell)(\lambda)$.
3. For each $\lambda \in dom(\Delta(\textbf{any}))-\{\textbf{from}\}$, it holds that $\Delta(l)(\lambda) \sqsubseteq_\pi \Delta(\textbf{any})(\lambda)$, and that $\Delta(l)(\textbf{any}) \sqsubseteq_\pi \Delta(\textbf{any})(\textbf{from})$.

The first condition is not too restrictive, because the use of **from** is really necessary only when no knowledge of the last node visited by processes is available (i.e. when using **any**). The second condition says that l grants to ℓ-processes (for $\ell \in dom(\Delta)$) no more privileges than those granted to its local processes, i.e. those processes statically allocated at l. Finally, the last condition is similar to the previous one, but applies to processes coming from any node; in this case, it is also required that processes coming from any node own over the source node no more privileges than those owned by local processes over any node.

Notice that the syntax of types allows locality variables to occur within types. Basically, they are used when specifying the type of a node dynamically created for referring localities that will be dynamically determined. By exploiting this feature, we can write processes like the following: $\textbf{in}(!u : ...)@... .\textbf{newloc}(v : [u \mapsto v \mapsto \{r\}])$.

3.3 Static Type Checking

For each node of a net, say $l ::^{\Delta} P$, the static type checker analyzes the operations that P intends to perform when running at l and determines whether they are enabled by the access policy Δ or not (in fact, it is enough to consider $\Delta(l)$). To this aim, a *type context* Γ is a function of the form $\mathcal{L} \cup \mathcal{U} \cup \{\textbf{any}\} \rightarrow_\text{fin} (\Pi \cup \emptyset)$. To update a type context with the type annotations specified within a template, we use the auxiliary function *upd* that behaves like the identity function for all fields but for formal fields binding locality variables. Formally, it is defined by:

$$upd(\Gamma, T) = \begin{cases} upd(upd(\Gamma, F), T') & \text{if } T = F, T' \\ \Gamma \uplus [u \mapsto \pi] & \text{if } T = \,! \, u : \pi, \\ \Gamma & \text{otherwise} \end{cases}$$

where $\uplus$ denotes the pointwise union of functions.

The type judgments for processes take the form $\Gamma \vdash_{\overline{l}} P$, where the domain of Γ includes all the localities and all the free locality variables in P. The set of bindings for the localities in Γ implements the access policy of l for the processes statically located at l, while the remaining bindings record the type annotations for the locality variables that are free in P. Intuitively, the judgment $\Gamma \vdash_{\overline{l}} P$ states that, within the context Γ, P can be safely executed once located at l.

Table 3. Type Inference Rules

$$\Gamma \vdash_{\overline{l}} \mathbf{nil}$$

$$\frac{\Gamma(\ell) \cup \Gamma(\mathbf{any}) \sqsubseteq_{\Pi} \langle o, p \rangle \qquad t \in \mathcal{T}(p) \qquad \Gamma \vdash_{\overline{l}} P}{\Gamma \vdash_{\overline{l}} \mathbf{out}(t)@\ell.P}$$

$$\frac{\Gamma(\ell) \cup \Gamma(\mathbf{any}) \sqsubseteq_{\Pi} \langle i, p \rangle \qquad T \in \mathcal{T}(p) \qquad upd(\Gamma, T) \vdash_{\overline{l}} P}{\Gamma \vdash_{\overline{l}} \mathbf{in}(T)@\ell.P}$$

$$\frac{\Gamma(\ell) \cup \Gamma(\mathbf{any}) \sqsubseteq_{\Pi} \langle r, p \rangle \qquad T \in \mathcal{T}(p) \qquad upd(\Gamma, T) \vdash_{\overline{l}} P}{\Gamma \vdash_{\overline{l}} \mathbf{read}(T)@\ell.P}$$

$$\frac{\Gamma(\ell) \cup \Gamma(\mathbf{any}) \sqsubseteq_{\Pi} \{e\} \qquad \Gamma \vdash_{\overline{l}} P}{\Gamma \vdash_{\overline{l}} \mathbf{eval}(Q)@\ell.P}$$

$$\frac{\Gamma(l) \sqsubseteq_{\Pi} \{n\} \qquad \Delta \text{ is } u\text{–well-formed} \qquad \Gamma \uplus [u \mapsto (\Gamma(l) - \{n\})] \vdash_{\overline{l}} P}{\Gamma \vdash_{\overline{l}} \mathbf{newloc}(u : \Delta).P}$$

$$\frac{\Gamma \vdash_{\overline{l}} P \qquad \Gamma \vdash_{\overline{l}} Q}{\Gamma \vdash_{\overline{l}} P \mid Q} \qquad\qquad \frac{\Gamma \vdash_{\overline{l}} P}{\Gamma \vdash_{\overline{l}} A} \text{ if } A \stackrel{\triangle}{=} P$$

Type judgments are inferred by using the rules in Table 3 that should be quite explicative. For operations **out**, **in**, **read** and **eval**, the inference requires the capability associated to the operation to be enabled by the capabilities owned over the target ℓ or over all the net sites. Instead, for operation **newloc**, the capability n must be owned by the site l executing the operation. Moreover, in this case, it is assumed that the creating node owns over the created one all the privileges it owns on itself (except, obviously, for the n capability).

We conclude this section by introducing the notion of *well-typed* net.

Definition 1. *A net N is* well-typed *if for each node $l ::^{\Delta} P$ in N it holds that Δ is l–well-formed and $\Delta(l) \vdash_{\overline{l}} P$.*

4   Operational Semantics and Type Soundness

The operational behaviour of μKLAIM nets can be formalized via a structural congruence and a reduction relation, see [22] for details. Here we just point out some crucial points.

The *structural congruence* gives a convenient way of rearranging the nodes of a net without affecting the behaviour of the net. It says that '$\|$' is commutative and associative, that **nil** and **0** are the identities for '$|$' and '$\|$' resp., and that process identifiers can be replaced by the processes in the body of their definitions.

The *reduction relation*, $\succ\!\!\longrightarrow$, specifies the basic computational steps and formalizes the informal behaviours sketched in Section 2. Because of the highly dynamic nature of our calculus, the operational semantics uses types to perform some dynamic checks, e.g., when processes migrate (to block migration of processes that do not comply with the security policy of the target node) and when node addresses are retrieved from the TS (to ensure that the local security policy enables correct usability of these addresses). In both cases, the check occurs in the premises of an inference rule thus, if it fails, the rule cannot be used in the inference (i.e. the corresponding net reduction step is blocked). In the rest of this section, we present details on these two specific points.

As regards the first check, the rule for process migration takes the form

$$\frac{\Delta'(l) \uplus (\Delta'(\mathbf{any})[l/\mathbf{from}]) \vdash_{\overline{\Pi}} Q}{l ::^\Delta \mathbf{eval}(Q)@l'.P \parallel l' ::^{\Delta'} P' \; \succ\!\!\longrightarrow \; l ::^\Delta P \parallel l' ::^{\Delta'} P'|Q}$$

where $\Delta'(\mathbf{any})[l/\mathbf{from}]$ denotes syntactic substitution of **from** with l in function $\Delta'(\mathbf{any})$. Hence, the premise of the rule says that the migrating process Q must be checked against the union of the privileges that the security policy Δ' of the target node l' assignes to processes coming from l and to processes coming from any node (in this last case, occurrences of **from** must be interpreted as l).

The second run-time check is invoked for establishing matching of a formal field $!u : \pi$ against a locality l' when performing **read/in** operations. The reduction rule for **in** is

$$\frac{match_{\Delta(l)}(\mathcal{E}[\![T]\!], et)}{l ::^\Delta \mathbf{in}(T)@l'.P \parallel l' ::^{\Delta'} \mathbf{out}(et) \; \succ\!\!\longrightarrow \; l ::^\Delta P[et/T] \parallel l' ::^{\Delta'} \mathbf{nil}}$$

where $\mathcal{E}[\![\cdot]\!]$ evaluates the actual fields of T by replacing each expression with the value corresponding to its evaluation (the rule for **read** is similar but leaves the tuple et in the TS of l'). If the match between the evaluation of the template and the chosen tuple succeeds, all the formal fields of T are replaced with the corresponding values of et in the continuation process P (written $P[et/T]$). In particular, the matching succeeds if for each formal field $!u : \pi$ the corresponding value l'' that will replace u is such that the security policy Δ of the node l where the **in/read** operation is performed allows local processes to perform all the operations enabled by π over l'', using if needed also the capabilities owned by l's static code over all the net. This control is implemented by the following matching rule (the remaining matching rules are standard and are omitted)

$$\frac{\Delta(l)(l'') \cup \Delta(l)(\mathbf{any}) \sqsubseteq_\Pi \pi}{match_{\Delta(l)}(!u : \pi, l'')}$$

Other than for these two checks, the operational semantics must take types into account for updating the security policy Δ of a node l when it creates a new (fresh) node l'. The semantics prescribes that l-processes can perform over l' all the operations that they can perform locally, eccept for **newloc**, and hence Δ is extended with $[l \mapsto l' \mapsto (\Delta(l)(l) - \{n\})]$.

Type Soundness. We can now state two standard results for type systems, namely, *subject reduction* and *type safety*. The former means that well-typedness is an invariant of the operational semantics; the latter means that well-typed nets are free from immediate run-time errors. In our framework, such errors would arise when processes attempt to execute operations that are disabled by the security policy of the node where they are running. We use predicate $N \uparrow l$ to express the presence in N of a node l with an illegal behaviour. The two properties together amount to saying that well-typed nets never give rise to run-time errors due to misuse of access privileges. Function $loc(N)$ returns the set of localities occurring in N and can be easily defined inductively on the syntax of terms, while $\rightarrowtail^*$ denotes the reflexive and transitive closure of $\rightarrowtail$.

Theorem 1 (Subject Reduction). *If N is well-typed and $N \rightarrowtail N'$ then N' is well-typed.*

Theorem 2 (Type Safety). *If N is well-typed then $N \uparrow l$ for no $l \in loc(N)$.*

Corollary 1 (Global Type Soundness). *If N is well-typed and $N \rightarrowtail^* N'$ then $N \uparrow l$ for no $l \in loc(N)$.*

Type soundness is one of the main goal of a type system. However, in our framework it is formulated in terms of a property requiring the typing of whole nets. When dealing with larger nets, it is certainly more realistic to reason in terms of parts of the whole net. Hence, we put forward a more *local* formulation of our properties and results. To this aim, we define the *restriction* of a net N to a set of localities D, written N_D, as the subnet obtained from N by deleting all nodes whose addresses are not in D. The wanted local type soundness result can be formulated as follows.

Theorem 3 (Local Type Soundness). *Let N be a net and $D \subseteq loc(N)$. If N_D is well-typed and $N \rightarrowtail^* N'$ then for no $l \in D$ it holds that $N' \uparrow l$.*

5   A Bank Account Management System

In this section, we use our approach to model the simplified behaviour of a bank account management system. For ensuring compliance with the security policy of the bank some aspects of our setting, such as the possibility of granting different privileges to processes coming from different source nodes and the dynamic type checking of mobile processes when they migrate, have proved to be crucial.

We suppose that a bank is located at a node with address l_B and can receive and manage requests coming from many users located at nodes with addresses $l_U, l_{U'}, \ldots$. The bank must provide the users with typical account managing operations: opening/closing accounts, putting/getting money in/from accounts, and making statements of accounts. For simplicity, we shall omit some details and technical operations that in reality take place, like, e.g., the charge of taxes, dealing with improper operations like the attempt of getting more money than that really available, ...

For the sake of readability, in the rest of this section we will omit trailing occurrences of process **nil**, and use parameterized process definitions (that can be easily implemented in our setting using **out/in** operations to pass/recover the parameters), integer values (to denote, e.g., amounts of money) and strings (to identify the various operations).

For permitting the bank to check the operations that users intend to perform, we assume that users cannot perform remote operations over l_B except for sending processes. Hence, if a user U wants to require an operation to the bank, it has to send a process to l_B (thus virtually moving to the bank) which will interact locally with the proper operation handler. The user process, once it has been accepted (i.e. after its compliance with the bank security policy has been checked), can require the operation by locally producing a tuple whose first field contains the name of the operation and whose second field contains the address of the user node (used to identify the user that made the request). Depending on the operation, the tuple could have other fields containing the amount of money involved in the operation and the account receiving the money.

The node implementing the bank is illustrated in Table 4. First, the bank creates a new node that will contain its clients accounts, stored as tuples of the form $(userAddress, amount)$. This node acts just as a repository for tuples and will not be used for spawning processes, thus it has assigned the empty type $\perp$. Then, five different handler processes, one for each kind of operation, are concurrently spawned. Each handler continuously waits for a request. When such a request arrives, the proper handler executes its task by remotely accessing the reserved locality and then reports locally a confirmation of action completion. The client process performing the request waits for such a confirmation and then brings it back to its original locality. This last operation is performed by means of a migration thus providing the user node with the chance of controlling the operation.

Notice that, by taking advantage of the semantics of μKLAIM operations, the simple handlers of Table 4 implement the mutual exclusion needed to ensure the correctness of concurrent operations over shared data. Indeed, once a handler H has withdrawn the tuple representing an account (i.e. once H has locked the account), in order to proceed in their tasks, all the other handlers have to wait for H to write the updated tuple (i.e. for H to release the lock).

The security policy Δ_B is so defined that 'sensible' operations over the accounts of a user U (like getting some money and reading/closing the account) can only be requested by l_U-processes, while operations like putting some money can be requested by processes coming from any node. Moreover, the only remote operation processes are allowed to perform is to came back to their source site. Therefore, a l_U-process can request to the bank sensible operations only over U's accounts and can deliver the confirmations only to l_U. Typical processes acting on behalf of a user U are illustrated in Table 5, where the parameter s denotes an amount of money and the parameter $l_{U'}$ denotes an account.

Table 4. The node implementing the bank

$l_B ::^{\Delta_B}$ **newloc**$(u : \perp).\big(OpenH(u) \mid PutH(u) \mid GetH(u) \mid ReadH(u) \mid CloseH(u)\big)$

where:

$OpenH(u) \stackrel{\triangle}{=}$ **in**$(\text{``open''}, !x, !y)@l_B.$
$\qquad\qquad (OpenH(u) \mid \mathbf{out}(x, y)@u.\mathbf{out}(\text{``}OKopen\text{''}, x, y)@l_B)$

$PutH(u) \stackrel{\triangle}{=}$ **in**$(\text{``put''}, !x, !y, !w)@l_B.$
$\qquad\qquad (PutH(u) \mid \mathbf{in}(w, !z)@u.\mathbf{out}(w, z + y)@u.\mathbf{out}(\text{``}OKput\text{''}, x, y, w)@l_B)$

$GetH(u) \stackrel{\triangle}{=}$ **in**$(\text{``get''}, !x, !y)@l_B.$
$\qquad\qquad (GetH(u) \mid \mathbf{in}(x, !z)@u.\mathbf{out}(x, z - y)@u.\mathbf{out}(\text{``}OKget\text{''}, x, y)@l_B)$

$ReadH(u) \stackrel{\triangle}{=}$ **in**$(\text{``read''}, !x)@l_B.$
$\qquad\qquad (ReadH(u) \mid \mathbf{read}(x, !y)@u.\mathbf{out}(\text{``}OKread\text{''}, x, y)@l_B)$

$CloseH(u) \stackrel{\triangle}{=}$ **in**$(\text{``close''}, !x)@l_B.$
$\qquad\qquad (CloseH(u) \mid \mathbf{in}(x, !y)@u.\mathbf{out}(\text{``}OKclose\text{''}, x, y)@l_B)$

$$\Delta_B \stackrel{\triangle}{=} [\, l_B \quad\mapsto [\, l_B \quad\mapsto \{i, o, r, n\},$$
$$\qquad\qquad\qquad \mathbf{any} \mapsto \{e\}\,],$$
$$\qquad\quad \mathbf{any} \mapsto [\, \mathbf{from} \mapsto \{e\},$$
$$\qquad\qquad\qquad l_B \quad\mapsto \{\,\langle\, o\,, \{\ (\text{``open''}, \mathbf{from}, -),$$
$$\qquad\qquad\qquad\qquad\qquad (\text{``put''}, \mathbf{from}, -, -),$$
$$\qquad\qquad\qquad\qquad\qquad (\text{``get''}, \mathbf{from}, -),$$
$$\qquad\qquad\qquad\qquad\qquad (\text{``read''}, \mathbf{from}),$$
$$\qquad\qquad\qquad\qquad\qquad (\text{``close''}, \mathbf{from})$$
$$\qquad\qquad\qquad\qquad\qquad \}\,),$$
$$\qquad\qquad\qquad\qquad \langle\, i\,, \{\ (\text{``}OKopen\text{''}, \mathbf{from}, -),$$
$$\qquad\qquad\qquad\qquad\qquad (\text{``}OKput\text{''}, \mathbf{from}, -, -),$$
$$\qquad\qquad\qquad\qquad\qquad (\text{``}OKget\text{''}, \mathbf{from}, -),$$
$$\qquad\qquad\qquad\qquad\qquad (\text{``}OKread\text{''}, \mathbf{from}, -),$$
$$\qquad\qquad\qquad\qquad\qquad (\text{``}OKclose\text{''}, \mathbf{from}, -)$$
$$\qquad\qquad\qquad\qquad\qquad \}\,\rangle$$
$$\qquad\qquad\qquad\qquad]$$
$$\qquad\qquad]$$

Table 5. Processes of a user U requesting bank operations

$OpenR(s) \stackrel{\triangle}{=}$ **eval**$(\mathbf{out}(\text{``open''}, l_U, s)@l_B.\mathbf{in}(\text{``}OKopen\text{''}, l_U, s)@l_B.$
$\qquad\qquad \mathbf{eval}(\mathbf{out}(\text{``}OKopen\text{''}, s)@l_U)@l_U)@l_B$

$PutR(s, l_{U'}) \stackrel{\triangle}{=}$ **eval**$(\mathbf{out}(\text{``put''}, l_U, s, l_{U'})@l_B.\mathbf{in}(\text{``}OKput\text{''}, l_U, s, l_{U'})@l_B.$
$\qquad\qquad \mathbf{eval}(\mathbf{out}(\text{``}OKput\text{''}, s, l_{U'})@l_U)@l_U)@l_B$

$GetR(s) \stackrel{\triangle}{=}$ **eval**$(\mathbf{out}(\text{``get''}, l_U, s)@l_B.\mathbf{in}(\text{``}OKget\text{''}, l_U, s)@l_B.$
$\qquad\qquad \mathbf{eval}(\mathbf{out}(\text{``}OKget\text{''}, s)@l_U)@l_U)@l_B$

$ReadR \stackrel{\triangle}{=}$ **eval**$(\mathbf{out}(\text{``read''}, l_U)@l_B.\mathbf{in}(\text{``}OKread\text{''}, l_U, !x)@l_B.$
$\qquad\qquad \mathbf{eval}(\mathbf{out}(\text{``}OKread\text{''}, x)@l_U)@l_U)@l_B$

$CloseR \stackrel{\triangle}{=}$ **eval**$(\mathbf{out}(\text{``close''}, l_U)@l_B.\mathbf{in}(\text{``}OKclose\text{''}, l_U, !x)@l_B.$
$\qquad\qquad \mathbf{eval}(\mathbf{out}(\text{``}OKclose\text{''}, x)@l_U)@l_U)@l_B$

The only possibility for a malicious node to illegally access U's accounts is to pass through l_U, using a process like $\mathbf{eval}(\mathbf{eval}(MaliciousReq)@l_B)@l_U$. Hence, U has to protect itself from these attacks by granting an e capability over l_B only to processes coming from totally trusted nodes: the security policy of l_U must contain the element $[l \mapsto l_B \mapsto \{e\}]$ only if U trusts the user located at l. However, U can trust l only if U trusts all l' trusted by l (in fact, a node trusted by l can send to l a process that is then allowed to spawn a process at U containing requests on U's accounts).

Finally, notice that only the handler processes can access the node dynamically created whose address, say l_S, is bound to u. Indeed, when such node is created, the operational semantics dynamically extends Δ_B with $[l_B \mapsto l_S \mapsto \{i, r, o\}]$ thus enabling all the processes initially allocated at l_B to perform **in/read/out** operations over l_S.

6 Concluding Remarks

We presented a new capability based type system for the calculus μKLAIM [21] which controls data/resource access and process mobility in a flexible and expressive way. It has been designed to supply real systems security features, e.g. granting different privileges to processes coming from different nodes and constraining the operations allowed over different kinds of data/resources. Due to the highly dynamic nature of distributed and mobile systems/applications, our framework uses a combination of static and dynamic type checking to guarantee compliance with net security policies. As a future work we plan to integrate in μKLAIM other security mechanisms, like e.g. those based on cryptographic techniques, both for the establishment of secure channels, and for process code security and authentication.

The choice of the process calculus μKLAIM [21], that is at the core of the programming language KLAIM [14] and hence is based on the Linda [19, 11] coordination model, is motivated by the fact that μKLAIM has a number of features that make it appealing also for network computing environments where, in general, connections are not stable and host machines are heterogenous. Indeed, it permits *time uncoupling* (tuples life time is independent of the producer process life time), *destination uncoupling* (the producer of a tuple does not need to know the future use or the destination of that tuple) and *space uncoupling* (communicating processes need to know a single interface, i.e. the operations over the tuple space). As shown in [17], where several messaging models for mobile processes are examined, the *blackboard* approach, of which tuple space based models are variants, is one of the most appreciated, also because of its flexibility. Evidence of the success gained by the tuple space paradigm is given by the many tuple space based run-time systems, both from industries, e.g. JavaSpaces [33, 2] and TSpaces [36], and from universities, e.g. PageSpace [13], WCL [31], Lime [29] and TuCSoN [28].

Many type systems for guaranteeing security properties have been proposed for process calculi with distribution and mobility, but, as far as we know, ours is the first one implementing such fine grained policies. Among those type systems more strictly related to security, we mention those disciplining the types of the values exchanged in communications [9, 3, 25], those for controlling Ambients [10] mobility and ability to be opened [6, 7, 27, 18, 12], that for controlling resource access via policies for mandatory access control [4], that for checking that all processes that intend to perform inputs at a given channel are co-located [37], that for controlling the effect of transmitted process abstractions over local channels [38], and that for restricting the mobility of values/processes only to some part of a distributed system [26]. We also applied the latter approach to μKLAIM, defining a type system that enforces security policies by confining mobility of processes/values; we left its presentation and the comparisons with the present setting for a full paper.

The research line closest to ours is that on the Dπ-calculus [25], a distributed version of the π-calculus equipped with a type system to control access rights of mobile processes over located resources (i.e. communication channels). Like μKLAIM, the Dπ-calculus relies on a flat net architecture; however, differently from μKLAIM, communication is local and channel-based, types describe permissions to use channels, and the net architecture is not independent from the processes involved. [24,30] present two improved type systems for the Dπ-calculus that permit establishing well-typedness of part of a net. This is similar to our local type soundness result that, however, has been obtained by using only local type information.

[37] presents D$\pi\lambda$, a process calculus that results from the integration of the call-by-value λ-calculus and the π-calculus, together with primitives for process distribution and remote process creation. Apart from the higher order and channel-based communication, the main difference with μKLAIM is that D$\pi\lambda$ localities are anonymous (i.e. not explicitly referrable by processes) and simply used to express process distribution. In [38], a fine-grained type system for D$\pi\lambda$ is defined that permits controlling the effect of transmitted process abstractions (parameterized with respect to channel names) over local channels. Processes are assigned fine-grained types that, like interfaces, record the channels to which processes have access together with the corresponding capabilities, and process abstractions are assigned dependent functional types that abstract from channel names and types. This use of types is similar to that of μKLAIM.

Finally, a number of process calculi base their security policies on transmission of encrypted data over communication channels so that only those processes knowing the proper keys can access these information. [1,34,5] present this approach in various settings, but none of them consider process distribution and mobility.

References

1. M. Abadi and A. Gordon. A calculus for cryptographic protocols: The spi calculus. *Information and Computation*, 148(1):1–70, 1999.
2. K. Arnold, E. Freeman, and S. Hupfer. *JavaSpaces Principles, Patterns and Practice.* Addison-Wesley, 1999.
3. M. Bugliesi, G. Castagna, and S. Crafa. Boxed ambients. In *TACS 2001*, number 2215 in LNCS, pages 38–63. Springer, 2001.
4. M. Bugliesi, G. Castagna, and S. Crafa. Reasoning about security in mobile ambients. In *Concur 2001*, number 2154 in LNCS, pages 102–120. Springer, 2001.
5. N. Busi, R. Gorrieri, R. Lucchi, and G. Zavattaro. Secspaces: a data-driven coordination model for environments open to untrusted agents. In *To appear in FOCLASA'02*, ENTCS, 2002.

6. L. Cardelli, G. Ghelli, and A. D. Gordon. Mobility types for mobile ambients. In J. Wieder-man, P. van Emde Boas, and M. Nielsen, editors, *Proceedings of ICALP '99*, volume 1644 of *LNCS*, pages 230–239. Springer, 1999.
7. L. Cardelli, G. Ghelli, and A. D. Gordon. Ambient groups and mobility types. In J. van Leeuwen, O. Watanabe, M. Hagiya, P. Mosses, and T. Ito, editors, *Proceedings of TCS 2000*, volume 1872 of *LNCS*, pages 333–347. IFIP, Springer, 2000.
8. L. Cardelli, G. Ghelli, and A. D. Gordon. Types for the ambient calculus. *Journal of Information and Computation*, 2002.
9. L. Cardelli and A. D. Gordon. Types for mobile ambients. In *Proceedings of POPL '99*, pages 79–92.
10. L. Cardelli and A. D. Gordon. Mobile ambients. *Theoretical Computer Science*, 240(1):177–213, 2000.
11. N. Carriero and D. Gelernter. Linda in context. *Communications of the ACM*, 32(4):444–458, 1989.
12. G. Castagna, G. Ghelli, and F. Z. Nardelli. Typing mobility in the seal calculus. In *Concur 2001*, number 2154 in LNCS, pages 82–101. Springer, 2001.
13. P. Ciancarini, R. Tolksdorf, F. Vitali, D. Rossi, and A. Knoche. Coordinating multiagent applications on the WWW: A reference architecture. *IEEE Transactions on Software Engineering*, 24(5):362–366, 1998.
14. R. De Nicola, G. Ferrari, and R. Pugliese. KLAIM: a Kernel Language for Agents Interaction and Mobility. *IEEE Transactions on Software Engineering*, 24(5):315–330, 1998.
15. R. De Nicola, G. Ferrari, and R. Pugliese. Types as Specifications of Access Policies. In Vitek and Jensen [35], pages 117–146.
16. R. De Nicola, G. Ferrari, R. Pugliese, and B. Venneri. Types for Access Control. *Theoretical Computer Science*, 240(1):215–254, 2000.
17. D. Deugo. Choosing a Mobile Agent Messaging Model. In *Proc. of ISADS 2001*, pages 278–286. IEEE, 2001.
18. M. Dezani-Ciancaglini and I. Salvo. Security types for mobile safe ambients. In *ASIAN Computing Sciece Conference - ASIAN'00*, volume 1961 of *LNCS*, pages 215–236. Springer, 2000.
19. D. Gelernter. Generative Communication in Linda. *ACM Transactions on Programming Languages and Systems*, 7(1):80–112, 1985.
20. L. Gong. *Inside Java 2 platform security: architecture, API design, and implementation*. Addison-Wesley, Reading, MA, USA, 1999.
21. D. Gorla and R. Pugliese. Resource access and mobility control with dynamic privileges acquisition. Research report, Dipartimento di Sistemi e Informatica, Università di Firenze, 2002. Available at
    `http://rap.dsi.unifi.it/~pugliese/DOWNLOAD/muklaim-full.pdf`.
22. D. Gorla and R. Pugliese. Enforcing Security Policies via Types. Research report, Dipartimento di Sistemi e Informatica, Università di Firenze, 2003. Available at
    `http://rap.dsi.unifi.it/~pugliese/DOWNLOAD/spc-full.pdf`.
23. G. M. Graw and E. Felten. *Securing Java*. John Wiley and Son, 1999.
24. M. Hennessy and J. Riely. Type-Safe Execution of Mobile Agents in Anonymous Networks. In Vitek and Jensen [35], pages 95–115.
25. M. Hennessy and J. Riely. Resource Access Control in Systems of Mobile Agents. *Information and Computation*, 173:82–120, 2002.
26. D. Kirli. Confined mobile functions. In *Proc. of the 14th IEEE Computer Security Foundations Workshop*. IEEE Computer Society, 2001.
27. F. Levi and D. Sangiorgi. Controlling interference in ambients. In *Proceedings of POPL '00*, pages 352–364. ACM, Jan. 2000.

28. A. Omicini and F. Zambonelli. Coordination for internet application development. *Autonomous Agents and Multi-agent Systems*, 2(3):251–269, 1999. Special Issue on Coordination Mechanisms and Patterns for Web Agents.
29. G. Picco, A. Murphy, and G.-C. Roman. LIME: Linda Meets Mobility. In D. Garlan, editor, *Proc. of the 21st Int. Conference on Software Engineering (ICSE'99)*, pages 368–377. ACM Press, 1999.
30. J. Riely and M. Hennessy. Trust and partial typing in open systems of mobile agents. In *Proceedings of POPL '99*, pages 93–104.
31. A. Rowstron. WCL: A web co-ordination language. *World Wide Web Journal*, 1(3):167–179, 1998.
32. F. B. Schneider, G. Morrisett, and R. Harper. A language-based approach to security. In *Informatics: 10 Years Ahead, 10 Years Back. Conference on the Occasion of Dagstuhl's 10th Anniversary*, number 2000 in LNCS, pages 86–101. Springer, 2000.
33. Sun Microsystems. Javaspace specification. available at: http://java.sun.com/, 1999.
34. J. Vitek, C. Bryce, and M. Oriol. Coordinationg processes with secure spaces. *Science of Computer Programming*, 2002.
35. J. Vitek and C. Jensen, editors. *Secure Internet Programming: Security Issues for Mobile and Distributed Objects*, number 1603 in LNCS. Springer-Verlag, 1999.
36. P. Wyckoff, S. McLaughry, T. Lehman, and D. Ford. TSpaces. *IBM Systems Journal*, 37(3):454–474, 1998.
37. N. Yoshida and M. Hennessy. Subtyping and locality in distributed higher order processes. In *CONCUR '99*, volume 1664 of *LNCS*, pages 557–572. Springer-Verlag, 1999.
38. N. Yoshida and M. Hennessy. Assigning types to processes. In *Proceedings of LICS'00*, pages 334–348. IEEE, Computer Society Press, June 2000.

Towards Using Possibilistic Information Flow Control to Design Secure Multiagent Systems

Axel Schairer*

German Research Center for Artificial Intelligence (DFKI GmbH)
Stuhlsatzenhausweg 3, 66123 Saarbrücken, Germany
schairer@dfki.de

Abstract. We show how security requirements, in particular confidentiality requirements, for a whole multiagent system can formally be decomposed into confidentiality requirements for the agents. The decomposition assumes that there is some control over, or trust in, a subset of the agents and that the platform is trusted to satisfy certain reasonable assumptions. It is generic over the internal execution model of the agents. The decomposition is carried out in full detail for one specific class of confidentiality requirements, yielding a theorem that can be directly applied to derive confidentiality requirements for single agents from the overall requirement. Similar decompositions for other global requirements or under slightly different assumptions about the platform can be carried out along the same lines.

For expressing security requirements we use an existing framework for possibilistic information flow control, profitting from, e.g., the framework's available composition results. The decomposition, because it is carried out formally and rests on a well-studied framework, is fully rigorous and the resulting property of the overall system is well-understood.

1 Introduction

In recent years, multiagent systems have been used for solving distributed problems. Instead of having a central instance that resolves conflicts over constrained resources or conflicts of different stakeholders' interests, these conflicts are resolved based on negotiations between separate agents. Because of conflicting interests, security requirements of the agents or their owners arise frequently [8, 2, 7]. One particular kind of security requirement, which is rather difficult to handle adequately, is confidentiality (or dually integrity) of information. Such requirements become even more important when confidential information is stored by agents that are located on mobile devices and engage in numerous and unforeseen communications. While many mechanisms to enforce, e.g., access control or message filtering for agents have been proposed, as yet less progress has been made in providing means to assess whether a given mechanism actually enforces a given confidentiality requirement, and what exactly the appropriate requirement is in a given scenario. This is unsatisfactory since the value of a mechanism

* This work was supported by the German Ministry for Education and Technology (BMBF), ITW-5064.

D. Hutter et al. (Eds.): Security in Pervasive Computing 2003, LNCS 2802, pp. 101–115, 2004.
© Springer-Verlag Berlin Heidelberg 2004

is *a priori* unknown, unless a good characterization can be given of the overall property that it enforces.

In this paper, we use an existing framework for possibilistic information flow control to formally state global confidentiality requirements for a system of autonomous agents running on a trustworthy platform. These requirements are decomposed into local confidentiality requirements for individual agents. Non-trivial requirements are derived for a subset of the agents: those that can be controlled or trusted by the party which requires confidentiality. This is carried out in full detail for one specific class of confidentiality requirements. Similar decompositions for other overall requirements or under slightly different assumptions about the platform can be carried out along the same lines. Each agent can independently be designed to meet its requirement obtained by the decomposition.

Using the proposed approach, and in particular its framework, has several main benefits over less principled approaches. Information flow control has been well-studied in the past. It is well-understood what a given requirement means and exactly what notion of confidentiality it expresses. Since the global requirements for the whole system and the local requirements for single agents are expressed formally, it can be proven rigorously that the local requirements are sufficient conditions for the global requirements to be satisfied and it is clear which assumptions, e.g. about the platform, need to be made. The proofs are simplified because quite general results concerning the formal relationship between different requirements and the conservation of properties over composition of systems are available. Local confidentiality requirements are expressed independently of the particular mechanism that an agent uses to enforce them. They are also independent of the execution mechanism that the agent is programmed in. Therefore, it is possible to design and implement agents independently (by independent parties) and still achieve a global confidentiality requirement if every agent reliably and demonstrably enforces its local confidentiality requirement. The framework also provides verification techniques in order to prove that an agent satisfies a local requirement. Finally, since the framework is very flexible, there are many extensions of the work we present here that can be tackled. Possible extensions include different confidentiality requirements than the ones we investigate in this paper, or a platform that offers services in addition to passing agents' messages.

The paper is organized as follows. In Sect. 2, we give an informal overview of the multiagent system model we use followed by a formal presentation. We then show how confidentiality requirements are expressed formally in Sect. 3, and in Sect. 4 how global requirements can be decomposed into local ones. Finally, we refer to related work and conclude.

2   Formalizing Multiagent Systems

We model a multiagent system as a set of agents that are executed in parallel on a platform. Agents are specified by their behavior. The execution mechanism that causes agents to display their specified behavior is intentionally left unspecified to obtain a model that is as general as possible. For instance, we do not care about whether agents run a deterministic or non-deterministic program, or whether a more declarative description of the expected behavior of agents is used. An agent is provided with initial data from the outside, e.g. from the owner of the agent, before it starts executing. We assume the platform to be trustworthy, i.e. we assume that it executes an agent's program as advertised and that it runs different agents in completely separated environments, except that it allows agents to communicate explicitly.

Agents can communicate with other agents by sending messages to an explicitly named receiving agent (we assume that agents know the names of other agents). We assume that messages can be passed on by the platform, but we do not make assumptions about whether or in which order messages that have been sent are in fact passed on. I.e. we only assume the platform does not invent messages or make them available to anyone else but the designated receiver.

Many details could be specified differently, e.g. values from the owner could be passed to the agent while it is executing rather than before it starts running, or there could be stronger guarantees by the platform with respect to the discipline with which it passes on messages between agents. As it turns out, these details do not make a difference for the decomposition of the requirements that we carry out in Sect. 4. In any case, since the decomposition is carried out with mathematical rigor, a different agent model can be used and the decomposition repeated to determine exactly whether the results we obtain in this paper are still applicable or whether they need to be adapted.

2.1 Formalizing Agents

We model agents by specifying their behavior in terms of their internal state and transitions that they can make from one state to another one. Transitions are labelled by events. While some transitions are internal to the agent, e.g. internal computation steps, others allow interaction between an agent and its environment, e.g. sending or receiving messages. For the rest of the paper, we fix a non-empty set of agents $\mathcal{A}$. Also we assume a fixed, non-empty set *Val*, which models the values that agents compute with and send as messages. The possible behaviors of a single agent $a \in \mathcal{A}$ are specified by a state-event system (SES) SES_a. An agent's initial state is specified by a set of named variables and externally motivated assignments to them using init-events, and a program, which is encoded in the transition Relation T_a.

Definition 1 (State-event system). *A state-event system is a tuple $SES = (E, I, O, S, s_0, T)$, where E is a set of events, $I \subseteq E$, and $O \subseteq E$ are input and output events, respectively, S is a set of states, $s_0 \in S$ is the initial state, and $T \subseteq S \times E \times S$ is the transition relation. We require I and O to be disjoint. Additionally, we require T to be the graph of a partial function from $S \times E$ to S.*

Definition 2 (Agent-SES). *An agent $a \in \mathcal{A}$ is defined by the state-event system $SES_a = (E_a, I_a, O_a, S_a, s_{a,0}, T_a)$. We define SES_a as follows. For each $a \in \mathcal{A}$, let Var_a be a set of named variables for a. Furthermore, let init, start, trans, send, rec, and internal be injective functions with disjoint codomains. Let I_a, O_a, and $Internal_a$ be defined by*

$$I_a = \{\text{init}(a, p, v) \mid p \in Var_a, v \in Val\}$$
$$\cup \{\text{start}(a)\}$$
$$\cup \{\text{trans}(b, a, v) \mid b \in \mathcal{A} \setminus \{a\}, v \in Val\}$$
$$O_a = \{\text{trans}(a, b, v) \mid b \in \mathcal{A} \setminus \{a\}, v \in Val\}$$
$$Internal_a = \{\text{send}(a, b, v) \mid b \in (\mathcal{A} \setminus \{a\}), v \in Val\}$$
$$\cup \{\text{rec}(a, b, v) \mid b \in (\mathcal{A} \setminus \{a\}), v \in Val\}$$
$$\cup \{\text{internal}(a, i) \mid i \in N_a\}$$

where $N_a \subseteq \mathbb{N}$ is an index of all possible internal events for a. Let PC_a be a set of program control points for the agent program of a, and let $Bool = \{\top, \bot\}$. We define

$$E_a = I_a \cup O_a \cup Internal_a$$
$$S_a = Bool \times PC_a \times (\mathcal{A} \times Val)^* \times (\mathcal{A} \times Val)^* \times (Var_a \longmapsto Val)$$
$$s_{0,a} = (\bot, l, [], [], \sigma) \quad \text{for some } l \in PC_a, \text{ and some } \sigma \in (Var_a \longmapsto Val).$$

Each state in S_a consists of a boolean flag that indicates whether the agent is running or is still in the initialization phase, a program counter that captures the local state of the agent program, two buffers for incoming and outgoing messages, and an assignment of values to the variables in Var_a. The transition relation T_a is defined by Fig. 1.

init(a, p, v) modifies $var(p)$
    pre: $running = \bot$
    post: $var'(p) = v$

start(a) modifies $running$
    pre: $running = \bot$
    post: $running' = \top$

trans(a, b, v) modifies out
    pre: $running = \top$
        $out = append([[(b, v)], rest)$
    post: $out' = rest$

trans(b, a, v) modifies in
    pre: $running = \top$
    post: $in' = append(in, [(b, v)])$

send(a, b, v) modifies out, pc
    pre: $running = \top$
        $\theta_a^s(pc, var, b, v)$
    post: $out' = append(out, [(b, v)])$
        $pc' = \psi_a^s(pc, var)$

rec(a, b, v) modifies in, pc
    pre: $running = \top$
        $in = append([[(b, v)], rest)$
        $\theta_a^r(b, pc, var)$
    post: $in' = rest$
        $pc' = \psi_a^r(pc, var, b, v)$

internal(a, i) modifies pc
    pre: $running = \top$
        $\theta_a^i(i, in, pc)$
    post: $pc' = \psi_a^i(pc, var)$

Fig. 1. Example definition of agent's transition relation T_a by pre- and postconditions. A statement specifies that in a given state $s = (running, pc, in, out, var)$, the events are enabled iff the conjunction of the preconditions are true in that state. It also specifies the successor state $s' = (running', pc', in', out', var')$ by the conjunction of the postconditions and additional frame axioms $x' = x$ for the state variables not mentioned in the "modifies"-slot.

The control- and dataflow of the agent program is determined by giving appropriate definitions for θ_a^s, θ_a^r, θ_a^i, ψ_a^s, ψ_a^r, and ψ_a^i in Fig. 1. The statement for, e.g., $rec(a, b, v)$ in Fig. 1 is read as follows: The transition can only be taken by agent a in state $s = (running, pc, in, out, var)$ if the agent is running, the input message queue in is non-empty (the first pending message is from b with content v), and the agent program allows messages from b to be received in the current state of a given by pc and var. If the transition is in fact taken by the agent then the message is deleted from the queue of pending input messages, and the agent goes into a new state, depending on the previous state and the message received. All other state variables, i.e. *running*, *out*, and *var*, are unchanged.

The intuition behind Def. 2 is the following: in each run of agent a, the agent takes an arbitrary number of init-events, followed by one start-event, followed by an arbitrary number of other events complying with the agent's program. send-events (rec-events) queue messages for delivery by the platform (access messages delivered by the platform, respectively), trans-events model the transmission of messages from one agent's output queue to the input queue of another agent. Note that the only inputs to an agent are init-, start-, and trans events and the only output events are trans-events. Except for init-events, no event is enabled before a start-event has occurred, and after a start-event has occurred, no further init- or start-events are possible. This is in accordance with our informal description of agents and the assumptions that the only way for agents to communicate is via message transmission. Different choices can be made if they describe the agent model for a specific application better. For the rest of the paper, we do not depend on all details of this agent specification. Instead, we use a less constrained (and therefore more general) definition given in the following section.

It is obvious that I_a and O_a are disjoint and that the only events that can be shared by several agents are trans-events. Also, a trans-event shared by two agents is an input-event of one and an output-event of the other. We will need these facts later on, so we state them as a lemma.

Lemma 1. *Let $a, b \in \mathcal{A}$ be two agents such that $a \neq b$. Then $I_a \cap O_a = \{\}$, $E_a \cap E_b = \{\mathrm{trans}(a, b, v), \mathrm{trans}(b, a, v) \mid v \in Val\}$, and $e \in E_a \cap E_b$ implies either $e \in (I_a \cap O_b)$ or $e \in (O_a \cap I_b)$.*

2.2 Formalizing Agents by Event-Systems

We will now model agents (and later on whole multiagent systems) by specifying their behavior in terms of finite sequences of events, so called traces. The agent's possible behaviors are modelled by a set of traces, without reference to the state of agents. The relationship to the specification in the preceeding section is that each state-event system induces a uniquely determined event system (ES). In particular, each agent specification according to Def. 2 induces an event system according to Def. 5 below. The following definitions follow the definitions used in the framework for possibilistic information flow control in [3], which we use later to express and decompose confidentiality requirements.

Definition 3 (Trace, sets of traces). *Let E be a set of events. A (finite) trace over E is a sequence $\tau \in E^*$ of events. We write $\langle e_1, \dots, e_n \rangle$ for the trace consisting of the* events $e_1, \ldots, e_n$ (in that order), and $\alpha.\beta$ for the concatenation of traces α and β. α is called a prefix of $\alpha.\beta$. A set of traces is said to be closed under prefixes if $\alpha.\beta \in Tr$ implies $\alpha \in Tr$.

Definition 4 (Event system). An event system is a tuple $ES = (E, I, O, Tr)$ where E is a set of events, $I \subseteq E$ is the set of input events, $O \subseteq E$ is the set of output events, and $Tr \subseteq E^*$ is the set of possible traces of ES. Again, we require I and O to be disjoint. Furthermore, we require Tr to be closed under prefixes.

Definition 5 (Agent-ES). Let init, start, trans, I_a, and O_a be defined as in Def. 2. Furthermore, let Internal$_a$ (for each $a \in \mathcal{A}$) be a set of events such that Internal$_a$ is disjoint from I_b and O_b (for all $b \in \mathcal{A}$) and that $a \neq b$ implies that Internal$_a$ and Internal$_b$ are disjoint. An agent $a \in \mathcal{A}$ is defined by an event system $ES_a = (E_a, I_a, O_a, Tr_a)$, where $E_a = I_a \cup O_a \cup$ Internal$_a$ and Tr_a is an arbitrary but fixed set of traces closed under prefixes.

The following definition provides the link between a state-event system and its induced event system.

Definition 6 (Event system induced by a state-event system). A state-event system $SES = (E, I, O, S, s_0, T)$ induces an event system $ES = (E, I, O, Tr)$, where Tr is defined as follows: A sequence of events $\langle e_1, \ldots, e_n \rangle \in E^*$ $(0 \leq n)$ is said to be enabled for the state-event system SES in state $s = s_1$ if there is a sequence of states $\langle s_1, \ldots, s_{n+1} \rangle \in S^*$ such that $T(s_i, e_i, s_{i+1})$ for all $1 \leq i \leq n$. Tr is defined as the set $Tr = \{\tau \mid \tau \text{ is enabled for SES in state } s_0\}$.

An event system ES_a induced by a state-event system SES_a given by Def. 2 trivially complies with our assumptions given for agent event systems in Def. 5.

2.3 Formalizing a System of Agents

A system of agents is modeled by several agents running in parallel, where trans-events are shared between sender and receiver. Formally, given a set of agents, we model the resulting multiagent system by a parallel composition of the event systems of the agents.

Definition 7 (Composition of event systems). Let $ES_1 = (E_1, I_1, O_1, Tr_1)$ and $ES_2 = (E_2, I_2, O_2, Tr_2)$ be event systems with $E_1 \cap E_2 \subseteq (O_1 \cap I_2) \cup (O_2 \cap I_1)$. The composition $ES = ES_1 \| ES_2$ of ES_1 and ES_2 is defined by $ES = (E, I, O, Tr)$, where $E = E_1 \cup E_2$, $I = (I_1 \setminus O_2) \cup (I_2 \setminus O_1)$, $O = (O_1 \setminus I_2) \cup (O_2 \setminus I_1)$, and $Tr = \{\tau \mid \tau \in E^*, (\tau|_{E_1}) \in Tr_1, (\tau|_{E_2}) \in Tr_2\}$. The projection $\tau|_X$ of $\tau \in E^*$ to $X \subseteq E$ is the trace resulting from τ by deleting from τ all events e not in X. Composition is associative, so we write $\|_{i \in I} ES_i$ for the parallel composition of all ES_i for $i \in I$, where I is a non-empty set. If I is the singleton set $\{i\}$, then we define $\|_{i \in I} ES_i$ to be ES_i.

Definition 8 (Multiagent system). Let $X \subseteq \mathcal{A}$ be a non-empty set of agents. The multiagent system $ES_X = (E_X, I_X, O_X, Tr_X)$ consisting of the agents in X is defined by $ES_X = \|_{a \in X} E_a$.

Lemma 2. ES_X *is well-defined. Furthermore, if* $X, Y \subseteq \mathcal{A}$ *are disjoint, then* $E_X \cap E_Y = \{\text{trans}(a, b, v), \text{trans}(b, a, v) \mid a \in X, b \in Y, v \in \textit{Val}\}$.

Proof. We show that ES_X is well-defined by an induction over the size of X. The base case is obvious. In the step case, $ES_{X'} \| ES_a$ for some $a \notin X'$ is well-defined because $E_{X'} \cap E_a \subseteq (O_{X'} \cap I_a) \cup (O_a \cap I_{X'})$ (induction over the size of X', using Lemma 1). Similarly, the other proposition can be shown by a double induction on the size of X and Y.   □

Two agents can only communicate via occurrences of their shared trans-events. These events are possibly constrained by the sending and the receiving agent. Therefore, the occurrence or non-occurrence of such events possibly allows sender and receiver to infer knowledge about the other agent's behaviour. The specification of Def. 2 in Sect. 2.1 is an example in which the receiver can infer that the sender has actually sent the message, but the sender does not learn anything about the receiver by sending a message.

3 Formalizing Confidentiality Requirements

In the rest of the paper, we look at a particular class of confidentiality requirements: given an agent a and some variable p, the initial value of p should be confidential for another agent b, i.e. information about the initial value should not be obtainable by b by communication with a directly, nor should it be obtainable by communications with other agents indirectly. The requirement does not change over time. This is expressed in terms of observations of b and their dependence on the confidential initial value of p. For a trace τ of the multiagent system ES_A, the observation of b is the projection of τ to the events in E_b. Assume the initial value of p in τ is v. If there is another trace τ' with a different initial value v' for p, and b's observations of τ' are the same as for τ, then b cannot distinguish the different initial values v and v' by its observations. We require that $\text{init}(a, p, v)$-events for arbitrary v cannot be distinguished by observations of b, because the initial value of p is determined by such init-events.

We chose Mantel's framework for possibilistic information flow properties MAKS (modular assembly kit for security properties) [3–5] to represent confidentiality requirements. Requirements are expressed as restrictions on the flow of information within a system and are specified by a security property, which consists of a view and a security predicate. A view captures the set of those events that are observable (or visible) and the set of those that are confidential. In the example above the observable events are the ones in E_b and the confidential ones are the $\text{init}(a, p, v)$ events. A security predicate specifies the exact semantics of what confidentiality means for a given view.

Definition 9 (View). *A view* $\mathcal{V}$ *for a set of events* E *is a disjoint, exhaustive partition* (V, N, C) *of* E. *Events in* $V \subseteq E$ *are called visible, events in* $C \subseteq E$ *are called confidential, and events in* $N = E \setminus (V \cup C)$ *are neither visible nor confidential.*

For a given view, the requirement that events in C should be confidential with respect to events in V is specified as a closure property of sets of traces. We use the properties $BSD_\mathcal{V}(Tr)$ and $BSIA_\mathcal{V}^\rho(Tr)$ defined in [5]. Let $\mathcal{V} = (V, N, C)$ be a view. Simplified, the intuition behind *BSD* (backward strict deletion) is that for each possible trace τ, the observation (i.e. $\tau|_V$) is also the observation for another trace τ', in which a confidential event $c \in C$ has been deleted. Thus, by observing $\tau|_V$, it cannot be determined that c has happened: the observation could as well be an observation of τ'. Similarly, the intuition behind *BSIA* (backwards strict insertion of admissible events) is that the observation $\tau|_V$ for a given trace τ is also an observation for a trace τ' that results from τ by inserting a confidential event. Only the insertion of admissible confidential events is considered by *BSIA* (which events are admissible is determined by a function ρ from views to sets of events). Otherwise the property would be too strong, because it would imply that confidential events are possible everywhere, which is typically not the case: in our example, the confidential init-events are only enabled before a start-event has occurred. In both cases, events neither in V nor in C can be different in τ and τ'.

Definition 10 (BSD, BSIA). *Let* $\mathcal{V} = (V, N, C)$ *be a view for a set of events* E *and* $Tr \subseteq E^*$ *be a set of traces. Furthermore let* ρ *be a function from views over* E *to subsets of* E. *The properties* $BSD_{\mathcal{V}}(Tr)$ *and* $BSIA_{\mathcal{V}}^{\rho}(Tr)$ *are defined by*

$$BSD_{\mathcal{V}}(Tr) \equiv \forall \alpha, \beta \in E^*, c \in C.$$
$$\beta.\langle c \rangle.\alpha \in Tr \wedge \alpha|_C = \langle \rangle$$
$$\implies \exists \alpha' \in E^*. \, \beta.\alpha' \in Tr \wedge \alpha'|_V = \alpha|_V \wedge \alpha'|_C = \langle \rangle$$

$$BSIA_{\mathcal{V}}^{\rho}(Tr) \equiv \forall \alpha, \beta \in E^*, c \in C.$$
$$\beta.\alpha \in Tr \wedge \alpha|_C = \langle \rangle \wedge Adm_{\mathcal{V}}^{\rho}(Tr, \beta, c)$$
$$\implies \exists \alpha' \in E^*. \, \beta.\langle c \rangle.\alpha' \in Tr \wedge \alpha'|_V = \alpha|_V \wedge \alpha'|_C = \langle \rangle$$

where $Adm_{\mathcal{V}}^{\rho}(Tr, \beta, e) \equiv \exists \gamma \in E^*. \, \gamma.\langle e \rangle \in Tr \wedge \gamma|_{\rho(\mathcal{V})} = \beta|_{\rho(\mathcal{V})}$. $Adm_{\mathcal{V}}^{\rho}(Tr, \beta, e)$ *determines whether the event* e *is admissible after the trace* β, *when only events in* $\rho(\mathcal{V})$ *are considered.*

The guarantee provided by *BSD* is that if an agent sees a sequence of events $\tau|_V$ then it cannot deduce that a confidential event $c \in C$ has occurred in τ. Similarly, the guarantee provided by the conjunction of *BSD* and *BSIA* is that if an agent sees a sequence of events $\tau|_V$ then it cannot deduce whether a confidential event $c \in C$ has or has not happened in τ. For more details and other possible properties see [3–5].

The intuitive global requirement that a's initial value of p be confidential for b can now be formalized by the view $\mathcal{V}_{\text{global}}^{a,p,b}$ and the property $SP_{\text{global}}^{a,p,b}$ below.

Definition 11 (Global confidentiality requirement). *Let* $a, b \in \mathcal{A}$, $a \neq b$, *and* $p \in Var_A$. *Let* $\mathcal{V}_{\text{global}}^{a,p,b}$ *be the view* (V, N, C) *over* E_A *defined by*

$$V = E_b \qquad C = \{\text{init}(a, p, v) \mid v \in Val\} \qquad N = E_{\mathcal{A}} \setminus (C \cap V)$$

and let $\rho^a(\mathcal{V}) = \{\text{start}(a)\}$. *The security property* $SP_{\text{global}}^{a,p,b}$ *is defined by*

$$SP_{\text{global}}^{a,p,b}(Tr) \equiv BSD_{\mathcal{V}_{\text{global}}^{a,p,b}}(Tr) \wedge BSIA_{\mathcal{V}_{\text{global}}^{a,p,b}}^{\rho^a}(Tr).$$

This formalizes that $\text{init}(a, p, v)$-events (for arbitrary v) are not inferable from events that are visible to b. The particular choice of ρ^a takes into consideration that $\text{init}(a, p, v)$-events are only enabled before a $\text{start}(a)$-event, so $BSIA^{\rho^a}$ only requires init-events to be insertable before a started running.

Other requirements can be formalized similarly. If, e.g., the communication between a and a' should be confidential for b, then this could be expressed by letting C be $\{\mathsf{trans}(a, a', v), \mathsf{trans}(a', a, v) \mid v \in \mathit{Val}\}$ instead of the definition of C given above. For the class of global confidentiality requirement given in Def. 11 and in the last remark, both $BSD_{\mathcal{V}^{a,p,b}_{\text{global}}}$ and $SP^{a,p,b}_{\text{global}}$ are useful for formulating requirements. Therefore, we have chosen to consider both BSD and the conjunction of BSD and $BSIA$ in parallel in the rest of the paper.

4   Decomposing Confidentiality Requirements

In the previous section, we have presented $SP^{a,p,b}_{\text{global}}$ as an example for a global confidentiality requirement for the whole multiagent system. We decompose this global requirement into local requirements for individual agents in several steps. (1) First, we strengthen the requirement such that it requires the initial value of p to be confidential not only for b but for a whole set Y of agents including b. We call the agents in the set Y the *observers*, and the remaining agents (i.e. those in $\mathcal{A} \setminus Y$) *friends*. The result $SP^{a,p,Y}_{\text{strengthened}}$ is again a global requirement for $ES_{\mathcal{A}}$. (2) In a second step, we decompose $SP^{a,p,Y}_{\text{strengthened}}$ into a requirement $SP^{a,p,X}_{\text{friends}}$ for the multiagent system ES_X consisting of the set of agents $X = \mathcal{A} \setminus Y$ and a requirement $SP^Y_{\text{observers}}$ for the multiagent system ES_Y consisting of the set of agents Y. As we will show, $SP^Y_{\text{observers}}$ is trivially fulfilled for arbitrary sets of agents Y. (3) Finally, we decompose the requirement $SP^{a,p,X}_{\text{friends}}$ into local requirements $SP^{V_{a'},C_{a'}}_{\text{local}}$ for each of the individual agents $ES_{a'}$ with $a' \in X$. Since $SP^Y_{\text{observers}}$ is trivially fulfilled, the conjunction of the local requirements $SP^{V_{a'},C_{a'}}_{\text{local}}$ for all $a' \in X$ logically implies the global confidentiality requirement $SP^{a,p,b}_{\text{global}}$. This result is stated more precisely in Theorem 1 at the end of this section.

We use results obtained for MAKS from [5]. The relevant results are given as Theorems 2, 3, and 4 in the Appendix for ease of reference.

Step (1). We strengthen the requirement $SP^{a,p,b}_{\text{global}}$ such that the initial value of p is confidential with respect to the observations that a coalition of agents in a set Y (with $b \in Y$) can make, i.e. that the initial value is confidential even if the agents in Y collaborate. The result is a requirement for the overall multiagent system.

Definition 12 (Strengthened confidentiality requirement). *Let $Y \subseteq \mathcal{A}$ be a set of agents such that $a \notin Y$, and let $p \in \mathit{Var}_a$. Let the view $\mathcal{V}^{a,p,Y}_{\text{strengthened}}$ be the view (V, N, C) over $E_{\mathcal{A}}$ defined by*

$$V = \bigcup_{b \in Y} E_b \qquad C = \{\mathsf{init}(a, p, v) \mid v \in \mathit{Val}\} \qquad N = E_{\mathcal{A}} \setminus (C \cup V).$$

The security property $SP^{a,p,Y}_{\text{strengthened}}$ is defined by

$$SP^{a,p,Y}_{\text{strengthened}}(Tr) \equiv BSD_{\mathcal{V}^{a,p,Y}_{\text{strengthened}}}(Tr) \wedge BSIA^{\rho^a}_{\mathcal{V}^{a,p,Y}_{\text{strengthened}}}(Tr).$$

Lemma 3. *Let $Y \subseteq A$ such that $b \in Y$ and $a \notin Y$, and let $p \in Var_a$. Then the following holds:*

$$BSD_{\mathcal{V}^{a,p,Y}_{\text{strengthened}}}(Tr_A) \text{ implies } BSD_{\mathcal{V}^{a,p,b}_{\text{global}}}(Tr_A) \tag{1}$$

$$SP^{a,p,Y}_{\text{strengthened}}(Tr_A) \text{ implies } SP^{a,p,b}_{\text{global}}(Tr_A) . \tag{2}$$

Proof. Let $(V_1, N_1, C_1) = \mathcal{V}^{a,p,b}_{\text{global}}$ and $(V_2, N_2, C_2) = \mathcal{V}^{a,p,Y}_{\text{strengthened}}$. Because of $b \in Y$ we have $V_1 = E_b \subseteq \bigcup_{b \in Y} E_b = V_2$ and $C_1 = C_2$. Thus, Theorem 2 is applicable, from which (1) and (2) immediately follow. $\square$

Step (2). We consider the multiagent system ES_A to be the composition of the two systems ES_X and ES_Y (where $X = A \setminus Y$). The requirement $SP^{a,p,Y}_{\text{strengthened}}$ is decomposed into a requirement $SP^{a,p,X}_{\text{friends}}$, which is a property of the multiagent system ES_X consisting of agents in X only, and a requirement $SP^Y_{\text{observers}}$, which is a trivially fulfilled property of the multiagent system ES_Y.

Definition 13. *Let X, Y be a disjoint exhaustive partition of A such that $a \in X$ and $b \in Y$, and let $p \in Var_a$. Let the views $\mathcal{V}^{a,p,X}_{\text{friends}} = (V_1, N_1, C_1)$ (for E_X) and $\mathcal{V}^Y_{\text{observers}} = (V_2, N_2, C_2)$ (for E_Y) be defined by*

$$V_1 = \{\text{trans}(a', b', v), \text{trans}(b', a', v) \mid a' \in X, b' \in Y, v \in Val\}$$
$$C_1 = \{\text{init}(a, p, v) \mid v \in Val\} \qquad N_1 = E_X \setminus (C_1 \cup V_1)$$
$$V_2 = \bigcup_{b \in Y} E_b = E_Y \qquad C_2 = N_2 = \{\} .$$

The security properties $SP^{a,p,X}_{\text{friends}}$ and $SP^Y_{\text{observers}}$ are defined by

$$SP^{a,p,X}_{\text{friends}}(Tr) \equiv BSD_{\mathcal{V}^{a,p,X}_{\text{friends}}}(Tr) \wedge BSIA^{\rho^a}_{\mathcal{V}^{a,p,X}_{\text{friends}}}(Tr)$$

$$SP^Y_{\text{observers}}(Tr) \equiv BSD_{\mathcal{V}^Y_{\text{observers}}}(Tr) \wedge BSIA^{\rho^Y}_{\mathcal{V}^Y_{\text{observers}}}(Tr)$$

where $\rho^Y(\mathcal{V}) = \{\}$.

Lemma 4. *Let a, p, b, X, Y be given as in Def. 13. Then the following holds:*

$$BSD_{\mathcal{V}^{a,p,X}_{\text{friends}}}(Tr_X) \text{ implies } BSD_{\mathcal{V}^{a,p,Y}_{\text{strengthened}}}(Tr_A) \tag{3}$$

$$SP^{a,p,X}_{\text{friends}}(Tr_X) \text{ implies } SP^{a,p,Y}_{\text{strengthened}}(Tr_A) . \tag{4}$$

Proof. Let a, p, b, X, Y be given as in Def. 13. Let $(V, N, C) = \mathcal{V}^{a,p,Y}_{\text{strengthened}}$, $(V_1, N_1, C_1) = \mathcal{V}^{a,p,X}_{\text{friends}}$, and $(V_2, N_2, C_2) = \mathcal{V}^Y_{\text{observers}}$. The following can be checked easily.

$$V \cap E_X = \{\text{trans}(a', b', v), \text{trans}(b', a', v) \mid a' \in X, b' \in Y, v \in Val\} = V_1$$
$$V \cap E_Y = E_Y = V_2$$
$$C \cap E_X = \{\text{init}(a, p, v) \mid v \in Val\} = C_1 \qquad C \cap E_Y = \{\} = C_2$$
$$N_1 \cap N_2 = \{\} \qquad N_1 \cap E_Y = \{\} \qquad N_2 \cap E_X = \{\} .$$

Define $ES = ES_X \| ES_Y$. Since composition is associative and $X \cup Y = \mathcal{A}$, we have $ES = ES_\mathcal{A}$, and by Theorem 3 the above are sufficient conditions for the following:

- $BSD_{\mathcal{V}^{a,p,X}_{\text{friends}}}(Tr_X)$ and $BSD_{\mathcal{V}^Y_{\text{observers}}}(Tr_Y)$ implies $BSD_{\mathcal{V}^{a,p,Y}_{\text{strengthened}}}(Tr_\mathcal{A})$.
- $BSIA^{\rho^a}_{\mathcal{V}^{a,p,X}_{\text{friends}}}(Tr_X)$ and $BSIA^{\rho^a}_{\mathcal{V}^Y_{\text{observers}}}(Tr_Y)$ implies $BSIA^{\rho^a}_{\mathcal{V}^{a,p,Y}_{\text{strengthened}}}(Tr_\mathcal{A})$,

  provided that both $BSD_{\mathcal{V}^{a,p,X}_{\text{friends}}}(Tr_X)$ and $BSD_{\mathcal{V}^Y_{\text{observers}}}(Tr_Y)$ are satisfied.

Both $BSD_{\mathcal{V}^Y_{\text{observers}}}(Tr_Y)$ and $BSIA^{\rho^a}_{\mathcal{V}^Y_{\text{observers}}}(Tr_Y)$, and therefore, $SP^Y_{\text{observers}}(Tr_Y)$, are trivially satisfied, because C_2 is empty (cf. Theorem 4). This implies both (3) and (4).   □

Step (3). We decompose the requirement $SP^{a,p,X}_{\text{friends}}$ to obtain requirements for individual agents in X. The overall idea is the following. Think of each agent a' in X as consisting of two independent parts $\overline{a}'$ and $\underline{a}'$, where the intuition is that the part $\overline{a}'$ (possibly) deals with the secret and the part $\underline{a}'$ does not. The intuition is that the overall system should be secure if no information can flow from any part $\overline{a}'$ (for $a' \in X$) to any part $\underline{a}''$ (for $a'' \in X$), and if no information can flow from any part $\overline{a}'$ (for $a' \in X$) to any agents that are not themselves in X. This vague idea is formalized as follows. The events of an agent $a' \in X$ are split into two sets $C_{a'}$ and $N_{a'}$. The occurrence or non-occurrence of events in C_a may depend on the confidential initial value of p. The occurrence or non-occurrence of events from $V_{a'}$ may not depend on the confidential initial value. Furthermore, constraints on these sets ensure that they constrain the flow of information in the way vaguely described above. The sets $V_{a'}$ and $C_{a'}$ themselves specify a confidentiality requirement on $ES_{a'}$ for each $a' \in X$, i.e. on single agents rather than collections of agents.

Definition 14. *Let X be a subset of $\mathcal{A}$ such that $a \in X$, $Y = \mathcal{A} \setminus X$, and $p \in Var_a$. For each $a' \in X$ let $C_{a'}, V_{a'}$ be a disjoint, exhaustive partition of $E_{a'}$ such that all of the following conditions are satisfied.*

1. *$\{\text{init}(a,p,v) \mid v \in Val\} \subseteq C_a$.*
2. *$e \in C_{a'}$ for some $a' \in X$ implies $e \notin V_{a''}$ for any $a'' \in X$.*
3. *$e \in E_Y$ implies $e \notin C_{a'}$ for any $a' \in X$.*

For each $a' \in X$ let $SP^{V_{a'},C_{a'}}_{\text{local}}(Tr_{a'})$ be defined by

$$SP^{V_{a'},C_{a'}}_{\text{local}}(Tr) \equiv BSD_{\mathcal{V}^{V_{a'},C_{a'}}_{\text{local}}}(Tr) \wedge BSIA^{\rho^{a'}}_{\mathcal{V}^{V_{a'},C_{a'}}_{\text{local}}}(Tr)$$

where $\mathcal{V}^{V_{a'},C_{a'}}_{\text{local}} = (V_{a'}, \{\}, C_{a'})$, and additionally $\rho^a(\mathcal{V}) = \{\text{start}(a)\}$ (as before) and $\rho_{a'}(\mathcal{V}) = \{\}$ for $a' \in X \setminus \{a\}$.

Lemma 5. *Let a, p, X and $C_{a'}, V_{a'}$ for all $a' \in X$ be given as in Def. 14. Then the following holds:*

$$(BSD_{\mathcal{V}^{V_{a'},C_{a'}}_{\text{local}}}(Tr_{a'}) \text{ for all } a' \in X) \text{ implies } BSD_{\mathcal{V}^{a,p,X}_{\text{friends}}}(Tr_X) \tag{5}$$

$$(SP^{V_{a'},C_{a'}}_{\text{local}}(Tr_a) \text{ for all } a' \in X) \text{ implies } SP^{a,p,X}_{\text{friends}}(Tr_X). \tag{6}$$

Proof. Let a, p, X and $C_{a'}, V_{a'}$ for all $a' \in X$ be given as in Def. 14, $Y = \mathcal{A} \setminus X$, and $(V, N, C) = \mathcal{V}^{a,p,X}_{\text{friends}}$. Let the auxiliary view $\mathcal{V}'_X = (V'_X, \{\}, C'_X)$ be defined by $V'_X = \bigcup_{a' \in X} V_{a'}$ and $C'_X = \bigcup_{a' \in X} C_{a'}$. Because of

$$C = \{\text{init}(a, p, v) \mid v \in Val\} \qquad \text{(Def. 13)}$$

$$\subseteq C_a \subseteq \bigcup_{a' \in X} C_{a'} = C'_X \qquad \text{(Def. 14(1), } a \in X)$$

$$V = \{\text{trans}(a', b', v), \text{trans}(b', a', v) \mid a' \in X, b' \in Y, v \in Val\}$$
$$\qquad \text{(Def. 13)}$$

$$= E_X \cap E_Y \qquad \text{(Lemma 2, } X, Y \text{ disjoint)}$$

$$\subseteq \bigcup_{a' \in X} V_{a'} = V'_X \qquad \text{(Def. 14(3), } V_{a'}, N_{a'} \text{ disjoint)}$$

we have $V \subseteq V'_X$ and $C \subseteq C'_X$. By Theorem 2 we conclude that $BSD_{\mathcal{V}'_X}(Tr_X)$ implies $BSD_{\mathcal{V}^{a,p,X}_{\text{friends}}}(Tr_X)$, and also that $BSD_{\mathcal{V}'_X}(Tr_X)$ and $BSIA^{\rho^a}_{\mathcal{V}'_X}(Tr_X)$ imply $BSIA^{\rho^a}_{\mathcal{V}^{a,p,X}_{\text{friends}}}(Tr_X)$. It is, therefore, sufficient to show

$$(BSD_{\mathcal{V}^{V_{a'}, C_{a'}}_{\text{local}}}(Tr_{a'}) \text{ for all } a' \in X) \text{ implies } BSD_{\mathcal{V}'_X}(Tr_X) \qquad (7)$$

$$(BSD_{\mathcal{V}^{V_{a'}, C_{a'}}_{\text{local}}}(Tr_{a'}) \text{ and } BSIA^{\rho^a}_{\mathcal{V}^{V_{a'}, C_{a'}}_{\text{local}}} \text{ for all } a' \in X) \text{ implies } BSIA^{\rho^a}_{\mathcal{V}'_X}(Tr_X) \qquad (8)$$

We prove (7) by induction over the size of X.

- *Base case.* For $X = \{a\}$ we have $ES_{\{a\}} = ES_a$ and $\mathcal{V}'_{\{a\}} = \mathcal{V}^{V_{a'}, C_{a'}}_{\text{local}}$. Therefore, (7) holds trivially.
- *Step case.* For $X = \{a'\} \cup X'$ (for some $a' \notin X'$) we use the fact that $ES_X = ES_{X'} \| ES_{a'}$ and Theorem 3. All views that are involved only have confidential or visible events, so the preconditions of the theorem dealing with N-events are trivially fulfilled, and the remaining preconditions can easily be checked:

$$V'_X \cap E_{X'} = V'_{X'}, \quad V'_X \cap E_{a'} = V_{a'}, \qquad C'_X \cap E_{X'} = C'_{X'}, \quad C'_X \cap E_{a'} = C_{a'}$$

Thus, Theorem 3 is applicable and from $BSD_{\mathcal{V}^{V_{a'}, C_{a'}}_{\text{local}}}(Tr_a)$ and the induction hypothesis $BSD_{\mathcal{V}'_{X'}}(Tr_{X'})$ we conclude (7).

For (8) the inductive argument is very similar. In the step case, there are two additional preconditions of Theorem 3, however. Because of $a' \neq a$ we have $\rho^{a'}(\mathcal{V}^{V_{a'}, C_{a'}}_{\text{local}}) = \{\}$ and thus $\rho^{a'}(\mathcal{V}^{V_{a'}, C_{a'}}_{\text{local}}) \subseteq \rho^a(\mathcal{V}'_X) \cap E_{a'}$ trivially holds. Similarly, because of $\rho^a(\mathcal{V}'_{X'}) = \{\text{start}(a)\} = \rho^a(\mathcal{V}'_X)$, the second precondition $\rho^a(\mathcal{V}'_{X'}) \subseteq \rho^a(\mathcal{V}'_X) \cap E_{X'}$ also trivially holds. $\qquad \square$

Overall Decomposition. The overall decomposition of the original requirement into local requirements of individual agents is now summarized in the following theorem.

Theorem 1. *Let $a \in \mathcal{A}$ be an agent and $p \in Var_a$. Let $b \in \mathcal{A}$ be an agent different from a. Let X be a subset of $\mathcal{A}$ such that $a \in X$ and $b \notin X$. Further, let sets $C'_{a'}, V'_{a'} \subseteq E_{a'}$ be given for each $a' \in X$ satisfying conditions 1–3 in Def. 14. Then the following holds:*

$$BSD_{V_{local}^{V_{a'}, C_{a'}}}(Tr_{a'}) \text{ for all } a' \in X \text{ implies } BSD_{V_{global}^{a,p,b}}(Tr_{\mathcal{A}})$$

$$SP_{local}^{V_{a'}, C_{a'}}(Tr_{a'}) \text{ for all } a' \in X \text{ implies } SP_{global}^{a,p,b}(Tr_{\mathcal{A}}).$$

Proof. This result immediately follows from Lemmas 3, 4, and 5.   □

We have thus presented a way to specify confidentiality requirements for individual agents from the set X that imply the overall global confidentiality requirements for the overall multiagent system. The decomposition involves finding suitable sets X and Y and suitable partitions of events of all agents in X. This is by no means trivial. However, Theorem 1 helps to cut down the search space tremendously compared to finding sufficient conditions for individual agents guaranteeing the global requirement from scratch.

5   Related Work

Biskup and Bonatti propose controlled query evaluation [1] as an answer strategy for agents, possibly refusing to give answers or lying. An observer cannot determine the secrets from the sequence of answers it directly receives because the answers would have been the same for different values of the secrets. Controlled query evaluation can be used to enforce confidentiality requirements for single agents.

Subrahmanian *et al.* [9] put forward definitions of confidentiality based on whether an observer can infer more about secrets after it has received a message than before it has received it. In this case one has to make explicit the inference mechanism of all the observers or to approximate it conservatively. When the mechanism is approximated, the proposed definition is only applicable to requests if the answer depends on the secrets. Whether it depends on the secrets has to be determined outside of the proposed framework.

Our formalization of multiagent systems and the general approach to relate local information flow requirements to global ones is strongly inspired by the work of Mantel and Sabelfeld in [6]. They link an existing notion of language based security for concurrent programs to an overall confidentiality property that prevents leakage of secret initial values of program variables.

6   Conclusions and Further Work

We have presented a general formalization of agents and multiagent systems as event systems. Using an existing framework for possibilistic information flow control we have formulated one particular class of global confidentiality requirements for the overall multiagent system and hinted at how other requirements can be formalized. The requirement was decomposed in detail into confidentiality requirements for a set of individual agents. The result is a theorem that can be used directly to conclude global requirements from local ones or, alternatively, to engineer local requirements that are sufficient for a global requirement to be satisfied. The process of decomposing the requirement also serves as an example of how similar requirements can be decomposed.

By using a well-understood, formal framework (MAKS) for our considerations, we profitted from the general results available for the framework, e.g. concerning comparison of different requirements and composing systems and requirements. The properties that we have used to express our requirements are well-studied and, therefore, it is clear exactly what requirements we have specified. Moreover, using a formal approach has allowed us to carry out the analysis and decomposition rigorously, rather than to invent *ad hoc* definitions of confidentiality.

We have focussed on deriving local security requirements for individual agents from global requirements, rather than on verifying individual agents wrt. their local requirements. However, verification techniques to demonstrate *after the fact* that a given system satisfies its confidentiality requirements are available within MAKS, e.g. unwinding [4]. For applying these techniques, the agents' execution model and programming language need to be chosen. In the future, we intend to look into ways to make this task easier in practice, e.g. by partially automating it.

References

1. J. Biskup and P. Bonatti. Confidentiality policies and their enforcement for controlled query evaluation. In *European Symposium on Research in Computer Security (ESORICS)*, 2002.
2. D. Hutter, H. Mantel, and A. Schairer. Informationsflusskontrolle als Grundlage für die Sicherheit von Multiagentensystemen. *Praxis der Informationsverarbeitung und Kommunikation*, 26(1), 2003.
3. H. Mantel. Possibilistic definitions of security – an assembly kit. In *Proceedings of the 13th IEEE Computer Security Foundations Workshop*, 2000.
4. H. Mantel. Unwinding possibilistic security properties. In *European Symposium on Research in Computer Security (ESORICS)*, 2000.
5. H. Mantel. On the composition of secure systems. In *Proceedings of the IEEE Symposium on Security and Privacy*, 2002.
6. H. Mantel and A. Sabelfeld. A generic approach to the security of multi-threaded programs. In *Proceedings of the 14th IEEE Computer Security Foundations Workshop*, 2001.
7. H. Reiser and G. Vogt. Security requirements for management systems using mobile agents. In *Proceedings of the 5th IEEE Symposium on Computers and Communications*, 2000.
8. I. Schaefer. Secure mobile multiagent systems in virtual marketplaces. A case study on comparison shopping. Research Report RR-02-02, Deutsches Forschungszentrum für Künstliche Intelligenz, DFKI GmbH, 2002.
9. V. S. Subrahmanian, P. Bonatti, J. Dix, T. Eiter, S. Kraus, F. Özcan, and R. Ross. Secure agent programs. In *Heterogeneous Agent Systems*, chapter 10. MIT Press, 2000.

Appendix

In the body of the paper, we have used the following theorems. These are reformulations of those parts of Theorems 1, 3, and 5 from [5] that we have used in this paper.

Theorem 2. *Let ρ, ρ' be functions from views in E to subsets of E, and $\mathcal{V} = (V, N, C)$ and $\mathcal{V}' = (V', N', C')$ be views in E such that $V \supseteq V'$, $C \supseteq C'$, and $\rho(\mathcal{V}) \subseteq \rho'(\mathcal{V})$.*

1. $BSD_{\mathcal{V}}(Tr)$ implies $BSD_{\mathcal{V}'}(Tr)$.
2. $BSD_{\mathcal{V}}(Tr)$ and $BSIA_{\mathcal{V}}^{\rho}(Tr)$ imply $BSIA_{\mathcal{V}'}^{\rho'}(Tr)$.

Theorem 3. *Let the event systems* $ES_i = (E_i, I_i, O_i, Tr_i)$ *(for* $i = 1, 2$*) and* $ES = (E, I, O, Tr) = ES_1 \| ES_2$, *and let* $\mathcal{V} = (V, N, C)$, *let* $\mathcal{V}_i = (V_i, N_i, C_i)$ *(for* $i = 1, 2$*) be views over* E *and* E_i, *respectively, such that* $V \cap E_i = V_i$ *and* $C \cap E_i \subseteq C_i$ *(for* $i = 1, 2$*),* $N_1 \cap N_2 = \{\}$, $N_1 \cap E_2 = \{\}$, *and* $N_2 \cap E_1 = \{\}$ *hold.*

1. $BSD_{\mathcal{V}_1}(Tr_1)$ *and* $BSD_{\mathcal{V}_2}(Tr_2)$ *imply* $BSD_{\mathcal{V}}$.
2. *If* $BSD_{\mathcal{V}_i}(Tr_i)$ *and* $\rho_i(\mathcal{V}_i) \subseteq \rho(\mathcal{V}) \cap E_i$ *(for* $i = 1, 2$*), then* $BSIA_{\mathcal{V}_1}^{\rho_1}(Tr_1)$ *and* $BSIA_{\mathcal{V}_2}^{\rho_2}(Tr_2)$ *imply* $BSIA_{\mathcal{V}}^{\rho}(Tr)$.

Theorem 4. *If* $C = \{\}$ *in* $\mathcal{V} = (V, N, C)$, *then both* $BSD_{\mathcal{V}}(Tr)$ *and* $BSIA_{\mathcal{V}}^{\rho}(Tr)$.

Authentication for Pervasive Computing

Sadie Creese[1], Michael Goldsmith[3,4], Bill Roscoe[2,3], and Irfan Zakiuddin[1]

[1] QinetiQ Trusted Information Management, Malvern, UK
{I.Zakiuddin,S.Creese}@eris.QinetiQ.com
[2] Oxford University Computing Laboratory
Bill.Roscoe@comlab.ox.ac.uk
[3] Formal Systems (Europe) Ltd.
{michael,awr}@fsel.com
http://www.fsel.com
[4] Worcester College, University of Oxford

Abstract. Key management is fundamental to communications security, and for security in pervasive computing sound key management is particularly difficult. However, sound key management itself depends critically on sound authentication. In this paper we review current notions of entity authentication and discuss why we believe these notions are unsuitable for the pervasive domain. We then present our views on how notions of authentication should be revised to address the challenges of the pervasive domain, and some of the new research problems that will arise. We end with some brief thoughts on how our revised notions may be implemented and some of the problems that may be encountered.

1 Introduction

1.1 Ambient Intelligence and Security

The Ambient Intelligence World. The pervasive computing paradigm fore- sees communicating and computational devices pervading all parts of our environment, from our physical selves, to our homes, offices, streets and so forth. Humans will be surrounded by intelligent and intuitive interfaces capable of providing information and communication facilities efficiently and effectively. Systems will recognise the presence of individuals, perhaps even their mood, in an unobtrusive manner, modifying their functionality according to changing needs. The huge numbers of communicating devices will provide and enable multiple dynamic networks at any one location. Users and their autonomous agents will be able to traverse these networks, passing seamlessly from one to another, coexisting in many at a single point in time, thus creating a truly ubiquitous intelligent computing environment.

In the future pervasive networking technologies will become commonplace within society and central to everyday life. Companies, organisations and individuals will increasingly depend on electronic means to store and exchange information in order to take advantage of ambient intelligence. Inevitably, many of these information transactions will be sensitive and critical.

D. Hutter et al. (Eds.): Security in Pervasive Computing 2003, LNCS 2802, pp. 116–129, 2004.

Appetite for Security. However, even in todays society information security is not taken as seriously as it should. There have been many 'sniffing' expeditions reported, aimed at locating and assessing the defences of wireless LAN networks[1]. Users frequently fail to initiate any form of security or information protection (not even well known encryption techniques). Citing such evidence, some security researchers have commented that it is not worth expecting users to care about security in the ambient intelligence world, since current attitudes are so sloppy.

But clearly people do care about both physical security (people protect their cars using locks) and information security (people protect their credit card numbers). There is building evidence that people are also becoming increasingly concerned about securing their privacy. A recent series by the U.K. newspaper The Guardian, 'Big Brother: Someone somewhere is watching you' [2], highlights the growing public debate surrounding personal privacy. One article details the results of a poll, conducted by ICM research, designed to measure people's attitudes to their privacy in an increasingly digital age. The results include the following: 58% of people in the U.K. don't trust the government to protect their privacy, 66% of people are worried about the security of their personal information travelling on the Internet, 72% of people would swap some functionality for security. Perhaps as computing becomes ubiquitous, and pervasive technologies become as common as motor cars, then security and privacy will grow in importance in people's minds.

1.2 Security Requires Authentication

Security is commonly divided into four categories:

- *authenticity:* that a claim (especially of an identity) is valid
- *confidentiality:* that secrets are only shared between authorised principals
- *integrity:* that data cannot be altered in an unauthorised way, and
- *availability:* that secrets are always eventually made available to authorised principals.

To achieve security we must be able to ensure that we can correctly identify the authorised principals. Underpinning this is our ability to confirm (i.e. authenticate) that claims for authorisation are correct.

A fundamental building block of secure systems is sound key management, by which we mean the secure and correct generation, distribution, storage, use and revocation of cryptographic variables. As the wireless research community gains momentum [3, 4], key management for the wireless world is seen as an important research challenge. But key management itself depends critically on authentication. Without sound authentication, sound key management is infeasible.

In short, authentication is a basic building block of security. And for this reason this paper presents our thoughts on what authentication will mean in the world of ambient intelligence.

---

[1] For example "Winning The New Wireless War", in [1].

1.3   Some Conventions

The range of types of device that will interact in the world of ubiquitous computing is very large (from laptops to pacemakers). So to simplify our terminology we'll use the term 'PDA' to refer to arbitrary devices with the wireless communications capability of a modern mobile phone and the computing resources of a modern laptop[2]. Our PDAs are each assumed to have a unique user/owner, though one user may certainly have several PDAs.

The problem of ensuring that a PDA is in use only by its rightful owner will be elided in the following discussion. This is a major simplification, but it does make it easier to think about authentication requirements and foster debate, which is our aim[3]. Let us also note that in the world of ubiquitous computing, devices (and agents) may act with significant autonomy from their human masters, and this partly justifies the simplification.

When some people are involved in secure multi-party transactions, then we'll call the collection of their PDAs the legitimate PDAs. Of course, legitimacy does not imply 'trustworthiness'; it only refers to the PDAs owned by the people taking part in the secure multi-party transaction. If a device is not legitimate, then it is (naturally) illegitimate.

1.4   Plan of the Paper

Section 2 provides a brief overview of traditional notions of authentication, setting the context for their subsequent deconstruction and revision. Section 3 provides two "case studies" of pervasive computing security, which highlight why traditional notions of authentication are inadequate (and indeed inappropriate). This is followed by our revision of authentication in, Section 4. The paper is primarily about requirements, but the penultimate section presents a few thoughts about how future notions of authentication may be implemented, and the security issues that we see as arising there.

2   A Glance at Traditional Authentication

Authentication concerns proving, to a verifier, the validity of a claim. Our principal interest is in entity authentication, which concerns proving the validity of a claimed identity. We concentrate on entity authentication because it is the basis of sound key agreement and authorisation. When we talk subsequently about "traditional" authentication we simply mean entity authentication.

The basic idea of entity authentication is deceptively simple: one principal wants to be sure that it is talking to (and only to) whomever it intends. However, the subject of formalising mutual entity authentication, where two or more principals authenticate themselves to each other, is notoriously difficult. The depth and difficulty come from

---

[2] Quite compact devices will have such capabilities in a few years, and devices may well have much greater capabilities, further in the future. However, a modern mobile phone and laptop form a sufficient basis for our discussion.

[3] Solutions such as those of Corner, [5], can address the device-to-user authentication problem.

the distributed, multi-party nature of mutual entity authentication. Typically, the requirement is that the beliefs, actions and actual achievements of all principals match [6, 7] despite malicious activity.

An identity is usually recognised by confirming that some known attribute of the subject is present. Humans have exceptionally powerful capabilities to recognise images and sounds, but in the electronic world identities are recognised by matching digital information. A representative, but not exhaustive, list of electronic means for entity authentication includes:

- shared secrets, including passwords,
- public key cryptography schemes, including both Public Key Infrastructures and Pretty Good Privacy[8],
- tokenisation,
- biometrics.

While these schemes appear quite diverse, for our discussion we can note that they share some basic assumptions and features. These will be the basis for our arguments against entity authentication, so we summarise them here.

Firstly, while authentication is a cornerstone of security, it does not provide any security on its own; rather, the security depends on *trust in the entity*[4]. Passwords or biometrics might correctly grant a user access to confidential data, but that data is secure only if the user is trustworthy. The same holds true for mutual entity authentication by crypto-protocols. I may have perfectly justified confidence that I have a keyed link with Alice, but I will only communicate sensitive data to Alice if I trust her.

Secondly, we noted identities are electronically confirmed by matching digital information. To implement entity authentication there must be a binding between a principal, or more precisely the identity of a principal and some recognising information (a password, PIN, and so forth), and there must be assurance that this binding is correct. An immediate consequence of this fact is that the recognising digital information and the binding has to be initialised, stored and managed securely. In general, any entity authentication scheme requires significant pre-existent trusted knowledge and infrastructure[5]. For instance, to use a password, or shared secret, all agents (human and electronic) must secretly agree the password, and of course be confident of whom they share it with. The challenges of maintaining and managing such information are great. The sometimes rickety services provided by PKIs[6] are now perhaps the most widely discussed example of the difficulties of managing the trusted information for entity authentication.

Finally, an obvious feature of entity authentication, is the essentially static and binary nature of the assurances it delivers. Clearly, a principal's claim to an identity is either true or false, a password either matches or it does not, and so forth. But this logical feature of entity authentication constrains the ways it can be used. If there is a need to grade levels of assurnace, then the facilities to do that (setting the minimum size of a password, for example) are rather limited.

---

[4] Thanks to Peter Ryan and Dieter Gollman for emphasising this point.

[5] Colin Boyd has a theorem, in [9], that entity authentication is impossible without pre-existent shared secrets. Maurer discusses and develops these ideas in [10].

[6] For instance, in March 2001, Microsoft announced that 2 digital certificates that were issued in it's name, by a highly trusted third party, were false.

3   What's Wrong with Traditional Authentication?

We will argue that for the pervasive world the current focus on authenticating identities will be misguided. The failings of entity authentication are partly because what it needs to assume will not be available, and partly because the assurances achieved by entity authentication will be of diminishing value.

The best way to elucidate our arguments is by some examples. The very nature of pervasive computing means that there are a lot of scenarios, but we will focus on two: using a public printer from a wireless device and a collection of PDAs bootstrapping a secure network. Both these examples have precedents in the literature. We hope to foster more active debate on the fundamentals of key management and authentication by focusing on these existing examples.

3.1   Using Public Printers, via a Wireless Link

For the first example imagine a user in a public place, like an airport, with a PDA. Suppose the PDA contains confidential data which the user wants to print out, and assume that the airport has a number of printers that can potentially service the user's needs. Ideally, the user wants to use a wireless link to send the confidential data securely to a chosen printer[7].

Balfanz et al.'s paper [11] is centred on this problem. They briefly discuss security aims (where we intend to dwell) and then they concentrate on a solution. Their proposal to secure the PDA to printer wireless link is based on the 'Resurrecting Duckling' of Stajano, [12]. Essentially, a keyed link is created by physical contact between the device and the printer. No pre-existent authentication mechanisms, like certificates, are needed; but securing the link does require users to touch their chosen printer with their PDA, on an appropriate physical interface. As such Balfanz et al.'s solution does 'bootstrap' a degree of security.

Nevertheless, the problem bears re-examination to understand better the security requirements, not least because it is a good example of wireless access to public utilities. In this example the security assurances that a user is likely to want are:

1. The confidential data on the user's PDA goes to the specific printer chosen by the user and to no other devices.
2. The printer treats the confidential data in a 'trustworthy' manner. Where trustworthy captures properties like guaranteeing that no other party has access to the data while it is resident on the printer, and (most likely) that the confidential data is deleted immediately after being printed.

Can traditional entity authentication meet these two requirements? For the first requirement the user might use entity authentication to ensure that the data only goes to the chosen printer. But this would mean that the user would need to have the printer's public key. And the user can only get the printer's public key after reliably determining

---

[7] Whilst this example is not particularly futuristic, the basic service model and security requirements will remain relevant in future pervasive environments.

the printer's name and then accessing a certification authority that serves the printer and whose certificates the user's PDA can recognise.

Reliable name resolution and access to useful certification information are both major assumptions about the world, which, as Balfanz et al. point out, are not likely to hold in the ubiquitous computing future. Obtaining the printer's name reliably will at best be impractical: will user's have to type in IP addresses of utilities into their PDA before using them? And it will be difficult to ensure the integrity of a claimed name of an arbitrary device. Even if the name could be determined reliably and easily, finding a useful public key for an arbitrary device, in an unspecified location, would require that every single device in the world is served by a small collection of PKIs. Furthermore, with wireless communications it may not be feasible to assume that a certification authority will be accessible.

Thus, for the first security requirement – namely that confidential data is received by the chosen device and no other – it appears that the *outcome* of traditional authentication could serve, but that it assumes things (viz. name resolution and certification) that will be increasingly difficult to provide. What about the second requirement, of ensuring that the printer treats the data in a trustworthy manner? We noted, in section 2, that for entity authentication to give security we need to trust the entity. In the pervasive domain, simply having a keyed link to an effectively arbitrary named device will give us no assurance about that device's trustworthiness. In effect the user still has to trust a random printer in an unknown place. Thus, entity authentication appears to be of very little value in delivering assurance about how the printer will behave. In fact, this type of assurance seems to fall outside the ambit of entity authentication.

Finally, it should be noted that a user may have varying degrees of concern for the information that needs to be sent to the printer. We noted the essentially binary nature of entity authentication, but a more useful capability will enable a user to grade the assurance provided.

The above reasons, for traditional authentication having limited value in the case of the PDA and printer, hold true more generally. In a pervasive computing environment these failings will become more acute.

3.2   Mesh Networks

For our second example imagine a set of people meeting in some place and wanting to work together securely. Of course, they will have their PDAs and so they will want these PDAs to form a 'secure' network. The users' PDAs are automatically legitimate (according to our original definition), but it is quite conceivable that the users will want to network securely with other devices in their vicinity, and these nominated devices must also be treated as legitimate. We'll take secure to mean that it is infeasible for any illegitimate device to decipher communication between the legitimate PDAs and peripherals. It may be possible to assume that the users' PDAs will be 'trustworthy'. However, when the users want to use other devices then their trustworthiness will probably need to be validated.

The problem is: how do the legitimate PDAs and other legitimate devices form a secure network (in the sense just mentioned) with minimal pre-existent trusted knowledge (such as valid certificates)? When the users are in an arbitrary place and want to use various devices from their environment, then this problem generalises the previous problem - of secure use of a public printer.

In the literature the simplest form of this problem is discussed by Asokan and Ginzboorg [13]. They discuss the problem of users with PDAs, in a closed meeting room, wanting to create a secure network across their PDAs. Their solution is based on protocols that use weak encryption to agree a strong encryption key. The basic idea is that the users agree a password and then they type that password into their PDAs. The legitimate PDAs are by definition those that have had the password input. This password makes the weak encryption key, which is, nevertheless, sufficient for the legitimate PDAs to agree a strong key - using the protocols that they present. Thus they provide a solution for bootstrapping security that requires no pre-existent electonic trust. In effect they have manual initialisation of trust, since the users are (implicitly) responsible for controlling the exposure of the password. It is also clear that their solution can be extended to include any device with a keyboard.

Asokan and Ginzboorg preface their solution with a brief discussion of the security requirement. They note that maintaining confidentiality with respect to identities, which can be achieved by authenticated key agreement, is not what is required here. Instead they propose that the security requirement (they use the term "prior context") is defined by location. To quote:
Only people present in this meeting room can read the messages that I send.

In other words, the legitimate PDAs are only those owned by people in the meeting room and only these should be able to decrypt the messages.

In this problem, trust stems from the fact that people in the room can see each other, and already know that they wish to share secrets. Security, in this location-centric context, is still predicated on trust in the PDAs and, in the more general case, in the nominated peripherals. However, imagine the room containing people who are less trusted than the others (perhaps some people know each other, but some are strangers). Whilst it remains true that principals only wish to share their secrets with principals in the room, they may also wish to authenticate the strangers. In this case the strangers will need to provide credentials, about themselves and their devices, to admit them to the secure multi-party session. Trusted Third Parties may be the means for obtaining added assurance, though what constitutes an acceptable credential is likely to vary.

To summarise the light this example sheds on entity authentication, trust is based largely on location and human contact, not on identity. Effective solutions to this example should be able to translate human trust into electronic trust quickly and easily (this is what the proposed solution, by Asokan and Ginzboorg does). If assurance is required concerning the behaviour of peripherals, then this example simply iterates the failing of entity authentication from the previous example. Finally, the inflexible binary assurance of entity authentication does not match the spectrum of assurances (and means of assurance) that may be needed in the future.

4   Revising Authentication for the Pervasive Domain

4.1   What Should We Authenticate?

The examples in the previous section tried to describe why, in the world of ubiquitous computing, entity authentication will neither be easy to achieve nor give the desired assurances. It will be impractical because device names will usually be indeterminate and it is unlikely that infrastructures to support certifying names of the huge numbers of devices will be available. Furthermore, entity authentication will not give the desired assurances, because critical to entity authentication is trust in the entity. When desiring secure interaction with an unknown entity, assurance of its identity is far less relevant than assurance that it is 'trustworthy', where the interpretation of trustworthy varies considerably according to the application.

Reflecting on the examples from Section 3 does yield some clues about how we might revise traditional notions of authentication. Firstly, a name is an attribute of an object, but only one of many. Entity authentication is predicated on the belief that the name is sufficient to infer the appropriate property of trustworthiness. In the world of ubiquitous computing few trustworthiness properties will follow simply from the name of an object.

But what about other attributes of objects? In both the examples in Section 3 it is clear that location is an important attribute. In the mesh network example physical location was fundamental to specifying the legitimate PDAs and devices, and indeed for the decision to trust the people taking part. Also, when the users want to connect to various peripherals in their locality, they might confirm the legitimacy of the choosen devices by seeking assurance of the type of device. Thus a printer might be asked to prove that it is in a specific location and that it is a printer. By authenticating these sorts of attributes we might have justifiable confidence in legitimacy.

But as we have noted, legitimacy does not necessarily imply any useful property of trustworthiness; usually it gives little assurance about what the device will do. People make decisions about who or what to trust based on experience, on various conventions (like referal) and even on 'instinct'. We can transfer the same trust model into the digital domain. I trust my computer to work as I expect because I have bought it from a trusted vendor or manufacturer. The software on board is from a trusted software developer. Continuing the transfer, if a user can authenticate the printer's manufacturer and the user trusts the manufacturer, then that might be a basis to trust the printer. Thus the attribute of manufacturer may also be important.

Certificates may be a viable means to prove a reliable manufacturer to a user. But it should be noted that even if it is decided to use this as a basis for trust it may be necessary to confirm that the printer retains its original dependability despite being in a public place for a protracted period. Thus there may be a need to exhibit trusted maintenence and tamper freedom.

Tamper freedom is part of the 'state' of a device (and the state of a device is also one of its attributes) and aspects of state may imply appropriate trustworthiness properties. Another important aspect of state might be that the device is not running another concurrent session, with someone else.

In general, by authenticating various attributes we would aim to confirm precisely which devices are legitimate. Having sufficient evidence of legitimacy we would then need a basis to trust what those devices are doing, or will do.

4.2   How Much Should We Authenticate?

Authenticating different attributes of an entity will give varying levels of assurance. These assurance levels will fluctuate depending upon the environment. For example, you can be more sure when you are in an environment where you can confirm the results of an authentication attempt. Consider the printer example described above. Verifying the location of the printer using GPS will be a much stronger form of authentication when you can see it and you know the coordindates of yor own location, because you can then make a judgement about your distance apart.

Clearly, there are many different levels of assurance possible. By authenticating sets of attributes (hereafter referred to as authentication sets) we are likely to gain more assurance than by authenticating only one. But assurance usually brings a cost. This cost may be in terms of financial price of implementing a particular authentication (high assurance could cost more to engineer), or the cost may be the time it takes a user to achieve assurance (this is likely to be a major factor). In some cases there may be no price too high, in others speed may be of the essence, or budget. Other sensible decision criteria could also be applied.

While it is clear that some sort of context aware, dynamic security policy will be required in the pervasive paradigm, it is not so clear how to define and implement one. We first need to devise metrics for comparing authentication sets, and find decision criteria reflecting our priorities (for instance, cost in time or money).

Consider Figure 1 below:

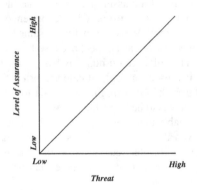

Fig. 1. A notional optimal level of assurance

This graph represents a notional optimal level of assurance, with respect to environmental threat. It is 'notional' in that it is proposed only as a starting point to discuss requirements. It is 'optimal' in the sense that the line defines the level of assurance that is just sufficient. Assuming that cost is related to assurance, the line captures the minimum costs that is likely to be incurred.

The horizontal axis represents a function of the threats that we want to guard against. In pervasive computing threats will vary from juvenile hacking, to corporate espionage, right up to cyber terrorism and government surveillance. The vertical axis represents the level of assurance that is required, this will be determined by a number of factors including:

- the criticality of the security service that we want to protect,
- the type of association that is being made.

This last will vary from a transient link (as is the case with a public printer), to on-going associations (with devices in the home or office), to long term or lifetime associations (for instance, a pacemaker). A further dimension to the type of association is the number of principals involved; group key management is significantly more complex than the two party case, and we can similarly expect multiparty associations to exacerbate the complexity of the required levels of assurance.

When developing or evaluating a security technology, or a security policy, all that really matters is that you possess at least as much assurance as is required. This simply means that the level of assurance achieved must be above the optimal line. In our naive representation this is just the shaded region in Figure 2.

Note that Stajano's work, on the 'Resurrecting Duckling' [12], is an avowedly low assurance solution, designed for low cost applications. As such, an evaluation of the Resurrecting Duckling should find it on the bottom left hand corner of the shaded region, on the graph in Figure 2. Given that researchers are already investigating low assurance solutions, it seems that an understanding of gradeable levels of assurance is necessary.

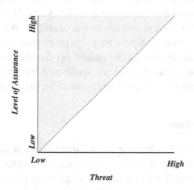

Fig. 2. The region of safe assurance levels

In summary to enable the flexibility that will be required the research community should aim to:

1. Establish metrics for comparing and quantifying the assurance levels gained from differing authentication sets.
2. Understand better what the optimal graph actually looks like.
3. Understand better the cost drivers and their impact, for each context.

A sound understanding of these subjects will form a basis for the flexible and dynamic security policies that the ambient intelligence world will need.

5   Thoughts on Future Implementations

The primary aim of this paper is to re-examine traditional notions of authentication and to suggest alternatives. Nevertheless, it is also worth some noting issues and problems regarding implementation.

5.1   Using Certificates

We noted above, in Section 4, that if it were possible to certify attributes such as the manufacturer of a device, then this may, in appropriate circumstances, provide assurances about how that device will behave. More generally, while the examples discussed above point away from entity authentication, that does not imply abandoning entity authentication. For instance, in the example of mesh networks the security requirement is defined with respect to locality, but there may be a need for the local mesh to connect securely to an infrastructure. Alternatively, the degree of trust that users have in the local group may vary and some users may need to supply additional credentials of trust, like certificates. Thus, when considering implementation attention first needs to be paid to the use of traditional authentication mechanisms in the pervasive domain.

Debate about the practicality of PKIs is an on-going subject. Questions of scalability are paramount: will PKIs simply not scale, or will it be possible to address scalability by making PKIs work together [14]? The debate should be extended to the use of certificates, and the value they add, in the pervasive domain. Wireless communications are fundamental to pervasive computing, and that means variable connectivity, so what use is a Certification Authority, if it is not always accessible? What trust will certificates carry, when their timely revocation will be even more problematic? How will certificates be used? Will certificates have to be issued per device, for its lifetime? It may be the case that some attributes can only be authenticated by certificates (static ones like manufacturer spring to mind). These questions must be explored.

5.2   Agent Based Solutions

Are there more direct ways of achieving confidence in what a device will do, other than relying on its manufacturer (and perhaps evidence of tamper freedom)? The mobile code community has invested effort into studying techniques for self-certifying code, where a software agent carries evidence that it will behave in a trustworthy manner [15]. Security for pervasive computing could use similar concepts (although it isn't clear how much will simply 'port'). For instance, hardware could be configured to send a hash of its configuration to devices it wishes to communicate with. Then policies may be implemented where devices will only interact with other self-certifying devices, whose hash is acceptable. If the assurance at the hardware level was sufficiently high, then this could be used to mitigate the assurance demanded at the network level.

Continuing to draw inspiration from the mobile code community, user friendly security could be enforced by having a mobile agent act on the user's behalf. A user's agent might certify that other devices are fit for interaction, in the senses that we have discussed. Such approaches would have the obvious drawback of needing to ensure that the agent runs correctly on the correct device. It may be observed that the 'which' and the 'what', that we mentioned in Section 4.1 have re-appeared, in this new context. Nevertheless, an agent approach may broaden the range of techniques that can be deployed, as well as yielding user friendly solutions.

5.3 Man-in-the-Middle Vulnerabilities

We have argued forcefully for a paradigm shift from authenticating names to a much broader and flexible notion of attribute authentication. However, it is worth giving thought to whether such a change of orientation will create fresh security vulnerabilities.

Our main concern has been that when a connection is established by something other than name there is a greater than usual danger of man-in-the-middle attacks. Here an attacker sits "in the middle" of a channel between two agents, passing the information on, but not giving any evidence that he is there. For instance, in the example of using the printer (from Section 3.1), if a PDA's wireless link to the printer, P, has a device-in-the-middle, D_M, then the PDA might be communicating with D_M, instead of P. To mask the interception D_M would still forward the user's messages onto P, and indeed pass P's response back to the PDA. If the PDA doesn't know P's identity, then it has no way of knowing that it is talking to D_M instead of P. In the case of the mesh networks it is possible for a set of n nodes to suffer a 'men-in-the-middle' attack, where each of the n nodes ends up connected to an attacking network of $n - 1$ nodes.

Entity authentication precludes man-in-the-middle attacks because each agent has proof of the identity of his interlocutor. If we pronounce entity authentication obsolete or impractical, then we need to think about the added risk of man-in-the-middle attacks, and how these risks may be averted.

An inevitable feature of a man-in-the-middle attack is that it adds a hop to each communication, and this gives a clue to avoidance. If we can introduce some feature in the protocol in which there is an inevitable loss of some resource or entropy from messages as they are passed around, then this would be a basis for avoidance. This could be the passage of time (for instance ensuring each authentication takes some measurable time in a way that is noticeable in the particular circumstance) or some use of watermarking or cryptographic hashing. Another might be each participant announcing in some way a sufficient piece of information about the agent or set of agents to which it is connected. So, in the case of the printer, we might get the printer to print out a banner page with the serial number of the device with which it is operating the protocol. Provided that the man-in-the-middle is using a public key certificate other than that of the originator, it will not be the man-in-the-middle's device number - assuming the protocol is properly designed). In the case of the PDAs, each node might be told a hash of the serial numbers of all the nodes in the network: they might then check that these all agree.

A further possibility is for some unambiguous description of a printer, say, to be conveyed by the protocol to the potential user. This description might be the printer's position, as certified by some especially precise form of GPS or some signed description by an authority the user trusts.

Note that all of the methods assume some way of passing information between nodes other than through the wireless network. The given examples are: reading a printout, listening to one's colleagues at a meeting, watching timed behaviour or even looking where a printer is (or, indeed, checking the integrity of its tamperresistant seal). In the work of Balfanz, et al. [11], physical contact is the means for a non-wireless exchange of information, and indeed this is another possibility. Given the breadth of the problem domain it seems impossible to state fixed methods. Nevertheless, the avoidance of man-in-the-middle (and indeed men-in- the-middle) attacks should be an important item on the future research agenda.

6 Conclusions

Enabling security will be critical to realising the exciting future of Ambient Intelligence. But sound key management will be critical to securing transactions in the world of ubiquitous computing. In the wireless security research community key management is seen as one of the fundamental problems and an area of active research [3, 4]. But key management itself depends fundamentally on sound authentication. Based on the past experiences of the security community (particularly in the area of key management) we claim that understanding and implementing authentication are among the most important challenges facing pervasive computing security.

Traditional authentication has concentrated on the notion of entity authentication, which provides assurance of who is the subject of a secure interaction. We have argued that the requirements to implement entity authentication are unlikely to be practical in the pervasive domain. Further, we have argued that the assurances delivered by entity authentication will be of limited value.

Instead of entity authentication we have argued that assurances are required of which devices are the subject of interaction and what those devices will do. These assurances may be achieved by 'authenticating' (or providing tamperresilient confirmation of) a much broader class of device attributes than name. For the pervasive domain it is clear that location is an important attribute, but many more attributes are likely to be required, including origin, aspects of current state, retention of original integrity, and more. Making this shift is likely to introduce many new challenges and create new security vulnerabilities, the increased likelihood of man-in-the-middle attacks being an important example. It is also clear that the requirements of which attributes to authenticate will vary from context to context.

A further concern is the rigid, binary nature of entity authentication. The much broader range of interaction will need more flexible security policies with richer gradations of assurance. Deciding upon the appropriate security policy will be crucial, and devising metrics to facilitate such a decision will be an important research topic.

The subject of security for ad-hoc and wireless networks is relatively new but the area is growing very fast [3], with key management being one of the major challenges. However, much of the research in this area focuses on engineering traditional approaches, based on certification (for example, [16]) or tokenisation (for example, [5]) to solve specific problems within the domain. Above we have discussed in detail the work of Balfanz et al. [11] and Asokan and Ginzboorg [13]. Both these papers concentrate on engineering solutions. Thus far we have seen little work that thinks specifically of how authentication needs to be deconstructed and revised. We hope it is clear that the concepts we have discussed underpin the on-going solution-oriented research. More importantly, we hope that this work will help to foster debate on the new security concepts for the Ambient Intelligence World.

Acknowledgements

The authors would like to thank give special thanks to Gavin Lowe for stimulating discussions, as well as to Peter Ryan, Dieter Gollman, Colin Boyd, Colin OHalloran and Nick Moffat.

References

1. *Information Security Management.* June 2002, published by Penton.
2. *The Guardian Newspaper.* 7th Spetember, 2002
3. http://www.crhc.uiuc.edu/ nhv/wise/
4. http://www.pampas.eu.org/
5. Corner, M. D. and B. D. Noble.Zero-interaction authentication. The *8th ACM Conference on Mobile Computing and Networking*, September 2002, Atlanta, GA.
6. Diffie, W., P.C.van Oorschot and M.J.Wiener, Authentication and Authenticated Key Exchange.Design, *Codes and Cryptography*, 2 (1992), pp 107-125.
7. Roscoe, A.W. Intensional Specifications of Security Protocols. *Proceedings of the 1996 IEEE Computer Security Foundations Workshop*, IEEE Computer Society Press, 1996.
8. Zimmerman, P. *The Official PGP Users Guide*. The MIT Press, 1995.
9. Boyd, C. Security Architectures Using Formal Methods. *IEEE Journal on Selected Areas in Communications*, Vol. 11, No. 5, 1993, pp. 694-701.
10. Maurer, Ueli and Pierre Schmid. A Calculus for Security Bootstrapping in Distributed Systems. *Journal of Computer Security*, vol. 4, no. 1, pp. 55-80, 1996.
11. Balfanz, Dirk, D. K. Smetters, P. Stewart and H. Chi Wong. Trusting Strangers: Authentication in Ad-hoc Wireless Networks. *Network and Distributed Systems Security Symposium*, 2002. Available from: http://www.isoc.org/isoc/conferences/ndss/02/proceedings/index.html
12. Stajano, F. and R. J. Anderson. The Resurrecting Duckling: Security Issues for Ad-hoc Wireless Networks. 7th Security Protocols Workshop, LNCS vol. 1796, Cambridge, UK.
13. Asokan, N. and P. Ginzboorg. Key Agreement in Ad-hoc Networks. Computer Communication Review, 2000. Available from:
    http://www.semper.org/sirene/people/asokan/research/index.html
14. http://www.dti-mi.org.uk/newweb/fiducia.htm
15. Vigna, G. Mobile Agents and Security. LNCS, July 1998.
16. Kong, J., P. Zerfos, H. Luo, S. Lu, L. Zhang. Providing Robust and Ubiquitous Security Support for Mobile Ad-hoc Networks. Proceedings of 9th International Conference on Network Protocols. IEEE Computer Society Press, 2001.

End-to-End Trust Starts with Recognition

Jean-Marc Seigneur, Stephen Farrell,
Christian Damsgaard Jensen, Elizabeth Gray, and Yong Chen

Distributed Systems Group, Department of Computer Science,
Trinity College Dublin, Dublin 2, Ireland
secure-tcd@cs.tcd.ie
http://www.dsg.cs.tcd.ie/

Abstract. Pervasive computing requires some level of trust to be established between entities. In this paper we argue for an entity recognition based approach to building this trust which differs from starting from more traditional authentication methods. We also argue for the concept of a "pluggable" recognition module which allows different recognition schemes to be used in different circumstances. Finally, we propose that the trust in the underlying infrastructure has to be taken into account when considering end-to-end trust.

1 Introduction

Weiser's vision of ubiquitous computing [33] will only become true when computing capabilities are woven into the fabric of every day life, indistinguishable from it. In ambient intelligence (AmI) environments [21], where ubiquitous computing[1], ubiquitous communication and intelligent user interfaces are combined, it has been envisaged [6] that real people would have a digital-self acting on their behalf. These digital entities are more likely to be artificial intelligence agents following the real person they are representing – kind of ubiquitous roaming entities. As in real life, these digital entities will encounter other previously unknown entities while roaming from place to place. Billions of entities – potentially any device with a digital heartbeat – are expected to spread in the surrounding environment. A fundamental question concerns the representation of entities including their naming and subsequent identification as well as their association with real-world principals. We believe that, in this context, it is more beneficial to take an approach based on entity recognition [26], rather than solely on traditional authentication schemes like PKI [9] or Kerberos [17].

Establishing the authenticated identity of the other party is not necessarily enough in pervasive computing, because identity conveys no a priori information about the likely behaviour of the other party. In many cases, it will be more useful to determine whether the other party is someone with whom one has interacted successfully in the past, whether the other party can provide a recommendation from a trusted third party (e.g., from a personal friend) or whether the other party has a generally good reputation.

In AmI environments, the question "When should a person cooperate, and when should a person be selfish, in an ongoing interaction with another person?" [2] will

---

[1] The pervasive computing magazine [8] treats ubiquitous computing and pervasive computing as synonyms; so do we.

D. Hutter et al. (Eds.): Security in Pervasive Computing 2003, LNCS 2802, pp. 130–142, 2004.

be extended to digital entities collaborating with other digital entities. To tackle this question, the concept of trust in computer systems is attracting increasing attention from the research community. Trust has been formalized as a computational model [18, 32], but the term trust means different things in different research communities, for example it may relate to trust in the underlying technology [3] or to trust between entities when they have to collaborate [11, 13]. We argue that end-to-end trust includes both types of trust – trust between parties and trust in the underlying infrastructure.

Usually, authentication is the first step to ensure security in distributed computing environments. In this paper, we concentrate on the authentication level, which is one part of the technical trust in our end-to-end trust model. We start by motivating the need for dynamic enrollment and defining the notion of entity recognition, and then map this to authentication in traditional systems. We then further develop the concept of end-to-end trust as required in pervasive computing environments and describe an end-to-end trust model. Finally, this model is applied for entity recognition.

2 The Need for Dynamic Enrollment in Pervasive Computing

In this section, we motivate and describe our entity recognition process.

2.1 Benefit of Pervasive Computing Comes from Unforeseen Interactions

The current IPv4 based Internet is likely to provide the foundation of any pervasive computing environment. However, mobile ad hoc networks (MANETs) are increasingly common [35] and bring interesting properties such as spontaneity. Mobile entities will have the chance to move and join networks in an ad hoc manner. In fact, as in real life, opportunities will be offered to entities roaming from place to place. These opportunities cannot be predicted because it is not known in advance where these entities will roam. Many other aspects are still unknown: even the scale of the networks of entities cannot really be evaluated; it is known that ad hoc networks will be possible but due to their nature we can not predict when they will be formed; nor can we predict which entities will interact together; etc. We can say that no individual organization will manage the whole; self-organization will have to emerge from these unmanaged networks along with new, previously unknown, features. The benefit of self-organized systems is that they can create higher level features [12]. Thus, pervasive computing will hopefully exhibit interesting properties to solve complex issues, where the diversity of entities opens the door for new opportunities. In the Resurrecting Duckling security policy model [29], ducklings have to take the risk to emerge from their shell in order to find their mother, who will look after them. In pervasive computing, the scenario is extended to other potentially caring entities such as friends but computational entities will not be able to identify friends without taking the risk to make friends of unknown entities. In MANETs, a node which is too far from an Internet gateway but has another node in wireless range, which is itself in range of the gateway, can only reach the gateway by forwarding packets to this node. Of course, the owner of this helping node can be unknown. In computing terms, the first risk will be to enroll unknown entities. A fundamental requirement for ubiquitous computing environments is therefore to allow for potential interaction with unknown entities.

2.2 Dynamic Enrollment

Generally, authentication schemes start with enrollment of entities. This task is often time consuming and requires explicit human intervention, e.g. from a system administrator. For example, integrating new users may involve considerable work and resources: a random initial secret may be sealed in an envelope and sent to the new user; it can be even worse for smart tokens, which can involve two separate activities – token programming and user management [27].

Usually, entities which have not been enrolled cannot interact. Collaboration is seen as a privilege that only specific entities can obtain, with the implicit assumption that it is known a priori which entities can obtain this privilege. The principle of least privilege is applied for interaction: some entities can interact; others cannot. In pervasive computing environments, collaboration should be possible between all entities; the most likely situation is that one of them has not previously enrolled. There is an inherent conflict between how enrollment is done in current computing systems and what is required for pervasive computing. This introduces the requirement for smooth dynamic enrollment, i.e. the door should not be closed to strangers, but instead any stranger showing up at the door might become an acquaintance. Since it is not known in advance which entities should get the privilege to collaborate, we argue that the principle of least privilege should not be applied for collaboration. We further argue that it is not possible to give pervasive entities exactly the privileges they really need. Instead, a practical approach, as in the real world, would be as follows: a small initial measure of trust is given to any entity so that it can be enrolled and begin collaborating, even though technically this gives permission to do things it should not be doing.

To allow for dynamic enrollment of strangers and unknown entities, we propose an entity recognition process. Table 1 compares the current authentication process (AP) with our entity recognition (ER) process.

There is no initial enrollment step at the beginning of the entity recognition process but this does not mean that enrollment cannot be done. Actually, in step E.3, if the entity to be recognized has never been met before, what will be retained is going to be reused the next time this entity is going to be recognized. Depending on the recognition scheme, it should be more or less transparent, i.e. more or less like the enrollment step in A.1. Thus, by moving down the enrollment step in the process, we emphasize that the door is still open for interacting with strangers and unknown entities. We can show that any authentication process can be integrated into an ER scheme (by doing enrollment at step E.3) and can also show that some ER schemes are not authentication schemes and thus that the class of authentication schemes is a proper subset of the class of entity recognition schemes. Further in this paper, we detail a "pure" recognition scheme – "A Peer Entity Recognition" scheme (APER).

A number of different sensing, recognition and retention strategies can be envisaged for entity recognition schemes. However, specifying retention strategies is the subject of ongoing work and beyond the scope of this paper. The detective work depends on which recognition scheme is used, for example, in the APER recognition scheme described in section 4.2, it may consist of sending a challenge/response.

By self-triggering (step E.1) we mean that the entity takes the initiative to start the recognition process in order to recognize potential surrounding entities, for example

Table 1. Authentication and entity recognition side-by-side

Authentication Process (AP)	Entity Recognition (ER)
A.1. Enrollment: generally involves an administrator or human intervention	
A.2. Triggering: e.g. someone clicks on a Web link to a resource that requires authentication to be downloaded	E.1. Triggering (passive and active sense): mainly triggering (as in A.2), with the idea that the recognizing entity can trigger itself
A.3. Detective work: the main task is to verify that the principal's claimed identity is the peer's	E.2. Detective work: to recognize the entity to be recognized using the negotiated and available recognition scheme(s)
	E.3. Retention (optional): "preservation of the after effects of experience and learning that makes recall or recognition possible" [30]
A.4. Action: the identification is subsequently used in some ways. Actually, the claim of the identity may be done in steps 2 or 3 depending on the authentication solution (loop to A.2)	E.4. Action (optional): the outcome of the recognition is subsequently used in some way (loop to E.1)

it may be starting the recognition scheme that involves the recogniser monitoring the network and selectively carrying out detective work on (some of) the identities that are observed. Step E.4 is optional since it is not required if the only objective is to gather recognition information. Step E.3 is also optional but the reason is different: recognition information need not be retained – say if the entity has been seen before.

To cope with scalability, we propose to forget about entities, that we have not collaborated with, after a certain time. Actually, the tremendous number of entities expected in a pervasive computing environment raises the question of how to scale entity recognition (or authentication) to billions of entities with potentially different distinguishing characteristics. In the next subsection, we describe how entities can be recognized by different means and represent different principals.

2.3 Virtual Anonymity

Our expectation is that entities are in general virtually anonymous to the extent that identity conveys little information about likely behaviour. What is important as a prerequisite is not really "Who exactly does this entity represent?" but "Do I recognize this entity as a trustworthy collaborator?" As there is no a priori information concerning likely behaviour; identity therefore does not imply privilege. We assume virtual anonymity and therefore we do not require (but do allow) the ability to establish the identity of a given entity in absolute terms, e.g. through globally unique and meaningful X.500 "distinguished names" [10]. The nature of MANETs makes it inherently difficult to rely on centralized or online servers. As an example, consider authentication based on Kerberos, which is based on the idea of having a global hierarchy of trust, where leaf and interior nodes trust their superior. This model does not work when the superior is not reachable, e.g. in MANETs where network partitions may be common. For a web of trust like PGP [36], there is still the question of whether trust [1, 5, 13] and recommendations [4, 14] are transitive. In fact, the entity itself is responsible for its final trust decision. In the end, the control should be in the owner's hands. Rather than relying on recommendation or reputation, entities can rely on their own previous interactions and past history with another entity as soon as the recognition is possible. This is why we simply require the ability to recognize other entities, e.g. through their name, location, digital signatures or other means. Collaboration amongst virtually anonymous entities is an approach to security in the global computing infrastructure. The Resurrecting Duckling security policy model [29] is an example of entity recognition; "ducklings" know their mother is the entity who sent the imprinting key when they were "born", i.e. they must be able to recognize the entity which sent the imprinting key, no more. Stajano speaks of anonymous authentication [28], which is also seen in other authentication work [4, 7].

To us, entities are virtually anonymous: any identifier can work as long as it allows for referencing the entity involved over the required lifespan. This means that the "real" identity in absolute terms is not needed. Through collaboration, trust will be associated with these identifiers. How does this trust information relate to the inherent trust of the identifier? Khare claims that there is trust in a name [16]. The next section explains what kind of inherent trust we expect in identifiers and what we mean by end-to-end trust.

3   End-to-End Trust Implications and Model

The first part of this section makes it clear that there is a layering of trust. Then, we explain how trust in the underlying technical infrastructure is linked with trust between entities to form end-to-end trust.

3.1   Acknowledging the Presence of Layers of Trust

Differences in the strength of authentication and recognition schemes obviously raise the question of trust in the underlying infrastructure. However, recognition is not the only technical piece of the infrastructure on which a trust assessment would be useful. In fact, trust at the entity level regarding interactions is meaningless if the low level information about the collaboration is invalid. There are therefore multiple layers of trust described below, which affect end-to-end trust. The overall trust level should be chosen at the application level. We first describe trust in technologies and follow this by describing a "higher" layer of trust, which is trust between entities.

Trust in the Technical Infrastructure. The trusted computing platform alliance (TCPA) [31] makes it clear that we can speak of trust in technical components. TCPA focuses on platform identity and integrity metrics to establish trust, which is defined as follows: "an entity can be trusted if it always behaves in the expected manner for the intended purpose" [30]. It is envisaged that the levels of integrity will be set either from experience or recommendation from experts and based upon either direct or indirect assessment of a platform.

We should also note that users ought not be bothered by a requirement that they frequently change security settings, since this would run counter to the requirement that ubiquitous computing should not monopolize the attention of the user [34].

Jøsang [15] gives another approach for assessing trust in underlying technologies based on a belief model, where trust is considered to be a subjective belief, a set of operators for combining beliefs and a combination of evidence such as for example security evaluation, security incidents, security advisory reports, system reputation, ISO 9000 certification or developer reputation. Again, the user should deduce from this evidence the trustworthiness of the system, which seems hard for security and technologically unaware users. Our specific focus, authentication, has even more work trying to define metrics to assess its trustworthiness [14, 22].

Trust between Entities. TCPA helps to deduce the trustworthiness in the underlying technology, partly thanks to collaboration between different on-line parties, e.g. a so-called "privacy CA". In return, as any collaboration implies, these different parties have to put more or less trust in their partners to allow for collaboration. Even if this trust assessment takes place at a higher level of abstraction – trust between entities – this highlights the fact that effectively a chain of trust is present in the background. Axelrod's question on real world cooperation [2] is transferred in pervasive computing as follows: when should an entity cooperate, and when should an entity be selfish, in an ongoing interaction with another entity? This time Marsh's model of trust [18] is a more relevant approach for this layer of trust. The SECURE project [24] aims at building secure environments for collaboration among ubiquitous roaming entities thanks to mechanisms based on the human notion of trust. A model for trust management is expected from this project. One may also mention Jøsang's work [13] or the use of a virtual trust currency, such as the trusto [25].

As mentioned above, dynamic enrollment as required in pervasive computing environments leaves the door open for any encountered entities to become an acquaintance. The question is now how to evaluate trust in such open and dynamic environments?

3.2   End-to-End Trust Model

We have identified layers of trust which can be divided into two main categories: trust in the underlying technology and trust between entities. The point is that these layers form an end-to-end trust, a chain of layers of trust. The overall trust is the result of how much trust is found at each level. Whether the final level of trust is acceptable or not is a separate issue. Some benefits of pervasive computing applications make it worth relying on not-so-trustworthy underlying technologies; there is a trade-off between what can be obtained and what can be lost. This trade-off has to be acknowledged and made clear. Our view is to set up a threshold at the end of the trust chain, most likely the application layer, which would indicate how much trust is required. This threshold may be represented by a value in the range [0,1], 1 for full trust and 0 for no need of trust.

A similar approach has been proposed in different authentication metrics [22]. In some way, it is equivalent to setting the trust level in an ASP.NET Web applications [20], even though in that case the trust "granularity" is coarser – consisting of only four levels: full, high, low, none. More complex metrics, such as Jøsang's subjective ones [14, 15], may be implemented at a later stage. To reach this threshold, trust at each layer has to be taken into account. This requires being able to evaluate the end-to-end trust, which is the result of trust in technology and in other entities.

For trust in the underlying technology, we could use metrics, dynamically calculated or statically defined by a group of experts, as detailed above in this paper.

For trust in entities, trust would be calculated based on the human notion of trust, probably thanks to direct observations, past history, and careful use of recommendation and reputation.

Again, as a starting point, we think of converting these two trust values on a scale between 0 and 1, where trust may be interpreted as the probability that an entity behaves in the expected manner for the intended purpose. Since both of these types of trust have no inheritance, we assume they are independent. This suggests the use of the following formula.

$$End\text{-}to\text{-}end\ trust = f(Trust\ in\ infrastructure,\ Trust\ in\ entities)$$

which can be as simple as:

$$End\text{-}to\text{-}end\ trust = (Trust\ in\ infrastructure) * (Trust\ in\ entities)$$

This formula acknowledges the idea that in pervasive computing the security properties of the underlying infrastructure are more or less strong, e.g. MANETs may come easily but they can also go easily. Indeed, to get the full potential of pervasive computing, the risks of using not-really-trustworthy environments have to be considered explicitly. Nevertheless, the above model helps to keep in mind that a risk has been taken. The next section shows how this can be applied for authentication in pervasive computing.

4   End-to-End Trust Model Applied at the Source – The Authentication Level

One of the foundations of security is authentication. Stajano [28] emphasized that without being sure with whom an entity interacts, the three fundamentals properties - confidentiality, integrity and availability - can be trivially violated. As explained at the beginning of this paper, in some cases, absolute security will not matter and weak recognition schemes may be used in order to still be able to collaborate, this is a choice to be made at the application level. This section explains how this will be applied for recognition by following the model described at the end of the previous section. Recognition is only one piece of the underlying technical infrastructure. However, other mechanisms have to be trusted after recognition, e.g. secure communication over networks after authentication. We consider the problem of implementing our approach for other parts of the underlying infrastructure as beyond the scope of this paper and we only explain how trust in the recognition scheme is reported into the end-to-end trust. We therefore assume secure communication channels for any collaboration that follows recognition.

First, we give an overview of the difference in trust for entity recognition schemes in pervasive computing. Then, we present a "pure" entity recognition scheme (APER). Finally, we give a coarse-grained description of our design and expected implementation.

4.1   Recognition Schemes with Different Technical Trust

Since any authentication scheme can follow the entity recognition process explained above, we already support a considerable set of "legacy" entity recognition schemes: symmetric and asymmetric keys, biometrics... Moreover, the openness required for enrollment suggests many more schemes to come, e.g. the APER scheme described in the next subsection.

On the other hand, each recognition solution will have to be assessed concerning its trustworthiness. Actually, we think of setting up a static value between 0 and 1 for each recognition scheme implemented. This value would be the consensus between different security experts concerning individual technologies, but other means may be used such as integrity metrics. The short list below gives an example of which value may be used for different recognition schemes based on the average attack space (AAS) [27]. These values are neither definitive nor reviewed but they are helpful to demonstrate the idea.

In 1999, the company RSA Security recommended to use public keys (PK) of at least 768 bits, which has an AAS of 76 bits but that can be attacked off-line. Well-designed biometrics, those that can only be attacked interactively, are considered strong when the false acceptance rate (FAR) is around 1 in 1000000 [27]. So, we consider that schemes respecting at least the latter criterion would get near to 1. Biometrics with higher FAR would get a value in proportion with the criteria for strong biometrics (e.g. a FAR of 1/100000 would get 0.1). With higher FAR, enrollment can be achieved more dynamically because learning phase is simpler. Imprinting with strong key (e.g. 128-bit AES, which gives an AAS of 127 bits [27]) in the Resurrecting Duckling scheme [29] would get near to 1 because it respects our criteria when off-line attacks are possible.

4.2   A Peer Entity Recognition Scheme (APER)

The APER scheme (pronounced "ape-er", based on the word "aping", meaning imitating) is designed to be usable to recognise peers on a network. It is explicitly not designed to associate an identity with the recognised peer, other than in terms of the cryptographic artefacts involved in the protocol. However, it does not prevent higher-layer code from associating an identity with the recognised peer (which is where identity can more usefully be handled).

APER assumes that the network supports some form of "broadcast" or "multicast" messaging, for example using IP broadcast or multicast addresses, or adopting an application layer broadcast approach.

APER has not (yet) undergone peer review for its security properties, therefore we only indicate the properties we assume it to have, which is fine for current purposes since the scheme is really a proof-of-concept for the "recognition is enough" argument. It is certainly clear that other schemes with similar properties can be developed.

There are two roles distinguished in APER, the recogniser and claimant (though any party can take on any role). The basic approach is for the claimant to occasionally (according to its own schedule) broadcast a digitally signed packet (a "claim") and for the recogniser to be able to challenge the claimant as desired. However, in contrast to most such schemes, it is also considered useful and, though weaker, often sufficient for the recogniser not to issue challenges, but simply to recognise the peer on the basis of correctly signed (and, perhaps, co-dependent) claims.

When a challenge is issued, producing a correct response to the challenge requires the claimant to possess the private key used to sign some previous claims. The recogniser can then much more safely (re-)associate the public key with the claimant's network address or other context information. The claimant may optionally include some context information (e.g. time, network-address, application-layer naming) in claims.

There is one further "trick" used in order to increase the recogniser's confidence that the claimant was responsible for previous claims. In order to provide evidence that the claim is "fresh", and not, e.g. copied from some other broadcast network, the claimant is required to (where possible) include within its claim the hashes over the last "n" claims which were seen on the network (by the claimant). If the recogniser has also seen one of these (the recogniser is assumed to record its own set of recently received claim hashes) then the recogniser can treat the claim as being "fresh".

So, we end up with three levels of recognition, any of which can be sufficient, depending on the end-to-end trust level set. Each level will have some associated parameters (e.g. the number of claims seen), which may also impact on how the recognition is treated. The levels are:

- Level 1: Claimants signature verified over a set of recently seen claims
- Level 2: Level 1 and claimants recent claims are "fresh", based on the "last-n-hashes" mechanism
- Level 3: Level 2 and the claimant successfully responded to a challenge

We describe the scheme in an algebraic notation in Table 2.

For key hygiene and other reasons a claimant may own as many key pairs as it wishes. However, for application and storage limitation reasons it will be beneficial for a claimant to reveal to a recogniser that it "owns" two keys. This is done by creating a new pair of claims in which the "that" field of one contains the value of the "this" field of the other and vice-versa. The recogniser can then treat the pair of recognised entities as one. If the application context requires, the recogniser can ask the claimant to do this by sending along a pair of "this" values which it would like to see bound. Clearly, this key binding can be extended to arbitrary sets of keys, and we term such sets key-chains. A useful way to ensure this binding is for the "this" and "that" values to be hashes of the "pointed-at" public keys or claims.

It may be argued that by associating context information (e.g. a network address) with the public key, we are really authenticating that information and that therefore the context information is taking the part of an identity. That, however, is not the case, as can be seen if we consider a case where a network address is included in a claim in the presence of a network address translation (NAT) box, where the claimant and

Table 2. APER scheme

Item	Description
"{x}y"	A digitally signed form of "x", verifiable using (and containing) public key "y"
"a,b"	The comma is used for catenation. "a,b" is the catenation of a and b
[x]	An optional field is enclosed in square brackets
C	Claimant
R	Recogniser
n, n',n"	Nonces, i.e. a long (say 128 bits) random values
PuC	A public key claimed by C
PrC	A private key that ought to be C's
Ctxt	(optional) Context information, e.g. time, network address, application scope
fresh	A value which provides evidence that the claim is "fresh", in this case, this contains the last-n-hashes value (during a bootstrapping sequence this may be empty)
this, that	Identifiers for claims used when binding claims together
c	A claim, c={n,[ctxt],fresh,[this,that]}PuC
chal	A challenge to C chal=n'
Resp	A response to chal. Resp={n",hash(chal)}PuC

recogniser will "see" different network addresses. (Note: we are not recommending either inclusion of addresses, nor NAT, but just using those to show that recognition can work where authentication is problematic, at best!)

That brings us to considerations of the overall strength and security of APER. As we said we are not providing proofs at this stage (since they are not needed for the main argument of this paper), but we claim that APER:

1. Provides a strong recognition scheme when challenges are issued.
2. Requires an attacker to compromise a claimant's private key to succeed in a useful attack against a real claimant.
3. Provides a useful recognition scheme even for recognisers who do not issue challenges. In particular, if a recogniser associates a quality of recognition with each claimant for which claims have been seen (using an algorithm which is yet to be developed, but probably based on the time-span over which claims with this key-chain have been seen), then the scheme is such that spoofing an application layer identity can be made arbitrarily hard by the recogniser.

5 Pluggable Recognition Module – High-Level Design

Ubiquitous computing environments mostly imply MANETs but also include all other kinds of networks as well, most obviously the current IPv4 Internet for which many authentication protocols have been developed to verify the identity claimed by a principal. Most of these authentication schemes assume a managed network. Open and dynamic environments with heterogeneous parties do not have network managers in the sense assumed, or even proper infrastructure in the case of MANETs. Adaptability to an entity's capabilities but also to the legacy authentication schemes is therefore required. For this reason, we are investigating an entity recognition module into which different recognition schemes can be plugged. The design of that pluggable recognition module (PRM) will be based on extending the Pluggable Authentication Module (PAM) [23]. PAM allows for the use of different legacy authentication schemes: Kerberos, smart cards, etc. In order to get dynamic enrollments, policies – regarding which authentication scheme or combination of authentication schemes should be used – cannot require an administrator to be effective. For pervasive computing, the degree of auto-configuration has to be increased. To achieve this, the appropriate recognition scheme must be negotiated either explicitly or implicitly (e.g. perhaps selected by an application). This negotiation should make use of the degree of trust needed which is set by the application. Choosing a weak recognition scheme, maybe one allowing for highly dynamic enrollment, will be possible but this choice will impact the end-to-end trust; the highest level of trust possible will be as high as the level of trust in the underlying technology. In doing so, privacy of the to-be-recognized entity can be taken into account during the negotiation. Certainly, if an authentication mechanism is not trustworthy, data exchanged cannot be really considered "private". In addition, the security of the recognizing entity is somehow protected because the end-to-end trust takes into account the technical infrastructure. Our approach implicitly takes into account that recognition impacts trust. Dynamic enrollment is possible because technical trust is taken into account. Therefore, as part of any recognition scheme, meta-data should be included to achieve a sufficient level of confidence in the recognition. We will have to create this feature in our PRM because PAM does not provide it.

6 Conclusion

Pervasive computing needs smooth dynamic enrollment to get the full benefits from spontaneous interactions with previously unknown entities. This unconditional enrollment creates a risk that should be made explicit, so that it can be taken into account. Under certain circumstances, due to limited capabilities of entities or the ad hoc nature of collaboration – the technical infrastructure available may be limited as well, and especially, the security of the underlying infrastructure can be very low. In fact, even seamlessly integrated in pervasive computing environments, the intermediate technical infrastructure is still a concern of trust. However this is only one layer of the end-to-end trust. Trust is also envisaged to facilitate opportunistic collaboration among ubiquitous digital roaming entities. Through continued collaboration, trust between such entities would be built and evolve. This notion takes place at the level of entities where technical components are abstracted. Trust in the underlying infrastructure and trust between entities form the end-to-end trust. Each layer has to be taken into account to assess the whole.

The foundation of computer security has been built upon authentication. With this view, for initial collaboration to be possible, it is first necessary to know with whom the interaction occurs. However, we argue that it is sometimes sufficient to find out whether previous collaboration has ended successfully rather than to get a precise identity without information about the likely behaviour of the entity. Therefore, entity recognition provides a more general basis for dealing with end-to-end trust. Pervasive computing requires a pluggable recognition module into which more or less secure/dynamic schemes can be plugged. However, it is essential to acknowledge how far each scheme should be trusted by reflecting their implicit impact on the end-to-end trust.

There are remaining issues in this approach such as the correlation of trust associated with identifiers based on different recognition schemes but pointing to one unique entity. Although combining a sequence of more or less trusted recognition schemes can aid against spoofing, the ease of building Byzantine attacks in such open environments is another problem. Weak recognition schemes make it really hard to ensure accountability. Another open issue is the question of how to trigger recognition, especially in case of self-triggering? This requires a trade-off between computing power spent for recognition and for other relevant processing.

This work is sponsored by the European Union which funds the IST-2001-32486 SECURE project.

References

1. Abdul-Rahman, A. and Hailes, S.: A Distributed Trust Model. In: Proceedings of the 1997 New Security Paradigms Workshop, pp. 48-60, ACM, (1997).
2. Axelrod, R.: The Evolution of Cooperation. ISBN 0-465-02122-0, Basic Books Publishers, (1984).
3. Blaze, M., Feigenbaum, J., and Keromytis, A. D.: Keynote: Trust Management for Public-Key Infrastructures. In: Proceedings of the Cambridge 1998 Security Protocols International Workshop, pp. 59-63, Cambridge, England, (1998).
4. Blaze, M., Feigenbaum, J., and Lacy, J.: Decentralized Trust Management. In: Proceedings of the 17th IEEE Symp. on Security and Privacy, pp. 164-173, IEEE Computer Society, (1996).
5. Christianson, B. and Harbison, W. S.: Why Isn't Trust Transitive?. In: Proceedings of the Security Protocols International Workshop, University of Cambridge, (1996).
6. Ducatel, K., Bogdanowicz, M., Scapolo, F., Leitjen, J., and Burgelman, J.-C.: That's what friends are for. Ambient Intelligence (AmI) and the IS in 2010. In: the congress of Innovations for an e-Society, Challenges for Technology Assessment Berlin, Deutschland, 17 - 19 Oktober 2001, (2001).
7. Ellison, C.: The Trust Shell Game. In: Bruce Christianson, Bruno Crispo, William S. Harbison and Michael Roe (Eds), Proceedings of the 6th International Workshop on Security Protocols, Lecture Notes in Computer Science, ISBN 3-540-65663-4, pp. 36-40, Springer, (1998).
8. IEEE: Pervasive computing. IEEE Magazine, http://www.computer.org/pervasive/.
9. IETF: Public-Key Infrastructure (X.509).
   http://www.ietf.org/html.charters/pkix-charter.html.
10. ITU: The Directory: Overview of Concepts, Models and Service. ITU-T Rec. X.500, Information Technology - Open Systems Interconnection, (1993),
    http://www.itu.int/home/index.html.
11. Jensen, C. D.: Secure Collaboration in Global Computing Systems. In: ERCIM News, vol. 49, (2002).
12. Johnson, S.: Emergence. ISBN 0-140-287-752, (2001).
13. Jøsang, A.: The right type of trust for distributed systems. In: Proceedings of the 1996 New Security Paradigms Workshop, ACM, (1996).

14. Jøsang, A.: A Subjective Metric of Authentication. In: J.- J. Quisquater, Y. Deswarte, C. Meadows, and D. Gollmann, editors, ESORICS'98. Louvain-la-Neuve, Belgium, Springer-Verlag, (1998).
15. Jøsang, A. and Knapskog, S. J.: A Metric for Trusted Systems. In: Proceedings of the 21st NIST-NCSC National Information Systems Security Conference, (1998).
16. Khare, R.: What's in a Name? Trust. 4K Associates, (1999), http://www.4k-associates.com/IEEE-L7-names-trust.html.
17. Kohl, J. and Neuman, B. C.: The Kerberos Network Authentication Service (Version 5). Internet Request for Comments RFC-1510, (1993).
18. Marsh, S.: Formalising Trust as a Computational Concept. PhD Thesis, Department of Mathematics and Computer Science, University of Stirling, (1994), http://citeseer.nj.nec.com/marsh94formalising.html.
19. Merriam-Webster: Merriam-Webster's Collegiate Dictionary. Website, http://www.m-w.com/.
20. Microsoft: .NET Framework General Reference: trust Element. Website, (2001), http://msdn.microsoft.com/library/default.asp?url=/library/en-us/cpgenref/html/gngrftrustsection.asp.
21. Philips: Philips Ambient Intelligence. Website, http://www.research.philips.com/InformationCenter/Global/FArticleSummary.asp?lNodeId=712.
22. Reiter, M. K. and Stubblebine, S. G.: Authentication Metric Analysis and Design. In: ACM Transactions on Information and System Security, vol. 2(2), pp. 138–158, (1999).
23. Samar, V. and Lai, C.: Making Login Services Independent of Authentication Technologies. Sun Microsystems, (1995), http://java.sun.com/security/jaas/doc/pam.html.
24. SECURE: Secure Environments for Collaboration among Ubiquitous Roaming Entities. Website, http://secure.dsg.cs.tcd.ie.
25. Seigneur, J. M., Abendroth, J., and Jensen, C. D.: Bank Accounting and Ubiquitous Brokering of Trustos. In: 7th Cabernet Radicals Workshop, (2002), http://citeseer.nj.nec.com/seigneur02bank.html.
26. Seigneur, J.-M., Farrell, S., and Jensen, C. D.: Secure ubiquitous computing based on entity recognition. In: Ubicomp'02 Security Workshop, Göteborg, (2002), http://www.cs.tcd.ie/Jean-Marc.Seigneur/publications/secureubicomper.pdf
27. Smith, R. E.: Authentication: from passwords to public keys. ISBN 0-201-61599-1, Addison Wesley, (2001).
28. Stajano, F.: Security for Ubiquitous Computing. ISBN 0470844930, John Wiley & Sons, (2002).
29. Stajano, F. and Anderson, R.: The Resurrecting Duckling: Security Issues for Ad-hoc Wireless Networks. In: Proceedings of the 7th International Security Protocols Workshop, pp. 172-194, (1999).
30. TCPA: TCPA Design Philosophies and Concepts Version 1.0. White paper, Trusted Computing Platform Alliance, (2000), http://www.trustedcomputing.org/docs/designv1_0final.pdf.
31. TCPA: Trusted Computing Platform Alliance. Website, http://www.trustedcomputing.org/.
32. Weeks, S.: Understanding Trust Management Systems. In: IEEE Symposium on Security and Privacy, Oakland, (2001).
33. Weiser, M.: The Computer for the 21st Century. Scientific American, (1991), http://www.ubiq.com/hypertext/weiser/SciAmDraft3.html.
34. Weiser, M. and Brown, J. S.: Designing Calm Technology. In: PowerGrid Journal, v 1.01, (1996).
35. Wexler, J.: Wi-fi world. Network World, (2002), http://www.nwfusion.com/wifi/2002/main.html.
36. Zimmermann, P. R.: The Official PGP User's Guide. ISBN 0-262-74017-6, MIT Press, (1995).

Embedding Distance-Bounding Protocols within Intuitive Interactions

Laurent Bussard and Yves Roudier

Institut Eurecom
Corporate Communications
2229, route des Crêtes BP 193
06904 Sophia Antipolis, France
{bussard,roudier}@eurecom.fr

Abstract. Although much research was conducted on devising intuitive interaction paradigms with pervasive computing devices, it has not been realized that authentication, an important need in this context, has a strong impact on the ease of use. More specifically, distance-bounding protocols are necessary in some of the most interesting scenarios in pervasive computing. This article describes a drag-and-drop interaction paradigm that enables strong authentication by embedding such a protocol within personal authentication tokens. This article also discusses how this paradigm can be used as the basis for performing user-friendly pervasive multi-party secure interactions.

1 Introduction

The pervasive computing paradigm relies on the establishment of relations between several appliances embedding invisible electronic processors and human users authenticated through some digital identifier, potentially none of these entities trusting each other. Authentication requirements are thus clearly renewed in the pervasive computing world: it is the interaction of several entities, some virtual, and some real, that should be secured, rather than the identity of a single virtual party. In addition, the context, time, and location of an interaction is essential to some pervasive transactions.

Security properties like trust, non-repudiation, access control, or privacy have to be redefined in relation with authentication. We have shown in [2] that existing approaches like [7] and [4] are not sufficient when strong authentication is expected and we have proposed a solution based on distance-bounding protocols. This paper further investigates how such protocols may be embedded within an intuitive interaction paradigm.

Section 2 describes the security and usability requirements that are specific to pervasive computing, in particular the new authentication requirements in pervasive systems. Section 3 presents the distance-bounding protocols necessary for authentication and their implications for artifacts. Section 4 finally discusses how to devise a user-centric and user-friendly interaction embedding such a protocol and presents several security mechanisms adapted to pervasive security scenarios.

D. Hutter et al. (Eds.): Security in Pervasive Computing 2003, LNCS 2802, pp. 143–156, 2004.
© Springer-Verlag Berlin Heidelberg 2004

2   Application Requirements: Usability vs. Security

It is well known that security can have a strong impact on usability. Security leads to more complex protocols, requires users action such as entering a password, and sometimes relies on additional tokens such as smart cards. In pervasive computing, when interacting with artifacts, the situation is even worse: as shown in [2] and reminded in Section 3, touching artifacts during authentication is the only way to ensure strong yet flexible authentication. Transparently securing pervasive computing environments, which have important usability and security requirements, is challenging.

2.1   Usability of the Environment

Interactions between users and artifacts can be complex but have to stay as transparent and intuitive as possible. If some service requires the explicit interaction of users with real-world objects, this interaction should be rendered as intuitive as possible.

Discovery and advertisement [12] approaches impose the selection of virtual representations of surrounding devices: it is obviously neither transparent nor intuitive to select a printer in a list on one's PDA when it stands in front of the user and could be directly selected by touching it.

Physical contact with the device whose service is required may be constraining in the sense that it has to be within physical reach, but is extremely intuitive for the user; rooms containing devices out of reach might even be equipped with authentication switches alike light switches. However, plain physical contact lacks the details provided by a computer interface, which suggests that combining both approaches might be relevant.

Multi-party interactions involving multiple devices and/or multiple users should be possible in pervasive environments. Most paradigms essentially focus on two party interactions scenarios, but scenarios of sales typically involve two people and one device for instance.

2.2   Security Requirements

Securing interactions between users and artifacts is mandatory as soon as resources have to be protected. Access Control is necessary to verify the rights of users interacting with the environment. It can be based on access control lists or on capabilities (e.g. authorization certificates [10]).

Pervasive computing environments are shared by numerous users. It is the reason why it is necessary to account for their respective actions and to keep a proof that some critical interaction happened. In this context, non-repudiation can be required for establishing user liability.

Artifacts have an important role in pervasive computing and it is thus necessary to have a way to verify their characteristics. For instance, an interaction may require that the rights of an artifact or who its owner is be verified. The establishment of trust relationships has to be investigated as well. For instance, Public Key Infrastructures (PKI) are useless in open environments (i.e. without a priori trust).

In addition, standard security protocols that are used in the Internet, Intranets, or e-commerce rely on connected models where it is always possible to reach a Trusted Third Party (TTP) such as a Bank or a Certificate Revocation List (CRL) for security checks. In pervasive computing environments, some artifacts are put together and start collaborating over personal area networks. Personal devices as well as self-standing appliances do not necessarily have access to remote servers or trusted third parties. In this case, security checks have to be adapted.

Last but not least, finding a way to ensure security without bothering users is not trivial. Prompting the user for credentials such as passwords each time he interacts with his environment is not a credible solution and does not fit with the expected transparency or "pervasiveness". Section 4 proposes a new user-centric approach based on personal tokens with contact interface that are used to touch devices in order to dynamically and securely create relationships. In this solution, the user is authenticated and his rights are used during the operation.

2.3   Strong Authentication in Pervasive Environments

Pervasive computing environments seem to head for totally wireless interactions, supposedly simplifying the interactions between artifacts. Unfortunately, wireless networks make it easier to snoop on some protocol or to attack it by inserting malicious traffic. *Artifact authentication* is thus an essential security feature.

Two divergent points of view have been developed in former works. The first one is concerned with providing a unified and informative interface to all services and artifacts. It relies on a purely virtual representation, accessible on a PDA for instance, in which the user chooses the service or specific artifact that he wants to make use of. In such an approach, traditional techniques of authentication and key distribution apply quite straightforwardly. This approach however does not bridge the gap between the theoretical representation of the environment and the reality of it: no proof is given that the printer in front of the user is the one that the PDA says should be in this room.

The other approach attempts to authenticate physical artifacts in the user environment. The problem of this category of interaction thus becomes to know if the user is really dealing with the right artifact or if the real service is embedded in this artifact. Work on constrained channels [7] and the Smart-Its Friend project [4] proposed solutions for authenticating parameters that characterize a context of interaction. As acknowledged in these works however, those approaches are *"only usable in situations that do not require strong authentication"*. Furthermore, the feedback provided to the user is very limited if only existent.

Depending on the criticality of the resources accessed or of the goods exchanged, it can be sufficient to base the access control or the transaction on weak authentication. However, pervasive computing will lead to numerous payment or micro-payment schemes and access to critical resources will take place in some applications. This paper aims at answering the following question: *Is it possible to define user-friendly interactions in pervasive computing environments requiring strong authentication?*

3   Pervasive Authentication and Distance

Common authentication and access control problems are not enough to deal with in the most open pervasive computing environments, where nothing is known about the surrounding devices. This section discusses the importance of determining the location together with classical authentication and the implication of this requirement in pervasive computing environments.

3.1   Attacking Location = Attacking Pervasive Authentication

Authenticating a user or finding his privileges commonly means deploying asymmetric cryptography and certificates, for instance, identity certificates and authorization certificates. Certificates contain the user's public key and some of his attributes, those data being signed by a trusted entity, the certification authority. When the user wants to access a resource, he presents his certificates and, thanks to a challenge-response protocol, proves that he knows the private key corresponding to the public key embedded in the certificate. In this scheme, protecting the private key is mandatory because anybody having access to it can impersonate the owner of this key i.e. use his identity and his rights. Figure 1 describes this attack: a token M_1 protects the private key K_{S-M_1} and is necessary to access resources. If K_{S-M_1} can be extracted, clones ($C_1 \cdots C_n$) can be created and can access resources that M_1 is authorized to access.

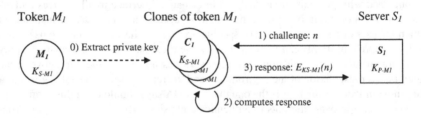

Fig. 1. Impersonation attack by stealing the private key

Generally, the private key is protected by a tamper-resistant token (e.g. a smart card) ensuring that the private key cannot be stolen. Moreover, it is necessary to generate the key pair within the token to ensure that only the public key can be known outside. Combining asymmetric cryptography and tamper-resistant modules ensures that a given physical token has to be involved during the certificate verification, i.e. during the challenge-response protocol, and ensures that the attack described in Figure 1 cannot occur.

However, this solution relies on the assumption that the authenticated device is talking directly to the verifier. Man-in-the-middle attacks between virtual entities, as assumed in classical protocols, are usually prevented by encrypting communications based on the public key of the impersonated entity. In pervasive computing however, such attacks occur between physical entities. Applications that involve the delivery of goods or authenticating the location of a person or token are thus vulnerable to this class of attack, a scenario that is quite different from that of classical protocols. This type of attack thus happens to be a major threat in pervasive computing environments since even though the real artifact or token may be involved in the authentication process, its physical location is not assured at all.

Figure 2 shows that even with tamper-resistant modules, it is possible to implement proxies that forward challenges and responses between the token and the entity verifying its attributes.

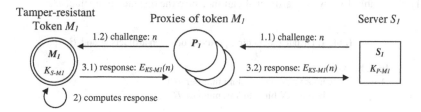

Fig. 2. Man-in-the-middle attack against a tamper-resistant token

Two solutions can be used to prevent proxy attacks and to offer strong authentication of artifacts: the artifact can be isolated when verifying that it knows a secret, or its vicinity can be determined with a distance-bounding protocol. The former approach is implemented to let automated teller machines (ATM) authenticate credit cards but it is not flexible enough to be used in most pervasive computing applications. The present work investigates how distance-bounding protocols can be integrated within simple interactions.

In many pervasive computing transactions, proximity and location verification are required during authentication of artifacts. For instance, a location stamping service can be necessary to prove the user or an artifact presence at a given place and time. If the location stamping service is implemented through a constrained channel, a peer-to-peer location sharing attack [2] can be mounted in order to obtain the stamp from anywhere: an accomplice of the attacker just needs to have access to the constrained channel (e.g. being in front of the location-stamp service) so that he can act as a proxy. Isolating the artifact is possible but may quite impede the user-friendliness or increase the cost of the solution. Distance-bounding protocols make it possible to prove that a given artifact is really present without resorting to its full isolation.

3.2 Distance-Bounding Protocols

A distance-bounding protocol associates a distance measurement and cryptographic properties in order to prove that a secret is known within a physical area. To ensure fast enough exchanges (i.e. a few nanoseconds), dedicated hardware interfaces and one-bit messages are required.

The artifact A wants to verify that the artifact B has some properties. B can show a certificate signed by a trusted certification authority (CA) which certifies that the owner of the public key K_{P_B} has some properties. The distance-bounding protocol is used to verify that the entity knowing the private key K_{S_B} is close enough and is not involved in a proxy attack.

The probability of successful attack can vary depending on the protocol used. In this paper, we will not use our initial proposal [2], but rather [1], which exhibits a lower probability of successful attack. This scheme, which was devised in the context of network authentication, can also be used for pervasive environments. One-bit challenges and one-bit responses being used, the probability of a successful attack during a single round is high: $1/2$. Using N rounds ensures that the probability of successful attack is $(1/2)^N$. Table 1 show how artifact A can measure the distance to artifact B.

Table 1. Distance-bounding protocol between artifacts A and B

1)   Initialization
1.1) A Choose a N bits random number R_A
1.2) B Choose a N bits random number R_B

2)   Rounds   (for $i \in \{1 \cdots N\}$)
2.1) A Start measuring round trip time
2.2) $A \Rightarrow B$ $R_A[i]$
2.3) $A \Leftarrow B$ $R_B[i]$
2.4) A Verify round trip time

3)   Verification
3.1) $A \leftarrow B$ $SIGN_B(R_A, R_B)$ where $SIGN_X(Y) = E_{K-S_X}(H(Y))$

During rounds $1 \cdots N$, the dedicated interface ($\Rightarrow$) is used and the response time is measured in order to evaluate the distance between A and B. Dedicated hardware and one-bit exchanges allow a few nanoseconds round trip time. If B cannot provide R_B to another artifact, the protocol can be used to prove that B is present. This protocol proves to A that it is in contact with an entity knowing K_{S-B}. If this is combined with tamper-resistant modules to protect the private key storage and use, A can be sure that it is in front of B. Within this paper, this protocol is symbolized by $A \rightsquigarrow B$. Mutual distance-bounding protocol ($A \leftrightsquigarrow B$) means that both A and B have verified that they have just been in contact.

To summarize, Security in Pervasive Computing relies on Certificates, Tamper-Resistant Modules, and Distance-Bounding Protocols:

$$SPC = CERT + TRM + DBP$$

3.3   Implementation Constraints

Different parameters have to be taken into account when implementing distance-bounding protocols. First, such protocols rely on a large number of simple rounds at each of which the probability of a successful attack is quite high. Such a protocol is thus difficult to be rendered fault-tolerant and has to be implemented on a noiseless channel.

Broadcast media such as radio are thus seemingly out of question for implementing these protocols.

In addition to these technical problems, radio does not offer a way to precisely select a (physical) artifact, which is essential for the user who wants to authenticate a precise device and not any device that can listen and answer to his requests. Contact based approaches are better in this respect, except when a user may want to access a device fixed to the ceiling. Alternately, a directive technique like the use of a laser may allow contacting wirelessly a precise artifact. It should be noted however that the laser performs two different tasks at the same time. It first selects a precise artifact and measures its physical distance, like the plugging in a contact based approach. It is then used to implement a distance-bounding protocol, therefore checking that the logical entity is effectively embodied in that artifact through the measurement of the time taken to transmit a secret. Performing these two tasks suggests a difficult technological integration.

Finally, mutual authentication is often expected and, in this case, the selection process has to be bi-directional. Again, defining a wireless approach based on lasers seems difficult in that case. The easiest solution is to use contact based approaches, be they electrical or optical.

In the following sections, we assume that each artifact offers a dedicated contact based interface for distance-bounding protocols (look at [2] for more details). Users that want to authenticate artifacts can touch them with a trusted artifact (PDA, electronic ring, etc).

4 Pervasive Security Mechanisms

As explained in Section 3, an electric contact is the easiest if not the only reasonable way to reach a strong authentication of pervasive computing artifacts. The requirement for a contact has a major impact on the possible secure interactions that can be defined. However, it fits well with scenarios involving a direct contact between users and artifacts. This section presents a solution that combines the use of tamper-resistant tokens and distance-bounding protocols in order to secure intuitive interactions between human beings and artifacts.

4.1 Presence of User

Distance-bounding protocols can be used to verify that an artifact is physically present. When it is necessary to check if a human being is present during a transaction or to deliver a proof of location, it is in fact the presence of his token that is verified, the token being for instance an electronic ring [9] that can be worn by the user. Tokens may potentially carry numerous rights such as accessing office, house, car, communication, and entertainment services, and may be used to sign documents, for payment, or to delegate rights. However, even such tokens can be stolen: directly authenticating the user of a token is thus critical. PIN codes are generally used to unlock tokens such as SIM cards. However, in pervasive computing, it is not possible to rely on passwords for each interaction because it suppresses intuitiveness. Two mechanisms can be proposed to diminish the threats on the personal token: when the interactions are done online, it is possible to create a token revocation list; when the interactions are done offline it is necessary to lock the token periodically. Both rely on surrounding artifacts: the former needs a terminal to add the token to the revocation list; the latter requires a way to delegate the right of unlocking the token to another artifact. For instance, an e-ring could be unlocked by entering a PIN code on a cell-phone or by touching a given finger print reader.

In the following, we will assume that each user U carries a personal token T_U that identifies him and that is used to interact with surrounding artifacts. We propose to implement tokens as tamper-resistant electronic rings with dedicated distance-bounding interface. They can be used for protecting the private key K_{S_U} of their owner and to select other artifacts by touching them.

Each artifact A_i has its own private key $K_{S_{A_i}}$. It is possible to provide rights to an artifact by defining an authorization certificate. The features and the owner of an artifact may also be defined by attribute certificates.

4.2   Seamless Trust

Trust relationships are bi-directional and often asymmetric. When using an artifact, it is necessary to verify whether it can be trusted. And, when lending an artifact or providing some service, abusive usage must be prevented.

Pervasive computing requires the most transparent interaction semantics in order to remain intuitive: touching a device holds such a promise. For instance, a user may plug his ring into an ATM in order to be authenticated and retrieve money. If he wants to prevent proxy attacks, the setup will be slightly more complex so that, for instance, he gets warned with a blinking led on his ring that the device he believes to be an ATM is potentially a fake because it cannot associate a certificate issued by a bank with a distance-bounding protocol. In addition, interesting interactions often involve three or more artifacts. For instance, the user can have to connect two artifacts using his ring.

This paper focuses on scenarios in which there exists a form of *a priori* trust that can be based on a public key infrastructure or a web of trust. For instance, interactions with ATMs rely on the knowledge of the bank's public key; working with artifacts owned by another company requires the prior establishment of relationships.

The following subsections describe how the *drag-and-drop* metaphor can be recycled to implement several security mechanisms that often come up in pervasive scenarios: how to be sure that an artifact conforms to some specification? How to enable an artifact to perform some access on behalf of a user? How to provide some proof about an operation? Finally, how to be sure of the ownership of an artifact and how to transfer it?

4.3   Verifying Attributes of Artifacts

Data are often associated with a physical object, be it a comment associated to paintings in a museum or the expiring date of some food. Protecting those data against forgery requires certifying and linking them to the artifact thanks to a distance-bounding protocol. For instance, when someone buys an artifact, let's say a pervasive Swiss watch or a pervasive box of pills, it is necessary to verify that the manufacturer did actually certify this artifact. Mechanisms ensuring that artifacts (or at least the chips associated to these artifacts [7]) cannot be cloned and that they are physically present are required. Certification can be based on a PKI, a web of trust, or ad-hoc mechanisms.

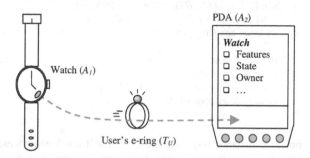

Fig. 3. Drag-and-drop to show attributes of an artifact

Requirements. This approach relies on the following hypotheses:

- Tamper-resistant hardware are available
- Hardware interfaces dedicated to distance-bounding protocols are deployed.
- Everybody has a unique personal token (e-ring) that is used for authentication and interactions.

A tamper-resistant token takes care of its owner's private key. Each artifact has its own asymmetric key pair that allows their certification (features, rights, owner). Strong authentication of users and artifacts is ensured by asymmetric cryptography and a distance-bounding protocol. Figure 3 shows how a drag-and-drop mechanism can be used to intuitively display the characteristics of an artifact. This protocol ensures that the displayed data correspond to the artifact that has been touched (e.g. the watch). The user trusts his token to perform a distance-bounding protocol with the artifact. The artifact can be verified anonymously using the token, hence protecting the user privacy. Alternately, the artifact can require the user identity or an authorization to control access to its services or resources.

Protocol Description. Table 2 describes how a drag-and-drop protocol can be used between two artifacts in order to verify attributes of the first one.

The user touches the two artifacts in succession with his token. The protocol is described in two parts: drag, which is the interaction between the token T_U and the artifact A_1, and drop, which is the interaction between the token and another artifact A_2. In 1.2, T_U receives a certificate describing A_1 signed by a Certification Authority (CA). In 1.3, T_U verifies that the touched artifact knows the private key $K_{S_{A1}}$ corresponding to the certified public key $K_{P_{A1}}$. As a result of the drag operation, the token has the proof that *it touched an artifact knowing $K_{S_{A1}}$* and that *CA certifies that the entity knowing $K_{S_{A1}}$ has some attributes*. In 2.1, T_U drops the certificate of A_1 to A_2. It is certified by T_U.

Table 2. Basic drag-and-drop protocol between two artifacts

1) Drag
1.1) $T_U \rightarrow A_1$ <Get description>
1.2) $T_U \leftarrow A_1$ $CERT\text{-}A_1 = CERT_{CA}(K_{P_{A1}}, attributes)$
                where $CERT_X(Y) = Y, SIGN_X(Y))$
1.3) $T_U \rightsquigarrow A_1$ Distance-bounding protocol

2) Drop   (before timeout)
2.1) $T_U \rightarrow A_2$ <Put description>:
                $CERT_{TU}(T_U$ touched $A_1, CERT\text{-}A_1)$
2.2) A_2 Display description of A_1

On a side note, the distance-bounding protocol, for it involves nonces, provides a one-time proof that the token is in contact with the owner of the secret key each time it is performed. No additional nonce or timestamp is required in the derived protocol. In any case, a timer should be available in the token to cancel operations if the drag is not performed after some timeout.

This scheme can be extended. For instance, in 1.2, mutual authentication could be required in order to provide access control so that A_1 only delivers description to authorized tokens. In this case, there is an obvious tradeoff between access control and privacy, that is, can anonymous drag be used or not.

4.4 Pervasive Access Control

In pervasive computing environments, the initialization of services has to be as transparent as possible. Figure 4 shows how an MP3 player should be connected to a headset: the user drags the song from one artifact to the other and dynamically creates a new relationship. In this context, secure pairing of artifacts can be achieved thanks to the drag-and-drop metaphor.

However, access control can be required and it can be necessary to know who is performing the drag-and-drop in order to verify his rights and possibly to charge him. Artifacts receive rights, for instance, an MP3 player can be allowed to pay up to a given amount when downloading a song. Bob can authorize Alice to drive his car or enter his house by providing a credential to her token.

Figure 4 shows how artifacts can be dynamically associated by a user. It is necessary to take into account the rights and ownership of the user and of the involved artifacts to define the rights of the artifact, how long they will remain in effect, etc.

The MP3 player and the headset know that a given user touched them one after another. They can then use a wireless medium to establish a connection and enable the headset to play some music according to the rights of this user.

Requirements. It is necessary to use a distance-bounding protocol to ensure that only the touched artifact (i.e. the headset) will receive the access to the service delivered (i.e. music delivered by the MP3 player). When the interaction leads to more strategic access rights (i.e. confidential data or physical access), it becomes mandatory to verify who

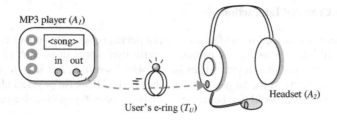

Fig. 4. Drag-and-drop to initiate a new relationship

receives the authorizations. The protocol is similar to Section 4.3. However, after the drop operation, A_2 is able to contact A_1 through a wireless medium such as Bluetooth in order to establish the service.

Protocol Description. Table 3 is an extended version of the basic drag-and-drop protocol defined in Table 2. It ensures mutual authentication and mutual proof of contact.

Table 3. Drag-and-drop protocol to start a service between two artifacts

1) Drag
1.1) $T_U \rightarrow A_1$ <Get description>
1.2) $T_U \leftarrow A_1$ <Require mutual authentication>
1.3) $T_U \rightarrow A_1$ $CERT\text{-}T_U = CERT_{CA_1}(K_{P_U}, attributes)$
1.4) $T_U \leftarrow A_1$ $CERT\text{-}A_1 = CERT_{CA_2}(K_{P_{A1}}, attributes)$
1.5) $T_U \rightsquigarrow A_1$ Mutual distance-bounding protocol

2) Drop   (before timeout)
2.1) $T_U \rightarrow A_2$ <Put description>
            $CERT_{T_U}(T_U \text{ touched } A_1, CERT\text{-}A_1)$
2.2) $T_U \leftarrow A_2$ <Require mutual authentication>
2.3) $T_U \rightarrow A_2$ $CERT\text{-}T_U$
2.4) $T_U \leftarrow A_2$ $CERT\text{-}A_2 = CERT_{CA_3}(K_{P_{A2}}, attributes)$
2.5) $T_U \rightsquigarrow A_2$ Mutual distance-bounding protocol

3) Service
3.1) $A_2 \rightarrow A_1$ <Negociate service>

After step 1, T_U knows which device has been touched by user U and artifact A_1 is waiting for a service call. After step 2, artifact A_2 knows that user U touched successively (i.e. within a given timeout) artifacts A_1 and A_2. In 2.1, A_2 received the attributes of A_1, including its network address. During step 3, A_2 gets in touch with A_1 to negotiate the service. Both have been touched by the same user and thus can use his rights or charge him when delivering the service.

4.5   User Centered Interactions

Previous sections focused on artifacts, but many pervasive scenarios rather emphasize user centered interactions, and in particular, multi-user interactions. Part of the trust and rights associated to a device relates in fact with its owner, and it is necessary to bridge the gap between the human being and his device. Because physical ubiquity is impossible, this task should also benefit from distance-bounding protocols as discussed in this section.

Non-repudiation.   Non-repudiation of interaction aims at proving that an interaction occurred between users and/or artifacts. Distance-bounding protocols are not sufficient to ensure non-repudiation. Indeed, after a distance-bounding protocol $A \rightsquigarrow B$, the artifact A verified that B is within some distance. However this information must be associated with a certain context: providing a non-repudiation service to a pervasive interaction may not only require certifying the identity of the involved parties, but also the time at which it occurred and the history of previous interactions, for instance. Different types of non-repudiation (e.g. order of interaction, initiator, target) can be integrated within the drag-and-drop protocol.

If two artifacts have to sign a proof of contact after performing a mutual distance-bounding protocol, it is necessary to ensure a fair exchange. Depending on the context, this issue can be solved directly by the tamper-resistant module within the involved artifacts or with a trusted third party.

Ownership Management.   A straightforward way to define trust levels is to base them on ownership. In that case, the level of trust depends on the type of an artifact and on its owner. Security policies can define whether a device owned by a friend or a partner company can be trusted enough to be involved in specific transactions. For instance, a corporate security policy could define that confidential data can be displayed on part-ners' displays but only the company's devices can be used to access secret data.

The management of ownership is also required to support the trading of artifacts. Ownership should be based on certificates too, the initial certificate being signed by the first owner, which could be the manufacturer. Such an imprinting could be similar to the approach proposed in [13]. When a user wants to trade an artifact, he has to use a distance-bounding protocol in order to verify that he becomes the owner of the device he is holding. It is possible to define intuitive interactions based on the drag-and-drop metaphor: for instance, the seller and the buyer could each touch the device in sequence and within a given timeout in order to change its ownership. When more complex exchanges are required (e.g. involving money), the semantics of the drag-and-drop is too poor. In this case, it may be necessary to extend these semantics with other artifacts able to display trading information (e.g. a PDA).

Proof of Context.   Accurate location and proximity information is very important to secure pervasive computing environments. For instance, an employee may obtain access rights whenever he enters the building of his corporation.

Proxy attacks should especially be expected in short range or personal area networks (e.g. W-LAN) which are notoriously insecure with respect to location. Protocols based on distance-bounding would be more than useful for instance for employees in a meeting room. Each of them could touch the meeting table with their e-ring to become part of a meeting group. Physically authenticated members would then receive a group key allowing them to share some data, for instance as long as they are together. Without the use of a distance-bounding protocol, one member of the group could act as a proxy and let someone, who is not in the meeting room, become a legitimate member of the group and have access to group identity based functions.

Users can also use proof of location to subsequently prove that they went somewhere or meet someone. The history of their actions may then serve to elaborate a key infrastructure or to deduct a trust level for their devices.

5   Conclusion and Future Work

Protection against impersonation attacks requires the association of asymmetric cryptography, tamper-resistant modules, and distance-bounding protocols. This combination makes it possible to verify whether one is really interacting with an identified appliance. The implementation of a distance-bounding protocol also implies the use of a small personal token able to perform cryptographic operations yet portable. However, authentication alone is not enough, especially because users manipulate appliances, not virtual services or cryptography.

The proposal made in this paper is to integrate the authentication phase performed with the personal token together with an intuitive model of interaction with appliances. This paper illustrates the use of the simple and familiar drag-and-drop paradigm to introduce security mechanisms specific to pervasive applications like managing the ownership of a device or manually performing access control between two artifacts.

The scenarios depicted in this paper essentially assume that every artifact has a network connection that can be used to connect to a trust infrastructure. Yet, the drag-and-drop approach developed can be useful to alleviate this limitation. For instance, personal token may be exploited as a repository for certificates: users would thus bring a small part of the public key infrastructure with them. It should be noted that in general, trust remains difficult to achieve in a decentralized situation where replay attacks on the services offered by an appliance are likely to happen because of the distributed nature of the system. We are currently developing one-time certificates to address this issue.

The *a priori* trust assumption that is made in the scenarios presented in this paper is correct in many business situations. However, open pervasive environments can be envisioned where this assumption does not hold because there is absolutely no prior relationship between users or appliances. Signing a transaction may as well be devoid of any legal liability in scenarios where the user travels to a country with a different legislation. We are investigating new mechanisms to deal with such open trust scenarios.

Finally, the protection of the user privacy [11] is a rather critical issue in pervasive computing [8] that may seem in contradiction with authentication. The one-time certificate mechanism mentioned above might just help dealing with an appliance without revealing one's identity.

References

1. Brands S. and Chaum D.: Distance-bounding protocols (extended abstract). EUROCRYPT 93, volume 765 of Lecture Notes in Computer Science, pages 344-359. Springer-Verlag, 1994, 23-27 (May 1993).
2. Bussard L., Roudier Y.: Authentication in Ubiquitous Computing, Ubicomp 2002, Workshop on Security in Ubiquitous Computing, (Sept 2002).
3. Covington, M.J.,. Moyer, M.J., and Ahamad, M.: Generalized Role-Based Access Control for Securing Future Applications. In 23rd National Information Systems Security Conference (2000).
4. Holmquist, L.E., Mattern F., Schiele B., Alahuhta P., Beigl M., and Gellersen H.W.: Smart-Its Friends: A Technique for Users to Easily Establish Connections between Smart Artefacts, In Proc. of UBICOMP 2001, Atlanta, GA, USA (Sept. 2001).
5. Kagal L., Finin T., and Joshi A.: Trust-Based Security in Pervasive Computing Environments. In IEEE Computer Volume 24, Number 12, pages 154-157. (December 2001).
6. Kahn J.M., Katz R.H., and Pister K.S.J.: Next Century Challenges: Mobile Networking for 'Smart Dust'. In MOBICOM, pages 271-278, (1999).
7. Kindberg T., Zhang K., and Shankar N.: Context authentication using constrained channels. In Proceedings of the IEEE Workshop on Mobile Computing Systems and Applications (WMCSA), pages 14–21, (June 2002).
8. Langheinrich M.: Privacy by design- principles of privacy-aware ubiquitous systems. In ubicomp2001, volume 2201 of LNCS, pages 273-291, (2001).
9. Meloan S.: Inside the Java Ring event. http://java.sun.com/features/1998/07/ring-project.html
10. Network Working Group: Request for Comments 2693: SPKI Certificate Theory, (September 1999).
11. Pfitzmann A., Köhntopp M.: Anonymity, Unobservability, and Pseudonymity - A Proposal for Terminology. Workshop on Design Issues in Anonymity and Unobservability (2000).
12. Richard G.G.,: Service Advertisement and Discovery: Enabling Universal Device Cooperation, IEEE Internet Computing, vol. 4, no. 5, (September/October 2000).
13. Stajano F. and Anderson R.: The Resurrecting Duckling: Security Issues for Ad-hoc Wireless Networks, 7th International Workshop on Security Protocols Proceedings, (1999).

Trust Context Spaces: An Infrastructure
for Pervasive Security in Context-Aware Environments

Philip Robinson and Michael Beigl

Telecooperation Office, Institut für Telematik, Universität Karlsruhe
{Philip,Michael}@teco.edu

Abstract. The issue we have focused on in the broad area of security for Pervasive Computing is maintaining trust in an interactive environment. Our solution is based on the premise that computers and implicit interaction mechanisms must function in accordance with the explicit parameters of physical human-human interaction. Otherwise, this results in imbalances between the physical and virtual worlds, which leads to "windows of vulnerability". Our solution presented requires an infrastructure of pervasive and context sensing technology, to provide entity mapping, policy and trust management services. We also investigate generating cryptographic keys using the context available The underlying technology is based on the Smart-Its context sensing, computation and communications platform.

1 Introduction

A primary driving force behind ubiquitous and pervasive computing research is the focus on bridging the divide between real-world-oriented tasks and the interfacing of facilitating technology [23, 32]. Want et al state in their 1999 paper [31], "There has long been a discontinuity between the rich interactions with objects in our physical world and impoverished interactions with electronic material." The narrowing of this discontinuity is primarily attributed to developments in Wearable and Smart-Appliance computing technologies [10]. They transform our computing experience into a more personal yet more personalize-able one. They allow a measure of freedom from location with respect to availability of services, yet the rendering of these services may be dependent on the location. Our identities are represented or impersonated by the devices we carry [9], such that we, our physical documents, and other physical artefacts often possess what is known as a "virtual counterpart" [20].

We believe that many security issues in Pervasive Computing stem from the difficulty of coordinating the symbiosis of physical and virtual entities or counterparts. In section 2, we elucidate this premise of "Virtual-Physical Imbalances and Security Vulnerability" by way of scenarios. Section 3 evaluates other existing work relevant to this theory, while section 4 presents our proposed solution called "Trust Context Spaces", including the goals, components and technology. We conclude with our expectations, intended contributions and scope for future work.

D. Hutter et al. (Eds.): Security in Pervasive Computing 2003, LNCS 2802, pp. 157–172, 2004.

2   Virtual-Physical Imbalances: Opening Security Vulnerability Windows

Security starts with an analysis of risks. It is then the means by which we seek to limit access to items or knowledge that have some value to us. The extremities of these limitations range from oneself to a group of trusted peers. The benefits of electronic media including data organization, querying and exchange, facilitate more efficient collaboration and generation of business decisions and notifications. In pervasive computing, this may however include interaction with devices and services without the same owners, and no prior knowledge of the character or background of each other's impersonated identity [15]. Brown et al in [5] define six categories for pervasive context-aware applications, namely, proactive triggering of events, streamlining interaction, memory for past events, reminders for future events, optimising patterns of behaviour, and sharing experience. These sorts of applications enhanced with implicitly communicated context information may cause unintended leakage of information, even if there was an explicit physical effort to avoid this. The two scenarios below are characterized by more than one of the pervasive categories given above.

2.1   Imbalances within Personal Areas

When I choose to pack my personal items away in my brief case, this is an indication that no one is to see them. If this physical action is not equally and thoroughly supported by the virtual world, then this is a potential point of vulnerability that may be exploited by an outsider. We refer to such situation as "implicit sharing of resources". That is, while we use implicit interactions to gain some benefit of services, it often comes with the sacrifice of implicitly forfeiting my right to control the access to the piece of information distributed [27]. However, the result of completely forgoing implicit interaction leads to an overload of management tasks and frequent interrupts. Consider if I have to be worried about maintaining the secure environment of the physical documents in my desks, the physical keys that I carry around in my pocket, coupled with the numerous passwords and PINs that I carry around in my head [2]. This is clearly an administrative overload from the perspective of security, and something that we need to consider in our research. In any event, it is still in a person's best interest and within their rights to be confident in both the physical and virtual provisions of security.

Security is not only about protecting oneself (privacy), but also about groups collectively protecting their resources and knowledge produced during meetings and other form of interaction.

2.2   Imbalances within Shared Environments

We considered a further situation where information is explicitly shared within an assumed controlled and trusted setting and environment. However, the interaction that leads to distribution of electronic meeting articles may be implicit from the perspective of the pervasive computer systems at work [7, 9, 26]. Such is the case when a presentation is shared with a defined group of attendees, through graphics, text and voice. These

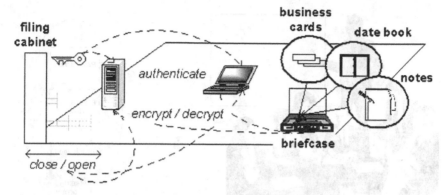

Fig. 1. Example of how physical artefacts may be mapped to virtual/ electronic applications and data, depicting a metaphor for explicit indication of need-for-privacy or personal security.

media elements may also be captured in electronic form for storage, reuse, or recording of what occurred in the presentation. The participants also have digital identities as their personal devices may impersonate them, or there was some issuance of group IDs or personal tokens during a registration phase, prior to the meeting.

During this meeting, it may so happen that subgroups wish to exchange information within a separate context not included in the main stream of discussion. From a device and application perspective, creation of a new session and hence security context would be necessary. This would entail generation and distribution of new session keys for the subgroup. Group management (Join| Leave | Parse | Merge) is therefore an undertaking for both the physical and virtual systems at work, as participants possibly come and go [16]. Furthermore, consider unofficial people entering the room at untimely intervals, causing disruption to the proceedings and becoming privy to information perhaps not intended for their knowledge. Very likely scenarios for imbalance between virtual and physical worlds that may occur include an electronic presentation continuing to be displayed, even though the physical presentation has been put on pause, devices continue to interact in spite of the cessation of interactive activity among their real-world peers, or electronic files have been locked away (devices turned off or files logically encrypted), yet their physical information equivalents remain in the open.

Sharing of interactive context and therefore the need to establish a Trust Context Space can be as a result of being in the *same place* and the *same time*, in *different places* but at the *same time*, in the *same place* but at *different times*, and finally, in *different places* and at *different times*. Nevertheless, as Brown et al state, "...a user should be able to retrieve [context] information about who was present at a meeting while they were present, but not to find out who came and went after they had left" [5].

2.3 Security Vulnerabilities

Arbaugh et al suggest two state models in [3], representing system vulnerability lifetime and system state with respect to vulnerability. Vulnerability is said to go through the

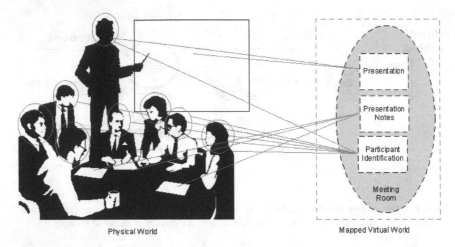

Fig. 2. People and artefacts in group meetings may also have physical/ virtual mappings.

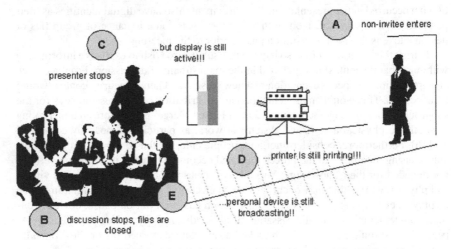

Fig. 3. Meeting scenario showing imbalance between virtual and physical worlds.

phases of birth to death, with the possible intermediate states surrounding the discovery and correction of the causative flaws. Accordingly, a system is said to be "hardened" when its integrity, expected usage and behaviour remain consistent, "vulnerable" when potentially weakening flaws are discovered, and "compromised" when the discovered flaw is exploited at least once. The goal of systems design and management from the perspectives of safety and security are to first curtail the existence of vulnerabilities, minimise the time the system spends in the state of vulnerable, or to recover in a timely manner if the system has reached a state of compromised.

What is special about security vulnerabilities in pervasive computing? While this is a very application-dependent question, there are some broad characteristics that do have immediate implications for security. Firstly, pervasive computing facilitates a greater overlap of virtual application and physical context, resulting in a larger interactive context [1, 4, 26]. The interactive context includes communications, processing, storage and I/O, which all influence the way that security is realized. Secondly, and consequently, the scope for implicitly shared information has become wider as context-awareness has become a more prominent feature of pervasive systems. Figure 4 depicts these anomalies.

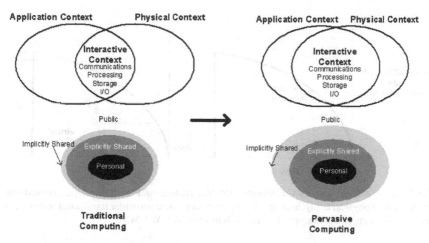

Fig. 4. Change in security considerations, moving from traditional to pervasive computing. These two concepts go together to define a Trust Context Space.

2.4 Pervasive Security Vulnerability Windows

Based on this look into the state-of-affairs, we describe security vulnerability windows in pervasive computing as the instances where information is implicitly shared with other peers through an inconsistency in the interactive context. This may be resultant from the sequencing of events in the physical world, including actions with explicit security implications, not being interpreted by the virtual world correctly or timely. Consider two people that have just discovered each other and are now at the stage of making decisions pertaining to trust; however, their personal devices are already interacting and exchanging pieces of information. This may be applied to the scenarios described earlier, where the people in the physical environment have made a decision not to share presentation information with an outsider, yet this was not the total reflected response of the virtual elements. Figure 5 gives a graphical representation of this.

In order for at least two peers to form an interactive relationship, or form a communications channel, they typically go through the phases of peer discovery, which is followed by some form of authentication, evaluation of trust, and channel assembly based on the policy for the communication. The final stage is of course a termination of communications. The issues in pervasive computing for spontaneous authentication, authorisation and trust are being addressed in the ad hoc networking and nomadic computing communities [33, 18, 11]. However, what we want to deal with a bit more is the effects of implicitly ordered invocation of these actions by the virtual counterpart, without proper guidance and sanctioning by the physical counterpart. This leads to weak forms of authentication and weak bases for determination of trust, and consequent weak constraining of any communications channels.

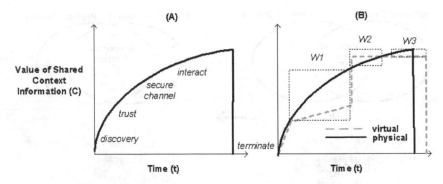

Fig. 5. Example State charts for Collaborative Context Transitions. Plot (B) is a superimposed plot of virtual over physical entity, highlighting the instances where particular transitional imbalances are cited, and depicted as Security Imbalance Windows (W1, W2, W3).

Having deliberated over this issue, we have two research agendas within the area of pervasive security; firstly, to *minimize the occurrence of security vulnerability windows*, and secondly, to *constrain the ill effects of implicit sharing of information*. Section 3 goes on to present our foundation themes that we considered.

3   Principles and Related Work

Within our lab, we have had practical experience with developing and using applications with multiple sensors for validation of situations and association of entities and events [4, 10]. Our first experiment with using simple sensor reading to associate items was the Smart-Its friends prototype [10], which allows a simple everyday activity, such as shaking, to create a logical association between items shook in the same instance, pattern and speed. This led us into investigations of combining more context variables (or sensor readings) into deriving association patterns, and coined this work the "generation of a *Context Key*". The use of this concept is outlined further in section 4, along with the required technology and experimental observations. Nevertheless, there is a wealth of research that we have found related to our concepts, and have evaluated their contributions to a solution for the issues we have highlighted.

3.1   Security through Physical Artefacts

Smart Cards represent a well-secured and limited interface device for transporting a person's virtual identification [8]. Therefore, when a person uses a Smart Card to open a door, it may trigger simultaneous virtual events associated with that person physically and explicitly announcing their authenticated presence. Furthermore, their well-known use in GSM mobile equipment to contain a user's credentials allows a network operator to react if the person's virtual identity has been stolen or involved in irresponsible use of resources. The field of Biometrics can also be considered as an even more intimate use of physical artefacts (our own bodies) in creating a link to our virtual identities. Fingerprints, retina scans and even more obscure things like footsteps [24] are used or are being further researched as ways of uniquely identifying a personality. The pervasiveness of fingerprint or retina scanners is a bit questionable, but having more loosely coupled sensors is more relevant for our work.

3.2   Secure Group Management (Secure Multicast)

The scenario described in section 2.2 indicated to us that some of the resources for tackling virtual-physical imbalances were to be found in the secure multicast community. There are two major techniques used to manage and exchange security context information amongst groups. One technique uses public key concepts, such as Diffie-Hellmann, to organize peers in a tree structure with the root being the overall group key [16]. However, peers remain autonomous with respect to generation of their private keys. Other techniques are based on symmetric cryptography, where n peers share a secret, such that at most two peers can reconstruct the entire group secret [29]. In any event, there are some criteria for good secure multicast key management techniques, which we endeavour to incorporate in our overall goals [16]. In summary they suggest that old members should not be capable of deriving the new group secrets (the context key in our case) and new members should not be able to derive those used before.

3.3   Virtual Identity Management

Perhaps if we have adequate means of coordinating our virtual identities then this is the solution to virtual-physical imbalances. The researchers at Freiburg University present a prototype that shows how a user-interface can change based on which identity the user assumes as a result of his context, primarily location [13]. Other research seeks to manage virtual identities through *pseudonyms* and *anonymity* [25]. That is, by providing a virtual counterpart identity that is not linkable to my legal and physical identity, one can be assured of a measure of privacy. An even more active concept of a virtual identity is the use of *mobile agents*, which can be described as nomadic executable content. They go from site to site and locally carry out transactions on behalf of their originating physical identity. The issues for security here are the risks of the mobile agent maliciously abusing the resources of visited hosts, and vice versa, the host altering or wrongfully depriving the agent's functionality. The streams of rebuttal research are either *passive preventative* – an agent is restricted to work in a trusted domain, *active preventative* – mathematical functions for obfuscating the functionality of the agent, while the host platform is either a tamper resistant, sandboxed operating system, or *detective* - agent activity is audited and mutual malicious behaviour is reprimanded [28,30]. We have comparable goals for identity management, trust and security through interrogation of the interactive context.

3.4 Privacy and Policy Management

Privacy has been one of the earlier security themes addressed within the area of pervasive and ubiquitous computing. We equate the concerns for privacy with what we have described as implicit sharing. Langheinrich states in [19], "...we must realize that our real-world presence cannot be completely hidden, or perfectly anonymized." His principles for maintaining privacy centre on notice, choice and consent, proximity and locality, and access and recourse. Having a feedback mechanism with regards to use of resources is also incorporated in our research agenda. Other recent work in privacy-enabling systems by the group from Berkley led them to deriving the theory of "Approximate Information Flows"[14]. From this they seek to detect when there are imbalances in the flow of information between communicating parties, or hoarding of private information, and aim for minimum information asymmetry as a matter of communications policy. Our work is complementary, in that we consider information asymmetry with respect to physical and virtual counterparts.

3.5 Context Information in Security

Looking into other context-based security research was a matter of fact. Noble and Corner describe "Transient Authentication" as a means of authenticating users with devices through a small, short-ranged wireless communications token that they wear. This therefore demonstrates the use of location (proximity) as authentication based on context [22]. Following authentication, Covington defines Environment Roles as a methodology for capturing context in authorization and access control models [6]. Kindberg et al go a step further and suggests that the context information itself should be authenticated [17]. Their work on context constrained channels suggests that communications channels are "send" or "received" constrained, based on some context predicate. As will be seen in our architecture, authentication and authorisation are not our primary uses of context information, but they are emergent properties of using a context key.

4   The Trust Context Space Architecture

A Trust Context Space represents the degree and state of trust within a certain interactive context (figure 4). It is therefore a mapping of physical and virtual application contexts, based on the nature of communications, processing, storage and I/O within the area of interaction. The operation of the architecture is therefore dependent on our quantification of an interaction context and criteria for determining trust. Our target platform for pervasive and ubiquitous computing involves wireless short-, medium- and long-ranged communications (therefore power and protocol-constrained broadcast), possibility for spontaneous networking protocols (bluetooth, IrDA, Wave-LAN), Networked Sensors (location, temperature, light, speed, etc), personal and shared devices and workspaces. When we say "environment", we typically refer to offices or other rooms that people share and interact using security-relevant data.

At this point we give a bit more details about the core technology used to facilitate context-awareness in the architecture, namely, the Smart-Its [10]. These are products of an ongoing project that supplies a hardware and software platform for integrating computing, sensing and communications capabilities into everyday objects.

Everyday objects include chairs, tables, doors, shelves and more. The Smart-Its contain their own operating system, processor (PIC 18F452 at 20 MHz, 5 MIPS), memory (32 program, 1.5 kB RAM, 8 kB FRAM), RF communications (868,35 ISM band, bandwidth 125 kbits/s) and a variety of integrated sensors, and they are programmable through an API. The available onboard sensors include audio (high-linear microphone and amplifier from 50 Hz – 20 kHz), light intensity (TSL 250 light sensor at 880 nm wavelength), temperature (Dallas DS1621 >>99% accurate between 0 – 40°C), and humidity (Hygrote SHS A3, 99% precision). As we have already built many different scenarios based on this technology, we leverage the platform for constructing the architecture specified here.

4.1   Technical Goals of the Architecture

The first goal of the architecture was to determine a well-reasoned means of evaluating trust. One analogy we used was the inherent willingness of people to trust acquaintances or even strangers, based on the fact that they have access to the same physical property. That is, based on the established guarantee of security by a well-enforced building, people tend to be more at ease with other peers they choose to interact with on the premises. This can be compared to establishing an intermediary trust reference, such as a CA (certificate authority) in PKIs (public key infrastructure). Therefore, our first architectural goal is to allow the trust of an entity to be derived from the overall sense of trust of the physical and virtual environment. Once the environmental sensors and systems detect or are alerted of a security imbalance, the overall trust changes and entities will then be notified of how to collectively redeem the overall environmental trust. Our practical implementation heavily depends on the precision of the sensors, the precision of the Analog/Digital interfaces and the computing power of the processors.

Nevertheless, in order for infringement of trust to be detected there must be some concrete rules or policies in place for stating conditions that must be maintained, and the evidence that must be produced to verify these conditions. Policies are defined by an administrator for access to the resources of the environment, while each entity is also responsible for managing their local policies. We therefore need a scalable methodology for specifying and negotiating policies, as the smart items and user devices are not as powerful as the workstations hosting the environment's services.

With reference to figures 1, 2 and 3, we also require a way of transferring real-world security primitives into the computational domain. That is, a means for the virtual counterparts to recognize explicit cues from the physical world, intended to counter disclosure of information. This is a clear requirement for incorporating the use of context awareness in a trust infrastructure. However, there are three things that we found must be considered when dealing with context information in security: firstly, security mechanisms are generally reliant on values that are not easily guessed and part of a wide field space, such as would be provided by finding the modulus of a large prime integer by a random number. Some elements of context have very little variability and hence may be easily guessed through basic knowledge and heuristics, which is not good if thinking to use them as the basis of a secret key. For example, temperatures in a building typically range between 19 and 25°C and light intensity is normally between 50 and 60 Hz. Secondly, sensor values can be quite variable even in closely co-located spaces e.g. the temperature near a window where the sun is shining through is warmer than next to the AC unit. Therefore forming implicit symmetric keys is a challenge using sensor values with these properties, without being restricted to very particular circumstances of very close collocation over an extended period of time. Thirdly, some sensor values may remain consistent over a long period of time, e.g. humidity, such that if one is thinking about a protocol with frequently refreshed key values that possess weak backwards dependability, this is a constraint.

Finally, with so many policies, regions of trust, smart items and sensors, the management of these environments where implicit sharing is allowed leans towards an administrative overload. The goal of using the context key is to define security mechanisms that are more integrated in everyday activity and not severe distractions from productive tasks, unless critically required to do so.

4.2   Architecture Components

The goals of the architecture may be summarized as ensuring that trust services are deployed appropriately and in a timely fashion. The components we derived are therefore our opinion of the basic infrastructure for managing context-based security and trust services. Our use of the term "appropriate" suggests that we do not seek to provide "security overkill", such that it becomes more of a task or hindrance than a service and support. With reference to figure 8, phases (A), (B) and (C) represent situations where differing expectations of security exists. Differing expectations therefore implies differing policies and mechanisms. The architecture diagram is presented below (figure 7); the role of each component becomes clear in the process description that follows.

(1) Communication. Explicit human - human (everyday interaction), human - smart item (I/O), and human initiated smart item – smart item (electronic communications) interactions are executed through established and defined interfaces. Objects in our environment use various communications channels. For example, the Smart-Its use a proprietary RF protocol called SPOT, which allows low power and low range communication, while PCs, laptops, and PDAs are either wired to the Ethernet, or connected via WaveLan. We therefore had to implement a Bridge between the Smart-Its communications protocols and the Ethernet/IP network to which the environment services are connected.

(2) Context Management. The **context management** components, serving each entity, coordinate sensor samples, collate the sensor values and semantically determine the interactive context. Therefore, the explicit interactions in (1) also generate implicit

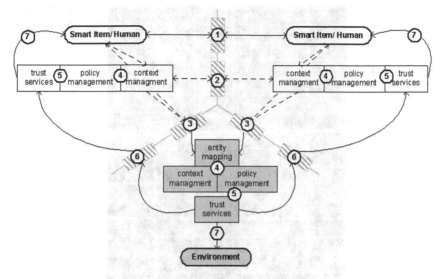

Fig. 6. Smart Environment where Trust Context Space Architecture manages security.

sensor information, which is used to derive the interactive context between the peers. This may also include implicit interaction of the context management component peers, as they share the same conditions. The context management components are the core application of the Smart-Its, which may be connected to the user devices as a peripheral over the serial interface. It is therefore during this implicit exchange that the context key between peers is locally, simultaneously and symmetrically calculated. The time of key generation is implicitly determined based on when the peers initiate physical interaction. However, at our stage of testing we still agree on the time that entities start to generate shared context, as the samples of the sensor signals used must be identical. Consider our experimentation and results using sound below:

The advantage of audio is its fast changing characteristic over time and the equal distribution over a closed area, e.g. a room. Furthermore audio signals do not spread beyond closed rooms and are therefore suitable for the scenarios aimed in this paper. Co-located audio signals are especially comparable from their frequency spectrum. In our approach we use an audio signal recorded over 3 seconds. Due to this long sampling time the shift of the signal resulting from the distance of the two microphones plays no role. Recording starts in all participating devices at exactly the same time (less than $10\mu s$ shift, guaranteed by the network protocol). Recorded signals are then transferred into frequency domain and normalised. The resulting distribution is divided into 11 500 Hz spectrums starting from 500 Hz. Each of the spectrums is rated a value between 0-7 and therefore contributes with 3 bits to the key (see figure 7). The overall length of the key is 33 bit. Although this key length seems to be inadequate for high security settings and also the 3 bit key-parts are not completely independent, we suggest that the key freshness is still an advantage. In our system we propose a change at least every

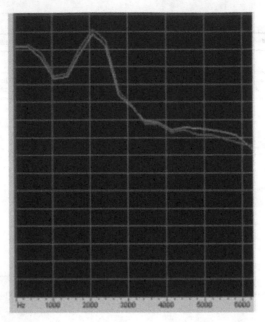

Fig. 7. A curve of the typical room noise in the Frequency domain recorded from two different sources inside the room.

60 seconds. A change of the key also eliminates the seldom error that two co-located nodes do not compute the same key.

(3) Entity Mapping. The sensors of the environment share the interactive conditions with all the interacting entities. Therefore, an active or aware environment may also be considered as an entity in itself, yet it has a constant interactive relationship (implicit and explicit) with its occupants. In a controlled environment, it is therefore possible for the application services of the environment to be aware of the location and other context factors of each entity. This means that it can generate the context key of any occupants and must therefore be provably trusted – recall the attacks on agents discussed in section 3.3. The **entity mapping** service creates a thread of execution per entity, which results in the instantiation of their virtual counterpart from the perspective of the environment. Our platform for the entity mapping service is the *RAUM* system [12]. The *RAUM* orders related location information in a tree-structure, with the root containing the semantics and Cartesian coordinates of the overall area of interest. Entities in the environment may then be located by following a path through the tree.

(4) Policy Management. Policies are specified and enforced locally (autonomously) per entity as well as environmentally (hierarchical constraints). Sloman broadly categorizes policies as either *obligation* (what a subject must do) or *authorization* (what a target allows) [28]. The **policy management** component is registered with its corresponding context management component, to be informed of key states of interactive context.

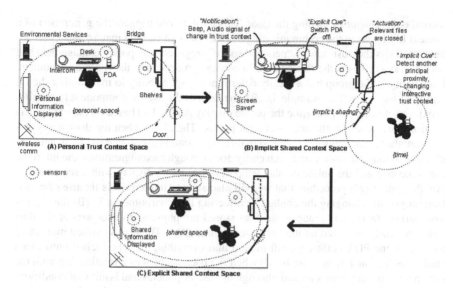

Fig. 8. Visualization of transitioning trust states, and reorganization facilitated by the Trust Context Spaces architecture.

Currently, we conceive these being related to location (Known? Trusted?), communication (Range? Authenticated? Encrypted?), interacting peers (Known? Trusted?), group enrolment (Explicit? Trusted?), and time (Scheduling Conflicts?). We also include a policy called an *introspective policy*, which is a form of obligation policy that states conditions and controls for an entity's internal reconfiguration based on the context. Access controls or authorization policies then state conditions and controls for how interacting entities can use the resources of another.

(5, 6, 7) Trust Service Management – Conditions and Evidence. The recipient of policy decisions is the **trust services** manager, which controls the invocation of services for handling authentication, authorisation and confidentiality. It is this component's task to present the appropriate interface and request for evidence that policy-specified conditions are met. Evidence may include passwords, certificates, public keys, and in the circumstances where it is warranted, the context key. The environmental services also go through this process of introspective policy enforcement followed by definition of access controls. In its role as overall "interactive context monitor", the environment's trust services also provide feedback to the entities regarding the trust state of the overall interactive context. Upon receiving obligation policies from respective trust services, each entity makes autonomous decisions or negotiates on how it will provide the evidence required to continue interactions in a manner that is acceptable by the overall environment.

An environment is most trusted by an occupant after a period of adjustment and familiarization, or if they have made explicit efforts to reinforce the areas of apparent insecurity. With reference to figure 8 (A), the room's principal user has obtained his trusted environment by closing the door. This explicit cue triggers the generation of a context key between the communicating devices (task of context management component), and sets the trust state to "personal space" (registered by policy management and trust services). This is the formation of a context group within the room environment. Each entity in the group has a locally determined responsibility to maintaining the integrity of the group. For example, in (B), the door is the logical component to monitor proximity of other people, while the public display parses data based on the parameters of disclosure stated by the access control policy. Therefore, when the door entity notices another person entity arrive, it signals to the context group that the trust state has changed to implicit shared, and each entity goes through reconfiguration – the intercom alerts the user and the public display temporarily hides its display with a screen saver. Another interesting procedure that we will also seek to implement is the use of actuation (physically changing the context by affecting the environment). In (B) the shelf is also part of the context group as the files stored are physical counterparts of the data being currently displayed on the public screen and PDA. The user's explicit movement to turn off the PDA is then a confirmation that everything is to be locked until given further notice. Such is the case in (C) when the user establishes a relationship with the new peer to the environment, and, through the use of policies and issuing of conditions to the peers by the trust services, the trust state is resolved to shared, and new context keys are generated. The ability to reorganize, resolve and accommodate are therefore the summarized administrative goals of the Trust Context Space.

5 Conclusion

In this paper we have introduced another viewpoint of the issues in security for pervasive computing, where we have shown examples of the loss in synchronization of interactive context between virtual and physical counterparts resulting in security vulnerabilities. As a direction towards solving these issues, we have also presented our experience with the use of context information in generating symmetric keys between peers, bypassing the need to implement a complicated distribution mechanism. To manage the generation of these keys and the formation of groups, the Trust Context Space architecture was derived.

We currently use our technology as a test-bed for the use of context in security, starting in a very controlled or active environment. We see this as an incubator for virtual identities, and thus a more practical environment to study their complexities. In terms of scalability, we envision complex Trust Context Space architectures being constructed by hierarchically grouping active environments. This stems from our designation of an active environment as an entity in itself. However, we are also thinking about how the use of context in security is suited to an uncontrolled environment, such as in infrastructure-less public spaces with no sensing architecture or presence of an online trust reference.

Furthermore, there are still some weaknesses of this approach and other functionalities that we do not wish to overlook. Firstly, there is the question of sensor integrity and detection of tampering. We refer to these situations as "perceptive attacks", where an adversary maliciously alters the sensor readings to report false context data. Secondly, we have only managed to generate a 33-bit key with sound, within an environment of possibly small entropy field space. By today's standards this is not a challenge to hack, but we have also stated that the situation in which we use these keys makes a difference. Researchers at Bell Labs and Carnegie Mellon are also working along a related research path, as presented in [21], where they state that the use of simple pass-phrases by users does not provide sufficient entropy to form the basis for a cryptographic key (subject to dictionary attack). Therefore, their approach has been to analyse the variance in how the pass-phrase is spoken as opposed to the content of the pass-phrase alone. We also believe that functionally combining more than one aspect of the context can lead to better-sized keys within larger field spaces.

References

1. Abowd, Dey, Brown, Davies,Smith and Steggles, "Towards a better understanding of context and context-awareness", (panel statements), Handheld and Ubiquitous Computing, (H.-W. Gellersen, Ed.), Springer, Berlin, pp. 304-307, 1999.
2. Anderson, *Security Engineering: A Guide to Building Dependable Distributed Systems*, pp 38, Wiley 2001
3. Arbaugh, Fithen, McHugh, *Windows of Vulnerability: A Case Study Analysis*, IEEE Computer, December 2000, pp 52-59
4. Beigl, Gellersen, Schmidt, "MediaCups: Experience with Design and Use of Computer Augmented Everyday Artefacts", Computer Networks, Special Issue on Pervasive Computing, Vol. 35, No. 4, March 2001, Elsevier, p. 401-409
5. Brown, Burleson, Lamming, Rahlff, Romano, Scholtz, Snowdon. *Context-awareness: some compelling applications*, December 2001, Retrieved from http://www.dcs.ex.ac.uk/~pjbrown/papers/acm.html Feb 2003
6. Covington, Long, Srinivasan, Dey, Ahamad, Abowd, *Securing Context-Aware Applications Using Environment Roles*, SACMAT 2001, Copyright 2001 ACM
7. Dourish, P. and Bellotti, V., Awareness and Coordination in Shared Workspaces, Proceedings of CSCW'92, 107-114.
8. Hendry, Smart Card Security and Applications. Artech House, 1997
9. Holmquist, Falk, Wigstroem, Supporting group collaboration with interpersonal awareness devices, Personal Technologies", Vol. 3, pp. 13 - 21, 1999
10. Holmquist, Mattern, Schiele, Alahuhta, Beigl, Gellersen, Smart-Its Friends: A Technique for Users to Easily Establish Connections between Smart Artefacts, Proc. of UBICOMP 2001, Springer 2001
11. HuBaux, Buttyan, Capkun. The quest for security in mobile ad hoc networks. In Proc. ACM MOBICOM, Oct. 2001.
12. Hupfeld, Beigl, Spatially aware local communication in the RAUM system, Proceedings of the IDMS, Enschede, Niederlande, October 17-20, 2000, pp 285-296
13. Jendricke, Kreutzer, Zugenmaier, Pervasive Privacy with Identity Management, Workshop on Security in Ubiquitous Compiting , UBICOMP2002, September 2002
14. Jiang, Hong, Landay, "Socially-Based Modeling of Privacy in Ubiquitous Computing", UbiComp 2002, Springer LNCS 2498, pp 176-193
15. Kagal, Finin, Joshi, "Trust-Based Security in Pervasive Computing Environments". IEEE Computer, December 2001
16. Kim, Perrig, Tsudik, Communication-efficient group key agreement, in Proceedings of IFIP SEC 2001.

17. Kindberg, Zhang. Context authentication using constrained channels. HP Labs Tech. report HPL-2001-84. 2001.
18. Kong, Zerfos, Luo, Lu, Zhang Providing robust and ubiquitous security support for mobile ad-hoc networks. In Proc. IEEE ICNP, pages 251–260, 2001.
19. Langheinrich, "A Privacy Awareness System for Ubiquitous Computing Environments", UbiComp 2002, Springer LNCS 2498, pp 237-245
20. Langheinrich, Mattern, Romer, and Vogt. „First Steps Towards an Event–Based Infrastructure for Smart Things". In Ubiquitous Computing Workshop, PACT 2000.
21. Monrose, Reiter, Li, Lopresti, Shih. Toward Speech-Generated Cryptographic Keys on Resource Constrained Devices. in Proceedings of 11th USENIX Security Symposium, 2002
22. Noble, Corner. The case for transient authentication. Presented at the 10th ACM SIGOPS European Workshop, September 2002
23. Norman, "The Invisible Computer", MIT Press, 1999
24. Orr, Abowd, The Smart Floor: A Mechanism for Natural User Identification and Tracking, Georgia Institute of Technology, 2000
25. Reiter, Aviel D. Rubin. Crowds: Anonymity for web transactions. DIMACS Technical Report, 97(15), April 1997. 22
26. Schmidt, Implicit Human-Computer Interaction through Context, Personal Technologies, June 2000, pp. 191-199
27. Schmidt, Beigl, "New Challenges of Ubiquitous Computing and Augmented Reality", 5th CaberNet Radicals Workshop, 5-8 July 1998, Valadares, NR. Porto, Portugal
28. Sloman, Lupu. Policy Specification for Programmable Networks. Networks (IWAN'99), Springer Verlag Lecture Notes in Computer Science 1999
29. Stadler. Publicly verifiable secret sharing. In EUROCRYPT '96, vol. 1070 of LNCS, pp. 191–199. Springer Verlag, 1996.
30. Strasser, Rothermel, System Mechanisms for Partial Rollback of Mobile Agent Execution. In: Proceedings of the 20th International Conference on Distributed Computing Systems (ICDCS 2000), IEEE Computer Society, Los Alamitos, California, pp. 20-28
31. Want, Kenneth, Fishkin, Gujar, Harrison, Bridging Physical and Virtual Worlds with Electronic Tags, Proceedings of CHI'99, ACM Press, April, 1999
32. Weiser, "Some Computer Science Issues for Ubiquitous Computing", PARC 1993
33. Zhou, Haas, Securing ad hoc networks, IEEE Network, vol 13 pp. 24 - 30, 1999

Time Constraint Delegation for P2P Data Decryption

Tie-Yan Li

Infocomm Security Department,
Institute for Infocomm Research (I^2R),
Singapore 119613
litieyan@i2r.a-star.edu.sg

Abstract. Large amount of digital content would be stored safely in peer-to-peer network, with encrypted format. Being requested, a cipher text is downloaded from certain peer and decrypted by a delegated decryptor to obtain the clear text. Observing the need for this new kind of delegation decryption service, we propose a novel time constraint delegation scheme for decrypting p2p data in this paper. The new features of the delegation scheme are that: it uses a flexible secure mobile agent solution without designated delegation server; the time constraint conditional parameter is clearly bound with the protocols; and the computation complexity is greatly reduced by replacing public key computation with hash function. We elaborate the protocol design as well as its security, extensions and properties. Potential applications in content delivery network and pervasive computing scenarios are depicted.

1 Introduction

Peer-to-peer (p2p) network, as a huge data storage space, becomes very popular recently. Data content from one peer can be stored in other peers due to insufficient storage spaces, weak computing capability or expensive network bandwidth. Content Delivery Network (CDN) substantially reduces the amount of Internet infrastructure required to maintain a global web presence. Content providers maintain a minimal "source" copy and CDN service providers, e.g. EdgeSuite of Akamai [1], provide global delivery, load balancing and content storage - enabling businesses to focus valuable resources on strategic, rather than technical issues. Most of the digital contents are stored in clear text and shared with other peers. Whilst private data that is not meant to be shared freely should be encrypted and then distributed. For instance, an online magazine, would still like to keep confidential of their content while serving them only to those subscribed. Being requested, the encrypted content can be fetched and decrypted by the original encryptor.

In case the original encryptor is not always on-line, i.e. a pervasive device may be connected to the network but lacking computing power make it unable to process large amount of computing tasks, of potential interest is a delegation method for decryption. The original encryptor generates a delegation decryption key and sends it to the delegator. With it, the delegator can decrypt any content encrypted by the original encryptor. This process highly decreases the dependence on the encryptor and increases data availability. Obviously, as a new value added service, the delegation decryption service is a

D. Hutter et al. (Eds.): Security in Pervasive Computing 2003, LNCS 2802, pp. 173–186, 2004.

necessary compensation for p2p data sharing. Thus, the integrated services can build a concrete p2p solution that could be very useful especially when practically applied into the emerging application areas like Content Delivery Network and pervasive computing environments.

The technique of delegating decryption discussed about is actually the research area of proxy cryptography, which has been studied for years in many approaches (i.e. [6–8]). Recently in [5], a conditional delegation decryption method was given. A proxy server can cooperate with the delegation check server to decrypt a cipher text. While the scheme is interesting as it departs the delegation key into two portions, it is not convincing for assigning a designated delegation server initially. Their scheme also suffers from no clear condition statement and unnecessary public key computation. Notice these drawbacks, in this paper, we propose a new scheme, namely time constraint decryption delegation. The scheme is more flexible as it removes the designated delegation server with a mobile agent on trusted platforms. The dependency on designated server is decreased. Moreover, the "condition" mentioned in [5] is replaced by a time constraint parameter. Hash chains are generated in which each hash value denotes one time unit. Within the two protocols - delegation key generation protocol and delegation decryption protocol, computations are significantly reduced by computing hash functions instead of public key computation. Meanwhile, the new protocols may also defend against a set of attacks such as "replay attack", "colluding attack" and "DDoS attack". In sum, the new properties for the delegation scheme are:

- No designated delegation server: In place a secure and flexible mobile agent solution.
- Clearer embedded condition: Time constraint condition parameter.
- Replacing public key computation with hash functions: Computation complexity is greatly reduced.
- New mechanisms such as delegation certificate and authentication are accomplished in the protocols: Security of protocols is enhanced.

The rest of the paper is organized as: section 2 introduces the related work. The proposed scheme is elaborated in section 3, in which the model, assumptions and protocols are addressed. Informal security analysis and extended scheme are discussed. Section 4 sketches two scenarios for using the scheme. At last, we conclude the paper and point out the future directions.

2   Previous Work

Proxy Cryptosystem: The primitive method of delegating decryption is to "decrypt and re-encrypt". The original message is disclosed to the delegator and two different encrypt/decrypt key pairs are used, which make it inefficient at all. The concept of proxy cryptosystem was first introduced in [6] where a proxy key is generated and used for decrypting without accessing the original message. In their paper, Mambo et. al. proposed two proxy cryptosystems based on ElGamal cryptosystem and RSA cryptosystem, respectively. These schemes are more efficient than the old one. Follow on, [7] and [8] added innovative properties of proxy cryptography.

[7] introduces the "divertibility" property of proxy protocols and "atomic" property of proxy cryptosystem. The proxy cryptosystems in [6] are not "atomic" since they need to hide the transforming functions and forward "specific" ciphertexts. Compensating [7] where only symmetric proxy functions were given, [8] proposed asymmetric proxy functions under quorum controlled. One interesting feature in their approach is the "translation certificate" that makes the correct translation between encryptions publicly verifiable.

Conditional Delegation: The approach [5] proposed a different model compared with the above models, where the delegation happens only on a single server. In their conditional cryptographic delegation protocols, the delegation key is departed into two portions and disseminated to two parties: the delegation check server and the proxy server. By conducting the two-party protocol with delegation check server, the proxy server can finally decrypt the ciphertext. However, the designated server may reduce the flexibility of the model, the condition is not clearly coupled with the protocols and the unnecessary public key computation limit its practicability. Our proposed scheme in this paper improves greatly towards these drawbacks.

P2P Data Sharing: Apart from the delegation service addressed in this paper, nowadays, many researches studied different issues (i.e. Digital Right Management (DRM), authentication) related to p2p data sharing. Different from tamper resistant solution in typical DRMs, [9] described new escrow services and incentives for p2p users. Many complex cryptographic techniques such as encryption, hashing and error-correction codes are used. By using the escrow service, the subscribers will be given economic incentives for keeping the content within the community. In [10], the authors described a self-healing distributed security architecture that allows the authentication and access control for distributed cache. From an infrastructure viewpoint, it explored the solution of how to protect the network architecture of delivering private data. Although dealing with different issues, these services are devoted to create a more secure and convenient p2p data sharing environment.

3   Scheme

3.1   Model

The role model of our scheme is shown in figure 1. The participants are the Sender (S), the Delegator (D), the Proxy (P) and the User (U). If the sender is off-line, it will dispatch a mobile agent (A) on Trusted Agent Platforms (TAP) for conducting the delegation protocols continuously. In our model, the peer-to-peer network provides the TAPs, delegation platforms (D) and proxy servers (P).

In fig. 1, the basic procedure will be like the following:

0. Firstly, U subscribes at S for certain interested digital content. Suppose the payment process of the requested services has passed. U will obtain the confirmation from S (i.e. a certification valid from t_1 to t_2) as well as a delegation key.

1. S prepares the message M and encrypts it into a cipher text C with its public key. The cipher text C is then sent to D for disseminating into the p2p data sharing network.

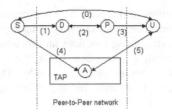

Fig. 1. Model

2. The p2p network could typically be used as a content delivery network that can be feed with a large scale of files. By default, CDN providers may maintain it with load balancing, traffic analysis or bandwidth management, etc. At last, C will be copied anywhere and be available for downloading from many proxy servers.
3. A user U may download C from certain proxy and ask for the decryption.
4. If U is a registered user and S is online, it will contact S for conducting the delegation decryption protocol and obtain M directly.
5. If S is not online, S will dispatch a mobile agent (A) to a trusted environment. The delegation decryption protocol will be conducted between U and A. U can also obtain M if protocol is completed successfully.

The roles aforementioned between the sender and the delegator can be overlapped: S may be assigned for registration and D will generate the delegation key. The same goes to the proxy and user for exchanging the decryption tasks.

3.2 Assumptions

The consideration of using mobile agent lies in that it will make the scheme more flexible. Otherwise, a trusted server must be assigned for conducting the delegation protocol. However, if a trusted server is also shutdown or under DDoS attack (therefore, it cannot provide services), the scheme will be stopped. The propriety of automatically roaming on various platforms makes mobile agent an ideal technique as a pervasive operating object. Unfortunately, mobile agent suffers from security threats [13] coming from its residing platform. Till now, the research on protecting the mobile agent from malicious hosts is still hot, but unsatisfied. It is very hard to keep any secret of an agent if the residing host is malicious. Toward these issues, on one side, we put as less important as possible information on mobile agent, thus less loss caused when compromised. On the other side, one basic assumption of our scheme is on the Trusted Agent Platform (TAP) where the mobile agent resides on. Therefore, we assume that the TAP will give the mobile agent an execution environment satisfying the following requirements:

1. The agent body will not be copied.
2. Agents' executions as well as communications are secured and not recorded.
3. Agents are protected against insider or outsider attacks.
4. Agent must be migrated securely to another safe platform and resume functioning when its residing platform is shutting down or compromised.

In fact, the assumptions 1, 2 and 3 drawn above are not difficult for a well-behaved TAP. Most of the current secure mobile agent platforms can achieve these goals. As for assumption 4, in case of one platform is compromised, the agent can also be resumed either by backup mechanism or from the original server.

3.3 Preliminary

Notation

p: a large prime number, its length is greater than 512 bits.

g: a generator for Z_{p^*}.

(v, s): a pair of public and private key of S, in which $v = g^s \bmod p$, where $s \in_R Z_{p-1}\backslash\{0\}$.

m: the original message.

(c_1, c_2): the encrypted message, where $c_1 = g^r \bmod p$, $c_2 = mv^r \bmod p$; $r \in_R Z_{p-1}\backslash\{0\}$.

$H(.)$: a secure one-way hash function. Such as SHA [3].

ElGamal cryptosystem. In ElGamal cryptosystem, a message m is encrypted into (c_1, c_2). In order to decrypt it with s, compute $m = c_2/c_1^s$. A proxy cryptosystem based on ElGamal cryptosystem was originally proposed in [6], where an original decryptor delegates its decrypting operation to a designated decryptor - proxy decryptor. In using Elgamal cryptosystem, we compute $H(m)$ and attach it to m to generate $M = m|H(m)$. Message M will then be encrypted into the ciphertext (C_1, C_2). Further on, when decrypted, m can be verified by its hash value.

Indeed, our scheme may employ any public key cryptosystem with homomorphic property[1], we select ElGamal cryptosystem [4] for protocol elaboration.

Hash chain. A one-way hash chain is constructed as $H^i(n) = H(H^{i-1}(n))(i = 1, 2, \ldots)$ where $n = H^0(n)$ is a random number as the root of the hash chain. Due to the property of one-way hash function, it is computationally infeasible to compute $H^{i-1}(n)$ from $H^i(n)$. We construct two hash chains as the building block of our protocols.

In figure 2, we use two hash chains to denote the timing constraints. For example, a user U subscribes for certain online content with valid time period ranging from t_0 (starting time) to t_v (ending time). Let hash chain H_1 (its root is $n_1 = H^0(n_1)$) denotes the ending time line and hash chain H_2 (its root is $n_2 = H^0(n_2)$) denotes the starting time line. The user U will be given $H_2^{(t_0)}$ as her starting time and $H_1^{(t_v)}$ as the ending time. Note that $H_2^{(t_0)}$ is equal to $H^j(n_2)$ (given j at the same point indicated by t_0) on the second hash chain. And, the two hash chains have the same time interval (t) to synchronize the two time line (t is selected according to various scenarios, i.e. it can be chosen as one day, and for a valid period of one year, nearly 365 hash values must be

---

[1] I.E. An additive homomorphic cryptosystem is defined as: Encryption function E is additively homomorphic if there is an efficient algorithm $PLUS$ to compute $E(x + y)$ from $E(x)$ and $E(y)$.

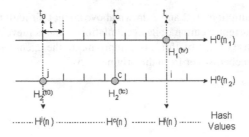

Fig. 2. Two hash chains

pre-computed). We also assume that the time clocks at S and U is loosely synchronized (we give method in section 3.4.2 in case two time clocks are not strictly synchronized). In sum, we have the following equations:

1. At point i of the hash chains or time t_v: $H_1^{(t_v)} = H^i(n_1)$; $H_2^{(t_v)} = H^i(n_2)$;
2. At point j of the hash chains or time t_0: $H_1^{(t_0)} = H^j(n_1)$; $H_2^{(t_0)} = H^j(n_2)$;
3. The same goes to point c or current time t_c;
4. At any two adjacent points or the time interval t: the two points must be $H^i(n)$ and $H^{i-1}(n)$.

3.4   Protocols

Suppose a user U would like to subscribe at S. After the negotiation and payment processes, U is given a delegation key by conducting the delegation key generation protocol. The key can be used to decrypt any ciphertext encrypted by S by completing the delegation decryption protocol. This protocol can be conducted with S if S in online, or with A on TAPs that is dispatched by S via a secure (i.e. SSL) channel.

Delegation key generation protocol. Refer to fig. 3, U negotiates with S a valid time period (i.e. $t_0 \sim t_v$) for the subscription and pays for it. S creates a valid delegation certificate indicating the subscription and then computes the delegation key as follow:

- S generates a user specific key pair (U_{pub}, U_{pri}) for U.
- S generates U's delegation certificate $Cert_U = SIGN_S[U, t_0, t_v, U_{pub}]$, where U is the identity of the user, (t_0, t_v) is the valid time period and U_{pub} is the newly generated public key for U.
- S computes the delegation key $K_d = \langle s - H_2^{(t_0)}, H_1^{(t_v)} \rangle$.

S sends $(Cert_U, U_{pri}, K_d)$ to U via a secure channel. The certificate will be used for verifying the valid time period. The key pair (U_{pub}, U_{pri}) will be used to authenticate U. K_d will be used to decrypt the cipher text in the delegation decryption protocol.

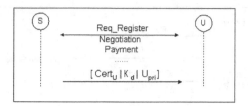

Fig. 3. Delegation key generation protocol

Delegation decryption protocol. Refer to fig. 4, at some time t_c, U wants to decrypt a cipher text (C_1, C_2).

1. U will send a decryption request to A (or S if S is online).
2. On receiving the request, A first send back a random number r to U.
3. U computes $SIGN_U(r)$ with it private key U_{pri} and sends it to S together with C_1 and its delegation certificate $Cert_U$ (indicating t_0 and t_v).
4. A will verify the certificate and further on, use U_{pub} in the certificate to verify $SIGN_U(r)$. If all the verifications are successful, A is sure that the communicating party is U. If the current time t_c satisfies $(t_0 < t_c < t_v)$, U's subscription is still valid.
5. Note that when A is dispatched, two values are taken with A: $(H_1^{(t_c)}, H_2^{(t_c)})$. With $H_2^{(t_c)}$ and the time period between t_0 and t_c, A computes $l = \lfloor (t_c - t_0)/t \rfloor$ (l is an integer). A can derive $H_2^{(t_0)} = H^l(H_2^{(t_c)})$.
6. A computes $C_A = C_1^{H_2^{(t_0)} + H_1^{(t_c)}}$. And sends C_A to U.
7. Given the current time t_c, U can compute $H_1^{(t_c)}$ from $H_1^{(t_v)}$ using the same method above.
8. U will use C_A to compute M in the following equation:

$$M = C_2 \cdot C_A^{-1} \cdot C_1^{-(s - H_2^{(t_0)} - H_1^{(t_c)})}$$

9. Since $M = m|H(m)$, U can verify m by computing its hash. If the verification is successful, U obtains m. If not (i.e. the time clocks at S and U is not strictly synchronized), U may try the two adjacent hash values of t_c on hash chain H_1. If these verification can pass, U can still obtain m. This additional steps can solve the strict time synchronization problem.

3.5 Security Analysis

In delegation key generation protocol, a basic requirement is that the original decryption key s be not disclosed to neither parties like U or A. Because knowing s means that all the ciphertexts encrypted by original encryptor can be decrypted. U is given $K_d = \langle s - H_2^{(t_0)}, H_1^{(t_v)} \rangle$ in the protocol. By keeping the two hash chains in secret, U does not know $H_2^{(t_0)}$ due to its randomness and can not derive s from it. Therefore, U cannot decrypt any ciphertext alone with the delegation key K_d.

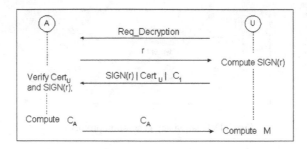

Fig. 4. Delegation decryption protocol

In delegation decryption protocol, A is dispatched with $(H_1^{(t_c)}, H_2^{(t_c)})$. Unless A reveals $H_2^{(t_c)}$ to U, U will never get s. The authentication procedure ensures that A and U are actually the two communicating parties. The verification procedure by A is to confirm that the subscription is still valid if $t_0 < t_c < t_v$. Additionally, since the hash chain root, (n_1, n_2), is generated and safely stored at S, A cannot get any subsequent hash values after the current time unit. If A discloses a $(H_1^{(t_c)}, H_2^{(t_c)})$ pair to the TAPs, TAPs can only use it within the current time interval. Thus, TAPs cannot pretend to be an honest party for conducting the protocol with U at a later time.

If U cannot get the decryption key s, to compute M from only the ciphertext (C_1, C_2) is equal to solving the discrete logarithm problem of the ElGamal cryptosystem. The proposed proxy cryptosystem has the same security level as the ElGamal cryptosystem.

Defending replay attack: the authentication procedure is necessary for defending against replay attack. Suppose another user U' intercepts the certificate of U in a former transaction. U' may use it to conduct the decryption protocol, but it cannot add a signature on r' with U 's private key U_{pri}. The protocol will refuse to proceed.

Defending colluding attack: suppose another user U' is colluding with U. They cannot obtain the decryption key s for the hardness of inverting the hash functions. If U' gives U its certificate and K_d' for U to obtain a longer valid time period, it will be detected at the certificate verification phase. Even multiple users cannot collude and obtain the decryption key s. Although TAPs are assumed trusted, in case TAPs collude with U, U can derive s with the knowledge of $H_2^{(t_0)}$ (refer to section 3.6). If the decryption key is revealed, S must update with a new key.

Defending DDoS attack: if A's residing platform is under DDoS attack, A will be resumed functioning at another platform within the TAPs, either by backup mechanism or by the responsive strategies. The extended scheme in section 3.6 could even tolerate the situation where less than t agents' platforms are compromised simultaneously.

3.6   Extensions

Since dispatching A with $(H_1^{(t_c)}, H_2^{(t_c)})$ may valid only for the current time interval, if S will be off-line for a longer time, A can be simply assigned a pair of hash value of a future time t_c'. Any pair of hash values between t_c and t_c' can be derived from $(H_1^{(t_c')}, H_2^{(t_c')})$.

All the assumptions are drawn on the trust on TAPs. In case the TAPs are compromised, the hash values (i.e. $H_1^{(t_c)}$, $H_2^{(t_c)}$) may be disclosed to U. U can now derive $H_2^{(t_0)}$ from $H_2^{(t_c)}$ and obtain s. If the decryption key is compromised, S must update with a new key. Hence, a new decryption key s' and a new hash chain H_2' are generated. U will be updated with a new portion of delegation key $(s' - H_2'^{(t_0)})$. The certificate for U's subscription and the other portion $H_1^{(t_v)}$ remains unchanged. In addition, all the ciphertexts encrypted by s must be deleted from the p2p network and re-encrypted with the new encryption key v'. This can be very inconvenient. Therefore, we employ a (t, n) threshold scheme (refer to [15]) to protect s, in which t out of n agents can decrypt the message together and any set of less than t agents can not compute the key. It may greatly reduce the trust on TAPs where less than t TAPs compromised are tolerant.

In this case, suppose for certain message M and its ciphertext (C_1, C_2) have a delegation decryption key at U and n hash values $(H_1^{(t_c)}, H_2^{(t_c)}, \ldots, H_n^{(t_c)})$ disseminated to n agents. To decrypt the ciphertext, t out of n agents must correctly conduct the decryption protocol. The message can be decrypted on collecting t valid results. The protocols are described as follow:

Quorum controlled delegation key generation protocol. For the simplicity of protocol, suppose the valid time of the user is from t_0 to eternity. Let $\Lambda = (A_1, A_2, \ldots, A_n)$ denotes the group of n agents. S will generate n hash chains $(H_1, H_2, \ldots, H_n)$and compute $(H_1^{(t_0)}, H_2^{(t_0)}, \ldots, H_n^{(t_0)})$. S forms a polynomial of degree n such that $f(0) = s$ and $f(i) = H_i^{(t_0)}$ (for each $i \in n$),

$$f(x) = \lambda_0(x) \times s + \sum_{i \in \Lambda} \lambda_i(x) \times H_i^{(t_0)} \mod q$$

where

$$\lambda_i(x) = \prod_{i \in \Lambda, i \neq j} (x - j)/(i - j) \mod q$$

is a function to compute the Lagrange coefficient.

Suppose t is the quorum number of agents required to conduct the decryption protocol together. S chooses a set of $n - t + 1$ integers $\Gamma = (i_0, i_1, \ldots, i_{n-t+1})$ from $Z_q \backslash (\Lambda \cup \{0\})$ and compute the delegation decryption keys K_d satisfy:

$$K_d = \{f(j) | j \in \Gamma\}$$

S then disseminates K_d to the user.

Quorum controlled delegation decryption protocol. At some time t_c, the user wants to decrypt a cipher text (C_1, C_2) with a set of agents $(A_1, A_2, \ldots, A_t)$. It will send C_1 to the agents in Λ and they will conduct the decryption protocol together with the user.

1. Each A will verify the certificate with S's public key v. If the certificates are valid and the current time ($t_0 < t_c$). U's subscription is still valid.
2. Note that when each A is dispatched, the hash value $H_i^{(t_c)}, (i \in \Lambda)$ are taken with A_i. With $H_i^{(t_c)}$ and the time period between t_0 and t_c, each A computes $l = \lfloor (t_c - t_0)/t \rfloor$ (l is an integer). For a subset of t integers $\Phi = (1, 2, \dots, t) \in \Lambda$. A_i can derive $H_i^{(t_0)} = H^l(H_i^{(t_c)})$ ($i \in \Phi$).
3. A_i computes $C_{A_i} = C_1^{H_i^{(t_0)}}$. And send C_{A_i} to L via a secure channel.
4. After collecting C_{A_i}, U can now compute M with the equation:

$$ M = C_2 \times C_1^{-\sum_{i \in \Gamma} \theta_i f_i} (\prod_{i \in \Phi} C_{A_i}^{-\theta_i}) $$

where

$$ \theta_i = \prod_{j \in \Gamma \cup \Phi, j \neq i} j/(j - i) \bmod q $$

Note that in the quorum controlled scheme, less than t agents colluding with U cannot decrypt the message. Even all n agents compromised cannot disclose the decryption key s without U.

3.7   Properties

Compared with the basic scheme of [5], our scheme has many improved features:

Firstly, there is no designated delegation server. Assigning a designated server is not flexible and practicable. If a designated server is broken down or replaced by another server, all the delegation keys generated before have to be updated. It is very inconvenient for a large group of users. More dangerously, if a designated server is compromised, the decryption key s could be disclosed. All the encrypted files have to be deleted from the p2p network and re-encrypted by a new key, which greatly reduce the reliability of the scheme. Our scheme uses a mobile agent solution that is more safe and reliable.

Secondly, we clearly defined time constraint condition as a component of the delegation keys taking part in protocols. In [5], the conditions are not clearly identified. It could be a generous solutions for all conditions superficially. However, the conditions are not closely coupled with the protocols. In our scheme, the subscription time period is tightly coupled within the certificate and the protocols. It will be much applicable for time binding applications. Other conditions, if exist, can be attached in the certificate sent to the user and checked by the sender on decrypting.

Thirdly, the overall system performance is improved by removing the unnecessary encryption/decryption computation. In [5], random number is encrypted for generating the delegation key and decrypted for resuming the original decryption key. By generating hash chains, the encryption/decryption computation is replaced by computing hash functions. The reusability of the hash chains further saves computing powers.

Moreover, the delegation can be controlled within certain time unit automatically. In [5], once the delegation server starts to provide the delegation services, it can do it freely without the control of S. Our scheme limits the delegation time within the current time unit (since one hash value denotes one time unit). A delegation server cannot pretend to be honest and conduct the protocols after the current time unit.

Last but not least, the decryption protocol of [5] demanded that the communication between the two parties be over a secure channel. This requirement is too strong as in our protocol, but not enough in their protocol. As to their protocol, it is necessary for protecting the computation result of the delegation server. However, it cannot defend against "replay attack" if it does not authenticate the users. As to our protocol, by authenticating the user, "replay attack" cannot be conducted successfully; by performing the decryption protocols, an attacker who intercepts all the exchanged data packets cannot derive the message M without the knowledge of the hash values.

4 Applications

In this section, we depict two p2p network scenarios that our proposed scheme can be adopted. The value added service of delegating decryption can be built to enrich the current solutions of content delivery network or to enhance the pervasiveness in wireless mobile networking environment.

4.1 Content Delivery Network

With the popularity of p2p network, a new service of delivering content among global network is now available. Utilizing the huge free (computing, storage and network) resources on Internet, content delivery network can delivery large amount of digital content efficiently and cost effectively. The EdgeSuite of Akamai, [1], is such a CDN solution. It provides an integrated suite of services for content and application delivery, content searching and personalization, business intelligence, and streaming media. The research issues such as searching, persist storage, load balancing and bandwidth management have been widely studied, i.e. the OceanStore project [12] at Berkeley.

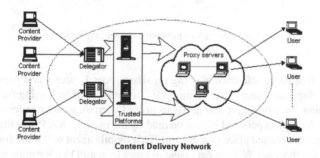

Fig. 5. Content Delivery Network

Figure 5 shows a content delivery network that provides storage service for various content providers (i.e. Music publishers, streaming companies or software distributors) and for the end users. With our proposed scheme, CDNs can now provide another value added service, **delegation decryption service**, to their customers. In this case, an online magazine will publish its encrypted content periodically to its subscribers. Within the valid subscription period, a subscriber may download the encrypted content from CDN and decrypt it with its delegation key. More flexible business models can be built based on our scheme, e.g. the delegation server can be functionally simple as TAPs for serving the mobile agents; the proxy servers within a CDN can delegate the decryption for online content.

4.2   Pervasive Computing

Pervasive computing has emerged as a new paradigm for future communication and computing services that will be available all the time, everywhere. The popularity of pervasive computing benefits from the rapid development of the relevant technologies such as wireless network, mobile computing, distributed computing and mobile agent techniques. For example, fluid computing [11] introduced an innovative middleware platform that enables seamless connectivity among multiple pervasive devices. Obviously, large scale of pervasive applications will be developed in the near future. Hereby, we describe how our scheme can be used in a **p2p conference system in a pervasive environment**.

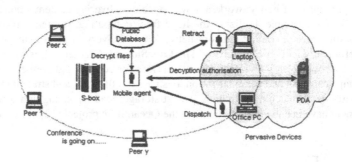

Fig. 6. P2P conference in a pervasive computing environment

In figure 6, a P2P conference is going on where peer 1, peer x and peer y are the participants. Suppose a peer (P) residing on its office PC will be leaving for an urgent important thing. Meanwhile, it still needs to provide certain assistance for the current meeting, i.e. decrypt its personal files to be read by the participants. P will first dispatch a mobile agent to a trusted place (e.g. S-box). This mobile agent will stand for its owner of attending the meeting. With its pervasive devices (e.g. a PDA), P can be updated the current conference status by its agent. In case of being requested a decryption operation, P can authorize its agent for decrypting. The proposed scheme is used here for fetching the encrypted files from a public database, decrypting the files and providing them to the conference. Since the agent has to do a lot of security sensitive operations, a trusted platform is critical and assumed here. The agent will also be retracted as long as P goes back online (e.g. with its Laptop). If the decryption must be confirmed by multiple participants, the quorum controlled scheme can be used. The agent will behave like the group coordinator in this case. After gathering enough confirmations, the message can be decrypted.

5 Conclusions and Future Work

In this paper, we proposed a new scheme of delegating decryption for encrypted p2p data. We believed that a new service of delegation decryption be necessary for complementing p2p data sharing services. We described the requirements of this service and elaborated our scheme in detail. The scheme consists of security building blocks such as ElGamal cryptosystem and hash chain. We provided two protocols, delegation key generation protocol and delegation decryption protocol, for constructing the decryption service. An informal security analysis and extensions on the basic scheme were discussed. Two scenarios, CDN and pervasive computing were provided to demonstrate the benefits obtained by using our scheme.

We will be implementing the proposed scheme on JXTA [2](an open source p2p platform) file sharing system and evaluate the overall system performance synthetically. We will also focus on proxy signature [14] for delegating the signing capability in p2p network.

Acknowledgements

I am grateful to Dr. Robert Deng for providing the authentication mechanisms and valuable comments. I thank Dr. Bao Feng and Dr. Zhou Jianying for discussion on Hash chain and applications. I Also thank the anonymous referees for their helpful reviews.

References

1. Akamai technologies Inc. EdgeSuite product. http://www.akamai.com
2. http://www.jxta.org
3. NIST FIPS PUB 180. *Secure Hash Standard.* NIST, May 1993.
4. T. El Gamal. *A public key cryptosystem and a signature scheme based on discrete logarithms.* In Proc. Of Crypto'84, pp. 10-18, 1984.
5. Y. Watanabe, M. Numao. *Conditional Cryptographic Delegation for P2P Data Sharing.* In proceeding of International Security Conference ISC 2002, LNCS 2433, pp. 309-321, 2002.
6. M. Mambo and E. Okamoto. *Proxy cryptosystems: Delegation of the power to decrypt ciphertexts.* In IEICE Trans. Fund. Electronics Communications and Comp. Sci. E80-A/1, pages 54-63, 1997.
7. M. Blaze, G. Bleumer, and M. Strauss. *Divertible protocols and atomic proxy cryptography.* In Proc. of EUROCRYPT'98, pages 127-144, 1998.
8. M. Jakobsson. *On quorum controlled asymmetric proxy re-encryption.* In Proc. Of PKC'99, pages 112-121, 1999.
9. B. Horne, B. Pinkas, and T. Sander. *Escrow services and incentives in peer-to-peer networks.* In Proc. of ACM EC'01, 2001.

10. J. Giles, R. Sailer, D. Verma and S. Chari. *Authentication for Distributed Web Caches*. ES-ORICS 2002, LNCS 2502, pp. 126-146, 2002.
11. Marcel Graf. *Demo: Fluid computing*. First International Conference, Pervasive 2002, Zürich, Switzerland, August 26-28, 2002.
12. OceanStore project. http://oceanstore.cs.berkeley.edu
13. Kristian Schelderup, Jon Ines, *mobile agent security-issues and directions*, ISN'99, LNCS 1597, pp. 155-167, 1999.
14. Masahiro Mambo, Keisuke Usuda, and Eiji Okamoto. *Proxy signatures: delegation of the power to sign messages*. IEICE Trans. Fund. of Electronic Communications and Comp Sci. E79-A/9 (1996) 1338-1354.
15. A. Shamir, *How to share a secret*. Communications of the ACM, vol. 22, no. 11, pp. 612–613, Nov. 1979.

SAOTS: A New Efficient Server Assisted Signature Scheme for Pervasive Computing

Kemal Bicakci and Nazife Baykal

Middle East Technical University, Informatics Institute,
06531 Ankara, Turkey
{bicakci,baykal}@ii.metu.edu.tr

Abstract. Two most important goals of server assisted signature schemes are to aid small and mobile devices in computing digital signatures and to provide immediate revocation of signing capabilities. In this paper, we introduce an efficient scheme named server assisted one-time signature (SAOTS) alternative to server assisted signature scheme introduced by Asokan et al. Extended the Lamport's one-time signatures by utilizing hash chains, this new scheme's advantages are two-folds; first of all, it is communication-efficient running in fewer rounds, two instead of three, secondly, verification of server's signature can also be performed off-line resulting in real-time efficiency in computation as well as flexibility in the public-key signature scheme to be used. The experiments we have conducted showed that at least 40% gain in performance is obtained if SAOTS is preferred.

1 Introduction

Handwritten signatures have long been used but the means to provide digital signatures for computer communications that are roughly equivalent to handwritten signatures on paper documents became available with the advances in modern cryptography. Whether we use a handwritten or a digital signature, there are three security services it provides:

- *Authentication* - assurance of the identity of the signer.
- *Data Integrity* - assurance that the document is not altered after it is signed.
- *Nonrepudiation* - blocking a sender's false denial that he or she signed a particular document, thus enabling the recipient to easily prove that the sender actually did sign the document.

While there are other means like message authentication codes (MACs) to ensure data integrity and authentication, digital signatures are better in one important respect. They can be used to solve the non-repudiation problem.

Most current techniques for generating digital signatures are based on public key cryptography, e.g., RSA [1] or DSS [2] . But, in general, it is well-known that these techniques cause significant delay in the computation especially if devices with limited computational capabilities are to be used e.g. mobile phones, palmtops etc. Secure ubiquitous information processing will be available in practice only if the computation delays of security primitives used are in acceptable range. One way to reduce the computation costs on these low-end devices is to get help from a verifiable and a powerful server. A verifiable server (VS) is the one whose cheating can be proven.

D. Hutter et al. (Eds.): Security in Pervasive Computing 2003, LNCS 2802, pp. 187–200, 2004.

On the other hand, increased use of digital signatures emphasizes the importance of effective and efficient revocation methods so that if a user does something that warrants revocation of his security privileges i.e. he might be fired or may suspect that his private key has been compromised, he should not generate valid digital signatures on any further messages (However, signatures generated prior to revocation may need to remain valid). In [3] [4], current revocation methods are discussed and as a conclusion they both state that immediate revocation is only possible if an online server is employed.

In this paper, we present a method called server assisted one-time signature (SAOTS) that is designed to provide more assist to small and mobile devices in computing digital signatures and to be more efficient especially in wide area network environments where network overhead is more significant. Like other methods based on VS idea, our proposed method also enable immediate revocation of signing capabilities.

The rest of the paper is organized as follows. Next section provides a brief summary of previous work on server assisted signature schemes. In section 3, we first give background material on one-time signatures and then as an alternative to previous schemes; we introduce SAOTS, which can be thought as an extension of one-time signature idea. Section 4 is for the analysis of our proposal where we explore the benefits and drawbacks. The implementation results in section 5 would be highly valuable for comparing the schemes with respect to the efficiency they provide in different environments. We end by summing up our work and discussing future possibilities for research.

2   Previous Work

The cryptography in the past has involved a secret key shared by the two parties. (Symmetric) encryption algorithms have served (and are serving) quite well for the purpose of secret communication. When the notion of digital signature is first suggested by Diffie and Hellman [5], the first thing came to minds was signing documents using symmetric encryption. This is possible only getting help from a trusted third party (TTP). The protocol works as follows:

1. The sender encrypts his document with the secret key it shares with the TTP.
2. TTP decrypts the document.
3. TTP appends a statement on the document saying that it has received the document from the sender.
4. TTP encrypts the appended document with the secret key he shares with the receiver and send it to him.
5. The receiver decrypts and reads the document and the statement of TTP.

One can easily prove that this protocol provides all the three security services asked from a digital signature but only if the parties fully trust the TTP (i.e. TTP can generate forged signature of any user in the system)[1].

Actually a variant of this idea where after getting the sender's request the (proxy) server on behalf of the sender generates a public-key signature has been proposed in a

---

[1] Note that this is a simplified picture since encryption by itself does not ensure authenticity however if the block cipher we use is in a mode of operation like OCB [17] then this provides both secrecy and authenticity.

recent paper [18]. In today's digital world, this kind of design based on a full trust on a third party is not apposite in most applications and that is why the term "verifiable server" is the key to understand the difference between the primitive design above and the methods we will go over next.

But before doing that, we should also mention the third alternative where a totally *untrusted* server is utilized i.e. the server only executes computations for the user. Now the goal of securely reducing computational costs on the sender's machine becomes more difficult to accomplish and in fact most of the schemes proposed have been found not to be secure. One exception is the interesting approach of [19]. While a more detailed comparison of our work and the server aided signatures of Jakobsson and Wetzel [19] would be highly beneficial, for now what we can say is that our scheme is better both in terms of number of rounds ([19] is also 3-round scheme as opposed to two rounds of our work) and the online computation requirements of the sender (public-key operations can be performed totally offline in our scheme).

The first work that aims to reduce the computational costs to generate digital signatures for low-end devices by employing a powerful VS is [6]. In [4], the authors extend this work by providing implementation results as well as other details of the scheme. The scheme in [3] also utilizes a server to generate signatures but their goal is not to minimize the computation cost on low-end machines but to provide fast revocation without losing transparency for those who verify signatures. This work also has the advantage of supporting revocation not just for signatures but for (public-key) encryption as well.

So, what we will do next in the following subsection is to briefly introduce server assisted signature (SAS) scheme of [6] and describe in the next subsection why it is not the perfect fit for environments where network overhead is significant or signature algorithms where verification is not faster than signing is to be used e.g. DSS [2]. We left the more detailed explanation to the original work [4] [6].

2.1 SAS Protocol Overview

There is an initialization phase in SAS where each user gets a certificate from an offline certification authority for K^n (the last element of a hash chain of length n) where

$$K^n = h^n(K) = h^{n-1}(K^{n-1}) \tag{1}$$

In Equation 1, $h()$ is a hash function like SHS [7] and $h^n(K)$ means we apply hash function $h()$ n times to an initial input K. In addition, each user should register to a VS (which has the traditional public-key based signing capability) before operation. Then the SAS protocol works in three rounds as illustrated in Figure 1:

1. The originator (O) sends $[h(m), ID_o, i, K^i]$ to VS where
   - $h(m)$ is the hash of the message (optionally $h(m)$ can be replaced by m).
   - ID_o is the (unique) identification number for the originator.
   - i is the counter initially set to $n - 1$. It is decremented after each run.
   - K_i is the ith element of the hash chain.

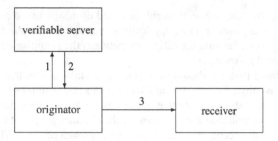

Fig. 1. Server assisted signatures operating in three rounds.

2. Having received O's request, VS checks the followings:
   - Whether O's certificate $(cert_o)$ is revoked or not.
   - Whether value of i is correct or not.
   - Whether $h^{n-i}(K^i) = K^n$ or in a more efficient way $h(K^i) = K^{i+1}$ since K^{i+1} has already been received.

   If these are all OK, VS signs $[Cert_o, h(m), i, K^i]$ and sends it back to O.
3. After receiving the signed message from VS, O verifies the VS's signature, attaches K^{i-1} to this message and sends it to the receiver (R).

   As far as receiver's verification is concerned, the authors in [4] propose two variations where in the light one, the receiver verifies VS's signature and checks whether $h(K^{i-1}) = K^i$ only and in the so called full verification, additionally he verifies O's certificate, checks whether $i < n$ and verifies whether $h^{n-i}(K^i) = K^n$.

2.2   SAS Protocol Weaknesses

Remember that the main motivation to design the SAS protocol is to decrease the time required to generate a signature. However in the above protocol, there are two issues that greatly decrease the performance. These are

1. *Network Overhead*: One of the cost factors of the SAS protocol is the round-trip delay between O and VS. To decrease the network delay or in other words to make the delay one-way instead of round-trip, if O attaches the hash element K^{i-1} to the first message he has sent to VS, an attacker can forge a signed message easily by modifying the message while in transit. As a result SAS protocol cannot be a two-round protocol just like the SAOTS protocol that will be introduced in the next section this is basically because the signature is not binded with the message itself in a two-round case. If the protocol is assumed to be running in a LAN environment, the network overhead is not significant and does not greatly affect the efficiency. However, in today's anywhere anytime nature of ubiquitous computing that kind of assumption is not valid anymore. A protocol, which operates efficiently in a WAN environment as well, would be more beneficial for our purposes.

2. *Verifying VS's signature*: In step 3 of the SAS protocol, before sending the signed message to R, O should verify the VS's signature otherwise a hostile attack cannot be noticed i.e. an attacker can change the message while in transit from O to VS and if VS signs this new message instead, O's revealing of K^{i-1} without verifying VS's signature will result a forged signature for the message the attacker has generated. If the VS uses RSA [1] signature scheme, where verification is much more efficient with respect to signing, this does not put a burden on the operation. However there are other popular digital signature schemes like DSS [2] where verification is at least as costly as signing so a protocol which offers lightweight signing without any restriction in the digital signature scheme used would be much more flexible and attractive.

3 SAOTS Description

3.1 One-Time Signatures

One-time signatures (OTS) provide an attractive alternative to public key-based signatures. Unlike signatures based on public key cryptography, OTS is based on nothing more than a one-way function (OWF). Examples of conjectured OWFs include SHS [7] and MD5 [8] (One-way functions can be constructed simply from a hash function where input length is set to be equal to the output length). OTSs are claimed to be more efficient since no complex arithmetic is typically involved in either OTS generation or verification.

The OTS concept has been known for more than two decades. It was initially developed by Lamport [9] and enhanced by Merkle [10]. Broadly speaking, a message sender prepares for a digital signature by generating a random number r, which is retained as the private value. He then securely distributes the hash of r, $h(r)$, where h is a hash function; this represents the public value and is used by receivers as the signature certificate to verify the signature. (These are also called anchor values.)

The signature is sent by distributing the value r itself. Receivers verify that this message could only be sent by the sender by applying h to r to get $h(r)$. If this matches the value for $h(r)$ in the signature certificate, then the OTS is considered to be verified, since only the sender can know r. This, in effect, allows the signing of a predictable 1-bit value (It also provides one-time entity authentication in one-time password schemes). In order to sign any 1-bit value, two random numbers $(r1, r2)$ are needed; this way, both $h(r1)$ and $h(r2)$ are pre-distributed but at most one of $(r1, r2)$ is revealed as a signature.

To sign an arbitrary length message by OTS, just like the public-key based signatures, we can reduce the length of the message m by computing $h(m)$ and then sign $h(m)$. However, in the above method where we need to reveal one random number for each bit, we need 128 if we use MD5 as the hash function and 160 random numbers if we use SHS (for the certificate, double the numbers). However this method is not optimum with respect to the length of certificates as well as the length of signatures. The authors in [11] realized that p out of m random numbers are sufficient to sign a b-bit length message if the following inequality holds for a given m and p.

$$2^b \geq C(m, p) = \frac{m!}{p! * (m-p)!} \tag{2}$$

It was also shown in [12] that for $b = 128$ (e.g. MD5), m must be at least 132, and each subset can be as small as size 64, since $C(132, 64) > 2^1 28$. For $b = 160$ (e.g. SHS), m must be at least 165 ($m = 164$ is just barely insufficient), with subsets of size 75.

Having determined the values of m and p, there is only one issue left to complete the signing with OTS, that is how to map a specific message to an OTS or in more concrete terms how to choose p out of m random numbers for the message in hand. Please refer to Appendix A for the discussion of how to obtain a valid mapping for a message. For our purposes it is sufficient to know that this mapping is not computationally heavy. It was also shown in the Appendix A that this costs less than one hash operation.

3.2   Server Assisted One-Time Signatures (SAOTS)

The OTS scheme described in subsection 3.1 requires the certificates for the OTSs to be distributed in a secure fashion. Since this is done most typically using a public-key signature, the benefit of using the quick and efficient hash functions is apparently lost.

However, Merkle also introduced a scheme whereby these signatures can be embedded in a tree structure [13], allowing the cost of a single public key signature (to sign the initial anchor values) to be amortized over a multitude of OTS. The problem in this formulation is the longer lengths of signatures. By employing a verifiable server, we now propose a new scheme called server assisted one-time signatures (SAOTS) that allows using one-time signatures more than once without an increase in the signature length. We will compare it to the server assisted signature (SAS) scheme in the next section.

There is an initialization phase in SAOTS similar to SAS where each user gets a certificate from an offline certification authority for the array of length m

$$K_0^n, K_1^n, K_2^n, \ldots K_{m-1}^n \tag{3}$$

Where m is chosen to be large enough to map the hashed message e.g. 165 if SHS is used to hash the message. Each element of the array is the last element of a hash chain of length n where

$$K_j^n = h^n(K_j) = h^{n-1}(K_j^{n-1}) \quad (for \ \ j = 0 \ \ to \ \ m-1) \tag{4}$$

In this equation, $h^n(K_j)$ means we apply hash function $h()$ n times to an initial input K_j.

Since only lightweight hash computations are required for the initialization, this would not put a burden on the setup delay of the protocol.

In addition, just like the SAS protocol, each user should register to a VS before operation. Then the SAOTS works in two rounds (as opposed to three rounds in SAS) as illustrated in Figure 2:

Note that $S^i = (K_{a_1}^i, K_{a_2}^i, K_{a_3}^i, \ldots, K_{a_p}^i)$ denotes the subset of the array of length p that maps the message to an OTS (composed of ith elements of hash chains).

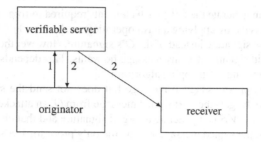

Fig. 2. Server assisted one-time signatures operating in two rounds.

1. The originator (O) sends $[h(m), ID_o, i, S^i]$ to VS where
   - $h(m)$ is the hash of the message (optionally $h(m)$ can be replaced by m).
   - ID_o is the (unique) identification number for the originator.
   - i is the counter initially set to $n - 1$. It is decremented after each run.
   - S_i is subset of ith elements of hash chains (that maps $h(m)$).
2. Having received O's request, VS performss the followings:
   - Checks whether O's certificate $(cert_o)$ is revoked or not.
   - Checks whether value of i is correct or not.
   - Computes the mapping of $h(m)$ or in other words finds out which subset S^i
     would correspond to the OTS of the message.
   - Checks whether for $(q = 1$ to $p)$ $h^{n-i}(K_{a_q}^i) = K_{a_q}^n$ or in a more efficient way
     $(q = 1$ to $p)$ $h(K_{a_q}^i) = K_{a_q}^{i+1}$ if $K_{a_q}^{i+1}$ has already been received (it depends on
     the previous message mapping).
   If these are all OK, VS signs $[Cert_o, h(m), i, S^i]$ and sends it back to both R and
   O at the same time.

After receiving the signed message from VS, both O and R verifies VS's signature. For secure operation, O should sign the next message only after this (off-line) verification. As far as receiver's verification is concerned, verifying only VS's signature corresponds to the light verification in the SAS protocol whereas a full verification can be defined similarly for SAOTS where the receiver verifies O's certificate, checks whether $i < n$ computes the mapping of $h(m)$ and verifies whether for $(q = 1$ to $p)$ $h^{n-i}(K_{a_q}^i) = K_{a_q}^n$.

4   Analysis

4.1   Security

We claim that SAOTS scheme achieves the same security level as the SAS scheme if the originator does not generate another signature without verifying VS's signature on the previous message. See [4] for the informal security analysis of server assisted signature schemes. If the originator sends a signed message with $(i - 1)^{th}$ elements of the hash chains before he gets the VS's signature of the previous one (with i^{th} hashes), the following attacks can be performed:

- An attacker can generate the (i^{th}) hash elements required to forge the signature on a different message by applying a hash operation on the $(i-1)^{th}$ hashes. He then inserts this new signature instead of the O's signature. However the attacker cannot generate a valid signature for any message he wants. This depends on the previous messages signed and the mapping algorithm.
- If VS gets the previous signed message but does not send the signature on this message before he gets the next signed message from O, an attacker cannot forge a signature but now VS can generate a forged signature and that cheating cannot be proven. For O, the signed message will be the only proof for VS's cheating.

Off-line verification of VS's signature before signing another message will be sufficient to avoid these attacks. Since VS has signed the O's signature with the ith hash elements, if an attacker sends a forged signature using the ith hash elements to VS, VS rejects this request (Look at the step 2 of the SAOTS protocol above) and the attack is not successful. The VS cannot even generate a forged signature because it has signed the genuine message previously.

Fast rates of signing is not required in most popular applications using server assisted signature protocols (like e-mail which was implemented in [4].) For applications where a faster rate of signing is demanded, SAOTS is flexible enough to perform the verification of VS's signature on-line instead of off-line. Alternatively we propose the following solution:

In the initialization phase, the user gets a certificate from an offline certification authority not for only one array of hash chains but for a multiple of them. For a secure operation, he should use different arrays sequentially in generating the signatures. Then, if there are n arrays, it is sufficient to get the VS's signature for the first message before generating a signature for the $(n+1)^{th}$ message. The drawback here is the increased setup cost.

4.2   Efficiency

Rule#5: You can buy more bandwidth but not lower delays. *A.S.Tanenbaum, Computer Networks 3rd Edition, page 564*

Table 1 shows the comparison of SAOTS and SAS schemes with respect to computation requirements on the participating entities. In this table, we show only the online computations (performed after the message is available) and ignore the off-line precomputation requirements e.g. preparing the hash chains, verifying VS's signature in SAOTS etc. Including only the on-line computations to this table is a reasonable action since in many applications the signer has a very limited response time once the message is presented but he can carry out costly computations between consecutive signings. In fact, the notion of "off-line/on-line signature" is so useful that special signature schemes solely based on this idea were proposed in the past [20].

In the receiver's computation we assume light verification and notice that the receiver needs to compute the hash of message before verifying the signature in both protocols. The server needs to perform m hashes on average to verify the OTS of O. How the value of m is calculated is given in Appendix B.

Table 1. Computation comparison of SAS and SAOTS protocols

H: hash computation
S: traditional signing by a public-key
V: verification of public-key based signature
M: mapping computation (costs less than one hash)

	SAS	SAOTS
Originator	$1H + 1V$	$1H + 1V$
Server	$1H + 1S$	$(m+1)H + 1M + 1S$
Receiver	$1V + 2H$	$1V + 1H$

Table 2 again makes a comparison between the two protocols but now in terms of communication efficiency. As seen from this table SAOTS provides more efficiency with respect to number of rounds but with an increase in the length of the messages exchanged. It will be experimentally shown in the next section that a decrease the number of rounds of the protocol is generally much more important than an increase in the bandwidth usage as far as communication efficiency is concerned.

Table 2. Communication comparison of SAS and SAOTS protocols

$[m]$: length of message m
X: [hash of message] + $[ID]$ + $[i]$ + $[K_i]$
Y: [hash of message] + $[Cert]$ + $[i]$ + $[K_i]$+[Public-key signature]
ID: identification number of originator
$Cert$: certificate of the originator
K_i: i^{th} hash in the hash chain of SAS protocol
h: [hash used in OTS]
p: number of hashes in the OTS signature

		SAS	SAOTS
Number of rounds		3	2
message	round 1	X	$X + (p-1)h$
length	round 2	Y	$Y + (p-1)h$
(in byte)	round 3	$Y + h$	-

Typical values of parameters: Here the algorithm used to hash the original message can be chosen to give a 160 bits output like SHS [7] with $m = 165$ and $p = 75$, whereas without having a bad impact on the security it provides, it is sufficient to use a 80-bit output hash algorithm in generating hashes for SAOTS or SAS operation because birthday attacks are not possible. One can employ a secure hash algorithm like SHS producing 160 bits output and folding the output of SHS with exclusive or to produce an 80-bit output. For the explanation of how birthday attacks work in digital signature schemes, please refer to some reference books [14]. The typical public-key signature length is 1024-bits if we use RSA [1] and 320-bits if we use DSS [2]. Lastly, we can assume the identification numbers of users are 2-bytes long (maximum number of users to share a VS is then 2^{16} and certificate lengths are 400-bytes long (highly dependent on the certificate format to be used as well the extensions included in the certificate).

5 Implementation and Experiments

To have a more concrete comparison of SAS and SAOTS, we have implemented both of them using MIRACL library [15]. A PC running Windows 2000 with an 800 MHz Pentium III and a 128 MB memory was chosen as the VS and a PC running Windows 95 with a 200 MHz Pentium I and a 32 MB memory was chosen as the originator's machine. Note that today's high-end PDA's and palmtops have a processor speed of 200 MHz. The compiler was Microsoft Visual C++ Version 6.0. We have conducted two experiments. One of them was over a 10 Mbit Ethernet LAN and the other was over the WAN (Internet) with a very long distance between machines. The client was running on Middle East Technical University in Ankara, Turkey and the VS was running on UCLA, Los Angeles, USA.

RSA with a 1024 bit key and SHS with a 160 bit output was used and $m = 165$ and $p = 75$ were the OTS parameters. The public key e of RSA was chosen to be 65537 since choosing $e = 3$ might cause some security vulnerabilities. Lastly, note that network delay measured for SAS was round trip time whereas for SAOTS it was one-way[2]. This is why the delay is smaller in SAOTS although the message transmitted is larger. Table 3 gives the performance measurements of cryptography primitives on two platforms used and Table 4 summarizes our findings of the experiments.

Table 3. Performance measurements of cryptography primitives (ms)

	Pentium III 800 Mhz	Pentium I 200 Mhz
SHS	0.028	0.156
RSA(verifying)	2.220	13.893
RSA(signing)	9.454	59.162

These experimental results show that at least 40% gain is obtained (in a LAN environment) if SAOTS is used instead of SAS protocol. $(24.831 - 14.922)/24.831 \cong 0.4$. It is straightforward to see that this gain will increase if

1. If the protocol is operating in an environment with greater network delays.
2. A public-key algorithm with a longer key (e.g. 2048-bit RSA) is to be used since as the verification time of public-key signature will increase, only the performance of SAS will get worse.
3. A public key algorithm where verification of the signature is not much more efficient than generating signature is used [2].
4. A more powerful server is used.

---

[2] The network delay for WAN has a big variance so the numbers given here are just for the purpose of giving a general idea.

Table 4. Experimental comparison of SAS and SAOTS protocols in LAN and WAN environments (ms)

	SAS	SAOTS
Originator's computation	14.049	0.256
Server's computation	9.482	14.122
Network delay (LAN)	1.3	0.8
Network delay (WAN)	260	140
Total time (LAN)	24.831	14.922
Total time (WAN)	283.531	154.122

We have also seen that there is a threshold for the network delay where signing in a traditional way and send the signed message directly to the receiver becomes more efficient for the user[3]. But SAS and especially SAOTS are still preferable in applications where a server needs to be utilized anyway e.g. e-mail, chat over a server etc.

6 Conclusion and Future Work

In this paper, we have proposed an efficient scheme named server supported one-time signature (SAOTS) alternative to server assisted signature (SAS) scheme introduced by Asokan et al. [6]. Having extended the Lamport's one-time signatures by utilizing hash chains, this new scheme's advantages with respect to SAS are two-folds:

1. It is communication-efficient running in a fewer rounds (2 instead of 3). This makes the protocol more flexible and suitable to be used in wide-area network environments as well where network delay is more significant. It is experimentally seen that the fact that the messages exchanged are larger in size does not result a degradation in performance.
2. To complete generating the signature, the originator does not need to verify a public-key based signature after the message to be signed is available. In other words, this verification also can be performed off-line.

The experiments we have conducted showed that at least 40% gain in performance is obtained if SAOTS is preferred over SAS. This gain would be much higher in environments where network delay is more significant.

We also argued that server assisted signature protocols are more promising where a server is a built-in element in the application. While it is easy to find such classical examples like e-mail, we need to explore more about the suitability in considerably new applications like e-publishing.

As a future work, we would like to focus more on the security analysis of SAOTS. We also plan to make a more detailed comparison of our work to the server-aided signatures of [19].

---

[3] The value of this threshold for the network delay is $59.162 - 23.531 = 35.631 msecs$ for SAS and $59.162 - 14.378 = 44.784 msecs$ for SAOTS.

In recent years researchers come up with new signature schemes which does not base on a public-key operation. One of them was the BIBA scheme proposed by A. Perrig [16]. BIBA's advantages are smaller signature lengths and faster verifying times. Designing and evaluating the performance of a server assisted BIBA signature is a promising future work.

Acknowledgments

We would like to thank Enver Cavus for his help on conducting the experiment over Internet with a machine in UCLA. We would also like to thank Albert Levi and Semih Bilgen for their helpful comments and discussions.

References

1. Ronald L. Rivest, Adi Shamir, Leonard M. Adleman: A Method for Obtaining Digital Signatures and Public-Key CryptoSystems. CACM, Vol. 21, No 2, February 1978.
2. National Institute of Standards and Technology (NIST): FIPS Publication 186: Digital Signature Standard (DSS), May 19, 1994.
3. D. Boneh, X. Ding, G. Tsudik, and B. Wong: Instantaneous revocation of security capabilities. In Proceedings of USENIX Security Symposium 2001, Aug. 2001.
4. X. Ding, D. Mazzocchi and G. Tsudik: Experimenting with Server-Aided Signatures. 2002 Network and Distributed Systems Security Symposium (NDSS'02), February 2002.
5. Whitfield Diffie and Martin Hellman: New Directions in Cryptography. IEEE Transactions on Information Theory, Volume IT-22, Number 6, November 1976.
6. N. Asokan, G.Tsudik, and M. Waidner: Server-supported signatures. Journal of Computer Security, vol. 5., no. 1, 1997.
7. National Institute of Standards and Technology (NIST): FIPS Publication 180: Secure Hash Standard (SHS), May 11, 1993.
8. Ronald L. Rivest: The MD5 message-digest algorithm. April 1992. RFC 1321.
9. L. Lamport: Constructing digital signatures from a one-way function. Technical Report CSL-98, SRI International, October 1979.
10. Ralph C. Merkle: A digital signature based on a conventional encryption function. In Carl Pomerance, editor, Proc. CRYPTO 87, pages 369–378. Springer-Verlag, 1988. Lecture Notes in Computer Science No. 293.
11. Kemal Bicakci, Brian Tung, Gene Tsudik: On constructing optimal one-time signatures. Proceedings of Fifteenth International Symposium on Computer and Information Sciences, ISCIS 2000, October 2000, Istanbul, Turkey.
12. Kemal Bicakci, Brian Tung, Gene Tsudik: How to construct optimal one-time signatures. In submission to Computer Networks, Elsevier Science journal.
13. Ralph C. Merkle: A certified digital signature. In G.Brassard, editor, Proc. CRYPTO 89, pages 218–238. Springer-Verlag, 1990. Lecture Notes in Computer Science No. 435.
14. A. Menezes, P. Van Oorshot, and S. Vanstone: Handbook of applied cryptography. CRC Press series on discrete mathematics and its applications. CRC Press, 1996. ISBN 0-8493-8523-7.
15. MIRACL Multiprecision Integer and Rational Arithmetic C/C++ Library: http://indigo.ie/~mscott/
16. Adrian Perrig: The BiBa one-time signature and broadcast authentication protocol. ACM Conference on Computer and Communications Security 2001, 28-37.

17. Phillip Rogaway, Mihir Bellare, John Black, and Ted Krovetz: OCB: A Block-Cipher Mode of Operation for Efficient Authenticated Encryption. Eighth ACM Conference on Computer and Communications Security (CCS-8), ACM Press, pp. 196-205, 2001.
18. M. Burnside, D. Clarke, T. Mills, A. Maywah, S. Devadas, and R. Rivest: Proxy-Based Security Protocols in Networked Mobile Devices. Proceedings of the 17th ACM Symposium on Applied Computing (Security Track), pages 265-272, March 2002.
19. M. Jakobsson, S. Wetzel: Secure Server-Aided Signature Generation. Proceedings of the International Workshop on Practice and Theory in Public Key Cryptography (PKC 2001), LNCS 1992, Springer, 2001.
20. S. Even, O. Goldreich and S. Micali: On-line/off-line digital signatures. Proc. CRYPTO 89, August 1990.

Appendix A: Encoding a Message for One-Time Signature

Given a vector R of m random numbers, and a V of subsets each containing p of those numbers, we have shown that we can sign any one of $C(m, p)$ distinct messages. In this appendix, we describe the mapping M between messages and the elements of V, and demonstrate how to compute them efficiently.

Assume that the domain of M is composed of 2^b messages, and we have a way of representing each of a message as a $b - bit$ integer k. Let any subset S in V be expressed as $R_{a_1}, R_{a_2}, R_{a_3}, \ldots, R_{a_p}$. Arrange the subsets in V such that their indices a_i are in ascending order. For example, for $m = 4$, $p = 2$, the subsets are ordered

$$\{R_1, R_2\}, \{R_1, R_3\}, \{R_1, R_4\}, \{R_2, R_3\}, \{R_2, R_4\}, \{R_3, R_4\}$$

Then the mapping $M(S, V)$ of each subset S is defined as the integer position of S in this list representation of V. For example, in the above case, $M(\{R_1, R_3\}, V) = 2$ and $M(\{R_3, R_4\}, V) = 6$. In general, for any n and p, the mapping of any subset $S = \{R_{a_1}, R_{a_2}, \ldots, R_{a_p}\}$, where $a_0 = 0$ and $a_1 < a_2 < \cdots < a_p$ is given by:

$$M(S, V) = 1 + \sum_{i=1}^{p} \sum_{j=n-a_i+1}^{n-a_{i-1}-1} \binom{j}{p-i} \tag{5}$$

Note that in order to compute the mapping for any subset, for a given n and p, we need only compute the binomial coefficients $C(j, p - i)$ for i from 1 to p, j from $p + 1 - i$ to $n - i$. Thus, each mapping requires $n - p - (n - a_p) = a_p - p$ additions.

Similarly, the mapping $M^{-1}(m, V)$ of a message represented by the integer m can be computed by subtracting binomial coefficients until zero is reached. This requires $a_p - p$ additions and comparisons. Pseudocode to do this conversion is as follows:

```
m₀ = m /* copy message to temporary value */
q = 1
for i = 1 to p do begin
while m₀ > C(n − q, p − i) do begin
m₀ := m₀ − C(n − q, p − i)
q := q + 1
```

end /* *while* */
$a_i := q$
$q := q + 1$
end /* *for* */

To put things in perspective, consider that a single SHS hash computation requires approximately 500 arithmetic operations. Thus, our mapping (in both directions) costs less than one SHS hash.

Appendix B: Average Number of Hash Computations Needed by the Server to Verify an OTS in SAOTS

For the OTS of a message, the server receives p out of m hashes. Let's call K^i any one of these hashes that is at depth i of the chain. To verify K^i, it requires any one of the next hashes in the chain (from $i + 1$ to n). If next hash (K^{i+1}) in the chain is available, then it needs only one hash operation to compute. If not the hash computation requirement will increase. The probability that K^{i+1} has been received is $(p/m = \alpha)$. So if we assume that n is a big number, average number of hash computations required for one hash will be approximated by

$$\sum_{k=0}^{\infty} \alpha(1 - \alpha)^k (k + 1) \tag{6}$$

Since $\alpha < 1$, this serial sum is equal to $1/\alpha$.

To find the total number of hash operations required, we need to multiply this number with p, then finally we find the average number of hash computations needed to verify an OTS in SAOTS protocol as

$$p * \frac{1}{p/m} = m \tag{7}$$

As an example, to map a 160-bit message, we can choose $m = 165$ and $p = 75$ where the server needs to do 165 hash computations to verify the OTS.

Security and Privacy Aspects of Low-Cost Radio Frequency Identification Systems

Stephen A. Weis[1], Sanjay E. Sarma[2], Ronald L. Rivest[1], and Daniel W. Engels[2]

[1] Laboratory for Computer Science
Massachusetts Institute of Technology
Cambridge, MA 02139, USA
{sweis,rivest}@mit.edu
[2] Auto-ID Center
Massachusetts Institute of Technology
Cambridge, MA 02139, USA
{sesarma,dwe}@mit.edu

Abstract. Like many technologies, low-cost Radio Frequency Identification (RFID) systems will become pervasive in our daily lives when affixed to everyday consumer items as "smart labels". While yielding great productivity gains, RFID systems may create new threats to the security and privacy of individuals or organizations. This paper presents a brief description of RFID systems and their operation. We describe privacy and security risks and how they apply to the unique setting of low-cost RFID devices. We propose several security mechanisms and suggest areas for future research.

1 Introduction

Radio Frequency Identification (RFID) systems are a common and useful tool in manufacturing, supply chain management, and inventory control. Industries as varied as microchip fabrication, automobile manufacturing, and even cattle herding have deployed RFID systems for automatic object identification. For over twenty years, consumer items have been identified with optical barcodes. One familiar optical barcode is the Universal Product Code (UPC), designed in 1973 [30] and found on many consumer products. More recently, RFID has made inroads into the consumer object identification market. Silicon manufacturing advancements are making low-cost RFID, or "smart label", systems an economical replacement for optical barcode.

RFID systems consist of radio frequency (RF) tags, or transponders, and RF tag readers, or transceivers. Tag readers *interrogate* tags for their contents by broadcasting an RF signal. Tags respond by transmitting back resident data, typically including a unique serial number. RFID tags have several major advantages over optical barcode systems. Tag data may be read automatically: without line of sight, through non-conducting materials such as paper or cardboard, at a rate of several hundred tags per second, and from a range of several meters. Since tags typically are a silicon-based microchip, functionality beyond simple identification may be incorporated into the design. This functionality might range from integrated sensors, to read/write storage, to supporting encryption and access control. Three example tags are shown in Figure 1.

D. Hutter et al. (Eds.): Security in Pervasive Computing 2003, LNCS 2802, pp. 201–212, 2004.

Fig. 1. A passive RFID tag, an RFID tag with a printed barcode, and dust-sized RFID microchips.

The potential benefits of a pervasive low-cost RFID system are enormous. World-wide, over 5 billion barcodes are scanned daily [8]. However, barcodes are typically scanned only once during checkout. By integrating a unified identification system on all levels of the supply chain, all parties involved in the lifespan of a product could benefit. This includes not only manufacturers and retailers, but also consumers, regulatory bodies such as the United States Food and Drug Administration (FDA), and even the waste disposal industry. The potential cost savings will likely make RFID tags one of the most widely deployed microchips in history, illustrated by the recent purchase of 500 million low-cost RFID tags by a major consumer product manufacturer [23].

Unfortunately, the universal deployment of RFID devices in consumer items may expose new security and privacy risks not present in closed manufacturing environments. Corporate espionage is one risk. Retail inventory labeled with unprotected tags could be monitored and tracked by a business' competitors. Personal privacy may also be compromised by extracting data from unprotected tags. Most consumers would prefer to keep the RFID tagged contents of their pockets or shopping bags private. Another risk is the violation of "location privacy": the tracking of an individual by the tags they carry.

Most manufacturing processes currently deploying RFID systems are for higher value items, allowing tag costs to be in the US\$0.50-US\$1.00 range. Tags priced in this range could support basic cryptographic primitives or tamper-resistant packaging, similar to many smart card designs. Unfortunately, to achieve significant consumer market penetration RF tags will need to be priced in the US\$0.05-US\$0.10 range and will need to be easily incorporated into most paper packaging. At this price range, providing strong cryptographic primitives is currently not a realistic option. Any viable tag and reader designs must take into account security and privacy risks, while not exceeding this low-cost range. This places the burden of supporting security on the readers, whose costs are less restrictive.

General low-cost RFID research is part of ongoing work at the MIT Auto-ID Center [21]. An overview of RFID systems and their security implications is available in [27]. Issues explored in the context of smart cards are most closely related to the resource scarce environment of RFID devices. Relevant security issues are addressed in a broad range of smart card and tamper resistant hardware literature. Cost and security trade-offs of smart cards are analyzed in [1]. RFID tags may operate in insecure environments or subject to intense physical attacks. An analysis of smart card operation in hostile environments is presented in [9]. An comprehensive overview of many physical attacks and countermeasures appears in [31]. Specific lower cost physical attacks are detailed in [2] and are part of ongoing research at the University of Cambridge's TAMPER Lab [29].

Many results pertaining to implementations of cryptographic primitives are relevant to RFID devices. Cautionary information regarding the implementation of AES in smart cards is presented in [7]. Being passively powered and relying on a wireless interface may make RFID devices especially susceptible to fault induction, timing attacks or power analysis attacks, highlighted in [4, 16, 15] and [14]. Location privacy risks present in Bluetooth technology and relevant to RFID systems are addressed in [12].

In this paper, Section 2 gives a brief introduction to RFID system components, describes the interface between tags and readers, and presents estimates of the capacities of current low-cost tags. Section 3 details various privacy and security risks of a low-cost RFID system deployed in everyday consumer items. Section 4 states assumptions about the security properties of a low-cost RFID system. Under these assumptions, Section 5 offers several proposals for addressing the concerns of Section 3, specifically a hash-based access control scheme in Section 5.1, a randomized access control scheme in Section 5.2, and an improved anti-collision algorithm in Section 5.3. Finally, Section 6 discusses open questions and areas for future research.

2   RFID System Primer

RFID systems are composed of three key elements:

- the RFID tag, or *transponder*, carries object identifying data.
- the RFID reader, or *transceiver*, reads and writes tag data.
- the back-end database associates records with tag data collected by readers.

Every object to be identified in an RFID systems is physically labeled with a tag. Tags typically are composed of a microchip for storage and performing logical operations, and a coupling element, such as an antenna coil, used for wireless communications. Memory on tags may be read-only, write-once read-many, or fully rewritable.

Tag readers *interrogate* tags for their contents through an RF interface. As well as an RF interface to the tags, readers may contain internal storage, processing power, or an interface to back-end databases to provide additional functionality.

Tags may either be *actively* or *passively* powered. Active tags contain an on-board power source, such as a battery, while passive tags must be inductively powered via an RF signal from the reader. The distance a reader may interrogate tags from is limited by the tag's power. Consequently, active tags may be read from a greater distance than passive tags. Active tags may also record sensor readings or perform calculations in the absence of a reader. Passive tags can only operate in the presence of a reader and are inactive otherwise.

Readers may use tag contents as a look-up key into a database storing product information, tracking logs, or key management data. Independent databases may be built by anyone with access to tag contents, allowing unrelated parties to build their own applications on any level of the supply chain. The back-end database may also perform functions on behalf of either the readers or tags.

Readers must be able to address a particular tag, or *singulate* it, from among a population of many tags. During singulation, multiple tags responses may interfere with each other, necessitating an anti-collision algorithm. Anti-collision algorithms may either be probabilistic or deterministic. A familiar probabilistic algorithm is the Aloha scheme [3, 20] used in Ethernet local area networks. In the tag-reader context, tags avoid collisions with other tags by responding to reader queries at random intervals. In the event of a collision, the culprit tags wait for another, usually longer, random interval before trying again. Higher densities of tags will result in a higher collision rate and degraded performance.

A simple deterministic algorithm is the binary tree-walking scheme. In this scheme, a reader queries all nearby tags for the next bit of their ID number. If the reader detects a collision then at least two tags among the population have different bit values in that position of the ID. The reader will send a response bit indicating which tags should continue with the protocol and which should cease responding. Each choice of bit represents choosing a branch in a binary tree. The leaves of the tree correspond to tag ID numbers. Assuming the tags have unique IDs, after walking to a leaf in the tree, a reader have singulated a tag. Benefits of binary tree-walking include simple tag implementation and efficiently broadcasting only the bits of an ID to singulate any tag.

A ubiquitous low-cost RFID system would most likely require the use of passive tags. Tight cost requirements make these tags extremely resource-scarce environments. Power consumption, processing time, storage, and gate count are all highly limited. A practical US$0.05 design, such as those proposed by the MIT Auto-ID Center [21, 26], may be limited to hundreds of bits of storage, roughly 500-5,000 gates and a range of a few meters.

The resources available in a low-cost RFID tag are far less than what is necessary for public key cryptography, even a resource-efficient scheme such as NTRU [11, 22]. Hardware implementations of symmetric encryption algorithms like AES typically have on the order of 20,000-30,000 gates [6], beyond what is available for an *entire* low-cost RFID design. Standard cryptographic hash functions such as SHA-1 [6] are also likely to be too costly for several years. Even the aptly named Tiny Encryption Algorithm [32, 33] is too costly for today's low-cost RFID tags, although may be feasible in the near future.

3   Security and Privacy Risks

RFID tags may pose security and privacy risks to both organizations and individuals. Unprotected tags may have vulnerabilities to eavesdropping, traffic analysis, spoofing or denial of service. Unauthorized readers may compromise privacy by accessing tags without adequate access control. Even if tag contents are protected, individuals may be tracked through predictable tag responses; essentially a traffic analysis attack violating "location privacy". Spoofing of tags may aid thieves or spies. Saboteurs could threaten the security of systems dependent on RFID technology through denial of service.

Any parties with their own readers may interrogate tags lacking read access control, although only within a relatively short tag read range of a few meters. While anyone could also scan nearby optical barcodes, they cannot do so wirelessly at a rate of hundreds of reads per second. The very properties making RFID technology attractive in terms of efficiency make it vulnerable to eavesdropping.

Aggregate logistics and inventory data hold significant financial value for commercial organizations and their competitors. A store's inventory labeled with unprotected tags may be monitored by competitors conducting surreptitious scans. Sales data may be gleaned by correlating changes over time. Individuals carrying items with unsecured tags are vulnerable to privacy violations. A nearby eavesdropper could scan the contents of your pockets or bag; valuable data to nosy neighbors, market researchers or thieves in search of ripe victims.

Another important privacy concern is the tracking of individuals by RFID tags. A tag reader at a fixed location could track RFID-labeled clothes or banknotes carried by people passing by. Correlating data from multiple tag reader locations could track movement, social interactions, and financial transactions. Concerns over location privacy were recently raised when a major tire manufacturer began embedding RFID tags into all their products [24]. Even if the tags only contain product codes rather than unique serial numbers, individuals could still be tracked by the "constellation" of products they carry. Someone's unique taste in brands could betray their identity.

In addition to threats of passive eavesdropping and tracking, an infrastructure dependent on RFID tags may be susceptible to denial of service attacks or tag spoofing. By spoofing valid tags, a thief could fool automated checkout or security systems into thinking a product was still on a shelf. Alternatively, a thief could rewrite or replace tags on expensive items with spoofed data from cheaper items. Saboteurs could disrupt supply chains by disabling or corrupting a large batch of tags.

4   RFID Security Settings and Assumptions

To address the security risks of low-cost RFID tags, we will first state a set of assumptions about the operation of the system. Assuming a minimalist approach, tags will be passive and provide only simple read-only identification functionality. We will arbitrarily assume our tags contain a few hundred bits of storage and have an operating range of a few meters.

In 2003, cost requirements dictate that low-cost tags may have 200-2000 gates available for security. This is far below what is feasible for standard public-key or symmetric encryption, including efficient algorithms such as NTRU or TEA [11, 32]. Furthermore, performance requirements dictate that at least 100-200 tags must be able to be read each second, which limits the clock cycles available for security protocols. Power consumption may also be a limiting factor, although highly dependent on the particular implementation.

We assume tag memory is insecure and susceptible to physical attacks [29, 31] revealing their entire contents. This includes a myriad of attacks such as shaped charges, laser etching, ion-probes, TEMPEST attacks, clock glitching and many others. Fortunately, these attacks require physical tag access and are not easily carried out in public or on a wide scale without detection. Privacy concerns are rather moot if someone can remove a tag or steal the item it is attached to without detection. The key point is that

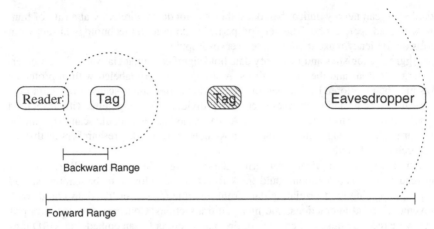

Fig. 2. Forward vs. Backward Channels: The reader will detect the nearby tag, but cannot detect the shaded tag. A distant eavesdropper may monitor the forward channel, but not the tag responses.

tags cannot be trusted to store long-term secrets, such as shared keys, when left in isolation.

Tags may also be equipped with a physical contact channel, as found on smart cards, for critical functions or for "imprinting" tags with secret keys [28]. Additionally, we may assume the tag packaging contains some optical information such as a barcode or human-readable digits. This information may corroborate tag data, as in the design presented in [13].

Tag readers are assumed to have a secure connection to a back-end database. Although readers may only read tags from within the short (e.g. 3 meter) tag operating range, the reader-to-tag, or *forward* channel is assumed to be broadcast with a signal strong enough to monitor from long-range, perhaps 100 meters. The tag-to-reader, or *backward* channel is relatively much weaker, and may only be monitored by eavesdroppers within the tag's shorter operating range. Generally, it will be assumed that eavesdroppers may only monitor the forward channel without detection. This relationship is illustrated in Figure 2.

Tags will be assumed to have a mechanism to reveal their presence called a *ping*. Anyone may send a ping, which tags respond to with a non-identifying signal. Tags are also equipped with a *kill* command rendering them permanently inoperable. The kill command may be assumed to be a slow operation which physically disables the tag; perhaps by disconnecting the antenna or short circuiting a fuse.

5   Security Proposals

5.1   Hash-Based Access Control

Accepting the resource limitations of low-cost tags, we offer a simple security scheme based on one-way hash functions [19]. In practice, a hardware-optimized cryptographic

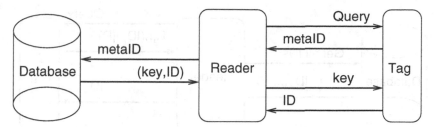

Fig. 3. Hash-Locking: A reader unlocks a hash-locked tag.

hash would suffice. Each hash-enabled tag in this design will have a portion of memory reserved for a temporary *metaID* and will operate in either a locked or unlocked state.

To lock a tag, a tag owner stores the hash of a random key as the tag's metaID, i.e. $metaID \leftarrow hash(key)$. This may occur either over the RF channel or a physical contact channel for added security. After locking a tag, the owner stores both the key and metaID in a back-end database. Upon receipt of a metaID value, the tag enters its locked state. While locked, a tag responds to all queries with only its metaID and offers no other functionality.

To unlock a tag, the owner queries the metaID from the tag, looks up the appropriate key in the back-end database and finally transmits the key to the tag. The tag hashes the key and compares it to the stored metaID. If the values match, it unlocks itself and offers its full functionality to any nearby readers. This protocol is illustrated in Figure 3. To prevent hijacking of unlocked tags, they should only be unlocked briefly to perform a function before being locked again.

Based on the difficulty of inverting a one-way hash function, this scheme prevents unauthorized readers from reading tag contents. Spoofing attempts may be detected under this scheme, although not prevented. An adversary may query a tag for its metaID, then later spoof that tag to a legitimate reader in a replay attack. A legitimate reader will reveal the key to the spoofed tag. However, the reader may check the contents of the tag (often collectively referred to as a tag's ID) against the back-end database to verify that it is associated with the proper metaID. Detecting an inconsistency at least alerts a reader that a spoofing attack may have occurred.

The hash-lock scheme only requires implementing a hash function on the tag and managing keys on the back-end. This is a relatively low-cost requirement and may be economical in the near future. This scheme may be extended to provide access control for multiple users or to other tag functionality, such as write access. Tags may still function as object identifiers while in the locked state by using the metaID for database lookups. This allows users, such as third-party subcontractors, to build their own databases and to take advantage of tag functionality without necessarily owning the tags. Unfortunately, since the metaID acts as an identifier, tracking of individuals is possible under this scheme.

5.2 Randomized Access Control

Preventing the tracking of individuals motivates an additional mode of operation. While in this mode, a tag must not respond predictably to queries by unauthorized users, but

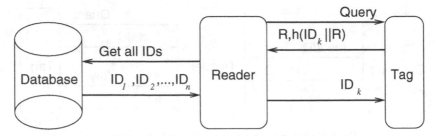

Fig. 4. Randomized Hash-Locking: A reader unlocks a tag whose ID is k in the randomized hash-lock scheme.

must still be identifiable by legitimate readers. We present a practical heuristic based on one-way hash functions, best suited for consumers with a small number of tags. We also offer a theoretically stronger variant based on pseudo-random functions (PRFs).

As in Section 5.1, tags are equipped with a one-way hash function, but now also have a random number generator. Tags respond to reader queries by generating a random value, r, then hashing its ID concatenated with r, and sending both values to the reader. That is, tags respond to queries with the pair $(r, h(ID||r))$, where r is chosen uniformly at random. This protocol is illustrated in Figure 4. A legitimate reader identifies one of its tags by performing a brute-force search of its known IDs, hashing each of them concatenated with r until it finds a match. Although impractical for retailers, this mode is feasible for owners of a relatively small number of tags.

This scheme may suffice in practice, but is not theoretically robust. The formal definition of a one-way function only establishes the difficulty of inverting the function output [19, 10]. There is no provision of secrecy, technically allowing bits of the input to be revealed. We must use a stronger primitive to ensure ID bits are not leaked.

To address this issue, suppose each tag shares a unique secret key k with the reader and supports a pseudo-random function ensemble, $\mathcal{F} = \{f_n\}_{n \in \mathbb{N}}$. When queried, tags will generate a random value, r, and reply with $(r, ID \oplus f_k(r))$. The reader will once again perform a brute-force search, using all its known ID/key pairs to search for a match.

A minor fix allows readers to only store tag keys on the back-end, without needing to also store the tag IDs. Tags may pad their ID its hash, and reply with $(r, (ID||h(ID)) \oplus f_k(r))$. Readers may identify tags by computing $f_k(r)$ for all their known keys, XORing it with the second part of the tag's response, and searching for a value ending in the form $(x||h(x))$. To anyone without the key value, the tag's output is random and meaningless.

It is unknown whether PRF ensembles may be implemented with significantly fewer resources than symmetric encryption. There may be no be practical difference in the context of low-cost RFID tags. Many symmetric encryption algorithms employ PRFs as a core building block in a Luby-Rackoff style design [18]. The minimal hardware complexity of a PRF ensemble remains an open problem [17].

5.3   Silent Tree Walking and Backward Channel Key Negotiation

One security concern is the strong signal of the reader-to-tag forward channel. Eaves-droppers may monitor this channel from hundreds of meters and possibly deriving tag

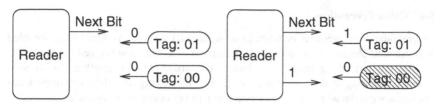

Fig. 5. Silent Tree Walking: The left-hand figure illustrates reading the first bit, which does not collide. The right-hand figure illustrates a collision. To singulate tag 01, the reader responds with "Last Bit" $\oplus$ "Tag 01" $= 0 \oplus 1 = 1$. Tag 01 proceeds, while the shaded tag 00 ceases the protocol.

contents. Of particular concern is the binary tree walking anti-collision algorithm, because the reader broadcasts each bit of the singulated tag's ID.

We present a variant of binary tree walking which does not broadcast insecure tag IDs on the forward channel and does not adversely affect performance. Assume a population of tags share some common ID prefix, such as a product code or manufacturer ID. To singulate tags, the reader requests all tags to broadcast their next bit. If there is no collision, then all tags share the same value in that bit.

A long-range eavesdropper can only monitor the forward channel and will not hear the tag response. Thus, the reader and the tags effectively share a secret, namely the bit value. If no collisions occur, the reader may simply ask for the next bit, since all tags share the same value for the previous bit. When a collision does occur, the reader needs to specify which portion of the tag population should proceed.

Since we assumed the tags shared some common prefix, the reader may obtain this prefix on the backward channel. The shared secret prefix may be used to conceal the value of the unique portion of the IDs. Suppose we have two tags with ID values $b_1 b_2$ and $b_1 \overline{b_2}$. The reader will receive b_1 from both tags without a collision, then will detect a collision on the next bit. Since b_1 is secret from long-range eavesdroppers, the reader may send either $b_1 \oplus b_2$ or $b_1 \oplus \overline{b_2}$ to singulate the desired tag without revealing either bit. Figure 5 illustrates a reader performing silent tree walking on two bits.

Eavesdroppers within the range of the backward channel will obviously obtain the entire ID. However, this silent tree walking scheme does effectively protect against long-range eavesdropping of the forward channel with little added complexity. Performance is identical to regular tree walking, since a tag will be singulated when it has broadcast its entire ID on the backward channel.

Readers may take advantage of the asymmetry of the forward and backward channels to transmit other sensitive values. Suppose a reader needs to transmit the value v to a singulated tag. That tag can generate a random value r as a one-time-pad and transmit it in the clear on the backward channel. The reader may now send $v \oplus r$ over the forward channel. If eavesdroppers are outside the backward channel, they will only hear $v \oplus r$, and v will be information theoretically secure.

Another deterrent to forward channel eavesdropping is to broadcast "chaff" commands from the reader, intended to confuse or dilute information collected by eavesdroppers. By negotiating a shared secret, these commands could be filtered, or "winnowed", by tags using a simple MAC. This procedure is detailed in [25].

5.4   Other Precautions

Several other measures may be taken to strengthen RFID systems. First, RFID-enabled environments should be equipped with devices to detected unauthorized read attempts or transmissions on tag frequencies. Due to the strong signal strength in the forward channel, detecting read attempts is fairly simple. Deploying read detectors helps identify unauthorized read requests or attempts to jam tag operating frequencies.

Another measure to detect denial of service is to design tags which "scream" when killed, perhaps by transmitting a signal over a reserved frequency. RFID enhanced "smart shelves" may be designed to detect the removal of items, unauthorized read attempts or the killing of tags.

To enable end users to access the functionality of tags affixed to items they have purchased, a master key could be printed within a product's packaging, possibly as a barcode or decimal number. A similar mechanism is proposed for banknotes in [13]. After purchasing an item, a consumer could use the master key to toggle a tag from the hash-lock mode of Section 5.1 to the randomized mode of Section 5.2. The master key may also function as a key recovery mechanism, allowing users to unlock tags they have lost the keys to. Since the master key must be read optically from the interior of a package, adversaries cannot obtain it without obtaining the package itself. For further security, all functions using the master key could be required to use a physical contact channel, rather than RF.

Two final precautions take advantage of the physical properties of passively powered tags. First, readers should reject tag replies with anomalous response times or signal power levels. This is intended as a countermeasure to spoofing attempts by active devices with greater operating ranges than passive tags. Readers may also employ frequency hopping to avoid session hijacking. Passive tags may be designed such that their operating frequency is completely dictated by the reader. This makes implementing random frequency hopping trivial, since tags and readers do not need to synchronize random hops. Readers can just change frequencies, and the tags will follow.

6   Future Research

An area of research which will greatly benefit RFID security and privacy is the development of hardware efficient cryptographic hash functions, symmetric encryption, message authentication codes and random number generators. General advances in circuit fabrication and RFID manufacturing will lower costs and allow more resources to be allocated for security features. Continued research into efficient symmetric encryption algorithms, such as TEA [32, 33], may yield algorithms appropriate for low-cost RFID devices. One open question from Section 5.2 is whether pseudo-random function ensembles can be implemented with significantly less complexity than symmetric encryption. Designing efficient implementations of perfect one-way functions [5] may be a relevant avenue of research as well.

New RFID protocols resistant to eavesdropping, fault induction and power analysis need to be developed. The silent tree walking algorithm presented in Section 5.3 offers protection against long range eavesdropping, but is still vulnerable to nearby eavesdroppers and fault induction. It also requires that a population of tags share a common prefix unknown to eavesdroppers, which is not always a valid assumption. In general, readers and tags must be designed to gracefully recover from interruption or fault induction without compromising security.

With new technology advances allowing more features to be incorporated into tags, the line between RFID devices, smart cards, and general purpose computers will blur. Research benefiting RFID security today will aid in development of secure ubiquitous computing systems in the future. Recognizing inherent privacy or security threats of RFID systems will also help guide policy decisions regarding the obligations of RFID manufacturers and the privacy rights of end users.

Acknowledgments

Thanks to Peter Cole and Tom Scharfeld for RFID design contributions. Thanks to Levente Jakab and Simson Garfinkel for input and editorial review.

References

1. Martin Abadi, Michael Burrows, C. Kaufman, and Butler W. Lampson. Authentication and Delegation with Smart-cards. In *Theoretical Aspects of Computer Software*, pages 326–345, 1991.
2. Ross Anderson and Markus Kuhn. Low Cost Attacks on Tamper Resistant Devices. In *IWSP: International Workshop on Security Protocols, LNCS*, 1997.
3. Benny Bing. *Broadband Wireless Access*. Kluwer Academic Publishers, 2002.
4. Dan Boneh, Richard A. DeMillo, and Richard J. Lipton. On the Importance of Checking Cryptographic Protocols for Faults. In *EUROCRYPT'97*, volume 1233, pages 37–51. Lecture Notes in Computer Science, Advances in Cryptology, 1997.
5. Ran Canetti, Daniele Micciancio, and Omer Reingold. Perfectly One-Way Probabilistic Hash Functions. In *30th Annual ACM Symposium on Theory of Computing*, pages 131–140, 1998.
6. CAST Inc. AES and SHA-1 Cryptoprocessor Cores. http://www.cast-inc.com.
7. Suresh Chari, Charanjit Jutla, Josyula R. Rao, and Pankaj Rohatgi. A Cautionary Note Regarding Evaluation of AES Candidates on Smart-Cards. In *Second Advanced Encryption Standard (AES) Candidate Conference*, Rome, Italy, 1999.
8. EAN International and the Uniform Code Council. http://www.ean-int.org.
9. Howard Gobioff, Sean Smith, J. Doug Tygar, and Bennet Yee. Smart Cards in Hostile Environments. In *2nd USENIX Workshop on Elec. Commerce*, 1996.
10. Oded Goldreich. *Foundations of Cryptography*. Cambridge University Press, 2001.
11. Jeffrey Hoffstein, Jill Pipher, and Joseph H. Silverman. NTRU: A Ring-Based Public Key Cryptosystem. *Lecture Notes in Computer Science*, 1423:267–, 1998.
12. Markus Jakobsson and Susanne Wetzel. Security Weaknesses in Bluetooth. *Lecture Notes in Computer Science*, 2020:176+, 2001.
13. Ari Juels and Ravikanth Pappu. Squealing Euros: Privacy Protection in RFID-Enabled Banknotes. In *Financial Cryptography*, 2002. Submitted for publication.
14. Burton S. Kaliski Jr and Matt J. B. Robshaw. Comments on Some New Attacks on Cryptographic Devices. RSA Laboratories' Bulletin No. 5, July 1997. http://www.rsasecurity.com/rsalabs/bulletins/.
15. Paul Kocher, Joshua Jaffe, and Benjamin Jun. Differential Power Analysis. *Lecture Notes in Computer Science*, 1666:388–397, 1999.

16. Paul C. Kocher. Cryptanalysis of Diffie-Hellman, RSA, DSS, and other Systems Using Timing Attacks. Technical report, Cryptography Research, Inc., 1995.
17. Matthias Krause and Stefan Lucks. On the Minimal Hardware Complexity of Pseudorandom Function Generators. In *Theoretical Aspects of Computer Science*, volume 2010, pages 419–435. Lecture Notes in Computer Science, 2001.
18. Michael Luby and Charles Rackoff. How to Construct Pseudorandom Permutations from Pseudorandom Functions. *SIAM Journal on Computing*, 17(2):373–386, April 1988.
19. Alfred J. Menezes, Paul C. van Oorshot, and Scott A. Vanstone. *Handbook of Applied Cryptography*, chapter 1.9. CRC Press, 1996.
20. Robert M. Metcalfe and David R. Boggs. Ethernet: Distributed Packet Switching for Local Computer Networks. *Communications of the ACM*, 19(5):395–404, July 1976.
21. MIT. Auto-ID Center. http://www.autoidcenter.org.
22. NTRU. GenuID. http://www.ntru.com/products/genuid.htm.
23. RFID Journal. Gillette to Purchase 500 Million EPC Tags. http://www.rfidjournal.com, November 2002.
24. RFID Journal. Michelin Embeds RFID Tags in Tires. http://www.rfidjournal.com, January 2003.
25. Ronald L. Rivest. Chaffing and Winnowing: Confidentiality without Encryption. *CryptoBytes (RSA Laboratories)*, 4(1):12–17, Summer 1998.
26. Sanjay E. Sarma. Towards the Five-Cent Tag. Technical Report MIT-AUTOID-WH-006, MIT Auto-ID Center, 2001.
27. Sanjay E. Sarma, Stephen A. Weis, and Daniel W. Engels. RFID Systems and Security and Privacy Implications. In *Workshop on Cryptographic Hardware and Embedded Systems*, pages 454–470. Lecture Notes in Computer Science, 2002.
28. Frank Stajano and Ross Anderson. The Resurrecting Duckling: Security Issues for Ad-hoc Wireless Networks. In *7th International Workshop on Security Protocols*, volume 1796, pages 172–194. Lecture Notes in Computer Science, 1999.
29. TAMPER Lab. University of Cambridge Tamper and Monitoring Protection Engineering Research Lab. http://www.cl.cam.ac.uk/Research/Security/tamper.
30. Uniform Code Council. Homepage. http://www.uc-council.org.
31. Steve H. Weigart. Physical Security Devices for Computer Subsystems: A Survey of Attacks and Defences. In *Workshop on Cryptographic Hardware and Embedded Systems*, volume 1965, pages 302–317. Lecture Notes in Computer Science, 2000.
32. David J. Wheeler and Robert M. Needham. TEA, a Tiny Encryption Algorithm. Technical report, Computer Laboratory, University of Cambridge, 1995.
33. David J. Wheeler and Robert M. Needham. TEA Extensions. Technical report, Computer Laboratory, University of Cambridge, 1997.

Implementing a Formally Verifiable Security Protocol in Java Card

Engelbert Hubbers, Martijn Oostdijk, and Erik Poll

Nijmegen Institute for Information and Computing Sciences, University of Nijmegen,
P.O. Box 9010, 6500GL, Nijmegen, The Netherlands
{hubbers,martijno,erikpoll}@cs.kun.nl

Abstract. This paper describes a case study in refining an abstract security protocol description down to a concrete implementation on a Java Card smart card. The aim is to consider the decisions that have to be made in the development of such an implementation in a systematic way, and to investigate the possibilities of formal specification and verification in the design process and for the final implementation.

1 Introduction

Security protocols play a crucial role in pervasive computing, e.g. in ensuring authentication of different devices communicating over networks, or encryption of communications between these devices. There has been a lot of work on reasoning about security protocols over the past years, for example BAN logic [1] or state exploration based analysis using model checkers [2]. Still, there is a big gap between the abstract level at which such protocols are typically studied and the concrete level at which they are implemented. This is unsatisfactory since ultimately we are interested in properties of the concrete implementation.

This raises several questions: Which choices have to be made in the process of implementing a protocol and how do these affect the security of the implementation? Which properties of the abstract description also hold for a concrete implementation? What additional properties have to be worried about if for instance one of the agents participating in the protocol is running on a smart card and can therefore be subject to sudden loss of power at any moment?

Our aim is to investigate possible notations, techniques, and tools that can help in answering these questions. Rather than trying to make more precise what is meant by "the security of an implementation", the approach taken in this paper is to consider the kind of properties that we know how to specify and verify with today's tools and to see how these can contribute to secure protocol implementations.

This paper discusses a case study in refining a security protocol from the abstract description down to an actual implementation, where one of the agents is implemented on a smart card, using Java Card, a "dialect" of Java for programming smart cards. We investigate the choices that have to be made in this process by looking at formal descriptions of the protocol at different levels of abstraction and the properties we want to specify and verify.

D. Hutter et al. (Eds.): Security in Pervasive Computing 2003, LNCS 2802, pp. 213–226, 2004.

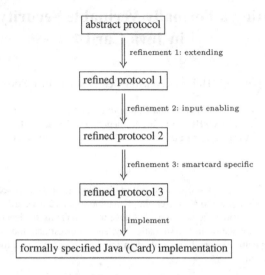

Fig. 1. Refinement overview

The relation between the abstract protocol description and the final Java implementation is shown in Fig. 1. Our long term goal is to prove that the implementation of the protocol ensures the security properties we are interested in. For the moment we have to content ourselves with

- accurately specifying the different refinements that lead from the abstract protocol to the implementation and making the design decisions underlying these refinements explicit; this is done in Section 3.
- using the formal specification language JML (Java Modeling Language [3]) and two tools that support JML, namely the runtime assertion checker for JML [4] and the static checker ESC/Java [5], to ensure that the Java code correctly implements the final refinement of the protocol; this is done in Section 4.

Section 2 first describes the abstract protocol that we want to implement.

2   The Abstract Protocol

For this case study we use the protocol for bilateral key exchange (BKE) with public key described in [6, § 6.6.6]. This protocol allows two agents to agree on a session key. One of the agents will be implemented as a so-called smart card applet, i.e. a program executing on a smart card. It could, for example, be running on a mobile phone SIM or a credit card. The other agent will be an off-card application, communicating with the smart card applet via a smart card reader and possibly some network connection. The protocol consists of three messages. In conventional notation for security protocols it reads as follows:

1. $B \rightarrow A : B, \{N_b, B\}_{K_a}$
2. $A \rightarrow B : \{f(N_b), N_a, A, K\}_{K_b}$
3. $B \rightarrow A : \{f(N_a)\}_K$

Here A and B are the two agents, N_a and N_b are the nonces (challenges) from A and B, and K_a and K_b are the public keys of A and B, respectively. The function f is a hash function and $\{\ldots\}_K$ denotes the data ... encrypted using key K.

Figure 2 presents an alternative description of the protocol as two simple finite automata, one for each agent. (These automata are almost identical, but in the course of introducing more implementation details the automata for the two agents will become different.) Initial states are indicated by extra circles. All transitions are labeled with messages and either a ?, in case of an incoming message, or ! in case of an outgoing message. This is standard CSP notation.

Principal A Principal B

Fig. 2. Abstract BKE protocol

We used Casper [7] in combination with the model checker FDR2 [8] to prove that this protocol does indeed ensure mutual authentication and secrecy of the session key.

The abstract protocol only describes the initial handshake between A and B that establishes a session key. It does not say how this session key is actually used afterwards. For an actual implementation we do of course want to use the session key to encrypt subsequent communications between A and B. Therefore we extend the protocol as follows:

1. $B \rightarrow A : B, \{N_b, B\}_{K_a}$
2. $A \rightarrow B : \{f(N_b), N_a, A, K\}_{K_b}$
3. $B \rightarrow A : \{f(N_a)\}_K$
4. $A \rightarrow B : \{\texttt{KeyOK}\}_K$
5. $B \rightarrow A : \{\texttt{Msg}\ldots\}_K$
6. $A \rightarrow B : \{\texttt{Msg}\ldots\}_K$

$$\vdots$$

$$2n.\ B \to A : \{\texttt{Msg}\ldots\}_K$$
$$2n+1.\ A \to B : \{\texttt{Msg}\ldots\}_K$$
$$2n+2.\ B \to A : \{\texttt{End}\}_K$$

Here KeyOK is an acknowledgment message sent to agent B in order to make sure that B knows he is allowed to send regular messages. This message is not really needed: if agent A would simply start to send a regular message using K, agent B could know that the suggested key has been accepted. The message End ends the session. This extension leads to the automata in Fig. 3. The modifications to the previous diagram are highlighted.

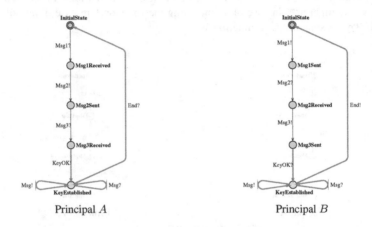

Fig. 3. Extended BKE state-transition diagram

3 Refinements

3.1 Anything That Can Go Wrong ...

Several things can go wrong during a protocol run:

1. We can get an *unsolicited message*. For example, agent A could be in its initial state and receive message[1] Msg3? from agent B, whereas it is expecting Msg1?. In this case we say that the agents are "out of sync", which is something that could happen as a consequence of messages being lost. Note that Fig. 3 does not specify what should happen if this situation occurs.
2. An *exception may be thrown while processing expected messages*. For instance, an agent may receive an *incorrectly encrypted message*. For example, agent B could receive a first response message of agent A that is not of the required form $\{f(N_b), N_a, A, K\}_{K_b}$.

---

[1] We assume that the messages are labeled so it is clear which message is received. In the Java Card implementation this is typically done by means of the so-called instruction byte.

3. An agent may fail to receive any message at all, due to a basic *failure of the communication channel* between the two agents.

Decision 1 *1. Receiving an unsolicited message ends the current session, i.e. an agent receiving an unsolicited message will move to its initial state. The only exception to this is if Agent A receives an unsolicited message* Msg1?; *in that case a new session will immediately start and Agent A will go to state* Msg1Received.
2. *In case an exception is thrown, for instance when an agent receives an* incorrectly encrypted message, *the agent will go back to its* InitialState *(and sends a special message* XcB! *back to the other agent).*
3. *An agent noticing a* failure of the communication channel *will go back to its* InitialState.

These decisions result in the new state-transition diagrams given in Fig. 4.

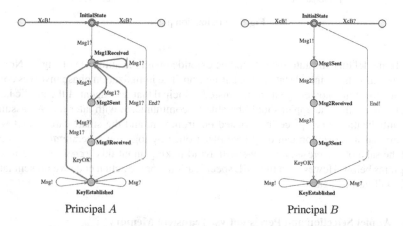

Principal *A*   Principal *B*

Fig. 4. Extended BKE state-transition diagram with exceptional behavior included

In order to keep these diagrams readable, two abbreviations are introduced. First, dummy states are introduced (indicated in Fig. 4 as the white states in the upper corners). Such a dummy state is to be seen as an abbreviation for all states. So, for example, from each state we have a transition to InitialState labeled XcB?. Without the upper right dummy state our diagram would be cluttered with five extra arrows.

Second, the label XcB? is an abbreviation for "all other messages", i.e. all possible messages that are not mentioned explicitly in the diagram. For example, consider the state Msg2Sent of agent *A* in Fig. 4. Two outgoing transitions, labelled with Msg3? and Msg1?, are drawn from this state. By the convention discussed above, there is also an implicit transition to InitialState labeled XcB?. Here XcB? now stands for any message other than Msg3? and Msg1?. So, from Msg2Sent we can move to Msg1Received by Msg1?, to Msg3Received by Msg3?, and to InitialState by any other message (i.e. Msg? or End? is received.

3.2 Initialization Phase

Before the protocol can be used, some initialization has to be performed: each agent has to get its private and public key, and has to know the public key of the other agent. All diagrams above start in the `InitialState` in which we assume the agents know all the relevant keys. In an actual implementation we will have to take care of this initialization phase.

Principal A   Trusted Principal

Fig. 5. Initialization phase

To model this, the automata should be extended with the automata of Fig. 5. Notice how this affects the initial state of the automaton. The initialization phase involves communication with another agent, some trusted principal that tells agent A the public keys of the agents that the applet should be able to communicate with later on. We assume the initialization takes place in a trusted environment, and the smart card applet will ensure that initialization can only take place once by toggling a *personalization flag*. For the sake of the presentation, we will avoid talking about this `PreBKE` state in the diagrams below. However, in the JML specifications for the actual code we present later on it will turn up again.

3.3 Applet Selection and Persistent vs. Transient Memory

Java Card smart cards are multi-application smart cards, which means that several applets can be installed on one smart card. As a consequence, before we can communicate with a Java Card applet on a smart card, we tell the smart card which applet we want to communicate with. This is done by sending a `select` command to the smart card.

Decision 2 *If the card has been issued, the resulting state after a* `select` *command is always* `InitialState`. *If the card has not been issued, the state will be* `PreBKE`.

There are two kinds of memory available on a smart card: there is *persistent* memory, EEPROM, which keeps its value if the card has no power, and there is *transient* memory, RAM, which loses its value as soon as the power supply to the smart card is interrupted. By default, all objects are allocated in persistent memory, but an applet can choose to allocate some fields in transient memory. Such fields will be reset to default initial value, e.g. 0 for numerical fields, by the smart card operating system when the card powers up.

Decision 3 *All session-oriented information such as nonces, the state of the protocol, and the session key are kept in transient memory. The other information like the card's id, public keys and the personalization flag is stored in persistent memory.*

3.4 Card Tears

A smart card applet can suddenly lose power due to a so-called *card tear*, e.g. when a card is removed from a card reader (or, in the case of a GSM SIM, when the battery of the mobile phone runs down). What should be the behavior of the smart card applet implementing agent A when a card tear happens? Of course, the applet will not be able to do anything after the card tear happens, as it will stop executing, but it can do something the next time the smart card powers up again and the applet is selected once again.

Decision 4 *It follows from Decisions 2 and 3 that after a card tear, the subsequent powering up, and selection of the applet, the new state is* InitialState *and of course all the transient memory is erased. This means that any session in progress is closed.*

Figure 6 later on makes these issues explicit. We have introduced two real states, CardInserted and CardReady, and one dummy state. As before, the dummy state can be seen as a union of all real states. So, the CardTear transition from this new dummy state to the state CardInserted can be taking from any state in the diagram. The name CardInserted may seem strange. The CardTear transition does not mean that after a card tear this automaton goes immediately to CardInserted. As soon as a card tear happens, the current session or the current automaton is stopped completely. Nothing will happen until the card is re-inserted again. In particular no transitions can be triggered during a card tear. Therefore this CardTear transition is only triggered at the re-insertion.

When the card is re-inserted the powering up takes place. In particular the terminal resets the card. The card responds to this by sending an Answer to Reset (ATR). After this the card is ready and waiting for a select command from the terminal.

3.5 Command-Response Pairs

Communication with a smart card uses the ISO7816 protocol, in which the terminal acts as a master and the smart card as a slave. The terminal sends *commands*, to which the card answers with a *response*. The messages sent between terminal and smart card are called APDUs (Application Protocol Data Unit) in ISO7816, which are just sequences of bytes. In our protocol agent A is implemented as a smart card and B as an application with access to the card terminal.

This means that all outgoing messages from A need to be triggered by an incoming message from B. And vice versa all incoming messages need to be followed by an outgoing message. Of course it would be possible to let agent A respond to all messages from B by sending a status word only. However, it seems more efficient to fill the response APDUs with the expected answers and a status word. For instance Msg1 will be implemented as a command APDU and `Msg2` will be implemented as the corresponding response APDU.

This choice has consequences for the states in the applet. After receiving `Msg1?` the applet will be in the state `Msg1Received`. However, before it tries to do anything else it will try to send back `Msg2!`. If this succeeds the resulting state will be `Msg2Sent`. If this fails the resulting state will be `InitialState`. In particular, this means the applet can never remain in state `Msg1Received` for any length of time, as the transition to this state –by a command APDU– will always be followed immediately by another transition out of this state –by the matching response APDU. This means that it is no longer possible for any incoming unsolicited message to be received in this intermediate state `Msg1Received`. Technically this means that some of the arrows in the diagram for agent A can now be omitted. However, because we used dummy states in our diagrams we do not see this in our representation. Only the interpretation of the notion of dummy state is weakened slightly.

Decision 5 *We need one extra response APDU* `Status!`*: it will act as a response to* `SelectApplet?`, `End?` *and* `XcB?`.

Below are the command-response pairs that may occur.

Commands	Msg1?	Msg3?	Msg?	End?	XcB?	SelectApplet?
Responses	Msg2!	KeyOK!	Msg!	Status!	Status!	Status!
	XcB!	XcB!	XcB!			

The way we implemented this affects the meaning of the message `Msg!`. Although it still appears in the diagram for principal A, it is now restricted to being used as an answer to the `Msg?` message. The applet will no longer be able to send `Msg!` on its own initiative! Furthermore, adding the necessary `Status!` response on the applet side implies also adding `Status?` on the terminal side.

Obviously the changes we have discussed here have an impact on the protocol as we presented it earlier. We need to add a single line:

$$2n + 3.\ A \to B : \{\texttt{Status}\}_K$$

Fig. 6 shows the corresponding state-transition diagram.

4   Using JML

This section considers the use of the Java Modeling Language (JML, see [3]) and tools that support JML to ensure that our Java (Card) implementation correctly implements the final refinement of the protocol discussed in the previous section. JML is a specification language that can be used to formally specify the behavior of Java programs.

4.1   JML Specifications

Fortunately, state-transition diagrams describing the required behavior of the agents can easily be translated into JML. (The only problem is how to deal with specifying the card tear mechanism; this is discussed in Section 4.4.)

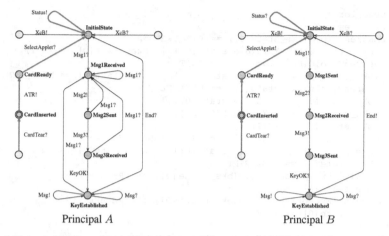

Fig. 6. Extended BKE state-transition diagram with exceptional behavior, card tear recovery, and paired APDUs included

In order to describe the rest of the diagram in Fig. 6 we use two instance variables. Namely the instance variable `personalized`, stored in persistent memory, that keeps track of whether the card has been issued or not, and the instance variable `bke_state[0]`, stored in transient memory, that records the state in the protocol. (In Java Card only arrays can be allocated in transient memory; therefore `bke_state` is a transient array of length 1.)

The diagrams of Figures 5 and 6 can be expressed by a combination of JML invariants, constraints, and method specifications.

In JML, as is usual, *invariants* are predicates which should be established by the constructor and preserved by the methods, i.e. invariants should hold after an invocation of a constructor, and both before and after any method invocation). E.g. the invariants in the JML specification below give the possible values of the applet state `bke_state[0]`, and the relation between this state and the `personalized` flag.

In JML *constraints* are relations that should be respected by all methods, i.e. the pre- and post-state of any method invocation should be in the relation specified by a constraint. E.g. the constraint in the JML specification below specifies that once a card has been `personalized`, it will remain `personalized` forever.

```
/*@ invariant
  @   bke_state[0] == PRE_BKE || bke_state[0] == INIT ||
  @   bke_state[0] == MSG1_RECEIVED || bke_state[0] == MSG2_SENT ||
  @   bke_state[0] == MSG3_RECEIVED || bke_state[0] == KEY_ESTABLISHED;
  @ invariant personalized <==> (bke_state[0] != PRE_BKE);
  @ constraint \old(personalized) ==> personalized;
  @*/
```

Based upon the automata in Fig. 5 and 6, and given these constraints and invariants, it is easy to give JML specifications for the methods that specify the desired flow of control. Below we give the method specification of the `process` method.

```
/*@ behavior
 @ requires true;
 @ ensures (\old(bke_state[0]) == PRE_BKE ==>
 @   (bke_state[0] == \old(bke_state[0]) || bke_state[0] == INIT));
 @ ensures (\old(bke_state[0]) == INIT ==>
 @   (bke_state[0] == \old(bke_state[0]) || bke_state[0] == MSG2_SENT));
 @ ensures (\old(bke_state[0]) == MSG2_SENT ==>
 @   (bke_state[0] == \old(bke_state[0]) ||
 @    bke_state[0] == KEY_ESTABLISHED ||
 @    bke_state[0] == INIT));
 @ ensures (\old(bke_state[0]) == KEY_ESTABLISHED ==>
 @   (bke_state[0] == \old(bke_state[0]) || bke_state[0] == INIT ||
 @    bke_state[0] == MSG2_SENT ));
 @ signals (Exception) (\old(bke_state[0]) == PRE_BKE ==>
 @    bke_state[0] == PRE_BKE);
 @ signals (Exception) (\old(bke_state[0]) != PRE_BKE ==>
 @    bke_state[0] == INIT);
 @*/
public void process(APDU apdu) throws ISOException
```

The method specification consists of a precondition (indicated by `requires`), post-conditions for normal termination (indicated by `ensures`), and postconditions for abnormal termination (indicated by `signals`). All `ensures` clauses should be considered together as a logical conjunction. The first `ensures` clause is specifically for the initialization phase. The `signals` clauses should be considered as a conjunction as well. There are two clauses here because we need to make a distinction between whether a card has been issued or not.

Below we give the specification of the `receiveMsg1` method. On the top level we see new keywords `also` and `exceptional_behavior`. The `also` splits the specification into two parts. The distinction is based upon the value of `bke_state[0]` on entry of the method. If this state is `PreBKE` the card has not been issued yet and hence an exception *must* be thrown and the resulting state will still be `PreBKE`. In any other state we allow this message to come in. If the receiving succeeds, the resulting state will be `Msg1Received`, otherwise an exception is thrown and the applet will go to `InitialState`. Note that this method has as a postcondition that the state will be `Msg1Received`. This state does not appear in the specification of `process`. This is because the `process` method will always call `sendMsg2` and this method will always change the state –either to `Msg2Sent` or to `InitialState`– before `process` terminates.

```
/*@ behavior
 @ requires bke_state[0] != PRE_BKE;
 @ ensures bke_state[0] == MSG1_RECEIVED;
 @ signals (Exception) (bke_state[0] == INIT);
 @ also
 @ exceptional_behavior
 @ requires bke_state[0] == PRE_BKE;
 @ signals (Exception) (bke_state[0] == PRE_BKE);
 @*/
private void receiveMsg1(APDU apdu) throws ISOException
```

4.2   Runtime Checking with the JML Tool

The JML runtime assertion checker [4] takes as input Java source files annotated with JML specifications. It augments the source files with runtime checks based on the JML specifications so that all invariants, constraints, pre- and postconditions are checked at runtime and any violation result in a special exception being thrown.

We used this tool to check the Java Card code of our applet against our JML specification. To do this we could not execute the code on an actual smart card, but we had to use a smart card simulator instead. (The reason for this is that the runtime assertion checker uses some Java API classes that are not part of the more restricted Java Card API, and are consequently not available on Java Card smart cards.) The smart card simulator we used was Sun's Java Card Workstation Development Environment (JCWDE).

In this setup we were able to find quite a few mistakes in our JML specification. Typically these errors were caused by forgetting to specify some of the implicit transactions from Fig. 6.

4.3   Static Checking with ESC/Java

ESC/Java [5], the 'extended static checker' for Java is a tool developed at Compaq SRC for automatically checking JML-annotated code[2]. The tool uses a theorem prover to automatically verify that assertions in Java code are correct, without any user interaction. The tool is neither sound nor complete, i.e. it can warn about possible violations of assertions that cannot happen, and fail to warn about possible violations of assertions that could happen. Still, the tool is very useful for debugging Java(Card) code and formal specifications, as it can provide quick feedback pointing out possible mistakes, especially since, unlike for runtime assertion checking, no test scenarios are needed for using ESC/Java. ESC/Java has already been used with great success in debugging Java Card source code, see [9].

The kind of JML specifications we have written are well within the range of what ESC/Java can handle. Running ESC/Java on our annotated applet pointed out several mistakes. For example, our initial JML specifications did not allow for the fact that on any point in the protocol the process method may receive a select APDU, in which case the applet reverts to the INIT state. In particular we did not find this mistake when we used the JML runtime assertion checker, simply because this possibility wasn't included in our test scenarios. On the other hand runtime assertion checking can deal with the actual contents of APDUs being sent, which is something ESC/Java cannot.

Note that ESC/Java requires ESC/Java specifications of the API classes used by the applet, such as the javacard.framework.APDU. Here we used the formal JML specifications for the Java Card API version 2.1.1, discussed in [10, 11] and available on-line via http://www.verificard.org.

4.4   Card Tears and Invariants

Card tears cause a special problem for invariants specified in JML. JML allows an invariant to be temporarily broken during the execution of a method. But if a card tear

---

[2] Actually, the specification language ESC/Java uses is a 'dialect' of JML.

should happen at such a point, this could cause problems later, when the applet continues its operation in a state where some of its invariants are broken.

Such problems will not show up in the runtime checking with the JML tool, as the simulator we use does not simulate card tears, and will also not show up in the static checking with ESC/Java, as ESC/Java has been designed for Java and does not take the peculiarities of Java Card into account.

There are three ways in which problems with a temporarily broken invariant at the moment of a card tear can be avoided:

1. The invariant could become re-established the next time the smart card powers up again, as a result of the resetting of all transient memory to its default initial value.
2. The invariant could become re-established when the applet is selected again, namely if the applet itself takes care to restore the invariant when it receives its select APDU.
3. Finally, Java Card offers a so-called *transaction mechanism*. By invoking special methods from the Java Card API one can turn any sequence of Java instructions into an atomic action. When the smart card powers up, the smart card operating system will roll-back to the pre-state of such a sequence of instructions if it has been interrupted by a card tear.

For every invariant in our JML specification we *manually* checked the following properties:

- Is this invariant ever temporarily broken during a method?
- If so, is the invariant re-established by one of the three mechanisms mentioned above ?

Because the Java Card transaction mechanism is not supported by the tools ESC/Java and JML, our applet does not use this functionality, and hence we never had to rely on the third way to re-establish invariants after a card tear listed above.

5   Conclusions

We started with an abstract description of a security protocol, for bilateral key exchange, for which we had earlier used Casper [7] and FDR2 [8] to prove its correctness. This paper describes how, based on a few explicit design decisions, we refined this protocol in several stages to an actual implementation, where one of the agents is implemented as a Java Card smart card applet. It should be stressed that our interest here is not the outcome of our decisions, but rather the decision making-process itself. The JML language was used for a formal specification of the Java Card code. It turns out that this specification can be systematically derived from the finite automaton in Fig. 6, the final refinement of the abstract protocol, that includes card tears and the handling of all possible exceptions that may arise. We have checked that the implementation meets these specifications, using runtime assertion checking with the JML tool, and doing static checking using ESC/Java.

Implementing a security protocol on a smart card involves some non-straightforward decisions: decisions 1, 2, 3, 4, and 5.

Both static checking and runtime checking turn out to be good methods to check JML specifications of applets. Although they will not notice all problems, they certainly help to improve the code and the specifications. Both methods have their own advantages and disadvantages, therefore it is a good idea to use both ESC/Java and JML, although they are not specific Java Card tools.

In [12] a list of important security properties for Java Card applets is presented. The JML specifications for our applet include several of these properties, e.g. 'service control' and 'error prediction', but not all of them. Some properties, most notably 'secure information flow', have been taken into account while coding, but cannot be specified in JML in any convenient way.

Future Work

The most important open question is how we can prove that the refinements of the protocol ensure the same security properties that the original protocol establishes. We can think of two ways to do this.

We already used the FDR2 model checker to prove that the original abstract protocol establishes authenticity and secrecy. We also tried to use it to check the same properties of our refinements of the protocol. However, FDR2 had problems with the recursion in these refinements, which allow infinite traces. It might be a good idea to spend some more time in defining this recursive CSP model. Maybe we could get FDR2 to prove that our security properties are valid for traces of a certain maximum length, which would give us some more confidence that the refinements preserve the properties of the original protocol.

Alternatively, we could investigate properties of the refinements between the different automata. For example, one obvious property that holds for the refinements is trace inclusion. Another property is that any trace that leads to the state KeyEstablished in the final refinement Fig. 6 will have a tail that leads to the state Msg3Received in Fig. 2. Intuitively, such properties seem sufficient to guarantee that our refinements preserve the security properties of the original protocol. However, we have not formally proved this yet.

It would be interesting to experiment with model checkers, such as Uppaal [13], to check interesting properties of the automata describing the protocol. (In fact, we already used Uppaal to draw all the diagrams in this paper.) Even if we are not able to check typical security properties, we might for example be able to rule out the possibility of deadlock.

Maybe it is worthwhile to develop new versions of ESC/Java and JML in order to cope with features specific to Java Card, such as the transaction mechanism and the possibility of card tears.

After static checking with ESC/Java and runtime checker for JML, the next step would be to prove the correctness of the JML specification with respect to the Java Card implementation using the LOOP tool [14], in combination with the theorem prover PVS [15]. See [16] for a discussion of examples of such correctness proofs. Such a formal verification would provide a much higher level of assurance that our implementation does indeed meet its specification than the checking with ESC/Java. However, it would also require much more effort, as such verifications are very labour-intensive. For the current JML specifications, we do not think such an additional effort would be worthwhile, as ESC/Java seems reliable enough when dealing with these kinds of properties.

References

1. Burrows, M., Abadi, M., Needham, R.: A logic of authentication. Proc. Royal Soc. **Series A, Volume 426** (1989) 233–271
2. Ryan, P., Schneider, S., Goldschmith, M., Lowe, G., A.W.Roscoe: The Modelling and Analysis of Security Protocols: the CSP Approach. Addison Wesley (2001)
3. Leavens, G., Baker, A., Ruby, C.: Preliminary design of JML: A behavioral interface specification language for Java. Technical Report 98-06q, Dep. of Comp. Sci., Iowa State Univ. (2002)
4. Cheon, Y., Leavens, G.: A Runtime Assertion Checker for the Java Modeling Language (JML). In Arabnia, H., Mun, Y., eds.: International Conference on Software Engineering Research and Practice (SERP '02), Las Vegas, Nevada, CSREA Press, June 2002 (2002) 322–328
5. Compaq Systems Research Center: Extended Static Checker for Java (2001) version 1.2.4, http://research.compaq.com/SRC/esc/.
6. Clark, J., Jacob, J.: A Survey of Authentication Protocol Literature: Version 1.0. http://www-users.cs.york.ac.uk/ jac/drareviewps.ps (1997)
7. Lowe, G.: Casper: A Compiler for the Analysis of Security Protocols (2001) version 1.5, http://web.comlab.ox.ac.uk/oucl/work/gavin.lowe/Security/Casper/.
8. Formal Systems: FDR2, Failures Divergence Refinement (2000) version 2.78, http://www.formal.demon.co.uk/FDR2.html.
9. Cataño, N., Huisman, M.: Formal specification of Gemplus's electronic purse case study. In Eriksson, L.H., Lindsay, P.A., eds.: Formal Methods Europe (FME). Volume 2391 of LNCS., Copenhagen, Denmark, Springer-Verlag (2002) 272–289
10. Poll, E., van den Berg, J., Jacobs, B.: Formal specification of the Java Card API in JML: the APDU class. Computer Networks **36** (2001) 407–421
11. Poll, E., van den Berg, J., Jacobs, B.: Specification of the JavaCard API in JML. In Domingo-Ferrer, J., Chan, D., Watson, A., eds.: Fourth Smart Card Research and Advanced Application Conference (CARDIS'2000), Kluwer Acad. Publ. (2000) 135–154
12. Marlet, R., Metayer, D.L.: Security properties and java card specificities to be studied in the secsafe project. Technical Report SECSAFE-TL-006, Trusted Logic (2001) Available from http://www.doc.ic.ac.uk/ siveroni/secsafe/docs.html.
13. Uppaal: An integrated tool environment for modeling, validation and verification of real-time system modeled as networks of timed automata, extended with data types (2002) version 3.2.11, http://www.uppaal.com.
14. Jacobs, B., et al.: Reasoning about classes in Java (preliminary report). In: Object-Oriented Programming, Systems, Languages and Applications (OOPSLA), ACM Press (1998) 329–340
15. Owre, S., Shankar, N., Rushby, J.M., Stringer-Calvert, D.W.J.: PVS System Guide. Computer Science Laboratory, SRI International, Menlo Park, CA, USA. (1999) Available at http://pvs.csl.sri.com/.
16. Breunesse, C.B., Jacobs, B., van den Berg, J.: Specifying and verifying a decimal representation in Java for smart cards. In Kirchner, H., Ringeissen, C., eds.: 9th Algebraic Methodology and Software Technology (AMAST). Volume 2422 of LNCS., St. Gilles les Bains, Reunion Island, France, Springer-Verlag (2002) 304–318

Cellular Automata Based Multiplier
for Public-Key Cryptosystem

Hyun-Sung Kim[1] and Kee-Young Yoo[2]

[1] Kyungil University, Computer Engineering,
712-701, Kyungsansi, Kyungpook Province, Korea
kim@kiu.ac.kr
[2] Kyungpook National University, Computer Engineering,
702-701 Daegu, Korea
yook@knu.ac.kr

Abstract. This paper proposes two new multipliers based on cellular automata over finite field. Finite fields arithmetic operations have been widely used in the areas of data communication and network security applications. First, a multiplier with generalized irreducible polynomial is implemented with MSB-first fashion. Then, new algorithm and architecture are proposed to reduce the size of the first multiplier. The algorithm and architecture uses the property of irreducible all one polynomial as a modulus. Since the proposed architectures have regularity, modularity and concurrency, they are suitable for VLSI implementation and could be used in IC cards because they have particularly simple architecture. They can be used as a basic architecture for the public-key cryptosystems.

1 Introduction

Finite field $GF(2^m)$ arithmetic is fundamental to the implementation of a number of modern cryptographic systems and schemes of certain cryptographic systems[1][2]. Most arithmetic operations, such as exponentiation, inversion, and division operations, can be carried out using just a modular multiplier or using modular multiplier and squarer. Therefore, to reduce the complexity of these arithmetic architectures, an efficient architecture for multiplication over $GF(2^m)$ is necessary.

In 1984, Yeh, et al. [7] developed a parallel systolic architecture for performing the operation $AB + C$ in a general $GF(2^m)$. A semi-systolic array architecture in [8] was proposed using the standard basis, whereas architecture to compute multiplication and inversion were represented using the normal basis [9]. A systolic power-sum circuit was presented in [10], and many bit-parallel systolic multipliers have been proposed. However, these multipliers still have some shortages for cryptography applications due to their system complexity. For the better complexity, Itoh and Tsujii [11] designed two low-complexity multipliers for the class of $GF(2^m)$, based on an irreducible all one polynomial (AOP) of degree m and irreducible equally spaced polynomial of degree m. Later, Fenn, et al. in [12] and Kim in [13] developed linear feedback shift register (LFSR) based multipliers with low complexity of hardware architecture using the property of AOP.

D. Hutter et al. (Eds.): Security in Pervasive Computing 2003, LNCS 2802, pp. 227–236, 2004.

Cellular automata (CA), first introduced by John Von Neumann in the 1950s, have been accepted as a good computational model for the simulation of complex physical systems [3]. Wolfram defined the basic classification of cellular automata using their qualitative and functional behavior [4], whereas Pries, et al. focused on the group properties induced by the patterns of behavior [5]. Choudhury proposed an LSB-first multiplier using CA with low latency [14]. However, all such previously designed systems still have certain shortcomings.

Accordingly, the purpose of this paper is to propose two new modular multipliers over $GF(2^m)$. Two multipliers deploy the mixture of the advantages from the previous architectures in the perspective of area and time complexity. First, a multiplier, denoted by GMM, is implemented with generalized irreducible polynomial. It uses MSB-first modular multiplication algorithm. Then, new algorithm and architecture are proposed to reduce the size of GMM. The algorithm and architecture uses the property of irreducible all one polynomial as a modulus. The proposed architectures can be used as a kernel circuit for exponentiation, inversion, and division architectures. These operations are very important part to implement public key cryptosystems. If we use the proposed multipliers to implement cryptosystem, we can get a great cryptosystem with low hardware and time complexity. They are easy to implement VLSI hardware and could be used in IC cards as the multipliers have a particularly simple architecture.

2   Background

This section provides the necessary operations in the public-key cryptosystem and a brief description of finite fields and cellular automata. These properties will be used to derive new multipliers.

2.1   Public-Key Cryptosystem

Elgamal proposed public-key cryptosystem[2]; it gets its security from the difficulty of calculating discrete logarithms in a finite field. To generate a key pair, first choose a prime, p, and two random numbers, g and x, such that both g and x are less than p, then calculate

$$y = g^x \bmod p \tag{1}$$

The public key is y, g, and p. Both g and p can be shared among a group of users. The private key is x. The Elgamal scheme using this property of equation 1 can be used for both digital signatures and encryption.

When designing ECC (Elliptic Curve Cryptosystem), the sum of two points on the elliptic curve requires a number of divisions, which can be computed using multiplication and a multiplicative inverse, $A/B = AB^{-1}$. An inverse can be regarded as a special case of exponentiation because $B^{-1} = B^{(2^m - 2)}$.

Therefore, modular exponentiation over finite fields is very critical operation to implement public-key cryptosystem as described in the above. So, it is necessary to see the operation in detail. Let C and M be elements of $GF(2^m)$, the exponentiation of M is then defined as

$$C = M^E, \ 0 \le E \le n \tag{2}$$

For a special case, $M = \alpha$. The exponent E, which is an integer can be expressed by $E = e_{m-1}2^{m-1} + e_{m-2}2^{m-2} + ... + e_1 2^1 + e_0$. The exponent also can be represented with vector representation $[e_{m-1}e_{m-2}...e_1e_0]$. A popular algorithm for computing exponentiation is the binary method proposed by Knuth [15]. The exponentiation of M can be expressed as

$$M^E = M^{e_0}(M^{2^1})^{e_1}(M^{2^2})^{e_2}...(M^{2^{m-1}})^{e_{m-1}} \tag{3}$$

Based on equation 3, an algorithm for computing exponentiations is presented as following algorithm.

[Algorithm 1] Knuth's Binary Method
Input : $M, E, f(x)$
Output : $C=M^E \bmod f(x)$

```
1:    T=M
2:    if (e_0==1) C=T else C=α^0
3:        for i=1 to m-1
4:            T=TT mod f(x)
5:                if (e_i==1) C=CT mod f(x)
```

The algorithm shows that the exponentiation can be performed with squaring in line 4 and multiplication in line 5. Modular squaring can be considered as a special case of modular multiplication, which has the same input for operand and operator. Next section presents new architectures for this modular multiplication with significantly low complexity of operations.

2.2 Finite Fields

A finite field $GF(2^m)$ contains 2^m elements that are generated by an irreducible polynomial of degree m over $GF(2)$. A polynomial $f(x)$ of degree m is said to be irreducible if the smallest positive integer n for which $f(x)$ divides $x^n + 1$ is $n = 2^m - 1$[6]. Let $f(x) = x^m + f_{m-1}x^{m-1} + ... + f_1 x^1 + f_0$ be an irreducible polynomial over $GF(2^m)$ and be a root of $f(x)$. Any field element $GF(2^m)$ can be represented by a standard basis such as

$$a = a_{m-1}\alpha^{m-1} + a_{m-2}\alpha^{m-2} + ... + a_0 \tag{4}$$

where $a_i \in GF(2)$ for $0 \le i \le m - 1$. $\{1, \alpha, \alpha^2, ..., \alpha^{m-2}, \alpha^{m-1}\}$ is an ordinary standard basis of $GF(2^m)$.

It has been shown that an all one polynomial (AOP) is irreducible if and only if $m+1$ is a prime and 2 is a generator of the field $GF(m+1)$ [11]. The values of m for which an AOP of degree m is irreducible are 2, 4, 10, 12, 18, 28, 36, 52, 58, 60, 66, 82, and 100 for $m \le 100$. Let $ff(x) = x^m + x^{m-1} + ... + x + 1$ be an irreducible AOP over $GF(2^m)$ and be the root of $ff(x)$ such that $ff(\alpha) = \alpha^m + \alpha^{m-1} + ... + \alpha + 1 = 0$. Then we have

$$\alpha^m = \alpha^{m-1} + \alpha^{m-2} + ... + \alpha + 1, \alpha^{m+1} = 1$$

The reduction is often performed using the polynomial $\alpha^{m+1} + 1$. This property of irreducible polynomial is very adaptable for PBCA architecture, which will be described in sub-section 2.3.

If it is assumed that $\{1, \alpha, \alpha^2, \alpha^3, ..., \alpha^m\}$ is an extended standard basis, the field element A can also be represented as

$$A = A_m \alpha^m + A_{m-1} \alpha^{m-1} + A_{m-2} \alpha^{m-2} + ... + A_0 \tag{5}$$

where $A_m = 0$ and $A_i \in GF(2)$ for $0 \le i \le m$. Here, $a = A \pmod{ff(x)}$, where $ff(x)$ is an AOP of degree m, then the coefficients of a are given by $a_i = A_i + A_m \pmod 2, 0 \le i \le m - 1$.

2.3 Cellular Automata

Cellular automata are finite state machines, defined as uniform arrays of simple cells in n-dimensional space. They can be characterized by looking at four properties: the cellular geometry, neighborhood specification, number of states per cell, and algorithm used for computing the successor state. Cells are restricted to local neighborhood interaction and have no global communication. A cell uses an algorithm, called its computation rule, to compute its successor state based on the information received from its nearest neighbors. An example is shown below for 2-state 3-neighborhood 1-dimensional CA [3-5].

Neighborhood state	:	111	110	101	100	011	010	001	000	
State coefficient	:	2^7	2^6	2^5	2^4	2^3	2^2	2^1	2^0	
Next state	:	0	1	0	1	1	0	1	0	(rule 90)
Next state	:	1	1	1	1	0	0	0	0	(rule 240)

In the above example, the top row gives all eight possible states of the 3-neighboring cells at time t. The second row is the state coefficient, while the third and last rows give the corresponding states of the ith cell at time $t+1$ for two illustrative CA rules. If the next state function of a cell is expressed in the form of a truth table, then the decimal equivalent of the out column in the truth table is conventionally called the rule number for the cell. The next state of the CA is determined by the current state and the rules that govern its behavior. Let the previous, current, and next state be s_{i-1}, s_i, and s_{i+1}. The two rules 90 and 240 result in the following:

$$\text{rule 90: } S_i^+ = s_{i-1} \oplus s_{i+1}, \text{ rule 240: } S_i^+ = s_{i-1}$$

where S_i^+ denotes the next state for cell s_i, and '$\oplus$' denotes an XOR operation.

In addition, CA is composed of Linear CA, Non-Linear CA, and Additive CA according to the operation rules applied between cells. Linear CA are restricted to linear rules of operation, which means that the next state of the machine can only be computed from the previous state using a linear operation, i.e., an XOR operation. Non-Linear CA is composed of XOR operation plus other operations, while additive CA is composed of only XOR and/or XNOR operations. CA is also classified as Uniform or Hybrid based on the rules applied. Uniform CA only has one rule, whereas Hybrid CA has two or more rules. Finally, CA can be referred to as named 1-dimensional, 2-dimensional, and 3-dimensional based on the structure of the array.

There are various possible boundary conditions, for example, a Null-Boundary CA (NBCA), where the extreme cells are connected to the ground level, a Periodic-Boundary CA (PBCA), where extreme cells are adjacent, etc.

The present state of a CA having m cells can be shown in terms of an m vector $v = (v_0 \ v_1 \ v_2 \ ... \ v_{m-1})$, where v_i is the value of cell i, and v_i is an element of $GF(2)$. The next state of a linear CA can be determined by multiplying the characteristic matrix with the vector in the present state, where the characteristic matrix denoted by T show all rules of the CA. If v^t is a column vector representing the state of the automata at the t-th instant of time, then the next state of the linear CA is given by $v^{t+1} = T \times v^t$.

$$T = \begin{bmatrix} 0 & 1 & 0 & 0 \\ 1 & 0 & 0 & 0 \\ 0 & 1 & 0 & 1 \\ 0 & 0 & 1 & 0 \end{bmatrix}$$

Fig. 1. Characteristic matrix for NBCA with rules (90, 240, 90, 240).

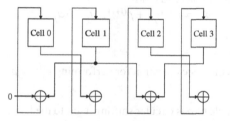

Fig. 2. One-dimensional 4-cell NBCA using rules (90, 240, 90, 240).

Fig. 2 shows a 4-cell 2-state 3-neighborhood 1-dimensional CA architecture using rules $\langle 90, 240, 90, 240 \rangle$.

3   Modular Multipliers

This section presents two new multipliers over $GF(2^m)$. These multipliers are based on cellular automata. First, we propose a new modular multiplier, denoted by GMM, using a generalized irreducible polynomial with the ordinary modular multiplication. Then, devise a new multiplication algorithm and a new multiplier, denoted by AMM, which uses the property of irreducible AOP as a modulus.

3.1   Generalized Modular Multiplier (GMM)

Let a and b be the elements over $GF(2^m)$ and $f(x)$ be the modulus. Then each element over ordinary standard basis is expressed as follows:

$$a = a_{m-1}\alpha^{m-1} + a_{m-2}\alpha^{m-2} + ... + a_0$$
$$b = b_{m-1}\alpha^{m-1} + b_{m-2}\alpha^{m-2} + ... + b_0$$
$$f(x) = x^m + f_{m-1}x^{m-1} + f_{m-2}x^{m-2} + ... + f_0$$

For steps 4 and 5 for modular exponentiation in Algorithm 1, the modular multiplication $p = ab \bmod f(x)$ can be represented with a recurrence equation with MSB (Most Significant Bit) first fashion as follows:

$$p = ab \bmod f(x)$$
$$= \{...[b_{m-1}a\,\alpha \bmod f(x) + b_{m-2}a]\alpha \bmod f(x) + ... + b_1a\}\alpha \bmod f(x) + b_0a \quad (6)$$

Following algorithm 2 shows the ordinary modular multiplication.

[Algorithm 2] Ordinary Modular Multiplication
Input   : $a, b, f(x)$
Output   : $p = ab \bmod f(x)$
Initial value : $p^{(m)} = (p^{(m)}_{m-1}, p^{(m)}_{m-2}, ..., p^{(m)}_0) = (0, 0, ..., 0)$

1:    for $i = m-1$ to 0 do
2:        for $j = m-1$ to 0 do
3:            $p^{(i)}_j = p^{(i+1)}_{j-1} + p^{(i+1)}_{m-1}f_j + b_ia_j$

The following is the basic operation for performing $p^{(i)}_j = p^{(i+1)}_{j-1} + p^{i+1}_{m-1}f_j + b_ia_j$ at step 3.

Operation 3-1: m-tuple of p is circular shifting 1-bit to the left as follows:

$$(p'_{m-2}, p'_{m-3}, ..., p'_{m-1}) \leftarrow (p_{m-1}, p_{m-2}, ..., p_1, p_0)$$

Operation 3-2: Multiply b_i to m-tuple of a, add it to m-tuple of p, and apply modular operation with $p^{(i+1)}_{m-1}f_j$ as follows:

$$(p_{m-1}, p_{m-2}, ..., p_1, p_0) \leftarrow (p'_{m-2}, p'_{m-3}, ..., p'_0, p'_{m-1}) + b_i(a_{m-1}, a_{m-2}, ..., a_1, a_0)$$
$$+ p'_{m-1}(f_{m-1}, f_{m-2}, ..., f_1, f_0)$$

In order to perform operation 3-1, the 1-dimensional PBCA having m cells is used which is the upper part with gray colored in Fig. 3. p is inputted into m cells of CA and CA has a characteristic matrix with all rules 170 for the operation 3-1. Fig. 3 shows the proposed generalized modular multiplier using PBCA with rules 170. It is possible to perform multiplication in m clock cycles over $GF(2^m)$.

Each cell has 2-AND (two 2-input AND gates) and 2-XOR (two 2-input XOR gates) except the last cell. It is because the last cell does not need one XOR operation since the last input always has the value of '0'.

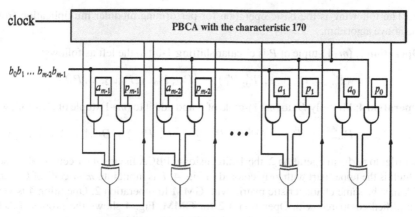

Fig. 3. Generalized modular multiplier (GMM).

3.2 AOP Modular Multiplier (AMM)

Let A and B be the elements over $GF(2^m)$ and $t(x)$ be the modulus which uses the property of an irreducible AOP. Then each element over extended standard basis is expressed as follows:

$$A = A_m\alpha^m + A_{m-1}\alpha^{m-1} + A_{m-2}\alpha^{m-2} + ... + A_0$$
$$B = B_m\alpha^m + B_{m-1}\alpha^{m-1} + B_{m-2}\alpha^{m-2} + ... + B_0$$
$$t(x) = \alpha^{m+1} + 1$$

From the recurrence equation 6, new modular multiplication $P = AB \bmod t(x)$ can be derived which applied the property of AOP as a modulus as follows:

$$P = AB \bmod t(x)$$
$$= [CLS(...[CLS([CLS(B_mA)] + B_{m-1}A)] + ...)] + B_1A)] + B_0A \quad (7)$$

Circular shifting 1-bit to the left is represented as $CLS()$ in equation 7. After the applying the property of AOP as a modulus, modular reduction is efficiently performed with just $CLS()$ operation.

Following shows the proposed modular multiplication with AOP as an irreducible polynomial.

[Algorithm 3] Proposed Modular Multiplication
Input   : A, B
Output   : $P = AB \bmod \alpha^{m+1}+1$
Initial value : $P^{(m+1)} = (P^{(m+1)}{}_m, P^{(m+1)}{}_{m-1}, ..., P^{(m+1)}{}_0) = (0, 0, ..., 0)$

```
1:   for i = m to 0 do
2:       Pⁱ = CLS(Pⁱ⁺¹)
3:       for j = m to 0 do
4:           P⁽ⁱ⁾ⱼ = P⁽ⁱ⁾ⱼ + BⱼAⱼ
```

The following is the basic operation for performing modular multiplication from the above algorithm.

Operation 2: $(m+1)$-tuple of P is circular shifting 1-bit to the left as follows:

$$(P'_{m-1}, P'_{m-2}, ..., P'_0, P'_m) \leftarrow (P_m, P_{m-1}, P_{m-2}, ..., P_0)$$

Operation 4: Multiply B_i to $(m+1)$-tuple of A and add it to $(m+1)$-tuple of P as follows:

$$(P_m, P_{m-1}, P_{m-2}, ..., P_0) \leftarrow (P'_{m-1}, P'_{m-2}, ..., P'_0, P\prime_m) + B_i(A_m, A_{m-1}, ..., A_0)$$

In order to perform operation 2, the 1-dimensional PBCA having $m+1$ cells is also used which is the upper part with gray colored in Fig. 4. P is input into $m+1$ cells of CA and CA has the same characteristic matrix with GMM for operation 2. Operation 4 is very simplified compared with Operation 3-2 for GMM. Fig. 4 shows the proposed AOP modular multiplier using PBCA with rules 170. It is possible to perform multiplication in $m+1$ clock cycles over $GF(2^m)$.

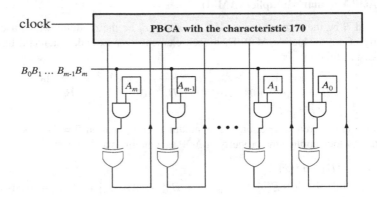

Fig. 4. AOP modular multiplier (AMM).

Each cell has one 1-AND and one 1-XOR (one 2-input XOR gate). AMM has more lower hardware complexity than GMM.

4   Analysis

Proposed two multipliers, GMM and AMM, were simulated using ALTERA MAX PLUSII simulation tool with FLEX10K device.

Table 1 shows a comparison between proposed and previous modular multipliers. For the comparison, it is assumed that n AND and n XOR represent n number of 2-input AND gate and XOR gate, respectively, and REG and Latch represents 1-bit register and latch, respectively. Comparison shows that the proposed architectures hybrid the advantages from previous architectures. Proposed two architectures, GMM and AMM, have

Table 1. Comparison for modular multipliers.

Item / Circuit	Function	Number of cells	Latency	Hardware Complexity	Critical Path
Yeh in [7]	$AB+C$	m	$3m$	$3m$ AND $2m$ XOR $11m$ Latch	AND+XOR
Chaudhury in [14]	$AB+C$	m	m	$2m$ AND $2m$ XOR $4m$ REG	AND+XOR
Fenn in [12]	AB	$m+1$	$2m-1$	$2m$-1 AND $2m$-2 XOR $2m+2$ REG	AND $+(\log_2 m)$XOR
Kim in [13]	AB	$m+1$	$2m+1$	$m+1$ AND m XOR $2m+2$ REG	AND $+(\log_2 m)$XOR
GMM	$AB+C$	m	m	$2m$ AND $2m$-1 XOR $3m$ REG	AND+2XOR
AMM	$AB+C$	$m+1$	$m+1$	$m+1$ AND $m+1$ XOR $3m+3$ REG	AND+XOR

good property in the perspective of hardware and time complexity compared with the architecture of Yeh. et al in [7]. Their architecture is based on systolic array. Chaudhury in [4] proposed multiplier based on cellular automata with LSB-first fashion. The multiplier has very similar property with GMM. But AMM reduced hardware complexity than Chaudhurys. Fenn et al. in [12] and Kim in [13] designed modular multipliers based on LFSR (Linear Feedback Shift Register) architecture. They both used the property of AOP as irreducible polynomial. The hardware complexity of their architecture is similar with AMM but AMM is very efficient for the time complexity.

5 Conclusion

This paper proposed two new modular multipliers over $GF(2^m)$. They are based on cellular automata, especially PBCA. First, a multiplier, denoted by GMM, with generalized irreducible polynomial was implemented based on the MSB-first algorithm. Then, new algorithm and architecture were proposed to reduce the size of GMM. New algorithm and architecture uses the property of irreducible all one polynomial as a modulus. Proposed multipliers hybrid the advantages from previous architectures.

Since the proposed multipliers have regularity, modularity and concurrency, they are suitable for VLSI implementation. The proposed multipliers can be used as a kernel circuit for public-key cryptosystem, which requires exponentiation, inversion, and division as their basic operation.

Acknowledgement

This research was supported by University IT Research Center Project.

References

1. I. S. Reed ,. T. K. Truong.: The use of finite fields to compute convolutions. IEEE Trans. on Information Theory. IT-21, pp. 208-213, Mar. 1975.
2. B. Schneier.: Applied Cryptography - second edition. John Wiley and Sons, Inc. 1996.
3. V. Neumann.: The theory of self-reproducing automata. Univ. of Illinois Press, Urbana London. 1966.
4. S. Wolfram.: Statistical mechanics of cellular automata. Rev. of Modern Physics. vol. 55, pp. 601-644, 1983.
5. W. Pries., A. Thanailakis., and H. C. Card.: Group properties of cellular automata and VLSI applications. IEEE Trans. on Computers. C-35, vol. 12, pp. 1013-1024, Dec. 1986.
6. E. R. Berlekamp.: Algebraic Coding Theory. New York: McGraw-Hill. 1986.
7. C. S. Yeh., S. Reed.,T. K. Truong.: Systolic multipliers for finite fields $GF(2^m)$. IEEE Trans. on Computers. vol. C-33, pp.357-360, Apr. 1984.
8. S. K. Jain., L. Song.: Efficient Semisystolic Architectures for finite field Arithmetic. IEEE Trans. on VLSI Systems. vol. 6, no. 1, pp. 101-113, Mar. 1998.
9. J. L. Massey., J. K. Omura.: Computational method and apparatus for finite field arithmetic. U. S. Patent application. submitted 1981.
10. S. W. Wei.: A systolic power-sum circuit for $GF(2^m)$. IEEE Trans. on Computers. vol. 43, pp. 226-229, Feb. 1994.
11. T. Itoh., S. Tsujii.: Structure of parallel multipliers for a class of finite fields $GF(2^m)$. Info. Comp. vol. 83, pp. 21-40, 1989.
12. S. T. J. Fenn., M. G. Parker., M. Benaissa., D. Taylor.: Bit-serial Multiplication in $GF(2^m)$ using irreducible all one polynomials. IEE. Proc. Comput. Digit. Tech. vol. 144, no. 6, Nov. 1997.
13. H. S. Kim.: Serial AOP Arithmetic Architecture for Modular Exponentiation. Ph. D. Thesis, Kyungpook National Univ. 2002.
14. P. Pal. Choudhury., R. Barua.: Cellular Automata Based VLSI Architecture for Computing Multiplication and Inverses in $GF(2^m)$. IEEE 7th International Conference on VLSI Design. Jan. 1994.
15. D. E. Knuth.: The Art of Computer Programming. Volume 2: Seminumerical Algorithms. Addison-Wesley, Reading, Massachusetts, 2nd edition. 1998.

Enlisting Hardware Architecture to Thwart Malicious Code Injection*

Ruby B. Lee, David K. Karig, John P. McGregor, and Zhijie Shi

Princeton Architecture Laboratory for Multimedia and Security (PALMS)
Department of Electrical Engineering, Princeton University
{rblee,dkarig,mcgregor,zshi}@ee.princeton.edu

Abstract. Software vulnerabilities that enable the injection and execution of malicious code in pervasive Internet-connected computing devices pose serious threats to cyber security. In a common type of attack, a hostile party induces a software buffer overflow in a susceptible computing device in order to corrupt a procedure return address and transfer control to malicious code. These buffer overflow attacks are often employed to recruit oblivious hosts into distributed denial of service (DDoS) attack networks, which ultimately launch devastating DDoS attacks against victim networks or machines. In spite of existing software countermeasures that seek to prevent buffer overflow exploits, many systems remain vulnerable.

In this paper, we describe a hardware-based secure return address stack (SRAS), which prevents malicious code injection involving procedure return address corruption. Implementing this special hardware stack only requires low cost modifications to the processor and operating system. This enables the hardware protection to be applied to both legacy executable code and new programs. Also, this hardware defense has a negligible impact on performance in the applications examined. The security offered by this hardware solution complements rather than replaces that provided by existing static software techniques. Thus, we detail how the combination of the proposed secure return address stack and software defenses enables comprehensive multi-layer protection against buffer overflow attacks and malicious code injection.

1   Introduction

As the number and networking capabilities of pervasive computing devices increase, built-in security for these devices becomes more critical. Hostile parties can exploit any of several security vulnerabilities in Internet-enabled computing devices to inject malicious code that is later employed to launch large-scale attacks. Furthermore, attacks involving billions of compromised pervasive computing devices can be much more devastating than attacks that employ thousands

* This work was supported in part by the NSF under grants CCR-0208946 and CCR-0105677 and in part by a research gift from Hewlett-Packard.

D. Hutter et al. (Eds.): Security in Pervasive Computing 2003, LNCS 2802, pp. 237–252, 2004.

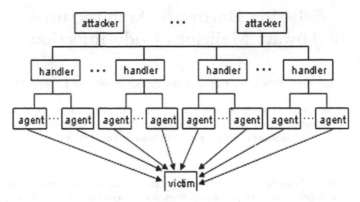

Fig. 1. Distributed denial of service attack network

or millions of traditional desktop machines. Malicious code is often inserted into victim computers by taking advantage of software vulnerabilities such as buffer overflows, which can alter the control flow of the program. In this paper, we propose a built-in hardware defense for processors to prevent malicious code injection due to buffer overflow attacks.

Buffer overflows have caused security problems since the early days of computing. In 1988, the Morris Worm, which resulted in large-scale denial of service, spread throughout the Internet using a buffer overflow vulnerability as one of its means of intrusion. The Code Red worm further exemplifies the severity of problems that buffer overflow vulnerabilities still cause today. Code Red and its variants, which stung companies over the summer of 2001, took advantage of a buffer overflow problem in Microsoft IIS. The total economic cost of these worms was estimated at $2.6 billion by Computer Economics [19].

Buffer overflow vulnerabilities also play a significant role in distributed denial of service (DDoS) attacks. In such attacks, an adversary compromises a large number of machines to set up a DDoS network that is later used to launch a massive, coordinated attack against a victim machine or network. A typical DDoS network is shown in Figure 1. An adversary controls one or more handler machines, which in turn command the agent machines (also called "zombies") that actually carry out the attack. This network structure allows an attacker to easily control a large number of machines and makes the attacker difficult to trace. Furthermore, as the number of pervasive computing devices grows rapidly, the potential destructiveness of DDoS attacks greatly increases.

Various tools are available that provide for the large-scale compromise of machines and the installation of DDoS attack software. These tools scan thousands of hosts for the presence of known weaknesses such as buffer overflow vulnerabilities. Susceptible hosts are then compromised, and attack tools are installed on the oblivious handler or agent machines. The compromised hosts can then be used to scan other systems, and this cycle of intrusion may be repeated indefinitely [11]. The tools differ in the types of attacks they execute and in the

Table 1. CERT buffer overflow advisories

Year	Advisories	Advisories involving buffer overflow	Percent buffer overflow
1996	27	5	18.52 %
1997	28	15	53.57 %
1998	13	7	53.85 %
1999	17	8	47.06 %
2000	22	2	9.09 %
2001	37	19	51.35 %

communication between nodes in the attack network, but all allow the attacker to orchestrate large-scale, distributed attacks [15, 16]. Popular attack tools include Trinity, trinoo, Tribal Flood Network (TFN) and TFN2K, and Stacheldraht [4].

Defending against DDoS attacks in progress is extremely difficult. Hence, one of the best countermeasures is to hinder attack networks from being established in the first place, and defending against buffer overflow vulnerabilities is an important step in this direction. Table 1 shows the percentages of CERT advisories between 1996 and 2001 relating to buffer overflow weaknesses. In 2001, more than 50 percent of CERT advisories involved buffer overflow. Furthermore, buffer overflow weaknesses play a very significant role in the 20 most critical Internet security vulnerabilities identified by the SANS Institute and the FBI [20].

The majority of buffer overflow exploits involve an attacker "smashing the stack" and changing the return address of a targeted function to point to injected code. Thus, protecting return addresses from corruption prevents many attacks. Past work addresses the problem through static and dynamic software methods, such as safe programming languages, operating system patches, compiler changes, and even run-time defense. However, the examination of potential solutions at the hardware architecture level is justified by the frequency of this type of attack, the number of years it has been causing problems, the continuing emergence of such problems despite existing software solutions, and the explosive increase of vulnerable devices.

We propose a hardware-based, built-in, non-optional layer of protection to defend against common buffer overflow vulnerabilities in all future systems. We detail how a hardware secure return address stack (SRAS) mechanism can be used to achieve this goal. The mechanism preserves a correct copy of every procedure return address for correct program control flow, and it provides a means of detecting buffer overflow attacks with high probability. Our proposal is a "hardware safety net" that should be applied in conjunction with safe programming techniques and compiler-inserted checking mechanisms to provide a multi-layered defense.

In Section 2, we describe the problem of return address corruption caused by buffer overflows. We summarize and compare past work in Section 3. In Section 4, we present a multi-layer software and hardware protection mechanism for buffer overflow attacks in pervasive computing devices. We describe the hardware architectural support for our proposal in Section 5. In Section 6, we discuss performance and implementation costs, and we conclude in Section 7.

2   Stack Smashing via Buffer Overflow

Most buffer overflow attacks involve corruption of procedure return addresses in the memory stack. During the execution of a procedure call instruction, the processor transfers control to code that implements the target procedure. Upon completing the procedure, control is returned to the instruction following the call instruction. This transfer of control occurs in a LIFO (i.e., Last In First Out) fashion, or properly nested fashion. Thus, a procedure call stack, which is a LIFO data structure, is used to save the state between procedure calls and returns. Compilers for different languages use the same stack format, and therefore a function written in one language can call functions written in other languages. We describe memory stack behavior for the IA-32 architecture [12], but the general procedures apply to all conventional ISAs.

The memory stack is typically implemented as a contiguous block of memory that grows from higher addresses toward lower addresses (as shown in Figure 2). The stack pointer (SP) is used to keep track of the top of the stack. When an item is pushed onto or popped off the stack, the SP is adjusted accordingly. Anything beyond the SP is considered to be garbage. We can reference data on the stack by adding an offset to the SP, and modifying the SP directly can either remove a batch of data or reserve space for a data such as local variables. The stack consists of a set of stack frames; a single frame is allocated for each procedure that has yet to return control to an ancestor procedure. The SP points to the top of the stack frame of the procedure that is currently executing, and the frame pointer (FP) points to the base of the stack frame for that procedure. To avoid destroying the value of the current FP upon calling a new procedure, the FP must be saved on entry to the new procedure and restored on exit.

Figure 2 illustrates the operation of the memory stack for the example program in Figure 3. The leftmost stack shows the state of the stack immediately preceding the call to g(). When function f() calls g(), a new stack frame will be pushed onto the stack. This frame includes the input pointers s1 and s2, the procedure return address, the frame pointer, and the local variables a and buf. Upon completing g(), the program will return to the address stored in g's stack frame; this address should equal the location of the instruction immediately following the call to g() in the function f(). The SP and the FP are also restored to their former values, and the stack frame belonging to g() is effectively popped from the stack.

Figure 4 illustrates a buffer overflow attack on the code listed in Figure 3. A security vulnerability exists because strcpy() does not perform bounds checking. In the function g(), if the string to which s1 points exceeds the size of buf, strcpy() will overwrite data located adjacent to buf in the memory stack. A malicious party can exploit this situation by strategically constructing a string

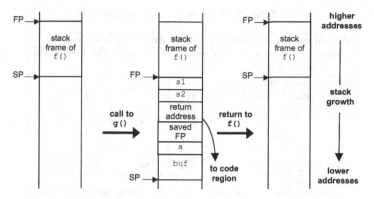

Fig. 2. Example of stack operation

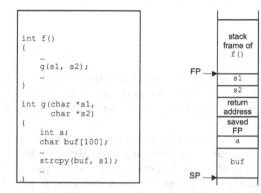

Fig. 3. Code example   **Fig. 4.** Buffer overflow attack

that contains malicious code and a corrupted return address. If s1 points to such a string, strcpy() will copy malicious code into the stack and overwrite the return address in g()'s stack frame with the address of the initial instruction of the malicious code. Consequently, once g() completes, the program will jump to and execute the malicious code instead of returning control to f(). There are many variations of this form of attack, but most rely on the ability to modify the return address [17]. For example, rather than the attacker injecting his own exploit code, the return address may be modified to point to legitimate, preexisting code that can be used for malicious purposes. In another variant, the malicious code inconspicuously installs agent software for a future DDoS attack and returns execution to the calling function f(). Thus, the program appears to execute normally, and the user is unaware that his machine may become a DDoS zombie in a future attack.

Table 2. Required system changes

Technique for defending against procedure return return address	Required system changes			
	Source code	Compiler	OS	Processor
Safe programming languages	Yes	Yes	No	No
Static analysis techniques	Yes	No	No	No
StackGuard	No	Yes	No	No
StackGhost	No	No	Yes	No
libsafe	No	No	Yes	No
libverify	No	No	Yes	No
Our SRAS proposal	**No**	**No**[a]	**Yes**	Yes

[a] Compiler changes may be required for certain programs to operate properly depending on the method used to handle non-LIFO
procedure control flow (see Section 5)

3　Past Work

Researchers have proposed many software-based countermeasures for thwarting
buffer overflow attacks. These methods differ in the strength of protection provided, the effects on performance, and the ease with which they can be effectively
employed.

One solution is to store the memory stack in non-executable pages. This
can prevent an attacker from executing code injected into the memory stack.
For example, Multics was one of the first operating systems to provide support
for non-executable data memory, i.e., memory pages with execute privilege bits
[14]. However, the return address may instead be redirected to preexisting, legitimate code in memory that the attacker wishes to run for malevolent reasons. In
addition, it is difficult to preserve compatibility with existing applications, compilers, and operating systems that employ executable stacks. Linux, for instance,
depends on executable stacks for signal handling.

Researchers have proposed using more secure (or safe) dialects of C and C++,
since a high percentage of buffer overflow vulnerabilities can be attributed to features of the C programming language. Cyclone is a dialect of C that focuses on
general program safety, including prevention of stack smashing attacks [10]. Safe
programming languages have proven to be very effective in practice. While programs written in Cyclone may require less scrupulous checking for certain types
of vulnerabilities, the downside is that programmers have to learn the numerous distinctions from C, and legacy application source code must be rewritten
and recompiled. In addition, safe programming dialects can cause significant
performance degradation and executable code bloat.

Methods for the static, automated detection of buffer overflow vulnerabilities
in code have also been developed [22, 23, 24]. Using such static analysis techniques, complex application source code can be scanned prior to compilation
in order to discover potential buffer overflow weaknesses. The detection mecha-

Table 3. Benefit and cost comparison

Technique for defending against procedure return address corruption	Provides complete protection[a]	Applies to many platforms	Application code size increase	Adverse performance impact
Safe programming languages	Yes[b]	Yes	Can be high	Can be high
Static analysis techniques	No	Yes	Varies	Varies
StackGuard	No	Yes	Low	Moderate
StackGhost	Yes	No	None	Low
libsafe	No	Yes	Low	Low
libverify	Yes	Yes	High	Moderate
Our SRAS proposal	Yes	Yes	**None**[c]	Low

[a] By "complete protection," we mean complete protection against buffer overflow attacks that directly corrupt procedure return addresses.

[b] Provided that programmers comply and write correct code.

[c] Depending on how non-LIFO procedure control flow is handled, some programs may experience a very small increase in code size (see Section 5).

nisms are not perfect: many false positives and false negatives can occur. Also, as true with Cyclone, these techniques ultimately require the programmer to inspect and often rewrite sections of application source code. Re-coding may also increase the total application code size.

StackGuard is a compiler-based solution involving a patch to gcc that defends against buffer overflow attacks that corrupt procedure return addresses [8]. In the procedure prologue of a called function, a "canary" value is placed on the stack next to the return address, and a copy of the canary is stored in a general-purpose register. In the epilogue, the canary value in memory is compared to the canary register to determine whether a buffer overflow has occurred. The application randomly generates the 32-bit or 64-bit canary values, so the application can detect improper modification of a canary value resulting from a buffer overflow with high probability. However, there exist attacks that can circumvent StackGuard's canaries to successfully corrupt return addresses and defeat the security of the system [2].

StackGhost employs the SPARC architecture's register windows to defend against buffer overflow exploits [9]. Return addresses that have stack space allocated in register windows are partially protected from corruption. The OS has the responsibility of spilling and filling register windows to and from memory, and once a return address is stored back in memory, it is potentially vulnerable. Various methods of protecting such spilled stacks are defined. Buffer overflow protection without requiring re-compilation of application source code is a benefit of StackGhost, but the technique is only applicable to SPARC systems.

Transparent run-time software defenses have also been proposed. The dynamically loaded libraries libsafe and libverify provide run-time defenses against stack smashing attacks and do not require programs to be re-compiled [1]. libsafe intercepts unsafe C library functions and performs bounds-checking to protect frame pointers and return addresses. libverify protects programs by saving a copy of every function and every return address in the heap. The first instruction of the original function is overwritten to execute code that stores the return address and jumps to the copied function code. The return instruction for the copied function is replaced with a jump to code that verifies the return address before actually returning.

The downside to libsafe is that it only defends against buffer overflow intrusions resulting from certain C library functions. In addition, static linking of these C library functions in a particular executable precludes libsafe from protecting the program. Implementations of libverify can double the code space required for each process, which is taxing for embedded devices with limited memory. Also, libverify can degrade performance by as much as 15% for some applications.

We compare past work in Tables 2 and 3. We observe that no existing solution combines the features of support for legacy applications (indicated by no changes to source code or the compiler), wide applicability to various platforms, low performance overhead, and complete protection against procedure return address corruption. Therefore, we propose a low-cost, hardware-based solution that enables built-in, transparent protection against common buffer overflow vulnerabilities without depending on user or application programmer effort in complying with software safeguards and countermeasures.

4   A Multi-layer Defense

We advocate a multi-layer approach to solving buffer overflow problems that lead to procedure return address corruption. By "multi-layer", we mean a combination of static software defenses and dynamic software or hardware defenses. Static software techniques include safe programming languages, static security analysis of source code, and security code inserted into executables at compile-time. Dynamic software security solutions include run-time defenses such as StackGhost, libsafe, and libverify. We present a dynamic hardware defense in the next section.

We categorize programs as new software and legacy software. With new software, the source code is available, so the programmer can apply static software techniques for defending against buffer overflows. In addition, the platform can provide dynamic software or hardware defenses to supplement these static techniques. Legacy software consists of compiled binary executables – the corresponding source code is no longer available. Hence, the only applicable protection for legacy software is dynamic (i.e., run-time) software or hardware defense. The dynamic software countermeasures described above may provide incomplete coverage (libsafe), only apply to a certain platform (StackGhost), or cause performance degradation and code bloat (libverify). Therefore, we recommend using a dynamic hardware countermeasure, which is designed to transparently provide protection for both new and legacy software.

We propose low-cost enhancements to the core hardware and software of future programmable machines that enable the detection and prevention of return address corruption. Such a processor-based mechanism would complement static software techniques in a multi-layered defense by overcoming some deficiencies of existing software solutions. Our proposed hardware defense provides robust protection, can be used in all platforms, causes negligible performance degradation, and does not increase code size. Since we require changes to processor hardware, our proposal is meant to be a longer-term solution. In the interim, software patches and defenses against buffer overflow vulnerabilities should continue to be applied when available.

5   The Processor-Based Defense

In instruction set architectures, procedure call and return instructions are clearly recognizable from other branch instructions. For instance, in many RISC ISAs, a branch and link instruction is identified as a procedure call, and a branch to the link register (such as R31) is identified as a procedure return instruction [18]. Furthermore, as explained in Section 2, procedure calls and returns occur in a properly nested, or LIFO, fashion. Since the processor can clearly identify call and return instructions, it can maintain its own LIFO hardware stack to store the correct nested procedure return addresses. The processor does not need to depend on the memory stack in which return addresses can be corrupted by external sources (that exploit software vulnerabilities such as buffer overflows).

We propose that security-aware processors implement a secure return address stack (SRAS) that preserves correct values of dynamic procedure return addresses during program execution. Only call and return instructions can modify the contents of the SRAS, and the processor can rely on the SRAS to provide the correct return address when executing a procedure return instruction. If the return address given by the SRAS hardware differs from that stored in the memory stack, then it is highly likely that the return address in the memory stack has been corrupted. In this event, the processor can terminate execution, continue execution using the correct address from the top of the SRAS, or issue a new invalid return address trap. With the SRAS, we can achieve our goal of thwarting buffer overflow attacks in which hostile code is injected into innocent hosts.

Our SRAS solution differs significantly in the security function it provides compared to the performance function provided by hardware return address stacks [13, 25] found in some high-performance processors like the Alpha 21164 [5] and the Alpha 21264 [6]. In these processors, the hardware return address stack provides a mechanism for branch prediction; the target address of a procedure return instruction is highly predictable, and thus it can be made available earlier in the pipeline. The processor uses a return address stack in conjunction with other mechanisms such as branch target buffers to perform branch prediction. Since branch prediction mechanisms are not expected to be 100% accurate, if the address predicted by the hardware return address stack differs from the return address saved in the memory stack, the processor assumes that the branch prediction is incorrect. It will "squash" instructions based upon the

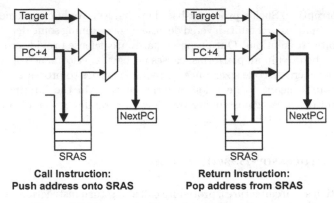

Fig. 5. SRAS operation for call and return instructions

address popped from the hardware return address stack and start fetching instructions beginning at the return address stored in the memory stack. Hence, in the event of return address corruption due to buffer overflow exploitation, existing processors will jump to the malicious code pointed to by the corrupted return address. In contrast, our SRAS solution places trust in the processor's hardware stack rather than in the memory stack, which can be modified by external sources.

5.1   SRAS Architectural Requirements

Supporting a Secure Return Address Stack mechanism in a processor requires a hardware return address stack (the SRAS itself), modification of the implementation of procedure call and return instructions to use the SRAS, and a method for securely spilling and filling of the contents of the SRAS to and from memory upon SRAS overflow or underflow. Since we do not require re-compilation or changes to programming languages and application source code, both legacy and new software can benefit from the security provided by these enhancements.

The hardware SRAS is simply an n-entry LIFO stack. We transparently modify the execution of procedure call and return instructions to place trust in the SRAS rather than the memory stack as follows. We maintain the ISA definitions and visible behavior of call and return instructions, but we alter the manner in which the processor executes call and return instructions to use the SRAS (see Figure 5). This enables protection for legacy programs as well as new programs. During the execution of a call instruction, the target of the procedure call is assigned to the next PC. Also, the return address (i.e., PC + 4 assuming the call instruction size is 4 bytes) is pushed onto the top of the SRAS. When a processor fetches a return instruction, the return address popped from the top of the hardware SRAS is always assigned to the next PC. The processor then determines whether the return address from the memory stack is the same as the return address popped from the SRAS. If these addresses differ, return address corruption (or some other error) has occurred, and the processor should take appropriate action.

A hardware SRAS structure contains a finite number of entries, which may be exceeded by the number of dynamically nested return addresses in the program. When this happens, the processor must securely spill SRAS contents to memory. We define the event in which the SRAS becomes full following a call instruction as overflow; the event where the SRAS becomes empty following a return is defined as underflow. The processor issues an OS interrupt to write or read SRAS contents to or from protected memory pages when SRAS overflow or underflow occurs. To prevent thrashing in some programs due to SRAS spilling and filling, we only transfer half (instead of all) of the SRAS entries to or from memory on an SRAS overflow or underflow.

This SRAS overflow space in memory is protected from corruption by external sources by only allowing the OS kernel to access spilled SRAS contents. The OS executes code that transfers contents of the SRAS to or from these protected memory pages; the application does not, and cannot, participate in SRAS content transfers. The kernel is responsible for managing the memory structures required to store the spilled SRAS entries for all threads running on the system. This is achieved by maintaining one stack of spilled SRAS return addresses for each process. In addition, the virtual memory regions that store the SRAS contents are mapped to physical pages that can only be accessed by the kernel. Hence, user-level application threads cannot corrupt the contents of their respective spilled stacks. Also, since the values popped from the SRAS must always be valid to preserve correct execution, the OS must transfer the SRAS contents to and from memory during context switches.

5.2   Non-LIFO Procedure Control Flow

If software always exhibited LIFO procedure control flow behavior, the SRAS would transparently provide hardware-based protection of return addresses for all programs. No compiler changes or recompilation of existing source code would be necessary: the system would provide protection for all legacy and future binary executables. Unfortunately, however, some existing executables use non-LIFO procedure control flow. For example, some compilers seek to improve performance by allowing certain procedures to return to an address located deep within the stack. The memory stack pointer is then set to an address of a frame buried within the stack; the frames located in between the former top of the stack and the reassigned stack pointer are effectively popped and discarded. Exception handling in C++ is one technique that can lead to such non-LIFO behavior.

Other common causes of non-LIFO control flow are the C setjmp and longjmp library functions. These functions are employed to support software signal handling. The longjmp function may cause a program to return to an address that is located deep within the memory stack or to an address that is no longer located in the memory stack. More specifically, a particular return address may be explicitly pushed onto the stack only once, but procedures may return to that address more than once. Note that tail call optimizations, which seem to involve non-LIFO procedure control flow, do not cause problems for the SRAS. Compilers typically maintain proper pairing of procedure call and return instructions when implementing tail call optimizations.

Our security proposal depends on the correctness of the address popped from the top of the hardware SRAS. Hence, the SRAS mechanism described so far does not accommodate non-LIFO procedure control flow. We can address this issue in at least four ways. The first option prohibits non-LIFO behavior in programs, providing the greatest security at the lowest cost but also the least flexibility. The fourth and last option disables the SRAS, providing the least security but the greatest flexibility for programs that exhibit non-LIFO behavior. There exist several possible alternatives between these two options that trade varying degrees of non-LIFO support for implementation cost and complexity. We present two of these possibilities: the second option described below relies on re-compilation, while the third option described below uses only dynamic code insertions. Both options only support certain non-LIFO behavior for cost and complexity reasons.

The first option is to implement the SRAS as described above and completely prohibit code and compiler practices that employ non-LIFO procedure control flow. This provides the highest degree of security against return address corruption. To support this option, we may need to rewrite or re-compile source code for certain legacy applications. Legacy executables that exhibit non-LIFO procedure calling behavior will terminate with an error (if not recompiled).

The second option is to permit certain types of non-LIFO procedure control flow such as returning to addresses located deep within the stack. This option requires re-compilation of some legacy programs. During re-compilation, the compiler must take precautions to ensure that the top of the SRAS will always contain the correct target address for an executed return instruction in programs that use non-LIFO techniques. We define new instructions, sras_push and sras_pop, which explicitly push and pop entries from and to the SRAS without necessarily calling or returning from a procedure. Compilers can employ these new instructions to return to an address deep within the SRAS (and to the associated frame in the memory stack) when using longjmp, C++ exception handling, or other non-LIFO routines.

The third option is to provide dynamic support for common non-LIFO behavior. This approach does not support all instances of non-LIFO behavior that the second option can handle via re-compilation, but it does allow execution of some legacy executables (where the source code is no longer available) that exhibit non-LIFO procedure control flow. First, we implement the sras_push and sras_pop instructions described above. We also need an installation-time or run-time software filter that strategically injects sras_push and sras_pop instructions (as well as other small blocks of code) into binaries prior to or during execution. The software filter inserts these instructions in recognized routines that cause non-LIFO procedure control flow. For instance, standardized functions like setjmp and longjmp can be identified at run-time via inspection of linked libraries such as libc. This option only handles executables that employ known non-LIFO techniques, however. For new manifestations of non-LIFO procedure control flow, the software filter may not identify some locations where the new instructions should be inserted.

The fourth option is to allow the users to disable the SRAS with a new sras_off instruction. This enables the execution of code that exhibits non-LIFO procedure control behavior as permitted in systems without an SRAS. In some situations (e.g., program debugging), a user may wish to turn off the SRAS and run insecure code. In other cases, the user may disable the SRAS to execute legacy code with unusual non-LIFO behavior.

Regardless of the method used to handle non-LIFO procedure control flow, we require that the SRAS be "turned on" by default in order to provide built-in protection. Our architecture definition stipulates that the SRAS is always enabled unless explicitly turned off by the user, at his own risk.

6   Performance Impact

We now analyze the implementation costs of our proposal. First, we investigate the performance degradation caused by the SRAS mechanism on typical programs. The SRAS does not impact the performance of procedure call and return instructions. Any performance degradation is due to spilling and retrieving the contents of the SRAS to and from memory during program execution. Although network-processing software is most vulnerable to buffer overflow attacks, the SRAS provides transparent protection for all applications, and therefore any SRAS-induced performance degradations apply to all software. Hence, we examine the performance impact of our SRAS solution on the SPEC2000 benchmarks [21], which are typically used to model a representative workload in processor performance studies.

We gather performance data using SimpleScalar version 3.0, a cycle-accurate processor simulator [3]. Our base machine model closely represents an ARM11 processor core, which is used in many network-enabled, embedded computing devices [7]. The ARM11 is a single-issue processor with 8 KB L1 instruction and data caches. Also, the ARM11 core supports limited out-of-order execution to compensate for the potentially high latencies of load and store instructions.

We simulate the execution of the first 1.5 billion instructions of 12 SPEC2000 integer benchmarks [21]. Our performance data is based upon the last 500 million instructions of each 1.5 billion instruction simulation in order to capture steady-state behavior. We obtain performance results for all 12 benchmarks and 6 SRAS sizes of 8, 16, 32, 64, 128, and infinite entries. Hence, we performed $12 \times 6 = 72$ simulations. To model the code executed by the OS upon SRAS overflow and underflow, we wrote a swapping and memory management routine in C. All of the benchmarks and swapping code were compiled using cc with -O2 optimizations.

We find that the performance degradation caused by SRAS swapping is negligible (i.e., less than 1%) for all the benchmarks when using SRAS sizes of 128 or more entries. When using a 64-entry SRAS, the only benchmark that suffers a non-negligible performance penalty is parser, which experiences a small performance degradation of 2.11%.

Next, we compare the implementation costs of our proposed processor-based solution to libverify, a dynamic software-based solution that provides robust security against procedure return address corruption. We do not consider Stack-Ghost and libsafe, for these solutions only function on SPARC platforms and only provide protection against buffer overflows in certain C functions, respectively. libverify does not require any changes to processors or hardware, which is an advantage over our proposal. Although our solution does require hardware enhancements, the necessary modifications are minor. In addition, many processors already contain a return address stack that would serve as the core of the SRAS.

Our SRAS solution causes a negligible performance penalty in the set of benchmarks examined, whereas libverify causes performance degradation as high as 15% in some common applications. Furthermore, our solution requires little or no expansion of executable code size. Since libverify copies functions to the heap at run-time, libverify can increase code size by a factor of two. Such code bloat can be very taxing for constrained devices in pervasive computing environments. Hence, our dynamic hardware-based solution is superior to dynamic software defenses from a performance perspective. As future processors are designed to include SRAS mechanisms, our dynamic hardware defense may be used to replace dynamic software defenses against procedure return address corruption.

7   Conclusion

Malicious parties utilize buffer overflow vulnerabilities to inject and execute hostile code in an innocent user's machine by corrupting procedure return addresses in the memory stack. Due to the growing threat of attacks such as distributed denial of service that exploit the rapidly increasing number of pervasive computing devices, addressing such buffer overflow vulnerabilities is a high priority for network and computer security. Although software-based countermeasures are available, a processor architecture defense is justified because major security problems stemming from buffer overflow vulnerabilities continue to plague computer systems.

We propose a built-in, non-optional, secure hardware return address stack (SRAS) that detects corruption of procedure return addresses. The SRAS mechanism only requires minor changes to the operating system and the processor, so legacy and new software can enjoy the security benefits without the need to modify application source code or re-compile the source, which may no longer be available. Also, the SRAS mechanism causes a negligible performance penalty in the applications examined. For greatest security, we suggest that new software disallow non-LIFO procedure control flow techniques. However, we describe compiler, OS, and hardware methods for supporting non-LIFO behavior when it is necessary. We also discuss the tradeoffs between security, implementation complexity, and software flexibility associated with supporting non-LIFO procedure control flow.

We describe a multi-layer software and hardware defense against buffer over-flow attacks. Our hardware-based solution should be applied in tandem with existing static software countermeasures to provide robust protection in pervasive computing devices. In future work, we will explore SRAS enhancements and alternative techniques for preventing buffer overflow and distributed denial of service attacks.

References

1. A. Baratloo, N. Singh, and T. Tsai, "Transparent Run-time Defense against Stack Smashing Attacks," *Proc. of the 9th USENIX Security Symposium*, June 2000.
2. Bulba and Kil3r, "Bypassing StackGuard and StackShield," *Phrack Magazine*, vol. 10, issue 56, May 2000.
3. D. Burger and T. M. Austin, "The SimpleScalar Tool Set, Version 2.0," *University of Wisconsin-Madison Computer Sciences Department Technical Report*, no. 1342, June 1997.
4. CERT Coordination Center, http://www.cert.org/, Nov. 2001.
5. Compaq Computer Corporation, *Alpha 21164 Microprocessor (.28μm): Hardware Reference Manual*, December 1998.
6. Compaq Computer Corporation, *Alpha 21264 Microprocessor Hardware Reference Manual*, July 1999.
7. D. Cormie, "The ARM11 Microarchitecture," available at http://www.arm.com/support/White_Papers/, April 2002.
8. C. Cowan, C. Pu, D. Maier, H. Hinton, J. Walpole, P. Bakke, S. Beattie, A. Grier, P. Wagle, and Q. Zhang, "StackGuard: Automatic Adaptive Detection and Prevention of Buffer-Overflow Attacks," *Proceedings of the 7th USENIX Security Symposium*, Jan. 1998.
9. M. Frantzen and M. Shuey, "StackGhost: Hardware Facilitated Stack Protection," *Proceedings of the 10th USENIX Security Symposium*, August 2001.
10. L. Hornof and T. Jim, "Certifying Compilation and Run-time Code Generation," *Proceedings of the ACM Conference on Partial Evaluation and Semantics-Based Program Manipulation*, January 1999.
11. K. J. Houle, G. M. Weaver, N. Long, and R. Thomas, "Trends in Denial of Service Attack Technology," CERT Coordination Center, October 2001.
12. Intel Corporation, *The IA-32 Intel Architecture Software Developer's Manual, Volume 2: Instruction Set Reference*, Intel Corporation, 2001.
13. D. R. Kaeli and P. G. Emma, "Branch History Table Prediction of Moving Target Branches Due to Subroutine Returns," *Proceedings of the 18th International Symposium on Computer Architecture*, pp. 34-41, May 1991.
14. P. A. Karger and R. R. Schell, "Thirty Years Later: Lessons from the Multics Security Evaluation," *Proceedings of the 2002 Annual Computer Security Applications Conference*, pp. 119-126, December 2002.
15. F. Kargl, J. Maier, and M. Weber, "Protecting Web Servers from Distributed Denial of Service Attacks," *Proceedings of the Tenth International Conference on World Wide Web*, pp. 514-525, April 2001.
16. D. Karig and R. B. Lee, "Remote Denial of Service Attacks and Countermeasures," Princeton University Department of Electrical Engineering Technical Report CE-L2001-002, October 2001.
17. klog, "The Frame Pointer Overwrite," *Phrack Magazine*, 9(55), Sept. 1999.

18. R. B. Lee, "Precision Architecture," *IEEE Computer*, 22(1), pp. 78-91, Jan. 1989.
19. J. McCarthy, "Take Two Aspirin, and Patch That System – Now," *SecurityWatch*, August 31, 2001.
20. The SANS Institute, "The SANS/FBI Twenty Most Critical Internet Security Vulnerabilities," http://www.sans.org/top20/, October 2002.
21. The Standard Performance Evaluation Corporation, http://www.spec.org/, Nov. 2001.
22. J. Viega, J. T. Bloch, T. Kohno, and G. McGraw, "ITS4: A Static Vulnerability Scanner for C and C++ Code," *Proceedings of the 2000 Annual Computer Security Applications Conference*, December 2000.
23. D. Wagner and D. Dean, "Intrusion Detection via Static Analysis," *Proceedings of the 2001 IEEE Symposium on Security and Privacy*, pp. 156-169, 2001.
24. D. Wagner, J. S. Foster, E. A. Brewer, and A. Aiken, "A First Step towards Automated Detection of Buffer Overrun Vulnerabilities," *Network and Distributed System Security Symposium*, Feb. 2000.
25. C. F. Webb, "Subroutine Call/Return Stack," *IBM Technical Disclosure Bulletin*, 30(11), April 1988.

Optimized RISC Architecture
for Multiple-Precision Modular Arithmetic

Johann Großschädl and Guy-Armand Kamendje

Graz University of Technology
Institute for Applied Information Processing and Communications
Inffeldgasse 16a, A–8010 Graz, Austria
{Johann.Groszschaedl, Guy-Armand.Kamendje}@iaik.at

Abstract. Public-key cryptosystems normally spend most of their execution time in a small fraction of the program code, typically in an inner loop. The performance of these critical code sections can be significantly improved by customizing the processor's instruction set and microarchitecture, respectively. This paper shows the advantages of instruction set extensions to accelerate the processing of cryptographic workloads such as long integer modular arithmetic. We define two custom instructions for performing multiply-and-add operations on unsigned integers (single-precision words). Both instructions can be efficiently executed by a $(32 \times 32 + 32 + 32)$-bit multiply/accumulate (MAC) unit. Thus, the proposed extensions are simple to integrate into standard 32-bit RISC cores like the MIPS32 4Km. We present an optimized Assembly routine for fast multiple-precision multiplication with "finely" integrated Montgomery reduction (FIOS method). Simulation results demonstrate that the custom instructions double the processor's arithmetic performance compared to a standard MIPS32 core.

Keywords: RSA Algorithm, Montgomery Multiplication, Finely Integrated Operand Scanning (FIOS), Multi-Application Smart Cards.

1 Introduction

Security and privacy are major concerns in the upcoming world of pervasive computing since publicly accessible wireless transmission channels are vulnerable to attackers. This necessitates to implement strong public-key cryptography (PKC) on non-traditional computing devices ("gadgets") like mobile phones, personal digital assistants (PDAs) or smart cards. Many public-key cryptosystems have in common that they involve arithmetic operations on very long integers, most notably modular multiplication. Typical operand lengths are 1024-4096 bits for "traditional" cryptosystems based on the integer factorization (IF) problem [1] or the discrete logarithm (DL) problem [2, 3], and between 192 and 521 bits for elliptic curve cryptosystems over prime fields GF(p) [4]. The computationally intensive nature of public-key cryptosystems is one of the reasons why they are difficult to implement efficiently on constrained devices like smart cards.

Recent 8-bit smart cards require a cryptographic co-processor to generate a 1024-bit RSA signature in less than a second. However, systems which use custom hardware for cryptography have significant drawbacks: they are not able to respond to advances

D. Hutter et al. (Eds.): Security in Pervasive Computing 2003, LNCS 2802, pp. 253–270, 2004.

in (side-channel) cryptanalysis or to changes in emerging standards. Other problems may potentially arise from the limited scalability of current-generation co-processors. In the context of cryptographic hardware, the term *scalability* refers to the ability to process operands of arbitrary size. Co-processors with a fixed-precision datapath (e.g. 1024-bit serial/parallel multiplier) do not scale very well, i.e. the co-processor has to be redesigned when the need for multiplication of higher precision arises[1]. Plus, a co-processor consumes power, adds to die size and increases total system cost.

On the other hand, software implementations of PKC are generally easier to upgrade and to adapt to new algorithms or larger key sizes. Furthermore, software offers a level of *flexibility* which is not available through conventional hardware implementations. Software implementations are flexible as they permit to use the "best" algorithm for the miscellaneous arithmetic operations involved in PKC. For instance, squaring of a long integer can be done almost twice as fast as multiplication of two different integers [6]. Hardware multipliers normally do not take advantage of special squaring algorithms since this would greatly complicate their architecture. Another example is modular reduction. Montgomery's algorithm [7] is very well suited for hardware and software implementation as it replaces the trial division with simple shift operations. However, certain special primes like the so-called *generalized Mersenne primes* (GM-primes) used in elliptic curve cryptography facilitate much faster reduction methods. For instance, the reduction of a 384-bit integer modulo the GM-prime $p = 2^{192} - 2^{64} - 1$ can be simply realized by additions modulo p [8]. A modular multiplier which performs the reduction operation according to Montgomery's method is not able to profit from GM-primes.

The market for processor-based smart cards is currently shifting from low-end 8-bit cards to 16 and 32-bit cards that are able to handle multiple applications [9]. Advanced security features (e.g. biometric techniques) and support of complex card operating systems such as *MULTOS* or *Windows for Smart Cards* demand greater processing power and memory capacity. The traditional 8-bit micro-controller cores like Intel's 8051 or Motorola's 6805 are getting more and more replaced by state-of-the-art 32-bit RISC cores [10]. High-performance RISC cores bring new opportunities in software cryptography that are not conceivable with 8-bit processors. The capability of handling 32-bit data words significantly improves the speed for the processing of long integer arithmetic [11]. By designing application-specific instruction set extensions, we combine the efficiency of hardware with the flexibility of software. These extensions blur the traditional line between general-purpose hardware (processor core) and application-specific hardware (e.g. crypto co-processor), resulting in fast yet flexible implementations of public-key cryptography.

In this work, we analyze how long integer modular arithmetic can be implemented efficiently on application-specific processors and what functionality is required to achieve peak performance. We define two special instruction set primitives which carry out calculations of the form $a \times b + c + d$, whereby a, b, c, and d are single-precision words (unsigned integers). These instructions can be easily integrated into a state-of-the-art RISC architecture by simple enhancements of the multiply/accumulate (MAC)

---

[1] Some recent multiplier architectures are scalable in both design and implementation, which means that a fixed-area multiplier can process operands of any length [5].

unit. We used the common MIPS32 instruction set architecture as a starting point for optimizing arithmetic performance. The application-specific instructions were defined and evaluated by applying hardware/software co-design techniques [12]. We developed a functional, cycle-accurate model of the processor core and the added hardware extensions. Both the modified core and the software routines for modular arithmetic have been co-simulated and co-verified with the *SystemC* hardware description language [13]. The proposed extensions entail only minor tweaks in the processor core but greatly speed up long integer modular arithmetic compared to a conventional software implementation on a standard MIPS32 core.

2 Background and Related Work

Cryptographic applications often spend most of their time executing a few time-critical code segments ("hot spots") with well-defined characteristics, making them amenable to processor specialization. The instruction set architecture (ISA) of application-specific processors is specifically tuned to the needs of the target application(s).

2.1 Application-Specific Processor Design

A recent trend in application-specific processor design is to extend an existing instruction set architecture (ISA) by special instructions for performance-critical operations [14]. Some microprocessor vendors and intellectual property (IP) providers license configurable and extensible processor cores to their customers [15]. By using a common base instruction set, the design process can focus on the application-specific extensions, which significantly reduces verification effort and hence shortens the design cycle. The results of this application-specific customization of a common base architecture are families of closely related and largely compatible processors. These families can share development tools (compilers, assemblers, simulators) and even binary compatible code which has been written for the common base architecture. Critical code portions are customized using the application-specific instruction set extensions [16, 17].

Instruction set extensions are generally tailored to a class of applications, called an application domain, like multimedia processing [18]. In recent years, multimedia instruction set extensions have become a prominent feature in desktop computers and workstations [19]. Major microprocessor vendors extended their processor's instruction sets to improve the performance of graphics and multimedia applications. Familiar examples include Hewlett-Packard's Multimedia Acceleration eXtension (MAX), Intel's MultiMedia eXtensions (MMX), Sun's Visual Instruction Set (VIS), and Motorola's AltiVec.

Instruction set extensions have also been designed to accelerate processing of cryptographic workloads, in particular secret-key cryptosystems [20, 21]. It was shown in [15] that the addition of four custom instructions to the Xtensa core can increase its DES encryption rate by a factor of between 43 and 72. The hardware cost of these extensions is roughly 4,500 gates.

2.2 Instruction Set Extensions for Public-Key Cryptography

Contrary to multimedia extensions, there exist only very few research publications concerned with optimized instruction sets for public-key cryptography. In the following, we briefly summarize the most significant contributions.

J.-F. Dhem proposed some simple modifications of the ARM7M architecture to obtain an "optimal" software implementation of long integer modular arithmetic [11]. He designed a $(8 \times 32 + 8 + 32)$-bit multiply/accumulate (MAC) unit which is able to "emulate" an entire $(32 \times 32 + 32 + 32)$-bit MAC unit. An early termination mechanism guarantees that a computation of the form $a \times b + c + d$ completes in minimum time. Given a clock frequency of 32 MHz, Dhem's implementation is able to execute a 1024-bit modular exponentiation in 480 msec when the Chinese Remainder Theorem (CRT) is used.

B. J. Phillips and N. Burgess introduced a different design approach in which special-purpose arithmetic hardware (i.e. co-processor) is exchanged for extra RAM [22]. All arithmetic operations are reduced to 32-bit additions, subtractions and binary shifts, and the processor is augmented with a small hardware enhancement to significantly accelerate accumulation of shifted multiple-precision numbers. They used signed sliding window algorithms for exponentiation, multiplication and reduction operations, respectively. A 1024-bit CRT-based modular exponentiation takes 887 msec on an enhanced ARM7 core clocked at 25 MHz. However, more than 2 kB of extra RAM and 2 kB of extra EEPROM memory are required to store the pre-computed tables of digit multiples and powers.

The instruction set of the IA-64 architecture developed by Intel and Hewlett-Packard has been optimized to address the needs of cryptography [23]. IA-64 can carry out an integer multiply-and-add $a \times b + c$ in the floating point unit, using the fixed-point XMA instruction with the FP registers interpreted as 64-bit integers. Leading vendors of microprocessors such as MIPS Technologies, Inc. or STMicroelectronics have developed special 32-bit RISC cores for smart cards (e.g. *SmartMIPS* [24], *SmartJ* [25]). These optimized cores feature advanced hardware security, small area, low power consumption, and instruction set extensions tailored to cryptographic workloads. However, the documents describing these extensions are confidential and hence no information about instruction set and microarchitecture is available to the public.

Previous work of the first author includes architectural enhancements to accelerate the execution of Montgomery multiplication [26]. The modular reduction operation was interleaved with the multiplication according to the so-called coarsely integrated operand scanning (CIOS) method [27]. However, a disadvantage of the CIOS method is that it contains two inner loops. The finely integrated operand scanning (FIOS) method allows to gain further performance improvements, which will be demonstrated in the following sections. The present paper also shows how to speed up multiple-precision squaring with the help of custom instructions, which was not considered in [26].

3 Algorithms for Multiple-Precision Arithmetic

Public-key cryptosystems involve arithmetic on integers that may be many hundreds, or even thousands, of bits long. Since no conventional microprocessor supports integer

---

Algorithm 1. Multiple-precision multiplication (school method)

Input: n-bit operands $A, B < 2^n$, $A = (a_{s-1}, \ldots, a_1, a_0)$, $B = (b_{s-1}, \ldots, b_1, b_0)$.
Output: $2n$-bit product $P = A \cdot B$, $P = (p_{2s-1}, \ldots, p_1, p_0)$.
 1: $P \leftarrow 0$
 2: **for** i from 0 by 1 to $s-1$ **do**
 3:    $u \leftarrow 0$
 4:    **for** j from 0 by 1 to $s-1$ **do**
 5:      $(u, v) \leftarrow a_j \cdot b_i + p_{i+j} + u$
 6:      $p_{i+j} \leftarrow v$
 7:    **end for**
 8:    $p_{s+i} \leftarrow u$
 9: **end for**

---

calculations of this size, we are forced to represent the numbers as multi-word data structures (e.g. arrays of 32-bit unsigned integers). Arithmetic operations on multiple-precision integers can be performed by means of software routines which manipulate these words using native machine instructions.

In this section we briefly summarize the basic algorithm for multiple precision multiplication. We present slightly modified versions of well-known algorithms for Montgomery multiplication and squaring. The inner loops of these algorithms have been adapted to better take advantage from the availability of a custom instruction which performs calculations of the form $a \times b + c + d$.

We use uppercase letters to denote long integers, while lowercase letters, usually indexed, represent individual words (digits). An n-bit non-negative integer A can be written as an ordered sequence of $s = \lceil n/w \rceil$ words of w bits each, i.e. $A = (a_{s-1}, a_{s-2}, \ldots, a_0)$. The typical value for w is the processor's native word size, which means 32 in our case.

3.1   Multiple-Precision Multiplication

Algorithm 1 illustrates the classical school method for computing a multiple-precision multiplication [6]. The algorithm contains an outer loop and a relatively simple inner loop which does the bulk of the computation. Any iteration of the inner loop executes an operation of the form $(u, v) \leftarrow a \times b + c + d$, the so-called *inner loop operation*. The tuple (u, v) denotes a double-precision word where both u and v are single-precision quantities representing the w most/least significant bits of (u, v), i.e. $(u, v) = u \cdot 2^w + v$. Note that the result of $a \times b + c + d$ does always fit into a double-precision word since

$$a \times b + c + d \leq 2^{2w} - 1 \quad \text{when } a, b, c, d \leq 2^w - 1. \tag{1}$$

Another point to consider is that $a \times b$ produces a double-precision number, and thus, the two additions are double precision. Consequently, the additions actually involve two instructions each since adding two single-precision numbers may produce a carry which needs to be processed properly. Some processors provide an "add-with-carry" instruction to facilitate multiple-precision addition.

The quality of the implementation of this inner loop operation is crucial to the algorithm's overall timing. Speeding up the inner loop through special-purpose hardware or an optimized Assembly implementation can result in dramatic performance improvements.

3.2 Montgomery Multiplication (FIOS Method)

An ingenious method for modular reduction was published by Peter L. Montgomery in 1985 [7]. Montgomery's algorithm takes advantage of the fact that $Z \cdot R^{-1} \bmod N$ is much easier to compute on a conventional microprocessor than the "exact" residue $Z \bmod N$. The factor R is referred to as *Montgomery radix* or *Montgomery residual factor*, and R^{-1} is the inverse of R modulo N. Montgomery's algorithm requires $R > N$ and $\gcd(R, N) = 1$. Generally, R is selected as the smallest power of 2 which is larger than N, i.e. $R = 2^n$ for an n-bit modulus N.

In order to describe the Montgomery multiplication algorithm, we first define the *N-residue* (or *Montgomery image*) of an integer $A < N$ as $\bar{A} = A \cdot R \bmod N$. It was demonstrated in [7] that the set $\{A \cdot R \bmod N \mid 0 \le A \le N-1\}$ is a complete residue system, i.e. it contains all numbers between 0 and $N-1$. If R and N are relatively prime, then there is a one-to-one relationship between any number A in the range $[0, N-1]$ and its corresponding N-residue $\bar{A}$ from the above set. Given two N-residues $\bar{A}$ and $\bar{B}$, the *Montgomery product* is defined as the N-residue

$$\bar{C} = \text{MonPro}(\bar{A}, \bar{B}) = \bar{A} \cdot \bar{B} \cdot R^{-1} \bmod N \tag{2}$$

Montgomery multiplication of $\bar{A}$ by $\bar{B}$ is isomorphic to the modular multiplication of A by B. For instance, it is easily verified that the resulting number $\bar{C}$ in Equation (2) is indeed the N-residue of the product $C = A \cdot B \bmod N$:

$$\bar{C} = \bar{A} \cdot \bar{B} \cdot R^{-1} \bmod N = A \cdot R \cdot B \cdot R \cdot R^{-1} \bmod N = A \cdot B \cdot R \bmod N = C \cdot R \bmod N$$

Montgomery's algorithm exploits this isomorphism by introducing a very fast multiplication routine to compute the Montgomery product, i.e. to compute the N-residue of the product of two integers whose N-residues are given [7, 27]. The conversion of A to $\bar{A}$ and vice versa can also be carried out on the basis of Montgomery multiplication:

$$\text{MonPro}\left(A, (R^2 \bmod N)\right) = A \cdot R^2 \cdot R^{-1} \bmod N = \bar{A} \tag{3}$$

$$\text{MonPro}\left(\bar{A}, 1\right) = \bar{A} \cdot 1 \cdot R^{-1} \bmod N = A \tag{4}$$

The factor $R^2 \bmod N = 2^{2n} \bmod N$ depends only on the modulus N and can be precomputed. In typical applications of Montgomery multiplication the conversions are carried out only before and after a lengthy computation like modular exponentiation. The overhead caused by conversion of numbers to/from their N-residues is therefore negligible.

Algorithm 2 shows the so-called *Finely Integrated Operand Scanning* (FIOS) method for computing the Montgomery product [27]. Since the reduction proceeds word by word, we need an additional quantity, n_0', defined as the inverse of the least significant word of N modulo 2^w, i.e. $n_0' = -n_0^{-1} \bmod 2^w$. The multiplications $a_j \cdot b_i$

Algorithm 2. Montgomery multiplication (modified FIOS method)

Input: n-bit modulus N, $2^{n-1} \leq N < 2^n$, operands $A, B < N$, $n_0' = -n_0^{-1} \bmod 2^w$.
Output: Montgomery product $P = A \cdot B \cdot 2^{-n} \bmod N$.

1: $P \leftarrow 0$
2: **for** i from 0 by 1 to $s-1$ **do**
3:    $(u, v) \leftarrow a_0 \cdot b_i + p_0$
4:    $t \leftarrow u$
5:    $q \leftarrow v \cdot n_0' \bmod 2^w$
6:    $(u, v) \leftarrow n_0 \cdot q + v$
7:    **for** j from 1 by 1 to $s-1$ **do**
8:       $(u, v) \leftarrow a_j \cdot b_i + t + u$
9:       $t \leftarrow u$
10:      $(u, v) \leftarrow n_j \cdot q + p_j + v$
11:      $p_{j-1} \leftarrow v$
12:    **end for**
13:    $(u, v) \leftarrow p_s + t + u$
14:    $p_{s-1} \leftarrow v$
15:    $p_s \leftarrow u$
16: **end for**
17: **if** $P \geq N$ **then** $P \leftarrow P - N$ **end if**

---

and $n_j \cdot q$ are both carried out in the same inner loop, and then the products are added to the current intermediate result. In this case, $(u, v) \leftarrow p_0 + a_0 \cdot b_i$ must be computed before entering into the loop since the quotient q depends on this value, which corresponds to unrolling the first iteration of the inner loop. The major advantage of the FIOS method over the *Coarsely Integrated Operand Scanning* (CIOS) method is that it contains only one inner loop which is iterated $s^2 - s$ times.

The FIOS method as described in [27] has the problem that it entails the addition of two $2w$-bit quantities (namely the two products $a_j \cdot b_i$ and $n_j \cdot q$), resulting in a $(2w+1)$-bit sum. This sum requires more than two words to store if the processor does not have a carry flag. The authors of [27] implemented an ADD function that performs the addition of a w-bit word to a word array and propagates the carry until no further carry is generated. Processors whose instruction set contains no "add with carry" instruction do not greatly benefit from the FIOS method. In other words, the advantage of having only one inner loop is counterbalanced by the requirement of the ADD function in the inner loop. Algorithm 2 illustrates a slightly modified version of the original FIOS method. The problem of carry propagation is tackled by using a "redundant representation" for the $w+1$ upmost bits of a $(2w+1)$-bit integer. This means that two w-bit words (termed t and u in Algorithm 2) represent a $(w+1)$-bit quantity. Consequently, three register are needed to store the temporary words t, u, and v. Similar approaches to overcome the carry-propagation problem have been reported in [11] and [28].

3.3 Multiple-Precision Squaring

Squaring is a special case of multiplication since both operands are the same and hence all cross-product terms of the form $a_i \cdot a_j$ and $a_j \cdot a_i$ are equivalent. They need to be

---

Algorithm 3. Multiple-precision squaring (Guajardo/Paar method [29])

Input: n-bit operand A, $0 \leq A < 2^n$, $A = (a_{s-1}, \ldots, a_1, a_0)$.
Output: $2n$-bit result $P = A \cdot A$, $P = (p_{2s-1}, \ldots, p_1, p_0)$.
1: $P \leftarrow 0$
2: **for** i from 0 by 1 to $s-1$ **do**
3:     $(u, v) \leftarrow a_i \cdot a_i + p_{2i}$
4:     $p_{2i} \leftarrow v$
5:     $t \leftarrow 0$
6:     **for** j from $i+1$ by 1 to $s-1$ **do**
7:         $prod \leftarrow a_j \cdot a_i$
8:         $(u, v) \leftarrow prod + t + u$
9:         $t \leftarrow u$
10:         $(u, v) \leftarrow prod + p_{i+j} + v$
11:         $p_{i+j} \leftarrow v$
12:     **end for**
13:     $(u, v) \leftarrow p_{s+i} + t + u$
14:     $p_{s+i} \leftarrow v$
15:     $p_{s+i+1} \leftarrow u$
16: **end for**

---

computed only once and then left shifted in order to be doubled. Consequently, an s-word squaring operation can be performed using only $(s^2 + s)/2$ single-precision multiplications, resulting in a theoretical speedup factor of almost two relative to conventional multiplication [30]. The inner loop of the classical squaring algorithm as described in [30] carries out calculations of the form $2 \cdot a \cdot b + c + d$. However, $2 \cdot a \cdot b$ returns a $(2w+1)$-bit result exceeding the range of a double-precision word by one bit, which poses a problem when implementing the algorithm in a high-level programming language.

Algorithm 3 illustrates a modified squaring algorithm introduced by J. Guajardo and C. Paar [29]. This algorithm solves the afore mentioned problem in a similar way as described in subsection 3.2, namely by using a redundant representation for the $(2w+1)$-bit quantity $2 \cdot a \cdot b + c + d$. Montgomery reduction can be easily integrated into the squaring operation (both "coarsely" and "finely" integration is possible). The inner loop of the squaring algorithm is executed $(s^2 - s)/2$ times.

3.4 Montgomery Squaring (FIOS Method)

The Guajardo/Paar squaring with finely integrated Montgomery reduction is illustrated in Algorithm 4. This algorithm (in the following denoted as FIOS Montgomery squaring) consists of two inner loops; each of them is iterated exactly $(s^2 - s)/2$ times. The first j-loop computes the product $n_j \cdot q$ required for reduction, whereas the second j-loop computes the sum of $n_j \cdot q$ and $2 \cdot a_j \cdot a_i$. Therefore, FIOS Montgomery squaring requires two extra words (t and x) in order to store a $(2w+2)$-bit quantity without loss of precision.

Note that there are several ways to implement FIOS Montgomery squaring. The version shown in Algorithm 4 is most efficient when the processor provides a fast (single-

---

Algorithm 4. Montgomery squaring (modified FIOS method)

Input: n-bit modulus N, $2^{n-1} \leq N < 2^n$, operand $A < N$, $n_0' = -n_0^{-1} \bmod 2^w$.
Output: Montgomery square $P = A \cdot A \cdot 2^{-n} \bmod N$.

1: $P \leftarrow 0$
2: **for** i from 0 by 1 to $s-1$ **do**
3:      $(u, v) \leftarrow a_i \cdot a_i + p_i$
4:      $p_i \leftarrow v$
5:      $t \leftarrow u$
6:      $q \leftarrow p_0 \cdot n_0' \bmod 2^w$
7:      $(u, v) \leftarrow n_0 \cdot q + p_0$
8:      **for** j from 1 by 1 to i **do**
9:          $(u, v) \leftarrow n_j \cdot q + p_j + u$
10:          $p_{j-1} \leftarrow v$
11:     **end for**
12:     $x \leftarrow 0$
13:     **for** j from $i+1$ by 1 to $s-1$ **do**
14:          $(u, v) \leftarrow a_j \cdot a_i + t + u$
15:          $t \leftarrow u$
16:          $(u, v) \leftarrow a_j \cdot a_i + x + v$
17:          $x \leftarrow u$
18:          $(u, v) \leftarrow n_j \cdot q + p_j + v$
19:          $p_{j-1} \leftarrow v$
20:     **end for**
21:     $(u, v) \leftarrow p_s + t + x + u$
22:     $p_{s-1} \leftarrow v$
23:     $p_s \leftarrow u$
24: **end for**
25: **if** $P \geq N$ **then** $P \leftarrow P - N$ **end if**

---

cycle) instruction for calculations of the form $a \times b + c + d$. In general, Montgomery squaring is only approximately 20% faster than Montgomery multiplication since the reduction operation $Z \bmod N$ requires the same effort regardless of whether Z is a square or a product.

4   Inner Loop Operation on the MIPS32 4Km

The MIPS32 architecture is a superset of the previous MIPS I and MIPS II instruction set architectures and incorporates new instructions for standardized DSP operations like "multiply-and-add" (MADD) [31]. MIPS32 is a 32-bit load/store architecture with 32 general-purpose registers (GPRs). The instruction set includes computational instructions, load and store instructions, jump and branch instructions, and co-processor instructions (see Table 1). MIPS Technologies, Inc. offers several implementations of the MIPS32 architecture, the MIPS32 4Km processor core being one of them [32]. The 4Km is widely used in digital consumer products, cell phones, and networking devices — application fields in which security becomes increasingly important.

Table 1. Some MIPS32 instructions with a symbolic description of their operations.

ADDIU rd, rs, c	Add Immediate Word (c is a 16-bit constant)	$rd \leftarrow rs + c$
ADDU rd, rs, rt	Add Unsigned Word (without Overflow)	$rd \leftarrow rs + rt \bmod 2^{32}$
BNE rs, rt, label	Branch on Not Equal	if $rs \neq rt$ then branch to label
LW rd, c(rt)	Load Word at RAM Address $(rt + c)$	$rd \leftarrow \text{memory}[rt + c]$
MADDU rs, rt	Multiply and Add Unsigned Word to (HI,LO)	$(HI, LO) \leftarrow rs \times rt + (HI, LO)$
MFLO rd / MFHI rd	Move from LO Reg. / Move from HI Reg.	$rd \leftarrow LO$ / $rd \leftarrow HI$
MTLO rs / MTHI rs	Move to LO Register / Move to HI Register	$LO \leftarrow rs$ / $HI \leftarrow rs$
MULTU rs, rt	Multiply Unsigned Word	$(HI, LO) \leftarrow rs \times rt$
SLTU rd, rs, rt	Set on Less Than Unsigned	if $(rs < rt)$ then $rd \leftarrow 1$, else 0
SW rs, c(rt)	Store Word at RAM Address $(rt + c)$	$\text{memory}[rt + c] \leftarrow rs$

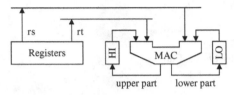

Fig. 1. MADD Instruction: $(HI, LO) = (HI, LO) + rs \times rt$.

Key features of the 4Km include a five-stage pipeline with branch control and single-cycle execution for most instructions, a fast multiply/divide unit (MDU) supporting single-cycle 32×16 MAC operations, and up to 16 kB of instruction and data caches (modified Harvard architecture). By having separate instruction and data caches, both an instruction and a datum can be fetched in a single clock cycle, enabling an instruction to be executed every cycle, even if that instruction also needs data. The MDU contains a separate pipeline for multiply and divide operations which works in parallel with the integer unit (IU) pipeline but does not stall when the IU pipeline stalls. According to [32], the MDU consists of a 32×16 Booth recoded multiplier, result/accumulation registers (referenced by the names HI and LO), a divide state machine and the necessary control logic. The MIPS32 architecture defines the result of a multiply operation to be placed in the HI and LO registers. Using MFHI and MFLO instructions, these values can be transferred to general-purpose registers (see Table 1). The MIPS32 has also a "multiply-and-add" (MADD) instruction, which is illustrated in Figure 1. The MADD instruction multiplies two 32-bit words and adds the product to the 64-bit concatenated values in the HI/LO register pair. Then, the resulting value is written back to the HI and LO registers. Various signal processing routines can make heavy use of that instruction, which optimizing compilers automatically generate when appropriate.

Figure 2 shows a hand-written Assembly routine for the inner loop operation $(u, v) \leftarrow a \times b + c + d$ using a MIPS32-like instruction set (see Table 1). At the beginning of the computation we assume that the single-precision words a, b, c, and d are stored in the registers Ra, Rb, Rc, and Rd, respectively. The first instruction adds the 32-bit value in register Rc to the value in Rd and places the result in Rv. Note that the ADDU instruction actually computes $c + d \bmod 2^{32}$, i.e. a possible overflow is ignored. The MIPS32 architecture has no explicit carry flag, and the instruction set does not con-

```
ADDU    Rv, Rc, Rd    # Rv = Rc + Rd
SLTU    Ru, Rv, Rc    # place carry bit in Ru
MTLO    Rv            # move Rv to LO
MTHI    Ru            # move Ru to HI
MADDU   Ra, Rb        # (HI,LO) = (HI,LO) + Ra * Rb
MFLO    Rv            # move LO to Rv
MFHI    Ru            # move HI to Ru
```

Fig. 2. Computing $(u, v) \leftarrow a \times b + c + d$ on the MIPS32 4Km.

tain an "add-with-carry" instruction. However, when the result of an ADDU instruction is less than either operand then we know that the addition produced an overflow. Instruction SLTU is used to set a "simulated" carry flag into register Ru. The $(w+1)$-bit sum of $c+d$ is then transferred to the register pair HI/LO. Instruction MADDU multiplies a by b and accumulates the product to the 64-bit concatenated values of HI and LO. Finally, the 64-bit result is copied to the general-purpose registers Ru and Rv.

Computing $(u, v) \leftarrow a \times b + c + d$ on a MIPS32 processor involves seven instructions if all operands are held in registers. The actual running time depends on the latency of the MADDU instruction. Given a (32×16)-bit multiplier, the MADDU instruction takes two clock cycles to complete, which results in an execution time of eight clock cycles. A fully parallel (i.e. single-cycle) (32×32)-bit multiplier reduces the execution time to seven cycles.

The instruction sequence depicted in Figure 2 occurs twice in the inner loop of the FIOS Montgomery multiplication (Algorithm 2). Furthermore, any iteration of the inner loop of Algorithm 2 requires three LW (load word) instructions in order to transfer the operands a_j, n_j, and p_j from memory to general-purpose registers. The operands b_i and q do not change during the iterations of the inner loop and can be held in the register file to avoid unnecessary memory accesses. At the end of the inner loop, a SW (store word) instruction performs the write-back of p_{j-1} to its location in memory. The increment of the loop counter j together with the branching takes another two instructions. In summary, the inner loop of Algorithm 2 consists of (at least) 20 MIPS32 instructions.

For a simple timing estimation let us assume that the MIPS32 4Km is an "ideal" RISC processor able to execute any instruction in one clock cycle (for sake of simplicity we do not consider cache misses, pipeline stalls, and load or branch delays). In such case, the inner loop of the FIOS Montgomery multiplication requires 20 clock cycles for one iteration. In the following section we demonstrate that minor enhancements of the MIPS32 architecture make it possible to execute the inner loop in 10 clock cycles.

5   Architectural Support for the Inner Loop Operation

Many RISC processors provide special instructions for calculating a sum of products — two operands are multiplied and the product is added to a cumulative sum. This operation is fundamental to a wide range signal processing routines like vector dot products or matrix multiplies. Therefore, almost every RISC core today includes a MAC unit for operations of the form $a \times b + c$, whereby the double-precision operand c is

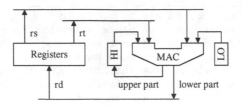

Fig. 3. MADDL instruction: $rd = (rs \times LO + rt + HI) \bmod 2^{32}$.

either stored in an accumulator or in a pair of registers. However, multiple-precision arithmetic would profit from a MAC unit that can compute $a \times b + c + d$ with all four operands being single-precision words.

Most MAC units originally designed for DSP/multimedia workloads can be easily extended to support multiply-and-add operations of the form $a \times b + c + d$. Our recent work [33] describes the design and implementation of a fully parallel $(32 \times 32 + 32 + 64)$-bit MAC unit based on an array architecture. The multiplier employs radix-4 Booth encoding to generate the partial products, and uses 3:2 counters to reduce the partial products to sum and carry vectors. All MIPS32 multiply-and-add operations (both signed and unsigned) can be performed with the MAC unit, along with the extra operation of the form $a \times b + c + d$. We point out that this extra operation causes almost no area or speed penalty. An implementation of the $(32 \times 32 + 32 + 64)$-bit MAC unit in 0.6 μm standard cells has a gate count of roughly $8,000$ and a delay of 25 ns [33].

The MAC unit of the MIPS32 4Km core includes a (32×16)-bit multiplier [32]. Replacing the original MAC unit with the extended one described in [33] entails a slight increase in silicon area since the area of a (32×32)-bit multiplier is twice the area of a (32×16)-bit multiplier. However, a fast (single-cycle) multiplier is vital for the efficient execution of arithmetic-intensive applications such as public-key cryptography. Therefore, it is prudent to sacrifice this additional area, the more so as a MAC unit is relatively small in relation to the processor core and other components like RAM or EEPROM.

5.1 Custom Instruction MADDL

As mentioned before, a conventional MAC unit can be easily extended to support calculations of the form $a \times b + c + d$. At a first glance, it seems that a custom instruction which implements the inner loop operation $(u, v) \leftarrow a \times b + c + d$ requires four source operands and produces a two-word result. The MIPS32, as most other RISC architectures, has a three-operand instruction format for the arithmetic/logical instructions (one destination register, two source registers). Consequently, the register file of most RISC processors has two read ports and one write port. The addition of extra read or write ports would necessitate some non-trivial modifications of the processor core.

In order to tackle this problem, we exploit the fact that two operands, b_i and q, do not change during the iterations of the inner loop of Algorithm 2. Our idea is to use the

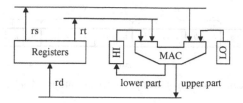

Fig. 4. MADDH instruction: $rd = (rs \times LO + rt + HI) \text{ div } 2^{32}$.

register LO as a "local cache" for the loop constants b_i and q, respectively[2]. Another property of the inner loop is that the result of the current multiply-and-add operation serves as an operand for the subsequent calculation. More precisely, the lower part v of the result of $a_j \times b_i + t + u$ (line 8) is used as an operand for the multiply-and-add carried out at line 10. Furthermore, the upper part u at line 10 is an operand for the calculations performed at line 8 during the next iteration of the inner loop. We can exploit this "data locality" by storing either the upper part or the lower part of (u, v) in register HI, depending on whether u or v is used as an operand in the next multiply-and-add operation. Now we are able to define an instruction with two source registers (rs, rt) and one destination register (rd), which we call MADDL (*Multiply and Add and write Lower part of result to destination register*). The MADDL instruction computes $rs \times LO + rt + HI$, treating all operands as 32-bit unsigned integers. The least significant 32 bits of the result are written to the destination register rd, and the most significant 32 bits are written back into register HI (see Figure 3). This instruction implements exactly the expression at line 10 of Algorithm 2.

5.2 Custom Instruction MADDH

The expression at line 8 of Algorithm 2 would profit from an instruction that directs the upper part of the result to a general-purpose register. Therefore, we define a second instruction which we call MADDH (*Multiply and Add and write Higher part of result to destination register*). The MADDH instruction works very similar to the MADDL instruction, i.e. MADDH does also carry out a computation of the form $rs \times LO + rt + HI$. The only difference is that MADDH writes the most significant 32 bits of the result to the destination register rd, whereas the lower part is written to register HI. This is illustrated in Figure 4.

6 Optimized Assembly Routines for the Inner Loop

In the following we present an optimized Assembly routine for the FIOS inner loop operation (Algorithm 2) taking advantage of the two custom instructions MADDL and MADDH.

---

[2] However, the contents of register LO must not be overwritten by temporary quantities during the multiplication. This has to be considered when using a MAC unit with a multi-cycle multiplier, as is the case with the original MIPS32 4Km core.

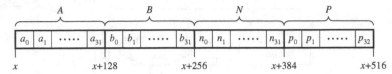

Fig. 5. Memory location of multiple-precision integers A, B, N, and P.

```
Loop:   LW      Ra, 0(Rj)        # load A[j] into Ra
        MTLO    Rb               # move Rb to LO
        MADDH   Rt, Ra, Rt       # Ra * LO + Rt + HI
        LW      Rn, 256(Rj)      # load N[j] into Rn
        LW      Rp, 384(Rj)      # load P[j] into Rp
        MTLO    Rq               # move Rq to LO
        MADDL   Rp, Rn, Rp       # Rn * LO + Rp + HI
        ADDIU   Rj, Rj, 4        # Rj = Rj + 4
        BNE     Rj, Rz, Loop     # branch if Rj != Rz
        SW      Rp, 376(Rj)      # store Rp to P[j-1]
```

Fig. 6. FIOS inner loop with instructions MADDL and MADDH.

6.1   Representation of Long Integers

Long integer arithmetic is generally characterized by a large number of memory accesses since operands of very high precision (e.g. 1024 bits) can not be kept in the register file. Therefore, it is desirable to minimize the overhead caused by address calculations. Long integers are typically represented by an array of single-precision words (unsigned integers). Given a 32-bit platform (i.e. $w = 32$), a 1024-bit integer can be stored in an array of $s = 32$ words.

Algorithm 2 computes $P = A \cdot B \cdot 2^{-n} \bmod N$, whereby the long integers A, B, N, and P occupy 516 bytes of memory if $n = 1024$. In our implementation, we place A, B, N, and P in contiguous locations in memory, as shown in Figure 5. When the word a_0 resides at address x (i.e. x is the starting address of array A), then let b_0 and n_0 have address $x+128$ and $x+256$, respectively, and p_0 shall be located at address $x+384$. The "bare" MIPS32 processors support a single addressing mode: *Indexed addressing*. In indexed addressing, an offset is encoded in the instruction word along with a base register. The offset is added to the base register's contents to form an effective address. Indexed addressing is useful when incrementing through the elements of an array as the addresses can be easily constructed at run-time.

6.2   Inner Loop of the FIOS Montgomery Multiplication

Figure 6 shows a hand-optimized Assembly routine for the inner loop of the FIOS Montgomery multiplication (Algorithm 2) utilizing the custom instructions MADDL and MADDH. The code is optimized for an operand length of $n = 1024$ bits and takes advantage of indexed addressing for fast address calculation. An inspection of Algorithm 2 reveals that the FIOS inner loop executes two multiply-and-add operations (lines 8 and

10); the first one takes b_i and the second one takes q as multiplier. These values are stored in registers Rb and Rq since they are needed in any iteration of the loop. Moreover, operands a_j, n_j and p_j are stored in registers Ra, Rn, and Rp, respectively. The temporary quantity t also occupies a register, namely Rt.

The Assembly routine basically implements the inner loop according to the pseudo-code illustrated in Algorithm 2. The first instruction loads the word a_j from memory into the register Ra. Instruction MADDH performs the computation of $a_j \times b_i + t + u$ and stores the upper part of the result in register Rt. The subsequent instructions load the operands n_j and p_j into the respective registers. Then, the MADDL instruction computes $n_j \times q + p_j + v$ and stores the lower part of the result in register Rp. The MTLO instructions are used to transfer the appropriate multiplier (either b_i or q) to register LO.

In our implementation, the loop count variable j is initialized with the address of a_1 and incremented by 4 each time the loop repeats. Thus, the value of j is actually the address of the current array element of A, i.e. the address of a_j. The loop finishes when j reaches the address of b_0, which means after 31 iterations in our example. Note that register Rz contains the address of b_0, and j is held in register Rj. The MTLO instructions are placed in the so-called *load delay slots*, and the store instruction (SW) is in the *branch delay slot*. MIPS processors implement a delay slot for load instructions, i.e. loads require extra cycles to complete before they exit the pipeline. For this reason, the instruction after the load must not "use" the result of the load instruction. MIPS branch instructions' effects are also delayed by one instruction; the instruction following the branch instruction is always executed, regardless of whether the branch is taken or not.

If a MIPS32 core contains a MAC unit with a (32×16)-bit multiplier, then the (32×32)-bit operations pass through the multiplier twice. In this case, MADDL and MADDH are multi-cycle instructions, meaning that they always force a stall of the IU pipeline in order to maintain their register file write slot. However, there are no pipeline stalls when the MAC unit consists of a fully parallel (single-cycle) (32×32)-bit multiplier. The instruction sequence depicted in Figure 6 can be executed in ten clock cycles, provided that the processor has a single-cycle MAC unit and that all operands are present in the data cache (i.e. no cache misses).

6.3   Inner Loops of the FIOS Montgomery Squaring

The FIOS Montgomery squaring (Algorithm 4) consists of two inner loops; the second one is more costly than the first one. The first j-loop can be efficiently implemented with the help of the MADDL instruction. This loop is identical to the inner loop of the CIOS Montgomery multiplication presented in [26]. An optimized Assembly routine for the first j-loop requires only six instructions and is executed in six clock cycles if there are no cache misses. Further information regarding this loop can be found in [26].

An implementation of the second j loop costs three LW instructions (for the operands a_j, n_j, and p_j), two MADDH instructions, one MADDL instruction, two MTLO instructions, and one SW instruction (for p_{j-1}). In addition, the increment of the loop count variable along with the branching takes another two instructions. Therefore, the second j-loop can be executed in eleven clock cycles. However, it must be considered that the two j loops are iterated only $(s^2 - s)/2$ times, making Montgomery squaring roughly 20% faster than Montgomery multiplication.

6.4 Simulation Results and Discussion

Simulations based on a functional, cycle-accurate model of the extended MIPS32 core have shown that a 1024-bit FIOS Montgomery multiplication executes in approximately 11,500 clock cycles. We point out that the usage of MADDL and MADDH instructions halves the execution time for the inner loop operation compared to an implementation with "native" MIPS32 instructions (see Figure 2). A 1024-bit squaring operation with finely integrated Montgomery reduction takes approximately 9,700 cycles. Thus, a 1024-bit modular exponentiation according to the "square and multiply" algorithm can be performed in slightly less than $16 \cdot 10^6$ clock cycles, which corresponds to an execution time of about 0.8 seconds when the processor core is clocked at 20 MHz[3]. If an RSA signature is generated once for a secure transaction — such as an ATM withdrawal — then a target time of around one second for the entire operation is tolerated by most users. However, a significant performance gain can be achieved by using an advanced exponentiation technique, e.g. addition chains or window methods [34]. The performance of RSA private key operations can be almost doubled when the *Chinese Remainder Theorem* is exploited [35]. Last but not least, software optimization techniques like loop unrolling would also help to reduce the execution time.

The FIOS method has some significant advantages over the CIOS method used in previous work [26]. For instance, the words p_j of the intermediate result must be loaded and stored only once instead of twice (see [26]). Moreover, the loop overhead (increment of the loop counter, branch instruction) has to be processed only once. In summary, the timing estimates presented in this paper are an improvement of 20% over the results of our previous work [26].

A serious problem to consider is that multiply and square operations produce different power traces. A careless implementation of the modular exponentiation could be exploited by an attacker to distinguish squares from multiplies. That way, the attacker can obtain the bits of the private key if the modular exponentiation is performed according to the binary exponentiation method (square-and-multiply algorithm). Some countermeasures against side-channel analysis have been proposed in the recent past, see e.g. [36].

7   Summary of Results and Conclusions

In this paper, we have shown that a simple enhancement of a MIPS32 processor core doubles its software performance in multiple-precision arithmetic. A 1024-bit modular exponentiation can be performed in approximately 0.8 seconds when the processor is clocked at 20 MHz. We achieved this result by defining only two additional instructions which can be easily integrated into common RISC architectures like the MIPS32. The area of a single-cycle (32×32)-bit multiplier (roughly 8k gates according to [33]) is rather marginal in relation to the processor core, and significantly less than the area of a crypto co-processor. All presented concepts (i.e. the extended processor core and the software routines) have been verified by co-simulation with the SystemC language.

---

[3] 20 MHz is a typical clock frequency for multi-application smart cards (Java cards).

We conclude that instruction set extensions allow fast yet flexible implementations of public-key cryptography. The general-purpose programmability of the processor provides the scalability of this approach, the specialization of the MAC unit provides the performance, and the universality of the proposed instructions enhances the flexibility. The primary advantage of software-based cryptography over hardware (i.e. crypto coprocessor for modular arithmetic) is the ability to fix bugs and to respond to changes in evolving standards. Even post-silicon design changes are possible by ROM mask modifications or by using external instruction memories.

References

1. Rivest, R.L., Shamir, A., Adleman, L.M.: A method for obtaining digital signatures and public key cryptosystems. Communications of the ACM **21** (1978) 120–126.
2. Diffie, W., Hellman, M.E.: New directions in cryptography. IEEE Transactions on Information Theory **22** (1976) 644–654.
3. National Institute of Standards and Technology (NIST): Digital Signature Standard (DSS). Federal Information Processing Standards Publication 186-2 (2000).
4. Blake, I.F., Seroussi, G., Smart, N.P.: Elliptic Curves in Cryptography. Cambridge University Press (1999).
5. Tenca, A.F., Koç, Ç.K.: A scalable architecture for Montgomery multiplication. In: Cryptographic Hardware and Embedded Systems — CHES '99. Vol. 1717 of Lecture Notes in Computer Science, Springer Verlag (1999) 94–108.
6. Knuth, D.E.: Seminumerical Algorithms. Third edn. Vol. 2 of The Art of Computer Programming. Addison-Wesley (1998).
7. Montgomery, P.L.: Modular multiplication without trial division. Mathematics of Computation **44** (1985) 519–521.
8. Solinas, J.A.: Generalized Mersenne numbers. Technical Report CORR-99-39, University of Waterloo, Waterloo, Canada (1999).
9. Dhem, J.F., Feyt, N.: Hardware and software symbiosis helps smart card evolution. IEEE Micro **21** (2001) 14–25.
10. ARM Limited: ARM SecurCore Solutions. Product brief, available for download at http://www.arm.com/aboutarm/4XAFLB/$File/SecurCores.pdf (2002).
11. Dhem, J.F.: Design of an efficient public-key cryptographic library for RISC-based smart cards. Ph.D. Thesis, Université Catholique de Louvain, Louvain-la-Neuve, Belgium (1998).
12. De Micheli, G., Gupta, R.K.: Hardware/software co-design. Proceedings of the IEEE **85** (1997) 349–365.
13. The Open SystemC Initiative (OSCI): SystemC Version 2.0 User's Guide. Available for download at http://www.systemc.org (2002).
14. Küçükçakar, K.: An ASIP design methodology for embedded systems. In: Proceedings of the 7th Int. Symposium on Hardware/Software Codesign (CODES '99), ACM Press (1999) 17–21.
15. Gonzalez, R.E.: Xtensa: A configurable and extensible processor. IEEE Micro **20** (2000) 60–70.
16. Gschwind, M.: Instruction set selection for ASIP design. In: Proceedings of the 7th Int. Symposium on Hardware/Software Codesign (CODES '99), ACM Press (1999) 7–11.
17. Wang, A., Killian, E., Maydan, D.E., Rowen, C.: Hardware/software instruction set configurability for system-on-chip processors. In: Proceedings of the 38th Design Automation Conference (DAC 2001), ACM Press (2001) 184–188.

18. Lee, R.B.: Multimedia extensions for general-purpose processors. In: Proceedings of the 1997 IEEE Workshop on Signal Processing Systems (SiPS '97), IEEE (1997) 9–23.
19. Lee, R.B.: Accelerating multimedia with enhanced microprocessors. IEEE Micro 15 (1995) 22–32.
20. Burke, J., McDonald, J., Austin, T.M.: Architectural support for fast symmetric-key cryptography. In: Proceedings of the 9th Int. Conference on Architectural Support for Programming Languages and Operating Systems (ASPLOS 2000), ACM Press (2000) 178–189.
21. Lee, R.B., Shi, Z., Yang, X.: Efficient permutation instructions for fast software cryptography. IEEE Micro 21 (2001) 56–69.
22. Phillips, B.J., Burgess, N.: Implementing 1,024-bit RSA exponentiation on a 32-bit processor core. In: Proceedings of the 12th IEEE Int. Conference on Application-specific Systems, Architectures and Processors (ASAP 2000), IEEE Computer Society Press (2000) 127–137.
23. Moore, S.F.: Enhancing security performance through IA-64 architecture. Technical presentation at the 9th Annual RSA Conference (RSA 2000). Presentation slides are available for download at http://developer.intel.com/design/security/rsa2000/itanium.pdf (2000).
24. MIPS Technologies, Inc.: SmartMIPS Architecture Smart Card Extensions. Product brief, available for download at http://www.mips.com/ProductCatalog/P_SmartMIPSASE/SmartMIPS.pdf (2001).
25. STMicroelectronics: ST22 SmartJ Platform Smartcard ICs. Product brief, available for download at http://www.st.com/stonline/prodpres/smarcard/insc9901.htm (2002).
26. Großschädl, J.: Instruction set extension for long integer modulo arithmetic on RISC-based smart cards. In: Proceedings of the 14th Int. Symposium on Computer Architecture and High Performance Computing (SBAC-PAD 2002), IEEE Computer Society Press (2002) 13–19.
27. Koç, Ç.K., Acar, T., Kaliski, B.S.: Analyzing and comparing Montgomery multiplication algorithms. IEEE Micro 16 (1996) 26–33.
28. Itoh, K., Takenaka, M., Torii, N., Temma, S., Kurihara, Y.: Fast implementation of public-key cryptography on a DSP TMS320C6201. In: Cryptographic Hardware and Embedded Systems — CHES '99. Vol. 1717 of Lecture Notes in Computer Science, Springer Verlag (1999) 61–72.
29. Guajardo, J., Paar, C.: Modified squaring algorithm. Unpublished manuscript, available for download at http://www.crypto.ruhr-uni-bochum.de/~guajardo/publications/squaringManuscript.pdf (1999).
30. Menezes, A.J., van Oorschot, P.C., Vanstone, S.A.: Handbook of Applied Cryptography. CRC Press (1996).
31. MIPS Technologies, Inc.: MIPS32™ architecture for programmers, Vol. I & II. Available for download at http://www.mips.com/publications/index.html (2001).
32. MIPS Technologies, Inc.: MIPS32 4Km™ processor core family data sheet. Available for download at http://www.mips.com/publications/index.html (2001).
33. Großschädl, J., Kamendje, G.A.: A single-cycle $(32 \times 32 + 32 + 64)$-bit multiply/accumulate unit for digital signal processing and public-key cryptography. Accepted for presentation at the 10th IEEE Int. Conference on Electronics, Circuits, and Systems (ICECS 2003), scheduled for December 14-17, 2003 in Sharjah, UAE.
34. Gordon, D.M.: A survey of fast exponentiation methods. Journal of Algorithms 27 (1998) 129–146.
35. Quisquater, J.J., Couvreur, C.: Fast decipherment algorithm for RSA public-key cryptosystem. Electronics Letters 18 (1982) 905–907.
36. Walter, C.D.: MIST: An efficient, randomized exponentiation algorithm for resisting power analysis. In: Topics in Cryptology — CT-RSA 2002. Vol. 2271 of Lecture Notes in Computer Science, Springer Verlag (2002) 53–66.

Visual Crypto Displays
Enabling Secure Communications

Pim Tuyls, Tom Kevenaar, Geert-Jan Schrijen, Toine Staring, and Marten van Dijk

Philips Research Laboratories, 5656 AA Eindhoven, the Netherlands

Abstract. In this paper we describe a low-tech and user friendly solution for secure two-way communication between two parties over a network of *untrusted* devices. We present a solution in which displays play a central role. Our approach guarantees privacy and allows to check the authenticity of information presented on displays. Furthermore, we provide the user with a secure return channel. To this end we propose to provide every user with a small *decryption display* which is, for example, integrated in a credit card and requires very limited computing power. The authentication and security are based on visual cryptography which was first introduced by Naor and Shamir in 1994. We solve some practical short-comings of traditional visual cryptography and develop protocols for two-way authentication and privacy in untrusted environments.

1 Introduction

As the world is moving into a real ambient intelligence environment, it is expected that telecommunication devices will be omnipresent and that they can be easily connected to a public network. In almost any situation and location it will be possible to check your bank account, place orders at the stock market, transmit pictures, etc. Moreover, to facilitate human interaction with these devices, most information will be presented in graphical form on a display.

In general, public networks have an open architecture and can easily be accessed. This causes a real threat to the authenticity of the information, its security and its privacy [7]. Imagine a scenario in which Alice wants to transfer money to a friend while she is on vacation. Via the access point in her hotel, she connects with her PDA to the web-site of her bank. As soon as she notices the small padlock in the corner of her Internet browser application, she starts the Internet banking session. She uses her Internet banking token (issued by the bank) for identification and for signing her money transfer order. This way of doing presents many risks. Although Alice thinks she is involved in a secure transaction with her bank (the padlock indicates a secure connection), in fact she might not be. For example, the server in the hotel might be setting up a man-in-the-middle attack and route traffic to a fake web-site that is controlled by the hotel itself [1]. If the hotel succeeds in this attack, transferred amounts and destination bank account of the transaction can easily be altered without notice to the user. A second risk is the fact that in earlier occasions Alice's PDA was connected to untrusted networks and might be contaminated with viruses, sniffer programs or Trojan horses and thus can not be trusted either [7]. Again this means that a secure connection might be compromised without notice to the user.

D. Hutter et al. (Eds.): Security in Pervasive Computing 2003, LNCS 2802, pp. 271–284, 2004.

Clearly, there is a large variety of cryptographic techniques available [10, 14] to ensure the authenticity and protect privacy when information is transmitted over a network. However, these techniques can not be applied straightforwardly for communication over untrusted networks since it is assumed that decryption is performed on a trusted device.

In this paper, we present solutions for the above mentioned problem. To provide integrity, authentication and confidentiality of messages that are transmitted through a public untrusted channel, a user will have to carry her own (trusted) *decryption display*. This display can easily be attached to a hand-held device[1] (e.g. mobile phone, PDA) or to another non-trusted terminal (e.g. ATM, PC in Internet cafe, etc.). Its main requirements are: cheap, low weight, limited computing power and small size. The decryption display is only equipped with simple dedicated hardware such as a pseudo random number generator and the interaction with the untrusted hand-held device is purely optical. Therefore there will be no means for Trojan horses or viruses to enter the decryption display.

Security problems related to the human-computer interface have also been investigated by Matsumoto [8, 9]. Their approach is based on visual images that have to be remembered by the user and therefore require an extra effort. Another approach to visual identification and authentication is that of [4]. Their solution suits well with larger screens and requires a trustworthy camera, but no integrity or confidentiality can be guaranteed.

This paper is organised as follows. The model and the problem setting will be explained in Section 2 and Section 3 gives a detailed explanation of the way an efficient visual cryptography system can be built by making use of the physical properties of light and Liquid Crystal Displays (LCD). Furthermore, in Section 4 protocols are developed to establish a private and authenticated two-way channel. In Section 5 we demonstrate the feasibility of the concept and we conclude in Section 6.

2   The Model and Problem Setting

2.1   The Model

In this section, we present an abstract model of the situation we have in mind (Fig. 1). The model consists of the following components:

- There is a human user, Alice who has the capabilities (vision, colour recognition) of a normal human being.
- There is a trusted computer TC (with normal computing power) that knows a secret key K associated with Alice[2].
- Both communicate with each other through an *untrusted network*, which can in principle have infinite computing power.
- Alice has a hand-held device H, which belongs to the untrusted network.

---

[1] The trusted display can be correctly aligned on the untrusted display by providing a solid frame into which it has to be entered or by equipping it with extra sensors which automatically read position information from the untrusted terminal. This will be a topic of further research.

[2] In some applications, TC can take the form of a trusted proxy [5].

– Alice has a personal *decryption display D* consisting of an (LCD) display equipped with an additional array of light sensitive sensors[3] and some hardware to do a minimal amount of computations. Furthermore, it holds the same secret key K as *TC*.

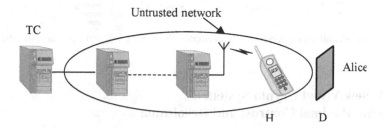

Fig. 1. Communication between Alice and *TC* over an untrusted network.

Alice wants to communicate with *TC* through her hand-held device H (e.g. PDA, mobile phone). The security of the solution that we propose makes use of the fact that Alice has two displays at her disposal (the display in H and decryption display D). *TC* will send only visually encrypted messages (using shared key K), to Alice. Alice's decryption display D will then generate the complementary randomised message according to the same key K. The message sent by *TC* will only be readable by Alice when she puts D on top of the display of H, on which the random pattern generated by *TC* appears. Note that the decrypted message is never available in electronic form.

2.2   The Problem

It will be the main topic of this paper to build a *Passive Two-Way Secure Authenticated Communication* channel *(PTWSAC)* in an untrusted environment using the model components of Section 2.1.

Definition 1. *A PTWSAC channel is a channel that allows for the following operations:*

– *Two way message authentication: the messages sent by* TC *are authenticated as well as the messages sent by Alice.*
– TC *can send secret messages of its choice to Alice (privacy).*
– *Alice can reply secretly to messages of* TC *but cannot send arbitrary messages of her own choice. This last property refers to the adjective 'passive'.*

Our results extend the visual cryptography system developed by Naor and Shamir in [11] and the protocols by Naor and Pinkas in [12], where transparencies are used to visually decrypt messages that are sent over an insecure channel. It was already recognised by the authors of [11] that such a system is only secure when each transparency is used only once, which makes their system rather impractical for general purposes.

---

[3] Light sensitive sensors can be easily and cheaply embedded in the pixels of an LCD display without reducing its picture quality.

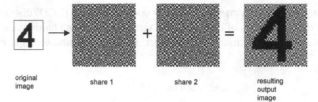

original
image   share 1   share 2   resulting
output
image

Fig. 2. Naor-Shamir visual cryptography example where every original pixel is split into four sub-pixels.

3 A New Visual Crypto System with Maximal Contrast and Resolution

3.1 Naor-Shamir Visual Cryptography

Visual cryptography was first introduced in [11] and further investigated in [12, 15, 17]. The basic idea is to split a (black and white) image into two shares (visual encryption) which are printed on transparencies. The original image is reconstructed when the two shares are superimposed (Fig. 2). This process is called visual decryption. The Naor-Shamir approach suffers from a number of drawbacks: i) reduced resolution and contrast, ii) a secure system for multiple messages requires the use of a large number of transparencies, iii) Alice has to verify that the presented share on the untrusted terminal is a true random pattern[4], iv) not very well suited for coloured pictures

3.2 Visual Cryptography Using Polarisation Properties of LCD Displays

In order to solve the problems with the Naor-Shamir approach, we propose to use the polarisation properties of light. A first proposal in this direction was made in [2]. Our idea on the other hand is to use an LCD display as a polarisation rotator. This allows easy key management and efficient reconstruction of gray-scale and colour messages.

An LCD display consists of three main parts: a bottom polariser, an LC layer (consisting of small individual LC cells) and a top polariser. Polarisers project the polarisation of the incoming light into one direction (e.g. horizontally). An LC cell rotates the polarisation of incoming light depending on the voltage applied to that cell.

The visual crypto system we propose, consists of the following components (Fig. 3): a first LC layer (LC1) with a polariser on the bottom but **not** on top and a second LC layer (LC2) with a polariser on top but **not** on the bottom. The LC layers form the shares of this visual crypto system.

Since a picture consists of pixels, we will explain the visual crypto scheme for a single pixel. In order to obtain a scheme for the total image, the single pixel scheme must be repeated for all the pixels in the image. We start with a construction for black-and-white images (Fig. 3) of which we show a demo in Fig. 4.

---

[4] This is to prevent an adversary from faking a message m by displaying a non-randomised version of m as a first share.

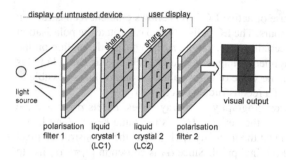

display of untrusted device   user display

light source

polarisation filter 1 | liquid crystal 1 (LC1) | liquid crystal 2 (LC2) | polarisation filter 2

visual output

Fig. 3. Visual cryptography by superposition of two liquid crystals. Cells in the liquid crystal layers that are indicated with an 'r' rotate the polarisation of light by $\pi/2$ radians.

Fig. 4. A hardware implementation that demonstrates the reconstruction method of Fig. 3.

Black and White Pixels. Incoming light from the light source (e.g. back-light) contains light waves with all possible polarisations that lie in the plane perpendicular to the propagation direction of the light beam. The first polariser (Fig. 3) blocks the vertical components and after the polariser all light is horizontally polarised. A liquid crystal cell to which no voltage is applied (indicated by 'r' in Fig. 3) rotates the polarisation of the incoming light by $\pi/2$. An LC cell to which a certain voltage is applied does not change the orientation of the polarisation. Depending on the polarisation of the light leaving the second LC cell, the last polariser generates a black or white output pixel. LC2 can hence determine the output intensity independently of the polarisation direction of light that is leaving from LC1. Consequently, overlaying two LC shares behaves like an XOR-operation, in contrast to Naor-Shamir visual cryptography where overlaying the shares behaves like an OR-operation. General secret sharing schemes that can be built with this XOR construction are presented in [16].

The shares of a pixel are generated as follows. Denote with α_1 and α_2 the angles of rotation of corresponding cells in LC1 and LC2 respectively. The total polarisation rotation of light that passes both LC cells equals $\alpha = \alpha_1 + \alpha_2$. Using the symbol I_r for the normalised intensity of the reconstructed pixel, we have

$$I_r(\alpha) = \cos^2 \alpha = \cos^2(\alpha_1 + \alpha_2) \ . \tag{1}$$

The decryption display D sets the angle α_2 to a value from the set $\{0, \pi/2\}$ according to the key K. As TC has the same key K (and hence knows α_2), he computes α_1 from the set $\{0, \pi/2\}$ such that $\alpha = \pi/2$ if the original pixel is black and $\alpha = 0$ or $\alpha = \pi$ if the original pixel is white.

It follows from the previous analysis that our scheme has the following advantages: i) Optimal resolution and contrast (since no sub-pixel patterns are used), ii) Elegant key updating mechanism by using the available electronics, iii) Alice does not have to verify the randomness of the image at H, since a non-randomised share produces a randomised reconstructed image. iv) Gray-scale and colour images can be efficiently reconstructed (shown below).

Gray Scales and Colours. The use of active LC layers allows efficient reconstruction of images with gray scales and colours. The LC cells in Fig. 3 can rotate the polarisation over an arbitrary angle within a certain range, say $[0, \pi/2]$ or $[0, \pi]$, depending on the construction of the LC and the applied voltage over an LC cell. In this case (1) holds with $I_\mathrm{r} \in [0, 1]$. Thus, by varying the value of α (or values α_1 and α_2) it is possible to change the intensity (gray scale) of a reconstructed pixel.

In order to implement visual cryptography with gray scales, D sets α_2 to a value from the interval $[0, \pi]$ according to the key K. TC has the same key K (and hence knows α_2) and computes α_1 such that the intensity I_r (Eq. 1) of the reconstructed pixel is equal to the intensity I_0 of the original pixel. Since α_2 is chosen in $[0, \pi]$, α_1 has to belong to the interval $[0, \pi]$ due to the π-periodicity of I_r in order to reveal no information. If we assume that $\alpha_1, \alpha_2 \in [0, \pi]$, then α_1 can be determined by Algorithm 1.

Algorithm 1	INPUT: $I_0 \in [0, 1]$, $\alpha_2 \in_R [0, \pi]$.
	OUTPUT: $\alpha_1 \in [0, \pi]$ such that $\cos^2(\alpha_1 + \alpha_2) = I_0$.
	1) compute $x = \arccos(|\sqrt{I_0}|)$; $\eta \in_R \{x, \pi - x\}$.
	2) if $\eta - \alpha_2 < 0$ then return $\alpha_1 = \eta - \alpha_2 + \pi$; exit.
	3) if $\eta - \alpha_2 \geq 0$ then return $\alpha_1 = \eta - \alpha_2$; exit.

The idea of gray scales described above can be extended to colours. One colour pixel (Fig. 5) is built from three sub-pixels each of which has a different colour 'back-light' (Red, Green and Blue) by applying a colour filter. As with gray scales, the intensity of each of the colours can be changed individually by changing the rotations α_R, α_G and α_B of the red, green and blue colour respectively. In this way, any colour can be generated.

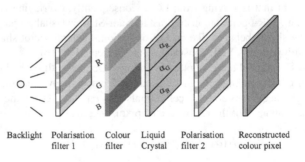

Backlight	Polarisation filter 1	Colour filter	Liquid Crystal	Polarisation filter 2	Reconstructed colour pixel

Fig. 5. Schematic construction of a transmissive colour pixel in a standard LCD display.

By applying Algorithm 1 three times per pixel, once for R, G and B, respectively, we can implement a colour visual cryptography system, without losing resolution. This stands in contrast to Naor-Shamir visual crypto systems as proposed in [13] and [17].

In a practical implementation, a pixel intensity can not have any value in $[0, 1]$ but is limited to a discrete set of k distinguishable values (e.g. $k = 256$). With k possible values for each colour component (R, G and B) a total number of k^3 colours can be displayed.

4 Building a PTWSAC Channel

4.1 Channels

In order to describe attacks on the system, we make a distinction between the communication from $TC \to$ Alice and the communication from Alice $\to TC$.

The main communication from $TC \to$ Alice will be based on the visual crypto system explained in Section 3.2. The light sensitive sensors in D provide TC with an additional low-bandwidth return channel to Alice, used for key synchronisation (see Section 5.1). The display of H receives from TC a set of voltages that has to be applied to the different LC cells the display consists of. Attacking this communication channel therefore means either trying to guess the message that is hidden in the set of voltages (secrecy) or trying to change the voltages (authentication).

The communication from Alice $\to TC$ makes use of a reverse channel established by presenting to Alice in the reconstructed image a keypad/ keyboard. Alice can then reply to messages from TC by clicking on the appropriate positions in the reconstructed keypad and the clicked positions are communicated back to TC. Attacking this communication line means either changing those positions in a clever way to fool Alice and TC or trying to guess the message that Alice sends to TC.

4.2 Authentication from $TC \to$ Alice

In Section 3.2 is explained how TC can encrypt images that can be decrypted by Alice. This message is secret by construction but not authenticated.

An impersonation attack is very difficult since the visual crypto system is a secret key system with a key length equal to the number of pixels which in practice is of the order of at least 100 bits. Therefore, the success probability of an impersonation attack by guessing the correct key can considered to be negligible[5].

In visual cryptography a substitution attack mainly consists of adding, deleting or modifying characters, which makes this attack a bit more subtle. Eliminating this attack in a strong sense is impossible but not necessary: an attacker can easily change one (or only a very few) pixels while being undetected and without changing Alice's interpretation of the message. Therefore, loosely spoken, we state the following requirements for a visual cryptography authentication protocol:

- An attacker is not able to add or remove characters that make sense to humans.
- An attacker is not able to change characters into characters of his choice.

For a precise and more formal definition of visual authentication, we refer to Appendix A.

The substitution attack problem is solved by the following procedure for messages from $TC \to$ Alice.

- The background of the images sent from $TC \to$ Alice consists of a pattern with many colour transitions. The colours are randomly chosen and the pattern is placed at a random position.

---

[5] Note that in a practical implementation, the security actually depends on the effective key length of the used Pseudo Random Number Generator (PRNG).

- Each character sent by TC is depicted in one single uniform randomly chosen colour.
- The message is shown on a random place on the screen.

If an attacker wants to change a character into another one, he has to know where the character is positioned in the image and add or remove an area of uniform colour. In order to derive an upperbound for the probability of a successful substitution attack, we assume that the background contains a pattern of randomly coloured grid cells, see for example Fig. 6.a. In this example the background is filled with triangular shaped grid cells (each grid cell consists of multiple pixels) on which the letter 'T' is displayed. Further we assume that the attacker knows the background *pattern* (i.e. where the colour transitions are) but not the specific *colours* of the grid cells. We denote by $\hat{c}$ the number of *partially* covered grid cells in the background of a shape (e.g. a character) that is to be removed by an attacker. With c we denote the number of *partially or completely* covered background grid cells by a shape to be added by an attacker (see Fig. 6.b). Note that in the example of Fig. 6, $\hat{c} = 33$ and $c = 38$.

The upperbound PU_{rem} for the probability of successfully removing an area of uniform predefined colour and the upperbound PU_{add} for the probability of successfully adding an area of uniform predefined colour are then given by

$$PU_{\text{rem}} = \left(\frac{1}{k^3}\right)^{\hat{c}} \quad \text{and} \quad PU_{\text{add}} = \left(\frac{1}{k^3}\right)^{c}. \tag{2}$$

We remind the reader that k^3 stands for the number of possible colours (see Section 3.2). The proofs of formulae (2) can be found in appendix A.

In general the system will be set up such that the attacker does not even know the background pattern nor the exact location of it (because it will be chosen differently for every message). Hence, Eqs. (2) are upperbounds for the probability of a successful substitution attack.

The protocol requires that Alice checks the colour uniformity of the characters and whether the background has the required format. This implies that in order to check authenticity of a message, Alice is in control herself.

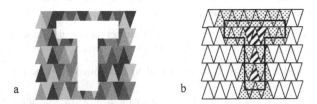

Fig. 6. (a) Example of the letter 'T' on a multi-coloured background using 5 gray scales. (b) The 33 partially covered grid cells (dotted) and 5 completely covered grid cells (striped) in this example.

We notice that when light sensitive sensors are present in each of the pixels of the decryption display, then the integrity of the communication channel from TC to the display of H can be based on message authentication codes (MAC) [10]. However, additional error correction codes need to be applied in order to be robust against pixel failures.

4.3 Secret and Authentic Channel (SAC) from Alice → TC

In this section, we will show how Alice can secretly reply in an authenticated way to messages from TC. We start with secrecy. In order to establish a private channel between Alice and TC, TC will send a visually encrypted message containing a picture of a randomised keypad/ keyboard (Fig. 7). The keypad is randomised in the sense that the characters are permuted in a random way but also the shape of the keypad might be randomised. This is done each time the keypad is sent to Alice. Moreover, we allow that a single character is displayed multiple times.

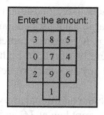

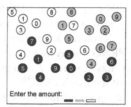

Fig. 7. Example of a randomised keypad.

Fig. 8. Example of various coloured keypads using three gray levels.

Alice enters a number (e.g. an amount) by clicking appropriate *locations* in the image. The coordinates of the locations selected by Alice are sent back to TC. An eavesdropper will get no information on the message because the locations of the characters are random and hence unknown to the eavesdropper which does not have the secret visual decryption key.

Although the above mentioned system establishes a private channel from Alice → TC, the replies are not yet authenticated. An attacker can for instance easily perform a *swap* attack. This means that he flips the positions of some of the characters (positions) that are sent back. It is clear that this attack has a high probability of being undetected by TC. More generally, he can insert new positions which have a non-negligible probability of being accepted by TC.

A straightforward way to eliminate the swap attack is by adding a *verification* protocol. In this protocol TC uses the authenticated channel from TC to Alice (explained in Section 4.2) to transmit the message that it has received from Alice together with a confirmation code. In order to confirm that TC indeed received what she had sent, Alice has to type in the confirmation code. TC checks whether Alice confirmed the message with the correct code. The verification protocol leads to an authenticated channel from Alice → TC at the price of extra interaction.

Another way of eliminating the attacks mentioned above, is given by the following protocol. Instead of sending one randomised keypad, TC sends various keypads, each in a different colour (Fig. 8) to Alice. Alice enters the different symbols of her message in the colours indicated by TC. In this way the *swap attack* is prevented. Denote with w the area of an indicated colour and with A the total display area (where a pixel is taken as the unit of area). Then the probability of performing a successful substitution attack becomes proportional to $\frac{w}{A}$ per symbol (with a proportionality factor smaller than 1). In order to reduce this probability further, Alice can be asked to type her message multiple times ($l > 1$) with different colour indications. In that case the success probability becomes proportional to $\left(\frac{w}{A}\right)^l$. The use of colours can be avoided by using different shapes instead.

5   Application

5.1   A Practical Problem: Key Synchronisation

Since the visual crypto system, developed in Section 3, acts like a one-time pad, both TC and Alice need synchronised keys. In order to avoid large databases containing the keys, we use pseudo random number generators, $PRNG(x, K)$ where x represents the state of the PRNG and K is the personal key that is secretly stored, in both TC and D. Hence, TC has to store for each user also the message key K_i which represents the current state of the user's PRNG[6].

In order to set up flexible key-synchronisation, we use the additional array of light sensitive sensors embedded in the pixels. Let K_i be the current key at TC and let h be a one-way hash function. TC uses K_i to visually encrypt the current message. At the bottom of the visually encrypted message, $h(K_i)$ is encoded in an optical signal that is modulated in the pixels of the complementary array[7]. D reads the encoded optical signal by using its light sensitive sensors. D performs the following algorithm, with K_j denoting the current key in D.

Algorithm 2	INPUT: $h(K_i)$.
	MEMORY: (K_j, j) with $j \leq i$.
	OUTPUT: update memory with (K_i, i), or no update.
	0) $x := K_j$ and $J := j$.
	1) while $h(x) \neq h(K_i)$ and $J - j < N$ do [8]
	2) $x := PRNG(x, K)$ and $J := J + 1$
	3) od.
	4) if $J - j < N$ then $memory := (x, J)$ else no update.

The algorithm updates D's key K_j until it is synchronised with the key of TC. The maximum number of possible attempts is given by N. We require that D's PRNG is

---

[6] Alice's security display D can be used in multiple applications by storing multiple personal keys (one for each application). Another option is implementing a proxy [5] (in that case TC represents Alice's proxy) such that only one personal key needs to be stored in the decryption display. The proxy will set up a secure communication to the application of Alice's choice.

[7] In order to avoid false detection of hashed keys, we can include a CRC check.

[8] If we replace this check by the requirement that $h(x)$ and $h(K_i)$ have a small distance to one another, then the algorithm is more robust against pixel failures.

only executed in algorithm 2. Hence, $j \leq i$ is an invariant of algorithm 2. Furthermore, TC's PRNG can only increase i such that $j \leq i$ is also an invariant of the protocol. In the case of a replay attack or a random message by an attacker, algorithm 2 will not make an update. After having performed algorithm 2, D can decrypt the message.

5.2 Communication Protocol

Based on the techniques developed in the previous sections, we describe the complete communication protocol.

Initialisation In order to initialise the system, Alice receives her decryption display D from TC. The PRNG in the display, D, is initialised in a certain state. This state is also secretly stored by TC together with the identity of the person it belongs to. A communication session starts with the following steps:

1. Using H, Alice notifies TC that she wants to start a communication session (by passing also her identity to TC).
2. TC looks up the PRNG and its state corresponding to the identity in its database.

Basic protocol We describe the basic protocol for establishing a PTWSAC.

1. Using their common key K_i, TC visually encrypts a message in an authenticated way as explained in Section 4.2.
2. Alice puts her trusted device D on top of H. D performs synchronisation algorithm 2. Alice checks whether the message sent by TC is authentic.
3. Alice answers the message of TC by clicking at the right positions in the keypad. She follows the protocol rules as developed in Section 4.3.
4. H sends the positions of the clicks to TC over the untrusted network.
5. TC interprets the received locations and possibly sends a verification message.
6. Alice replies on the verification message, if necessary.

6 Conclusions

In a world where information is an important commodity and should be available any time and anywhere, the integrity and confidentiality of the information and the security and privacy of the communication are important issues. In such a world the information will be presented in a user-friendly way, for example in graphical form on a display. However as devices like PDA's and cell phones are becoming more complicated and interconnected, they can no longer be trusted.

We present a solution for verifying the authenticity and confidentiality of information presented on untrusted displays based on visual cryptography. We propose some important practical technological modifications to the basic idea of visual cryptography leading to secure two-way communications. We replace transparencies with a small and cheap transparent LCD display. This enhances picture quality and allows for reconstructing colour images. The details of the visual crypto system presented in Section 3.2, are formulated as a mathematical model and are published in [16].

In order to extend the current solution to larger size displays, one can also make use of *flexible displays*. These are usually not made of Liquid Crystals. It will be investigated whether those materials offer interesting properties for the implementation of visual cryptography.

Acknowledgement

The authors like to thank the Oxygen project at MIT and M.T. Johnson for the stimulating discussions and G.J. Destura and Philips MDS Heerlen for the help with the demo.

References

1. M. Benham, *Internet Explorer SSL Vulnerability*, article on Thoughtcrime.org, August 2002, (see http://www.thoughtcrime.org/ie-ssl-chain.txt).
2. E. Biham, *Visual Cryptography with Polarisation*, Security Seminar, University of Camebridge, August 1997,
   (see http://www.cl.cam.ac.uk/Research/Security/seminars/1997/).
3. C. Blundo, A. De Santis and D. Stinson, *On the contrast in visual cryptography schemes*, Manuscript 1996.
   Available at ftp://theory.lcs.mit.edu/pub/tcryptol.96-13.ps.
4. M. Burnside, D. Clarke, B. Gassend, T. Kotwal, S. Devadas, M. van Dijk, R. Rivest, *The untrusted computer problem and camera-based authentication*, Springer LNCS2414, 2002.
5. M. Burnside, D. Clarke, T. Mills, A. Maywah, S. Devadas, R. Rivest, *Proxy based security protocols in networked mobile devices*, Proceedings SAC, 2002.
6. Case Western Reserve University, PLC group, *virtual textbook on liquid crystal displays*, http://abalone.cwru.edu/tutorial/enhanced/files/textbook.htm
7. J. Claessens, *Analysis and design of an advanced infrastructure for secure and anonymous electronic payment system on the Internet*, Ph.D. thesis, K.U. Leuven, December 2002.
8. T. Matsumoto, *Human identification through an insecure channel*, Theory and Application of Cryptographic techniques, 1991, 409-421.
9. T. Matsumoto, *Human-Computer Cryptography: An attempt*, ACM conference on Computer and Communication security, 1966, 68-75.
10. A. Menezes, P. van Oorschot, S. van Stone, *Handbook of Applied Cryptography*, CRC Press Inc., 1997.
11. M. Naor, A. Shamir, *Visual Cryptography*, Eurocrypt 94', Springer-Verlag LNCS Vol. 950, 1-12.
12. M. Naor, B. Pinkas, *Visual Authentication and Identification*, Crypto 97.
13. V. Rijmen, B. Preneel, *Efficient colour visual encryption or 'shared colors of Benetton'*, Presented at the rump session of Eurocrypt '96.
    Also available at http://www.esat.kuleuven.ac.be/~rijmen/vc/ .
14. G. Simmons, *A survey of information authentication*, in Contemporary Cryptography - The science of information integrity, IEEE Press, 379-419.
15. D.R. Stinson, *An introduction to visual cryptography*, presented at Public Key solutions '97.
    Available at http://bibd.unl.edu/~stinson/VCS-PKS.ps.
16. P. Tuyls, H.D.L. Hollmann, J.H. v. Lint, L. Tolhuizen, *Polarisation based Visual Crypto System and its Secret Sharing Schemes*. Available at the IACR Cryptology ePrint Archive, http://eprint.iacr.org/2002/194/.
17. E. Verheul, H. van Tilborg: *Constructions and properties of k out of n visual secret sharing schemes*, Designs Codes and Cryptography, 11, 179-196, 1997.

A   Visual Authentication

A.1   Definitions

By a visual authentication protocol the following is understood.

Definition 2 (Naor). TC *wishes to communicate to Alice an information piece* m, *the content of which is known to the adversary.*

1. TC *sends a message* c *to Alice which is a function of* m *and some shared secret information.*
2. *The adversary might change the message* c *before Alice receives it.*
3. *Upon receiving a message* c', *Alice outputs either FAIL or* $\langle ACCEPT, m' \rangle$ *as a function of* c' *and her secret information.*

In order to define the security requirements of a visual authentication system, we first note that the requirement that an adversary cannot convince Alice to receive any message different from the original message is much too strong. The change of one innocent pixel in the background for instance will with high probability not be detected by Alice. Therefore, we will only require that an adversary can not erase or enter symbols of his choice.

Definition 3. *Assume that Alice has the capabilities that are required from her for the protocol, that she acts according to the protocol and that the visual authentication system has the property that when the adversary is faithful, then Alice always outputs* $\langle ACCEPT, m \rangle$. *Let* Σ *be a set of messages that make sense to Alice (i.e. that she can understand). We call the system* $(\Sigma, (1 - p))$-*authentic if for any message* m *communicated from TC to Alice, the probability that Alice outputs* $\langle ACCEPT, m' \rangle$ *where* $m' \in \Sigma$ *is at most* p.

The definition implies that it is hard for an adversary to change a message m into a message $m' \in \Sigma$ that makes sense to Alice. The set Σ depends on the application. In order to prove authenticity in specific applications the set Σ has to be defined carefully.

A.2   Substitution Attack

In order to derive an upper bound on the probability of a successful substitution attack we make the following assumptions. The background of an image sent by the trusted party contains a more or less regular grid, for example as depicted in Fig. 6. Every grid cell (a triangle in Fig. 6) of this grid gets a uniform colour chosen randomly from the k^3 possible colours. We further assume that the attacker knows the exact position of the grid but not the colours of the grid cells. The goal of the attacker is to introduce a shape on this background of uniform colour. The size of this shape covers, completely or partially, c of the grid cells.

Recalling the mechanisms of visual cryptography based on polarisation (see Section 3.2), it is clear that an attacker can change the colour of a grid cell by changing the rotations of all the pixels in a grid cell with the same amount. However, because he does not know the secret key of Alice, he does not know to *which* colour he is changing the grid cell. Thus, if he wants to change the grid cell to a predefined colour, his success probability is $\frac{1}{k^3}$.

If we finally assume that pseudo random processes generating keys, colouring of the grid cells by the trusted party, etc. are truly random, then we can state the following lemma concerning the addition of a uniform shape.

Lemma 1. *Suppose an adversary wants to introduce a shape of uniform predefined colour covering c grid cells and that he knows the location of the grid cells but not the colour. Then, the attackers success probability is upper bounded by $\left(\frac{1}{k^3}\right)^c$.*

Proof. In order to get a uniform, predefined colour in the added shape, every (part of a) grid cell that is covered by the shape should be changed to the predefined colour. The probability to obtain the right colour for one grid cell equals $\frac{1}{k^3}$. Therefore, the probability of changing all the c grid cells to the correct colour is $\left(\frac{1}{k^3}\right)^c$.   □

Clearly, when the uniform colour of the added shape is not predefined, the probability becomes $\left(\frac{1}{k^3}\right)^{c-1}$.

By a similar reasoning we can derive an upperbound for the success probability of removing a shape. Here we make the same assumptions as above on the attacker's knowlegde on the position of the grid and the grid cells but we also assume that the attacker knows the exact location of the shape he wants to remove. In this case the probability depends on the number of grid cells which are *partially covered* by the shape. Changing a partially covered grid cell in one of uniform (arbitrary) colour, can be done with probability $\frac{1}{k^3}$.

Lemma 2. *Suppose an adversary wants to remove a shape of uniform colour partially covering $\hat{c}$ grid cells and he knows the location of the grid cells but not the colour. Then, the attackers success probability is upper bounded by $\left(\frac{1}{k^3}\right)^{\hat{c}}$.*

Proof. Grid cells that are completely covered by the shape to be removed can be easily turned into grid cells of a uniform colour by rotating their polarisations over an arbitrary angle. Therefore these pixels do not have to be taken into account. In order to be successful, an attacker has to change the colour of a partially covered grid cell, into a grid cell of a uniform but arbitrary chosen colour. Since the grid cell is partially covered his success probability is $\frac{1}{k^3}$ as explained above. Because he has to do this for $\hat{c}$ grid cells, his success probability becomes $\left(\frac{1}{k^3}\right)^{\hat{c}}$.   □

Security and Privacy in Pervasive Computing
State of the Art and Future Directions

Dieter Hutter[1], Werner Stephan[1], and Markus Ullmann[2]

[1] German Research Center for Artificial Intelligence GmbH,
Stuhlsatzenhausweg 3, 66123 Saarbrücken, Germany
{hutter,stephan}@dfki.de
[2] German Federal Office for Information Security,
Godesberger Allee 185-187, 53133 Bonn, Germany
markus.ullmann@bsi.bund.de

Abstract. This paper summarizes the ideas and results of three working groups that convened during the 1st International Conference on Security in Pervasive Computing. The scope of the workshop was to identify and discuss security and privacy issues specific to pervasive computing and how to address these issues with appropriate means.

1 Introduction

During the First International Conference on Security in Pervasive Computing in Boppard, an afternoon session was devoted to discuss the issues concerning security and privacy specific to pervasive computing. The discussion was organized into three parallel working groups of about 15 – 20 conference participants. Each of these working groups operated independently and came up with its own view on this issue and the organizers of the conference are pleased to merge the outcome of these discussions into this short summary[1].

As a starting point some central questions for pervasive computing were raised by the organizers:

- What are salient features of pervasive computing?
- How does pervasive computing create new security challenges?
- Which new security mechanisms are specific to pervasive computing?
- What are the most likely applications for pervasive computing and what specific security and privacy requirements arise from those applications?

Based on these discussions the three working groups were supposed to deduce and define consequences for future working strategies. The idea was to support researchers and research funding organizations in identifying new relevant fields in security and privacy of pervasive computing and to define new goals and topics for the upcoming Second International Conference on Security in Pervasive Computing in spring 2005.

---

[1] We are very grateful to various conference participants who supported us in memorizing the details of the discussions. In particular, we would like to thank Carl Ellison for providing us his detailed notes.

D. Hutter et al. (Eds.): Security in Pervasive Computing 2003, LNCS 2802, pp. 285–289, 2004.
© Springer-Verlag Berlin Heidelberg 2004

2   Salient Features of Pervasive Computing

Context-Awareness. Applications in pervasive computing actively explore physical location, available computer infrastructure and offered services running on such infrastructures to fulfill and enhance their ability to perform their designated task. Environments have to provide sensitive information necessary to perform tasks of an authorized application. Conversely, the application will adjust its behavior according to the settings of the environment. This means that the environment of an application has influence on the problem solving mechanisms selected by the application.

Invisibility and Non-intrusiveness. Pervasive computing aims at providing computers that users are unaware of. While nowadays work is organized around computers, pervasive computing will focus on user's tasks but not on the hardware to perform the tasks. Instead, the computing machinery will become more and more invisible and, as a consequence, more and more autonomous. Decisions have to be autonomously made by the application by means of previously agreed policies.

Mobility. Pervasive computing applications will be as mobile as their users. But unlike mobile code they will usually reside on a fixed platform (like a PDA) which is itself mobile. Thus, the platform operates in an unknown and untrusted environment. The communication to other systems is done more and more contactless using wireless communication technologies in a spontaneous manner (ad-hoc).

Boundedness of Resources. Pervasive devices have rather limited resources with respect to energy, memory, and computing capacity that hampers the use of some traditional security mechanisms. For instance, pervasive computing applications will be usually not able to access PKI-services that are available on line.

3   Security Challenges

To illustrate the type of security and privacy problems arising in a pervasive computing, the following application scenario was discussed:

A passenger waiting for his scheduled plane wants to print out some confidential papers residing on his PDA at the airport. Therefore his PDA negotiates via wireless LAN with the airport environment to get access to a printer in a locked room and to receive the access code for the printer room. The documents are printed and our passenger picks up the printouts at the printer room just in time to catch his flight.

This scenario raises various questions. In the first place PDA and airport environment have to agree on a common language to discuss the passenger's needs (format of the paper, double sided vs. single sided printing, etc). Semantic web languages like DAML-OIL might be a solution to this problem. However, both parties have also to agree on a common security policy (e.g. who has access

to the printer room in case of a malfunction? What happens to the misprints?).
If the passenger is not aware of the technology, how can he specify a security
policy in the first place ? Furthermore, how can our passenger trust the airport
environment in that it follows the agreed security policy and, for example, does
not make (electronic) copies of its own or does not transmit the confidential
document in plain text to the printer?

Privacy. In pervasive computing, personal equipment carried around will constantly communicate with stationary equipment without explicitly contacting
the user. Nowadays, mobile phones periodically inform base stations about their
location. In the future, active sensors implanted into clothes may, for instance,
inwardly contact receiving stations at the entrances of shopping malls or public
buildings. Vast amounts of personal data will be temporarily collected and may
result in a large, irrepressible distributed surveillance system. Furthermore, the
individuals might not be even aware of the collection of their personal data.

Location privacy is a new risk which is growing with the widespread use of
wireless communication. There is a need for means to enforce the need-to-know
principle and to ensure that data are only collected and stored for previously
agreed, specific purposes. It has been argued that this problem is closely related
to the enforcement of digital rights in multi-media industry where data (e.g.
music or movies) is only provided for viewing by a restricted circle of persons
during a limited time period.

Authentication and Accountability. The mobility of computing devices requires
spontaneous communication between previously unknown devices. For example,
PDAs will make use of service facilities offered by the actual computing environment (like printing, communication lines, etc.). Unlike standard computing, a
PDA and its environment will not be embraced by a common operating system
dealing with authentication, but are independent devices which have to negotiate about how to provide and use facilities. Resource boundedness limits the
use of common approaches like the use of a public-key infrastructure. Furthermore, services will be more and more requested on behalf of third parties which
gives rise to the problem of delegation and revocation of rights in a dynamically
changing environment.

Availability. A potential massive threat is a denial of service in a pervasive
world. In a pervasive computing environment, firewalls are getting useless as a
possible attacker will be part of the computing environment rather than being
an external intruder who might be stopped at the entrance.

4   Security Mechanism

Security Policies. In pervasive computing, devices depend on the successful operation of their computing environment. Security policies imposed by a user on
its personal device cannot be enforced without security guarantees of the environment. A specific security policy imposed by the user has to be (automatically)

decomposed into requirements of the involved devices: What does this security policy mean for each component and each electronic relationship in the whole system? Even if the first problem is solved, how can we propagate a specific security policy required by a component through all the dynamically assigned other components which are necessary to provide the requested functionality? Security policies will become dynamic and their instantiations will be a result of negotiations between the interacting devices.

Trust Management. In the future, devices will more and more operate in an unknown and potentially hostile environment. The question arises of how to establish trust in previously unknown devices or services within such environments. How can we trust in these devices that they really behave as specified in their advertised specification? Levels of trust and dynamic trust models are needed describing the mechanisms to grow or decrease trust. However, what are suitable actions initiating the growth or reduction of trust in a device? Are there means to detect misuse of trust by a device and possible imposition of sanctions against a device? How can we ensure liability in such a pervasive world?

Security Protocols. New kinds of security mechanisms are necessary to deal with the problem of restricted resources. For the authentication of pervasive devices new enhanced authentication procedures are required, which take into account the location of devices or the context of authentication.

Secure Computing Environments. The protection of pervasive devices will be a growing task in future [tamper resistant hardware, cryptographic support by the pervasive device, ..]. This is the case because the environment of the pervasive devices is unknown and untrusted.

5   Application Specific to Pervasive Computing

Talking about security from a perspective of applications or services means talking about the service itself. Today, the situation seems to be similar to the UMTS environment. Although there are lots of application scenarios, mostly the business cases are still missing in the discussions. The following enumeration sketches possible (security critical) applications in pervasive computing.

1. Transportation scenario: in public transportation the sale and control of tickets will be automated. Entering a train will automatically result in debiting the fare to the credit card. The PDA will negotiate about appropriate connection trains, collect information about the schedule, make appointments for dinner in the train, etc. Traveling by car, we will be automatically provided with routing and redirection information or our car will contact the nearest automobile dealer in case of an emergency and book a hotel in the surrounding. **Already today cars, trains and airplanes rely on systems that collect (performance) data of critical components, communicate them the a central surveillance center, and allow for remote maintenance procedures based on these data.**

2. Health-care scenario: Supervision at home is implemented with the help of active sensors attached to a patient which will monitor essential bodily functions and immediately contact physician in case of an emergency. Sensors attached to drugs will help to prevent wrong medications. Inside a hospital, medical records of patients, medical documentations or scheduling information can be presented on the PDA of a physician.

3. Home automation, media entertainment: Smart devices in these scenarios adapt there behavior to preferences of their users, like the music titles preferred at breakfast, are aware of the current situation,like the day of the week or the outside/room temperature, and keep a persistent state, like the content of the refrigerator. Devices might carry out computations and enforce certain rules, for example, to protect children in media entertainment. Based on their knowledge about user preferences as well as the current state and situation they are able to generate recommendations or even to initiate activities in a pro active way. Access to a global network enables the incorporation of non local information, like radio and television programs. The exchange (distribution) of information between local nodes is relevant in particular in media entertainment.

4. Office applications: employees wear active batches which allow the localization of individuals moving around the building. A computer system monitors the movements and automatically adjust the electronic infrastructure of a room to the needs of the attendee. Telephone numbers or computer sessions are redirected if an employee leaves the room and enters the next one.

5. Identification: Rather than being an application area of it's own identification of objects and persons is a necessary prerequisite for many services offered by ubicom solutions. Identification (and sensoring) is needed to bridge the gap between the physical environment and information stored in smart devices or central data banks accessed by these. Progress made in developing (passive and active) identification tags that are cheap and easy to access,like RFD tags, allows to include even objects from mass production into pervasive computing scenarios. Looking at security related services devices for the (automatic) identification and authentication of persons or objects are used to monitor or control access to certain resources, like rooms or computing devices, to provide anti theft protection for goods, and to automatically collect tolls and fees in transportation.

6   Conclusion

The technology of pervasive computing is changing. The above collection of new challenges, requested mechanisms and potential application areas are far from being complete but reflects the state of discussion at the workshop. The organizers intend to continue this vivid and fruitful discussion at the upcoming Second International Conference on Security in Pervasive Computing in Spring 2005.

Author Index

Lecture Notes in Computer Science

For information about Vols. 1–2849
please contact your bookseller or Springer-Verlag

Vol. 2887: T. Johansson (Ed.), Fast Software Encryption. Proceedings, 2003. IX, 397 pages. 2003.

Vol. 2888: R. Meersman, Zahir Tari, D.C. Schmidt et al. (Eds.), On The Move to Meaningful Internet Systems 2003: CoopIS, DOA, and ODBASE. Proceedings, 2003. XXI, 1546 pages. 2003.

Vol. 2889: Robert Meersman, Zahir Tari et al. (Eds.), On The Move to Meaningful Internet Systems 2003: OTM 2003 Workshops. Proceedings, 2003. XXI, 1096 pages. 2003.

Vol. 2890: M. Broy, A.V. Zamulin (Eds.), Perspectives of System Informatics. Proceedings, 2003. XV, 572 pages. 2003.

Vol. 2891: J. Lee, M. Barley (Eds.), Intelligent Agents and Multi-Agent Systems. Proceedings, 2003. X, 215 pages. 2003. (Subseries LNAI)

Vol. 2892: F. Dau, The Logic System of Concept Graphs with Negation. XI, 213 pages. 2003. (Subseries LNAI)

Vol. 2893: J.-B. Stefani, I. Demeure, D. Hagimont (Eds.), Distributed Applications and Interoperable Systems. Proceedings, 2003. XIII, 311 pages. 2003.

Vol. 2894: C.S. Laih (Ed.), Advances in Cryptology - ASIACRYPT 2003. Proceedings, 2003. XIII, 543 pages. 2003.

Vol. 2895: A. Ohori (Ed.), Programming Languages and Systems. Proceedings, 2003. XIII, 427 pages. 2003.

Vol. 2896: V.A. Saraswat (Ed.), Advances in Computing Science – ASIAN 2003. Proceedings, 2003. VIII, 305 pages. 2003.

Vol. 2897: O. Balet, G. Subsol, P. Torguet (Eds.), Virtual Storytelling. Proceedings, 2003. XI, 240 pages. 2003.

Vol. 2898: K.G. Paterson (Ed.), Cryptography and Coding. Proceedings, 2003. IX, 385 pages. 2003.

Vol. 2899: G. Ventre, R. Canonico (Eds.), Interactive Multimedia on Next Generation Networks. Proceedings, 2003. XIV, 420 pages. 2003.

Vol. 2900: M. Bidoit, P.D. Mosses, CASL User Manual. XIII, 240 pages. 2004.

Vol. 2901: F. Bry, N. Henze, J. Maluszyński (Eds.), Principles and Practice of Semantic Web Reasoning. Proceedings, 2003. X, 209 pages. 2003.

Vol. 2902: F. Moura Pires, S. Abreu (Eds.), Progress in Artificial Intelligence. Proceedings, 2003. XV, 504 pages. 2003. (Subseries LNAI).

Vol. 2903: T.D. Gedeon, L.C.C. Fung (Eds.), AI 2003: Advances in Artificial Intelligence. Proceedings, 2003. XVI, 1075 pages. 2003. (Subseries LNAI).

Vol. 2904: T. Johansson, S. Maitra (Eds.), Progress in Cryptology – INDOCRYPT 2003. Proceedings, 2003. XI, 431 pages. 2003.

Vol. 2905: A. Sanfeliu, J. Ruiz-Shulcloper (Eds.), Progress in Pattern Recognition, Speech and Image Analysis. Proceedings, 2003. XVII, 693 pages. 2003.

Vol. 2906: T. Ibaraki, N. Katoh, H. Ono (Eds.), Algorithms and Computation. Proceedings, 2003. XVII, 748 pages. 2003.

Vol. 2908: K. Chae, M. Yung (Eds.), Information Security Applications. Proceedings, 2003. XII, 506 pages. 2004.

Vol. 2910: M.E. Orlowska, S. Weerawarana, M.P. Papazoglou, J. Yang (Eds.), Service-Oriented Computing – ICSOC 2003. Proceedings, 2003. XIV, 576 pages. 2003.

Vol. 2911: T.M.T. Sembok, H.B. Zaman, H. Chen, S.R. Urs, S.H.Myaeng (Eds.), Digital Libraries: Technology and Management of Indigenous Knowledge for Global Access. Proceedings, 2003. XX, 703 pages. 2003.

Vol. 2912: G. Liotta (Ed.), Graph Drawing. Proceedings, 2003. XV, 542 pages. 2004.

Vol. 2913: T.M. Pinkston, V.K. Prasanna (Eds.), High Performance Computing – HiPC 2003. Proceedings, 2003. XX, 512 pages. 2003.

Vol. 2914: P.K. Pandya, J. Radhakrishnan (Eds.), FST TCS 2003: Foundations of Software Technology and Theoretical Computer Science. Proceedings, 2003. XIII, 446 pages. 2003.

Vol. 2916: C. Palamidessi (Ed.), Logic Programming. Proceedings, 2003. XII, 520 pages. 2003.

Vol. 2918: S.R. Das, S.K. Das (Eds.), Distributed Computing – IWDC 2003. Proceedings, 2003. XIV, 394 pages. 2003.

Vol. 2919: E. Giunchiglia, A. Tacchella (Eds.), Theory and Applications of Satisfiability Testing. Proceedings, 2003. XI, 530 pages. 2004.

Vol. 2920: H. Karl, A. Willig, A. Wolisz (Eds.), Wireless Sensor Networks. Proceedings, 2004. XIV, 365 pages. 2004.

Vol. 2921: G. Lausen, D. Suciu (Eds.), Database Programming Languages. Proceedings, 2003. X, 279 pages. 2004.

Vol. 2922: F. Dignum (Ed.), Advances in Agent Communication. Proceedings, 2003. X, 403 pages. 2004. (Subseries LNAI).

Vol. 2923: V. Lifschitz, I. Niemelä (Eds.), Logic Programming and Nonmonotonic Reasoning. Proceedings, 2004. IX, 365 pages. 2004. (Subseries LNAI).

Vol. 2924: J. Callan, F. Crestani, M. Sanderson (Eds.), Distributed Multimedia Information Retrieval. Proceedings, 2003. XII, 173 pages. 2004.

Vol. 2926: L. van Elst, V. Dignum, A. Abecker (Eds.), Agent-Mediated Knowledge Management. Proceedings, 2003. XI, 428 pages. 2004. (Subseries LNAI).

Vol. 2927: D. Hales, B. Edmonds, E. Norling, J. Rouchier (Eds.), Multi-Agent-Based Simulation III. Proceedings, 2003. X, 209 pages. 2003. (Subseries LNAI).

Vol. 2928: R. Battiti, M. Conti, R. Lo Cigno (Eds.), Wireless On-Demand Network Systems. Proceedings, 2004. XIV, 402 pages. 2004.

Vol. 2929: H. de Swart, E. Orlowska, G. Schmidt, M. Roubens (Eds.), Theory and Applications of Relational Structures as Knowledge Instruments. Proceedings. VII, 273 pages. 2003.

Vol. 2932: P. Van Emde Boas, J. Pokorný, M. Bieliková, J. Štuller (Eds.), SOFSEM 2004: Theory and Practice of Computer Science. Proceedings, 2004. XIII, 385 pages. 2004.

Vol. 2935: P. Giorgini, J.P. Müller, J. Odell (Eds.), Agent-Oriented Software Engineering IV. Proceedings, 2003. X, 247 pages. 2004.

Vol. 2937: B. Steffen, G. Levi (Eds.), Verification, Model Checking, and Abstract Interpretation. Proceedings, 2004. XI, 325 pages. 2004.

Vol. 2950: N. Jonoska, G. Păun, G. Rozenberg (Eds.), Aspects of Molecular Computing. XI, 391 pages. 2004.